Wives and P...

LEE HOLCOMBE is Associate Professor of History at the University of South
Carolina at Spartanburg.

In the 1870s Millicent Garrett Fawcett had her purse snatched by a young
thief in London. When she appeared in court to testify, she heard the young
man charged with 'stealing from the person of Millicent Fawcett a purse containing £1 18s 6d the property of Henry Fawcett.' Long after the episode she
recalled: 'I felt as if I had been charged with theft myself.'

The English common-law which deprived married women of the right to
own and control property had far-reaching consequences for the status of
women not only in other areas of law and in family life but also in education,
and employment, and public life. To win reform of the married women's
property law, feminism as an organized movement appeared in the 1850s, and
the final success of the campaign for reform in 1882 was one of the greatest
achievements of the Victorian women's movement.

Dr Holcombe explores the story of the reform campaign in the context of its
time, giving particular attention to the many important men and women who
worked for reform and to the debates on the subject which contributed greatly
to the formulation of a philosophy of feminism.

THE LADIES' ADVOCATE.

Mrs. Bull. "LOR, MR. MILL! WHAT A LOVELY SPEECH YOU *DID* MAKE. I DO DECLARE I HADN'T
THE SLIGHTEST NOTION WE WERE SUCH MISERABLE CREATURES. NO ONE CAN SAY IT WAS *YOUR*
FAULT THAT THE CASE BROKE DOWN."

reprinted from *Punch* 1867

Lee Holcombe

Wives and Property
Reform of the Married Women's Property Law in Nineteenth-Century England

UNIVERSITY OF TORONTO PRESS
Toronto and Buffalo

© University of Toronto Press 1983
Toronto Buffalo London
Printed in Canada

ISBN 0-8020-5573-7 (cloth)
ISBN 0-8020-6476-0 (paper)

Canadian Cataloguing in Publication Data

Holcombe, Lee, 1928-
   Wives and property

   Bibliography: p.
   Includes index.
   ISBN 0-8020-5573-7 (bound). – ISBN 0-8020-6476-0 (pbk.)

   1. Married women – England – History – 19th century.
   2. Women's rights – England – History – 19th century.
   3. Great Britain. Married Women's Property Act (1882).
   I. Title.

HQ1593.H64   305.4'2'0942   C82-095010-6

This book has been published with the help of a grant from
the Publications Fund of University of Toronto Press.

For Norma Adams,
Professor Emeritus of History,
Mount Holyoke College,
teacher and friend

Contents

Wives and Property

1

'The First Point in the Women's Charter' The Women's Movement and Legal Reform

In 1869 Susannah Palmer appeared in the Recorder's Court in London, charged with stabbing her husband. After years of brutal treatment at his hands she had left him, determined to support herself and her children in a new home. But her husband had found her, and seized and sold all her possessions, which legally belonged to him. Susannah Palmer was convicted and sentenced to prison, for she was the criminal, not the adulterous husband who had beaten and robbed her. A few years after this, Millicent Garrett Fawcett had her purse snatched by a young thief in London. When she appeared in court to testify against him, she heard the youth charged with 'stealing from the person of Millicent Fawcett a purse containing £1 18s. 6d., the property of Henry Fawcett.' Long afterward she recalled, 'I felt as if I had been charged with theft myself.' Such were two women's experiences of the common law relating to married women's property. One was a poor working woman who would have gone unnoticed in her time but for her tragic story. The other, happily married to a distinguished Cambridge professor and Liberal member of parliament, was for years one of the outstanding leaders of the women's suffrage cause in England.[1]

The stories of women as different as these two illuminate the arguments used by Victorian feminists in their demands for reform of the married women's property law and other legal reforms as well. On the one hand, the law often inflicted grievous practical hardships upon women. On the other, the law, regarding a woman as her husband's servant, even as his chattel, destroyed her independence, her identity, and her self-respect. Reform of the common law affecting married women stands out, therefore, as a major achievement of nineteenth-century feminism.[2]

Indeed, it can be argued that reform of the married women's property law was the most important of all the legal reforms won by feminists in the nineteenth century. In the history of English law, property and personal status have been closely linked, and the fact that under the law married women controlled no property, their husbands exercising control instead, necessarily reduced them to a subordinate and dependent legal status, deprived of the legal rights and responsibilities of men and unmarried women. Whether spinsters or widows, unmarried women enjoyed the same rights over property as men, with the single (but major) exception that possession of property did not qualify them to vote. It was not the fact of being female but the status of wife that entailed severe legal disabilities. But the great majority of women in England did marry and lose their property, and therefore did become legally subordinate to and dependent upon their husbands. Legally deprived of property, married women were also deprived both of power and of the civil rights of other citizens.

Highly important in themselves, the legal consequences of marriage had implications for the position of women far beyond the realm of law. For example, why should women be educated and trained to work as men were? They would marry and be taken care of, along with their property, by their husbands. Why should they be encouraged to take an interest in social problems and in public affairs? As married women they would have no practical means of helping to solve the problems of their time, and would be regarded legally as merely appendages of their husbands. Why, indeed, should not society generally, women as well as men, consider women to be inferior? The law held that they were. In short, as feminists always argued, the law affecting married women was degrading to all women.

It was for these reasons that one observer of the Victorian scene declared that 'the first point in the women's charter' should be reform of the married women's property law. It was not, he added caustically, 'so attractive and showy a subject as are voting, and speechmaking, and public showing-off of all the usual ridiculous kind,' but it had 'the merit of being useful, and the still greater merit of being quite simple and practicable, although, perhaps in the eyes of the rabid women's rights fanatics, this is its least recommendation.'[3] In fact, reform of the married women's property law was 'the first point in the women's charter.' Feminism as an organized movement made its appearance in England in the 1850s, and the feminists of this time, dedicated to winning reform of the laws affecting women, set as their first priority reform of the laws relating to the property of married women.

Reform of the married women's property law, and feminism itself, can be seen in one light as responses to the changing economic and social position of women in a time of rapid transition. They reflected the passing of a traditional, pre-industrial, and patriarchal society dominated by a landed aristocracy, and the advent of a modern industrialized society, increasingly secular, individualistic, and democratic. In this new society of the nineteenth century it was not quite clear what position women should have, but it was clear that old laws must be brought up to date to meet the needs of the time. In demanding reform of the married women's property law, feminists of the nineteenth century were fortunately not battling adverse intellectual elements. Rather, they were identifying themselves with some of the most important intellectual themes of the period.

The feminists' concern for the freedom and equality of women placed them in the mainstream of nineteenth-century liberalism. Owning John Locke as their godfather and tracing their history from the period of the Enlightenment and the French Revolution, liberals assigned supreme value to individual freedom and natural human rights – according to Locke, life, liberty, and property – and they condemned all social institutions that infringed upon those rights. Perhaps it was inevitable (certainly it was logical) that the Declaration of the Rights of Man in France was shortly followed by Mary Wollstonecraft's *Vindication of the Rights of Woman* in England.

At the same time, the feminists' denunciation of the marriage laws as being destructive of the happiness and welfare of the community identified them with the radicalism of the nineteenth century. Many English radicals, who reckoned Jeremy Bentham as their mentor, and James Mill and John Stuart Mill as perhaps his greatest disciples and spokesmen, used the criterion not of natural rights but of utility to test all institutions – were they or were they not conducive to the greatest happiness of the greatest number of the members of society? By such a test the marriage laws and many other laws as well stood condemned.

Feminists also saw clearly the close connection between the institution of private property and the legal inferiority of married women; they were much more closely akin to the socialists of their day than perhaps many of them realized or wanted to acknowledge. Karl Marx and Friedrich Engels, among a host of socialists of various descriptions, argued that there could be no improvement in the position of women until there was a complete transformation of that capitalist, bourgeois-dominated economy which was the basis of all social institutions and thus the cause of all social ills. Upholders of the existing social order might argue that the marriage laws had been established for the protection of women, but socialists maintained that these laws had actually been established for the protection of private property, and therefore must be abolished or greatly amended.

Finally, the feminists' concern to improve the character of women by improving those institutions, including marriage, which moulded women's character indicated their indebtedness to the evolutionism of their time. The ideas which Charles Darwin and others applied to natural phenomena to explain biological developments were applied (and sometimes misapplied) to explain social institutions and their influence upon the psychological development of individuals. In particular, Darwinism was applied to the study of law, and the appearance in 1861 of Sir Henry Maine's first great work, *Ancient Law*, was a landmark in legal literature. Maine argued that the history of law could be traced through various successive stages of evolution from barbaric to civilized times, and that this progress could be described as a movement from status to contract. All of this gave great support to the feminists' denunciations of the marriage laws as being archaic survivals from primitive times, and to their demands that these laws be amended so that married women would be treated as equal to others in legal rights, including the right to contract, and not treated as inferiors relegated to a special legal status.

In mounting their attacks upon the existing social order, feminists sought to destroy what may be called the patriarchal ideal of society. Despite the many dramatic changes taking place in the country – or more probably because of them – this ideal continued to have great appeal in Victorian times, and much was heard about the sanctity of the family dominated by the father. To many Victorians this traditional family seemed the only certain bulwark against a strange and hostile world. For them, marriage, sanctified by religion, was a sacrament, binding together two people for life, bestowing upon the one headship and control of the household, and requiring of the other and of their children submission and service. So constituted, the family was the essential building block of a civilized society. It was, indeed, a microcosm of the larger society, authoritarian in nature and carefully structured as to hierarchies and duties. So constituted, the family was also the basic unit of the economy, for work was carried on within the framework of the household and under the direction of the father, who controlled all the economic assets of family members for their benefit. In short, for many people patriarchy, or the subjection of women, as John Stuart Mill was to call it, embodied and enhanced all the essential religious and social virtues, and gave coherence to the country's economic life. As such, it had been buttressed by the provisions of the law.

But as the nineteenth century progressed, the patriarchal ideal came under increasingly severe attack. In the first place, there were many critics who, if they did not always denounce religion and the Church, did denounce the baneful influence of what they considered to be false religious ideas and the dominance of a Church which could no longer claim the allegiance of a majority of the population. Specifically, such critics denounced the traditional concept of marriage as a holy and indissoluble bond which gave the husband authority over the wife. They argued that the equality of human beings, including husband and wife, was the basic message of Christianity, and that marriage should be treated, legally at least, as merely a contract between equal partners having mutual rights and obligations.

Second, the patriarchal ideal was denounced as being subversive of the good of society generally. It was not true, critics urged, that a civilized society must be constituted on an authoritarian and hierarchical model, a model provided in microcosm by the patriarchal family. On the contrary, freedom and equality for all individuals were the true goals of a civilized society. But such goals could never be reached until the family itself, the first and most important school for citizens, was reconstituted, by law if necessary, to inculcate the social virtues. So reconstituted, the family would provide, in the relationship of husband and wife, a model of freedom and equality for their children to follow both in family life and in the wider life of society.

Finally, the patriarchal ideal was criticized for failing to take account of the changed economic realities of the day. By the mid-nineteenth century Britain had emerged as the first industrialized country in the world. As such, it had experienced all the economic and social dislocations associated with industrialization. One great and obvious effect of the growth of factory industry and large-scale commerce was the disruption of the small industrial and commercial enterprises carried on by families within the framework of the household. Families were atomized as the household ceased to function as an economic if not as a social unit. Men now went out of their homes to work, and their wives and children often followed them. Sometimes, indeed, women and children went out to work while men stayed home, unable to compete in the labour market with their lower-paid wives and offspring. Thus the economic position of married women was altered dramatically and irreversibly.

The decennial censuses taken in Britain furnish fascinating glimpses of the working out of these great economic changes in the country, although the census figures themselves are tantalizingly incomplete. When the first census was taken in 1801, the persons enumerated were asked to state the occupations of all those included in their households. But census officials considered the answers given to be valueless, for the men questioned returned all members of their families as being employed in their own occupations. The answers are more meaningful to us than they were to the officials of the time, for they illustrate the fact, or at least the general belief, that all members of the family comprised an economic unit. When the censuses of 1811, 1821, and 1831 were taken, no attempt was made to discover the number of individuals employed in different occupations; the figures showed instead the number of families engaged in different types of work. In 1831, for example, of a total of 2,911,874 families in England and Wales, 834,543 families were returned as being employed in agriculture, and 1,227,614 as employed in trade, manufacturing, and handicraft, leaving 849,717 families not employed or not classified.[4]

Still, the census takers persisted in their efforts to obtain a clearer picture of the occupational status of the population. In 1831 men over the age of twenty were enumerated in several occupational groups: agriculture; manufacturing, retail trade, or handicraft; banking, the professions, and education; non-agricultural labour; and domestic service. At the time no attempt was made to enumerate women according to their occupations, with the single major exception of domestic servants of all ages (not merely those over age twenty); the returns showed 560,979 of these women employed.[5] The census of 1841 finally broke completely with earlier practice, classifying individuals, both men and women, rather than families, by their occupations.

For forty years the census takers showed an interesting ambivalence about the position of married women in the country's economic life. The censuses of 1841 and 1851 included within the large general category titled 'without specified occupation or unoccupied' the classes of 'wife' and 'widow.' The census of 1861 included a large occupational category entitled 'domestic,' comprising 'wives,' 'widows,' 'children and relatives at home,' and 'scholars.' That of 1871 included an occupational category entitled 'wives,' and distinguished within it wives mainly employed in household duties and those generally assisting in their husbands' businesses. In the 1881 census and those of succeeding years, wives were again lumped into the category of persons without specified occupations. In short, the shifting census categories indicate the disappearance of the assumption that wives at home were productively employed although not working for wages.

At the same time, the census figures were showing with ever greater clarity that wives in increasing numbers were being employed for wages outside the home. For example, the census of 1851, the first to inquire into the 'conjugal condition' as well as the occupations of the population, revealed that there were in England, Wales, and Scotland 3,461,524 married women, of whom 830,141, or one in four, were employed outside the home, and these women constituted nearly 24 per cent of the total number of women employed in the country.[6]

It was the changing economic position of married women much more than philosophical arguments that undermined the Victorian ideal of patriarchy and led to reform of the married women's property law. Upholders of the patriarchal ideal might never be convinced by feminist arguments that marriage should represent a partnership of equals and that the family should serve as a school for democracy. But eventually they had to face the ugly fact that their principles did not coincide with practice – that there were in the country hundreds of thousands of married women who were not supported and protected by their husbands within the sheltering walls of home. Most of them, then, agreed with their critics that cases such as that of Susannah Palmer must not be allowed to happen – that even if it meant some sacrifice of the principles to which they still clung, the law relating to the property of married women must be amended.

While the philosophy of feminism flowered in the sympathetic intellectual climate of the nineteenth century, the legal reforms advocated and won by nineteenth-century feminists were but a part of a much wider movement for legal reform. Feminist attacks upon the laws applying to women reflected and exemplified that wide-ranging and corrosive criticism of the country's law and legal machinery which led eventually to a complete remoulding of the substance of the law and a thorough overhaul of the court system. To understand the legal context within which the feminists operated, and to trace the success of their efforts to reform the laws, it is necessary to consider the state of the English law and courts and the process by which both were reformed.[7]

There was, quite literally, no system of English law in the early nineteenth century. Instead there were four separate bodies of law administered in different sets of courts, each staffed by different groups of legal practitioners and judges, and each having its own avenue for appeals from its decisions. The country's superior courts exemplified this lack of system: they were scattered all over London, and some had no fixed place of meeting at all.

The common law was the first of the separate bodies of law. Originating in medieval times, this law had evolved as feudal law and local customs were moulded by the interpretations of royal judges and local magistrates throughout the country and were amended from time to time by parliamentary enactments. Hence the name – the law was common to all of England. The common law relating to property illustrates particularly well these medieval origins, for at first it dealt only with land and personal chattels – that is, tangible property capable of physical possession, the only property of importance in a feudal and agrarian society. To afford protection for such property, the common law early developed an elaborate system of writs for which plaintiffs could apply for the remedy of specific, clearly defined grievances. Only slowly and with difficulty did the common law come to recognize forms of property other than land and personal chattels. As a result, the legal rules applying to these various kinds of property were strikingly different.

The common law, being royal law, was administered by royal appointees. At the local level were the justices of the peace, unpaid and untrained magistrates drawn from the gentry of the countryside, who heard and decided the less important cases. According to the nature of the case, the justices sat singly, or in pairs at petty sessions, or together with all their fellow justices of the county at quarter sessions. The most important legal cases were heard by justices of the three superior common-law courts, based in London at Westminster Hall. These three courts, with their complements of puisne judges, were the Court of Queen's Bench and the Court of Common Pleas, each headed by a chief justice, and the Court of Exchequer, headed by a chief baron. Holding life peerages, these chiefs sat not only upon the bench but also in the House of Lords. Practising in these common-law courts were lawyers trained and called to the bar by one of the four ancient inns of court. Appeals from the decisions of any one of the three courts were heard by the judges of the other two courts sitting as the Court of Exchequer Chamber. Final appeal lay to the House of Lords. Because of its unique importance, London had its own legal machinery. Civil cases were heard by the judges of the three superior common-law courts. Criminal cases were tried in the Central Criminal Court, established in 1834 and including among its officials the judges of the three superior common-law courts, the lord chancellor, and the lord mayor, the aldermen, and the recorder of London.

The second great body of English law was equity. Like the common law, equity traced its origins to medieval times, when the king, exercising his prerogative as 'the fountainhead of justice;' acted to afford special relief to suitors as a 'matter of grace.' By the end of the fourteenth century equity had become the established recourse for suitors who, owing to the nature of their cases, which primarily involved what we would call contracts and torts, could not obtain justice from the common-law courts with their system of stereotyped writs.

The great development of equity and the expansion of its jurisdiction came in the seventeenth and eighteenth centuries. This was chiefly a response to the country's changing economic and social structure and its changing legal needs. In particular, various forms of property which were unprotected or inadequately protected by the common law – intangible property, including property held in trust and money invested in public funds and in company stocks and bonds – now made their appearance or grew significantly in importance, so that equity had to fill the breach. Actually, by the early sixteenth century a form of trusts called 'uses' had been developed by equity in order to separate legal and beneficial interests in land; but the Statute of Uses of 1535 effectively barred the equity courts from enforcing these trusts, which had made it possible for landholders to avoid the payment of feudal dues to the crown. By the mid-seventeenth century the modern trust, called a 'use upon a use,' had developed and was enforced in the equity courts. In addition, equity had exclusive jurisdiction in other matters conferred upon it in this period – jurisdiction in cases of bankruptcy, the administration of the estates of intestates, and the guardianship of lunatics and minors, the famous wards in Chancery.

Equity was administered exclusively by the Court of Chancery, headed by the lord chancellor. In medieval times the lord chancellor had been the king's secretary charged with special responsibility for legal matters. By the nineteenth century the lord chancellor was not only the highest judicial official in the kingdom but also an ex officio member of the cabinet and the presiding officer of the House of Lords. At the same time, the lord chancellor's official staff had grown, so that by the nineteenth century it was more accurate to speak not of the Court of Chancery as though it were a single tribunal but of the courts of equity which comprised the Court of Chancery. Suits in equity were heard first by one of the lord chancellor's special deputies, sitting in London at Lincoln's Inn – the master of the rolls, whose office dated back to the sixteenth century, or one of the three vice-chancellors, whose positions had been authorized (one in 1813 and the other two in 1842) in an attempt to clear the arrears of Chancery, since delays of as much as twenty years in deciding cases were not unknown. Practising in the courts of equity were lawyers who, like those practising in the common-law courts, had been trained at the inns of court and had chosen to specialize in equity practice. Appeals from decisions of the master of the rolls and the vice-chancellors lay originally to the lord chancellor, but after 1851 to a new Court of Appeal in Chancery which included, in addition to the lord chancellor, two specially appointed lords justices of appeal in Chancery. Final appeal could be made to the House of Lords.

To relieve the burdens upon the Court of Chancery, a special Court of Bankruptcy, including a chief judge and three other judges, was created in 1831. Appeals from this court's decision lay at first to the lord chancellor, but after 1851 to the Court of Appeal in Chancery and thence to the House of Lords. In 1869 the court was reconstituted as the London Court of Bankruptcy, headed by a chief judge, who was assisted by other judges of the superior courts appointed for the purpose by the lord chancellor. Appeals from the new court, as from its predecessor, lay to the Court of Appeal in Chancery and thence to the House of Lords.

The third great body of law in England was that which was based upon the Roman civil law and upon canon law and was administered by the ecclesiastical courts. In addition to exercising jurisdiction over the clergy of the Established Church in matters of doctrine and discipline, the ecclesiastical courts exercised exclusive jurisdiction in all matrimonial causes, so-called, and in all cases involving the wills of persons deceased. This jurisdiction reflected the powerful position of the Church in medieval times. Marriage was regarded as a sacrament of the Church, which naturally claimed authority over all related questions, such as the validity of marriages. Also, in the middle ages the Church claimed from its members, after their death as during their lifetime, a share of their worldly possessions, unless a document disposing of these possessions could be proved in a Church court to exist – hence the term probate. Because of the military and political obligations to the crown attaching to landholding in medieval times, the royal courts did not recognize wills disposing of land, which under the common law originally passed according to the feudal rules of primogeniture. The ecclesiastical courts were left to deal only with succession to the personal property of persons deceased; but in the seventeenth century they lost to the rival Court of Chancery their jurisdiction over the estates of intestates, retaining thereafter only their jurisdiction in probate and matrimonial causes.

The law of the Church was administered throughout the country in the courts of the bishops. Theoretically each bishop presided over his own court, but in practice his place was taken by a lay deputy who, like the lawyers practising before him, the so-called civilians, had been trained in Roman civil law and in canon law at one of the universities. From the bishops' courts, appeal lay to the courts of the archbishops of Canterbury and of York, and thence, under the provisions of an act of 1832, to the Privy Council.

There was one other relatively narrow and specialized body of law. This was maritime law, administered by the High Court of Admiralty in London, whose presiding judge, having no fixed quarters for his business, borrowed the court of the master of the rolls. In this court were decided cases arising in Britain and cases appealed from the vice-admiralty courts in the colonies. From this court, appeal lay to the Privy Council.

To sum up: in the earlier nineteenth century, English law and the machinery administering it, the fruits of centuries of evolution, were unsystematic and confused. Especially striking were the differences and possible conflicts between the courts administering the two most important bodies of English law, namely the common law and equity.

One major problem was that the jurisdictions of the different sets of courts were ill-defined and sometimes overlapping, with the result that concurrent proceedings might be possible in the same case in different courts. In these circumstances it was not unknown for a suitor to take his case, by way of appeal, all the way to the House of Lords, only to discover that he had begun in the wrong court and must begin again.

The case of a director of a joint-stock company furnishes a good example of the conflict and overlapping of jurisdictions. A company director could be considered both as an agent acting legally for others and as a trustee responsible for the management of others' property. Matters involving agency fell within the jurisdiction of the common-law courts, while matters involving trusts were within the jurisdiction of the courts of equity. Therefore a company director could be sued as an agent in a common-law court, or as a trustee in a court of equity, or he could be sued in both for the same offence.

In some cases a suitor could obtain one kind of remedy in one court and another remedy in another court, but not both together, so that he had to bring separate proceedings in two different courts. For instance, at law a plaintiff could obtain damages for breach of contract or for a tort committed against him, while in equity he could obtain an injunction (a court order forbidding the defendant to continue his existing or contemplated course of action) and could also obtain a decree (an order bidding the defendant do some act, a device that was particularly important in securing the specific performance of contracts).

Another problem related to that of conflicting and overlapping jurisdictions was the fact that courts differed in their choice of factors that were deemed relevant in deciding cases, and therefore they sometimes rendered conflicting decisions on the same sets of facts. An important principle of the equity courts, 'he who seeks equity must do equity,' meant in practice that a party pursuing a claim must permit the court of equity to examine all the circumstances of the case, and particularly the conduct of the parties, such conduct being always relevant. In contrast, the common-law courts considered only the factors relevant to specific claims, and the conduct of the parties might not be relevant at all. For example, in a case of alleged fraud, the common-law courts would determine merely whether a party was guilty of 'wilful intent to deceive,' while the equity courts would allow that party to plead in his defence such mitigating factors as 'mistake' and 'accident' or might consider him guilty of the broader offences of 'undue influence' or 'unconscionable behaviour.'

Finally, the various courts differed greatly in the form of their proceedings and even in the vocabularies they used. For example, in the common-law courts, civil proceedings, which were called actions, began with the application of a plaintiff for a writ to remedy a specific grievance. In the courts of equity, such proceedings, known as suits, began with a plaintiff's presentation of a petition setting forth his grievance. The common-law courts heard evidence given orally in court, while evidence in the courts of equity was given in the form of written depositions taken out of court by special commissioners. The verdict of a jury was the normal method of reaching a decision in the common-law courts, but in the courts of equity decisions were reached by the judge or judges alone. Also, the formalities and technicalities of each court's procedures had to be followed to the letter or else the case might be lost, whatever its merits.

Clearly the country's law and judicial machinery were in dire need of thoroughgoing reform, and the matter attracted the attention and engaged the energetic efforts of many of the most eminent lawyers and lay people of the time. Associations were organized, some to promote specific political and legal reforms, and others, such as the Law Amendment Society and the Social Science Association, to work for legal and social reform generally. Books and pamphlets poured from the presses, describing the deficiencies of the law and urging reforms. Even writers of fiction joined the cause. For example, Dickens's *Bleak House* (1853) can be viewed in one light as a lengthy diatribe against the Court of Chancery. However, Dickens, who began his working life as a law clerk in the 1820s, was not always accurate on points of law. In *The Old Curiosity Shop*, for instance, Daniel Quilp commits suicide, leaving no will, and his widow succeeds to his property; but at that time a suicide was considered a felon and a felon's property was forfeited to the crown; and even if he had not committed suicide his widow would have received only a part of his property. Likewise, in *Pickwick Papers* Mrs Weller makes a will of her property, but she could not have done so unless she had a marriage settlement in equity, which was unlikely for one in her social circumstances; without a settlement her property would have become her husband's at the time of their marriage, and she would have had no right to make a will without his consent.

In this climate of legal reform the substance of the law underwent sweeping revision. For example, the harsh criminal law was rendered more humane. The death penalty was abolished for dozens of offences and lesser punishments were instituted, while statutes were enacted to protect those brought to trial for crimes – such as acts granting the accused the right to be represented by counsel, to be informed of the crown's evidence against him, to call witnesses in his behalf, and to testify in his own defence.

The civil law likewise was thoroughly reformed. For example, the land law was amended to allow freer disposition of real property, to simplify conveyancing, to facilitate the registration of land titles, and to clarify the rules relating to the encumbering of land with debt. The foundations of modern company law were laid as public companies (those formed to execute undertakings of a public nature under special parliamentary sanction) were differentiated from ordinary commercial companies formed for profit, and as the latter were allowed to register and thereby automatically to be incorporated and enjoy the right of limited liability provided they met specified requirements with regard to their organization and financial dealings. The law of contract and tort was refined as, for example, the offences of libel, misrepresentation, and fraud were clarified. The laws relating to bankruptcy were also reformed; the long-standing distinction between traders and non-traders was abolished by the provision that every adult (except a married woman) and not only traders could be declared bankrupt, and imprisonment as a punishment for debt was done away with and the debtors' prisons emptied.

As the substance of the law was remoulded, so likewise the administration of the law was reformed. On the local level the justices of the peace never disappeared, but in this period their judicial powers, like their administrative duties, were whittled away. The Municipal Corporations Act of 1835 allowed the more important towns to appoint trained lawyers as stipendiary magistrates to act in the place of the justices in petty sessions, and to appoint trained recorders to replace the justices in quarter sessions. An act of 1846 created a countrywide system of five hundred county courts grouped into fifty-nine circuits, each having its own judge who dispensed justice at least once a month in each of the districts of his circuit. Originally the county courts were designed to provide a means for the easy recovery of small debts, but gradually their jurisdiction was greatly increased by the conferring upon them of jurisdiction over smaller bankruptcy cases and then of equity jurisdiction generally.

On the national level the first sweeping measures to reform the courts came in 1857. Two acts passed in that year transferred the jurisdiction of the ecclesiastical courts in marital matters and in matters of wills to newly created secular courts – the Court of Divorce and Matrimonial Causes and the Court of Probate. Both were headed by the same official, the judge ordinary, who like the judge of the High Court of Admiralty had no quarters of his own and borrowed those of the lord chancellor at Westminster Hall. Thereafter the civilians, those lawyers previously practising in the ecclesiastical courts, disappeared as a separate branch of the legal profession, merging with the lawyers practising in the other superior courts.

The decade of the fifties also saw the passage of other acts which, while important in themselves, were even more important as an indication of things to come. These acts were based upon the recommendations of a royal commission which had been appointed to study common-law procedure, and which advocated greater fusion of the common law and equity. (A series of acts had already been passed in the 1830s to ensure uniformity of procedure among the three superior common-law courts.) Now, in an attempt to bring into greater harmony the working of the common-law courts and the courts of equity, each set of courts had bestowed upon it some of the powers previously exercised only by the other. For example, the common-law courts were given the equitable power to issue injunctions and the right to allow equitable defences to be pleaded in cases before them; the courts of equity were empowered to take evidence orally as well as by written depositions and to award damages in cases of contract and tort in place of or in addition to their customary remedies of injunctions and decrees. Still, only a slight fusion of the common law and equity was effected; the Chancery judges generally opposed such a fusion unless it were made part of a larger scheme for remodelling the whole judicial system.

At last that large-scale remodelling came. In 1867 a royal commission, which included all the most eminent jurists of the time, was appointed to study the matter. The recommendations contained in its first report, issued in 1869, were enacted by the great Judicature Act of 1873 (36 & 37 Vict., c 66).

The Judicature Act completely reorganized the country's superior courts. All existing superior courts – the three common-law courts, the Court of Chancery, the High Court of Admiralty, the Divorce and Probate Courts, and the London

Court of Bankruptcy – were consolidated into one Supreme Court of Judicature, headed by the lord chief justice of England. This new Supreme Court was organized in two parts – the High Court of Justice and the Court of Appeal. The High Court exercised the jurisdiction of all the previous superior courts, whose judges now became justices of the High Court (with the restriction that they could no longer sit in the House of Commons as well as upon the bench), and it also heard appeals from local justices' petty and quarter sessions and from the county courts. For convenience, the High Court was organized in divisions retaining the names of the old courts, but by 1881 these had been consolidated into three divisions – Chancery, Queen's Bench, and Probate, Divorce and Admiralty. Appeals from decisions of the High Court were heard by at least three judges of the Court of Appeal. These judges were the lord chancellor, the master of the rolls, the lord chief justice of England, the president of the Probate, Divorce and Admiralty division of the High Court, any person who had ever served as lord chancellor and who consented to act at the lord chancellor's request, and up to five lords justices of appeal appointed by the crown. From the Court of Appeal final appeal lay to the House of Lords, which thenceforth could hear cases only if at least three of its specially qualified members were present. These members were the lord chancellor, two lords of appeal in ordinary appointed by the crown, and peers who held or had held high judicial office.

In addition to reorganizing the superior-court system, the Judicature Act provided for the creation of a single code of procedure for the Supreme Court. An appendix to the act included such a code of procedure. This was replaced by another code contained in an amending act of 1875, which provided that the rules of procedure could be further altered by a majority of the Supreme Court justices including the lord chancellor. Thereafter the rules and orders of procedure of the Supreme Court were published annually.

Finally, the Judicature Act of 1873 envisaged a fusion of the common law and equity. The act specifically empowered the Supreme Court to grant all remedies, whether legal or equitable, to which the parties in a case were entitled. More generally, the justices of the Supreme Court were to administer the rules of law and equity concurrently, being always guided by the principle that 'in all matters ... in which there is any conflict or variance between the rules of equity, and the rules of the common law, with reference to the same matter, the rules of equity shall prevail.' From that time until the present day, the Supreme Court, sometimes aided by parliament, has worked toward the goal envisaged by the act of 1873.

Of all the achievements of the Victorian age none was more impressive or important than its thorough reform of the English law and legal machinery. After decades of piecemeal reform there came at last a grand sweeping away of the clutter of courts administering distinct and sometimes conflicting bodies of law which had been inherited from earlier times. In their place was erected one Supreme Court responsible for administering a single system of law, or, as some would argue, one Supreme Court responsible for administering two major systems of law. An event in 1884 aptly symbolized this great achievement – the queen's official opening of the new Royal Courts of Justice in the Strand, where for the first time all the royal courts were gathered together under one roof.

It was in this period of thoroughgoing legal reform that amendment of the law relating to married women's property was demanded and at last achieved. Indeed, to illustrate the long-prevailing conflict between the common law and equity, no better example could be found than the state of the married women's property law. The reform of that law, the 'first point in the women's charter,' furnishes an excellent illustration of the trend of legal reform generally – the attempted fusion of the common law and equity, and the superseding of the law by equity in the case of conflict between them.

2

'The Virtual Slavery of Marriage' The Common Law and Married Women

... the revolt of women against the undue power of their husbands, against the virtual slavery of marriage has not been without cause. Not that they revolted, but that they have borne so long is the wonder.

ELIZA LYNN LINTON[1]

'In law husband and wife are one person, and the husband is that person.' This popular saying, generally ascribed to the great eighteenth-century jurist Sir William Blackstone, aptly summed up the common law relating to marriage.[2] Where matters of property were concerned, the unity of husband and wife meant that the law recognized the husband as the family's sole arbiter. Under the common law the property that a woman possessed or was entitled to at the time of her marriage and any property she acquired or became entitled to after marriage became her husband's to control. Moreover, if a woman who accepted a proposal of marriage sought, before the marriage took place, to dispose of any of her property without the knowledge and consent of her intended husband, the disposition could be set aside as a legal fraud. Were it otherwise, a man could be deprived of the property he had expected to acquire when he made his proposal. In addition, any will made by a single woman disposing of her property was revoked by marriage, as was a man's will, for the husband took over her property upon marriage and her testamentary capacity during marriage was severely limited. Finally, husband and wife could not make gifts to each other after marriage; by the act of marrying, a woman in effect made a gift of her property to her husband, while the fact that a married woman could not legally hold property prevented her husband from making over anything into her possession.

Historians of the law have speculated about the origins of the legal fiction of the identity of husband and wife, with its corollary that married women were deprived of property rights. Some have argued that the common law sought to embody the sacramental view of marriage held by the medieval Church – that marriage made two persons one flesh, and gave the husband dominion over the wife, meaning control of her person and property. Other historians have maintained that the common law, embodying the idea that marriage was for husbands a profitable guardianship of their wives' person and property, merely reflected the economic and social realities of the position of women in the middle ages, when the law developed. This seems the more persuasive argument as to the law's origins and purpose, especially in view of the fact that the extent of a husband's control over his wife's property depended upon the nature of that property.

The common law recognized four different categories of property and applied different rules to each, a reflection of the development over the centuries of various kinds of property which had to be given legal protection. The two most important categories were real property (property in land) and personal property, also called chattels personal, corporeal chattels, or choses in possession (tangible objects capable of physical possession other than land). In addition, there were two categories of property treated as neither real nor personal property but as intermediate between them and partaking of the character of both: chattels real, and chattels incorporeal, or choses in action.

Historians of the law have pondered the reasons for the legal distinctions between real and personal property. Some argue that the basic distinction derived from the common-law writs available to enforce the property rights of claimants. In legal terminology, real actions were available to enforce rights in rem, that is, the rights of a claimant to recover a thing itself, the best example being land. Personal actions were available for rights in personam, that is, the rights of a claimant to receive damages for another's interference with his property. In other words, the law classified property according to the kinds of writs used by claimants, not according to the kind of property. Others maintain that the legal distinction between real and personal property can be traced back to the division of jurisdiction between the royal courts and the ecclesiastical courts that took place in the thirteenth century. The royal courts administering the common law retained their interest in and jurisdiction over land and succession to land because of the military and political incidents then attaching to land tenure, but they lost to the ecclesiastical courts jurisdiction over succession to property other than land, whether under the provisions of wills or under the rules governing cases of intestacy. (In the seventeenth century the ecclesiastical courts, in turn, lost to the courts of equity their jurisdiction over the estates of intestates but retained their probate jurisdiction.) Still others argue that the legal distinction between real and personal property was simply due to the fact that in medieval times, when the law originated, land was both the chief form of wealth and the basic source of livelihood, and was of paramount importance to the upper classes of society. In contrast, personal property was small in amount and value, consisting of such things as household furnishings, clothing, farm implements, and livestock, and was important chiefly to the lower social classes.

Whatever the reasons for the distinction between real and personal property, the legal rules applying to these two categories of property were substantially different. The common law afforded married women considerable protection with respect to real property. It afforded no protection for their personal property.

Real property, the most important category of property recognized by the common law, was of two kinds. The first of these was freehold land. Originally this had been land held of the crown by members of the upper classes who, in return, lay under heavy military and political obligations. Gradually modified over the centuries, the holding of land by knight's service, as it was called, disappeared finally only in the late seventeenth century, when all land so held was converted into freehold land. The second kind of real property was copyhold land. This was originally land held of lords of the manor by persons whose rights and duties were regulated by the custom of the manor as set forth in a copy of the manorial records. This kind of property was not abolished until passage of the Law of Property Act of 1925, which provided for the conversion of copyhold land into freehold land by mutual agreement between landlords and tenants.

The possession of real property, whether land held in exchange for service to the crown or that held in return for service to the lord of the manor, entailed obligations which a woman alone was considered unable to discharge. She could not call out the feudal levies to follow the king to war, nor could she sit in the royal council. She could not cultivate her portion of the manorial lands or perform all the services required by the lord according to the custom of the manor. It was therefore natural that the common law should recognize a woman's husband as responsible in her stead for meeting the obligations imposed by landholding, and also natural that his responsibility carried with it rights – the right to assume sole management of her property and the right to receive and use freely all rents and profits from it.

At the same time the common law, by providing that a husband could not dispose of any of his wife's real property without her consent, made clear that he was merely the guardian of this property and not the legal owner. Any disposition of a married woman's land was accomplished by her and her husband acting jointly, by means of a legal device called levying a fine. Dating from the thirteenth century, this rather expensive process required that a married woman be examined in court separately from her husband to determine whether she freely agreed to the alienation of her land. The Fines and Recoveries Act of 1833, which was designed to simplify the procedures for alienating land, abolished fines and substituted for them the disposition of land by simple deeds, but the act still required that the wife must formally and separately acknowledge her consent. This requirement was abolished by the Law of Property Act of 1925. A woman whose husband alienated her land without her consent could, after his death, obtain a common-law writ of entry and regain possession of the property.

Originally the common law did not recognize the right to devise real property by will. Instead, succession to such property was governed by the feudal rules of primogeniture. But as land tenure in exchange for military service began to disappear, the law came to recognize the principle of testation with respect to land. The Statute of Wills of 1540 first permitted the devising of real property. It was enacted as a concession by Henry VIII after the Statute of Uses of 1535 had effectively abolished the early form of trusts, which had enabled landholders to escape their feudal services to the crown. Still, freedom of testation with regard to land was limited. Men could not devise their wives' real property by will – another illustration of the fact that they were legally only the custodians and not the owners of this property – and their freedom to dispose of their own lands by will was long restricted in order to protect the interests of their wives. Married women were specifically barred from devising their real property by will.

If a wife survived her husband, her real property remained hers legally and it reverted to her control absolutely. At the same time, by the ancient rights of dower and free-bench, she enjoyed a life interest in her husband's lands. These rights had developed in medieval times to compensate women for loss of control over their real property during marriage and, especially, to make provision for widows after their husbands' property had passed to the legal heirs. In earliest times the right of dower was a matter of private arrangement by the parties to a marriage, but by the thirteenth century the common law had come to recognize, and to enforce by appropriate writs, a widow's right to a life interest in one-third of the freehold lands (rather, lands that later became freeholds) which had been in her husband's possession at any time during their marriage. (Perhaps this was the origin of the husband's promise in the marriage service, 'With all my worldly goods I thee endow.') A widow's free-bench right, likewise recognized and enforceable by the law, was generally also a life interest in one-third of the copyhold lands which were in her husband's possession at the time of his death, although it might be a lesser interest, depending upon the custom of the manor. In the case of both dower and free-bench, a widow's right obtained whether or not a surviving child capable of inheriting the land had been born of the marriage. However, a widow lost her rights if her husband was guilty of treason and so forfeited his lands, or if she herself was guilty of treason, felony, or adultery.

These widows' rights were obviously a hindrance to the free disposition of land, and as such came under attack. From earliest times a man could bar his wife's free-bench right by alienating his copyhold land during his lifetime without her consent, since her right attached only to land in his possession when he died. He could also bar her right to dower, if she agreed to this, by levying a fine that conveyed to a third party his freehold land without any restrictions attaching to it. The Statute of Uses of 1535 provided that by an antenuptial agreement with her intended husband a woman could give up her dower right in exchange for a jointure – that is, a settlement of land upon her at least for her own lifetime. The Dower Act of 1833 in effect put an end to dower right, which by then was so rare as to be obsolete. (The act did not apply to a widow's free-bench right in copyhold land.) Under the act's provisions a husband could expressly bar his wife's right of dower, without her consent, by means of a deed conveying his freehold land during his lifetime or a will devising it after his death. If not expressly barred, a wife's dower right continued as before, except that it now attached only to the freehold lands her husband possessed at the time of his death and not to all such lands he had possessed at any time during marriage. The purpose of the Dower Act was to simplify conveyancing, and by the time of its passage there were ways whereby a man could provide property for his widow other than by encumbering his lands. But the act did leave widows unprotected in that it did not require a man to make some provision other than dower for his wife.

If a wife died before her husband, her real property passed not to him but to her heirs-at-law as specified by statute – her children and grandchildren or, failing these, her father or her mother and brothers and sisters. At the same time, a surviving husband had the right by the 'curtesy of England,' as it was called, to a life interest in his wife's lands. This right differed from a widow's dower and free-bench rights in her husband's lands in several ways. It meant a life interest in all of a deceased wife's freehold and copyhold lands, not an interest in only one-third of these. The husband's right depended upon the birth of a child of the marriage capable of inheriting the property, for whom he acted as guardian; strangely, his right was not extinguished if the child died before coming of age. A husband lost his right if he was guilty of treason or felony, but not if he was guilty of adultery. Finally, a wife could make no condition or disposition with respect to her real property so as to set aside her husband's right by the curtesy.

There remains to be considered a peculiar kind of land tenure under the common law, the tenancy by entireties. This tenure arose when land was conveyed to both husband and wife, and they became joint owners of the whole – the one exception to the legal rule that married persons never held land jointly. In this case neither spouse could dispose of the land separately, although they could dispose of it jointly under the provisions of the Fines and Recoveries Act of 1833, and neither could do anything to defeat the other's right by survivorship to possession of the whole property. It should be added that if real property was conveyed in shares to several persons, including a married couple, then the husband and wife took only one share and not two, under the common-law rule that they were not two persons but one. This long-standing rule relating to real property was, in the course of the nineteenth century, made applicable also to a married couple's share in personal property coming to them jointly.

While the common law relating to real property granted married women substantial protection, the law relating to personal property held that all such property that belonged to a woman at the time of marriage and all that she acquired after marriage were her husband's absolutely. He could use and dispose of this property in any way he chose during his lifetime without his wife's consent. He did not lose this property if she was convicted of felony, for it was no longer hers to be forfeited to the crown, although he forfeited it if he himself was guilty of felony. As the legal owner of this property he could, without his wife's consent, bequeath it by will. A wife could make a will bequeathing her personal property only with her husband's consent, and he could withdraw this consent at any time before the will was proved. A further complication was that if a husband died before his wife, any will she had made with his consent was revoked, and if she died without making another will she was held to have died intestate. If a wife died before her husband without making a will, her personal property became – or rather, remained – her husband's absolutely, to the exclusion of her children or other relatives.

The one exception to these rules relating to a married woman's personal property was that class of property legally termed 'paraphernalia' – that is, the clothing and personal ornaments that a woman possessed at the time of marriage or that her husband gave her during marriage. A husband could dispose of these items, like the rest of his wife's personal property, during his lifetime, but if he did not dispose of them they reverted to his wife's possession after his death, for he could not bequeath them by will and they did not pass under the rules governing cases of intestacy if he made no will. Still, a widow might be deprived of this property, for it was liable for the settlement of her husband's debts after his death, so that his creditors might take it.

As for the disposition of a man's personal property after his death, his wife had no claim to this property, including any he had acquired from her, against the provisions of his will. At one period in the middle ages the common law had held that a wife and children had certain rights in a man's personal property of which he could not deprive them by will, rights which were analogous to a widow's dower and free-bench rights in her husband's real property and which were likewise enforceable by common-law writs. Under the medieval rule of 'reasonable parts' a childless widow was entitled to one-half of her husband's personal property, and a widow with offspring was entitled to one-third while the child or children took one-third, so that a man could dispose freely only of the remaining half or third. But by the fourteenth century this rule began to disappear from the common law, and it became possible for a man to leave to his surviving wife and children no share at all in his personal property, including that which had come to him from his wife. This freedom of testation survived well into the twentieth century.

The medieval rule of 'reasonable parts' long applied in modified form only in the case of men who died without making wills, and was formalized with enactment of the Statutes of Distribution of 1670 and 1685. These acts provided that a widow with offspring would receive one-third of her husband's personal property and the child or children two-thirds, while a childless widow would receive half the property and the rest would go to the husband's near relatives – parents, brothers and sisters, and so on – or, if he had none, to the crown.

There remain to be considered the rights of married women with respect to the two other categories of property recognized by the common law as being somehow like, yet different from, real and personal property. The first of these categories, called chattels real, was land held under the terms of a lease for a specified period of time, whether for life or a series of lives or for a term of years, and was therefore distinct from freehold and copyhold land, which constituted real property. Since much house property was classed as leasehold land, this was a very large and important category of property indeed. Not until passage of the Law of Property Act of 1925 was provision made for the conversion of some leasehold land into freehold land. A married woman's chattels real were like her personal property in that her husband could sell or otherwise dispose of them during his lifetime; they were forfeited to the crown if he was guilty of treason or felony; and if his wife died before him without making, with his consent, a will disposing of them, they became his property absolutely. At the same time a married woman's chattels real were like her real property in that her husband, although he was entitled absolutely to the income and profits from them during his lifetime, could not dispose of them by his will; nor, if he died without a will, did they pass under the rules governing cases of intestacy, but instead reverted to her absolute possession and control if she survived him.

The second category of property recognized by the common law as lying between real and personal property was called chattels incorporeal, or choses in action. These, being personal claims by one individual against another or others, were incorporeal in that they were not tangible objects but they could, in the legal phrase, be reduced into possession – that is, they could be converted into money, thereupon becoming personal property or corporeal chattels. A complication was the distinction made between legal and equitable choses in action – those recognized by the common law and recoverable by actions in the common-law courts, and those recognized by equity and recoverable by suits in the courts of equity. Legal choses in action included, for example, simple contract debts, shares and bonds of joint-stock companies, patents and copyrights, and damages for injuries sustained through breach of contract and tort. A husband had the right to reduce into possession his wife's choses in action, thereby converting them into personal property which was his own absolutely, which he could dispose of as he pleased during his lifetime and bequeath by will, and which his wife could bequeath by will only with his consent. A married woman's choses in action were also like her personal property in that, if she died before her husband without making a will with his consent, they became her husband's absolutely – or, in more precisely legal terms, her husband had the right to serve as administrator of her estate and in that capacity to reduce her choses in action into possession, thereby becoming the absolute owner. A married woman's legal choses in action were like her real property in that her husband could not sell or dispose of them; they were not forfeited by his treason or felony; and if he died before her without reducing them into possession, they reverted to her ownership and control.

Despite the complexity of the legal rules relating to married women's rights in different categories of property, one fact stood out clearly and consistently – during marriage women had no property at their disposal; instead, their husbands assumed ownership or at least control of their property. Unlike single women and widows, who had the same property rights as men, except the right to vote, married women had legally no rights over property. Since property and status went hand in hand in English law, wives were reduced to a special status, subordinate to and dependent upon their husbands. In the words of Sir William Blackstone, 'By marriage the very being or legal existence of a woman is suspended, or at least it is incorporated or consolidated into that of the husband, under whose wing, protection and cover she performs everything, and she is therefore called in our law a *feme covert*.'[3]

The fact that a married woman had no property under her control, so that her legal existence was 'incorporated or consolidated into that of the husband,' meant in practice that her husband acted perforce as her legal representative. That is, in any legal action involving his wife, a man sued or was sued jointly with her if the cause of the action arose before marriage, or alone if the cause arose after marriage. Thus, while marriage gave a man wide powers over his wife's property and might therefore be a very profitable arrangement for him, it carried heavy responsibilities as well.

Upon marriage a husband assumed legal responsibility in all actions involving his wife that had arisen before their marriage. He became responsible for reducing her choses in action into possession – that is, taking legal action to recover any money owed to her – and the money recovered, being personal property, became his absolutely. At the same time, the husband became responsible for any debts his wife had incurred, any contracts she had entered into, and any torts she had committed before marriage; he was liable whether or not he had obtained property from her upon marriage, and liable to the full extent of his own property. If husband and wife were successfully sued with respect to her antenuptial obligations and failed to pay, both could be imprisoned, but as a matter of indulgence the court would order the wife released, since she could not legally acquire property with which to pay, while her husband remained in jail. Finally, the husband's liability to meet his wife's antenuptial obligations was a joint one only – that is, he could only be sued jointly with his wife during marriage, not sued alone after his wife's death even if he had become entitled to all of her property at her death. If the wife survived her husband, she again became liable to meet her antenuptial obligations, even if her husband's death left her without property at her disposal.

As his wife's legal representative, a man was likewise responsible in cases of tort involving her that arose after marriage. He sued in her behalf for damages due her as a result of torts committed against her, and the money recovered as damages became his absolutely. He was sued in her stead for torts she committed, and was liable for these whether or not he had acquired property from her upon marriage, and liable to the full extent of his own property. If a wife died before her husband, he was still liable to pay damages for her torts, but if a husband predeceased his wife, damages were not payable out of his estate; the wife became liable instead.

At the same time, a husband had the right to sue for damages in his own behalf for abrogation of his marital rights in two cases of torts involving his wife. The first of these was a case of criminal conversation, as it was called, in which a husband sought damages from another man who had committed adultery with his wife. The second was a case when damages were sought for loss of consortium, a word loosely defined as meaning a wife's 'comfort and society' or 'society and services.' Loss of consortium might result from the so-called enticement of a wife so that she left her husband or failed in her marital duty to him, or it might be caused by injuries sustained by a wife through an assault upon her or through an accident caused by another's negligence, in which case the damages collected by the husband for loss of consortium were in addition to, not in lieu of, the damages he obtained by suing in his wife's behalf. A wife, however, could not sue a woman guilty of adultery with her husband or sue another for loss of her husband's consortium; for, having no legal identity apart from her husband, she could not sue at all.

Finally, it should be pointed out that husband and wife could not sue each other in tort – as, for example, by attempting to collect damages for injuries suffered as a result of the other's negligence. This was so because legally they were not two persons but one – no person could sue and collect damages from himself. The husband already had legal ownership or control of his wife's property out of which her damages would be paid, and the wife could not legally hold personal property coming to her, including money paid as damages.

A husband was also legally liable upon contracts which his wife entered into during marriage, acting under the common law of agency. Technically a married woman could not enter into contracts in her own name, for she had no property under her control out of which her contracts could be satisfied, but since the late fifteenth century the common law had held that she could enter into contracts in her husband's name and as his agent. Still, from the time of Henry VIII the law had also held that a wife, merely as such, had no right to act as her husband's agent. Rather, her agency arose from her husband's express or implied consent. That is, a man could expressly authorize his wife to act as his agent (he could also expressly forbid her to do so), or his consent to her agency would be inferred from the fact that they lived together and she was in charge of managing their household. In like manner a man's agent might be his daughter, his sister, or a housekeeper who managed his domestic arrangements. Under the law of agency a wife could pledge her husband's credit with tradesmen for the supply of necessaries, as they were called, suitable to their station in life; the items normally considered necessaries were food, lodging, clothing, and medical attendance and medicines.

However, a husband might escape responsibility for contracts that his wife entered into in his name by successfully rebutting the presumption that she had been acting as his agent. He could, for example, prove that he had already provided all necessary supplies for the household; that he had paid his wife an allowance sufficient to enable her to obtain necessaries without pledging his credit; that his wife had extravagantly exceeded the authority he had given her; that he had expressly forbidden his wife to pledge his credit, although this fact was not known to the tradesmen concerned; or that the articles supplied were not necessary, in the sense that they were not suitable to his station in life. In each case it was for a jury to decide on the facts, for the law was clear – a husband, merely as such, could not be compelled to honour contracts his wife entered into.

The legal inability of married women to make contracts in their own names bore especially heavily upon those women who wished to carry on businesses or trades separately from their husbands for their own benefit. In medieval times a wife who was a 'separate trader' had been treated in many parts of the country as an unmarried woman with untrammelled property rights, but by the nineteenth century this privileged treatment had disappeared everywhere except in the City of London. A woman's marriage dissolved any partnership of which she was a member, and she could not enter into a partnership after marriage, for her husband assumed control of her property and she could not bind herself by any contract. After marriage a woman could carry on a business alone and separately from her husband if he agreed to her doing so, in which case he forfeited his legal right to ownership of her business assets. However, the wife's assets were still liable for the payment of her husband's debts, and her husband was liable upon her business contracts since she herself could not be held liable and could not be declared a bankrupt.

Finally, husband and wife could not contract with each other, for legally they were one person, the husband, who controlled the property of both. Also, contracts made by a man and woman who later married were voided, not technically but in effect, for during marriage neither spouse had legal remedies against the other – that is, they could not sue each other for breach of contract.

In this connection it should be pointed out that the legal principle of the unity of husband and wife had bearings upon the law of evidence in civil proceedings, such as might arise with respect to a married woman's torts and contracts. For centuries it had been the legal rule that none of the parties involved in a civil case could give evidence, the presumption being that an interested party would be tempted to commit perjury to influence the outcome of the case. Since husband and wife were legally one person, neither could testify in proceedings involving the other. However, an act of 1851 amended the ancient rule by allowing the parties in civil cases to give evidence, and another act of 1853 drew the logical conclusion from this by allowing the husband or wife of a party to testify as well. The purpose of the latter act was to tidy up the law of evidence, not to give greater legal rights to married women, but it was one small chip out of the enormous block of legal disabilities that weighed upon wives.

If husband and wife could not commit a tort against each other or contract with each other, neither could they steal from each other and be charged with larceny. This was so because larceny was legally defined as taking possession of goods without the owner's consent. Since a man became legally the owner or at least the custodian of his wife's property, clearly his appropriation of this property did not constitute a crime – he could not steal from himself. A woman who appropriated her husband's goods was presumed to be acting with his consent in her status of wife. However, decisions in a number of cases in the mid-nineteenth century indicated that larceny was in fact involved if a wife who took her husband's property had committed or intended to commit adultery; the act or the intention destroyed her status of wife and therefore ended her right to use her husband's property. Still, the wife in such a case could not be charged with larceny, although her lover might be charged as a receiver of stolen goods. In contrast, a man's actual or intended adultery did not end his rights in his wife's property.

Even if the law relating to larceny had been different, the law of evidence in criminal proceedings would probably have precluded successful prosecution of a husband or wife for stealing the other's property. An old and honoured rule of the law of evidence was that no person could be compelled to testify against himself. This meant in practice that husband and wife could not give evidence against each other, for under the legal principle that they were one person the giving of evidence by either would have been equivalent to self-incrimination. The Criminal Evidence Act of 1898, consolidating a number of earlier nineteenth-century acts which had allowed persons charged with certain criminal offences to give evidence in their defence, provided that the husband or wife of the accused could testify either for or against the accused. A decision of the House of Lords in 1912 interpreted the act to mean that a wife could give evidence against her husband even if he objected, but that she could not be compelled to testify against him if she objected to doing so.

The fact that the common law recognized the husband as the legal representative of his wife, responsible under the law for her actions during marriage, had important consequences not only with respect to his control of her property but also with respect to his control of her person. As an eminent nineteenth-century judge expressed it, 'For the happiness and honour of both parties it [the law] places the wife under the guardianship of the husband, and entitles him for the sake of both, to protect her from the danger of unrestrained intercourse with the world ...'[4] That is, the law considered the husband to be not only his wife's legal representative but also her moral guardian.

The husband's guardianship of his wife, and his legal responsibility for her, entailed his right to control her actions and to chastise her to keep her within the bounds of wifely duty. Since the late seventeenth century, courts had held that chastisement did not extend to physical punishment but meant only admonition of the wife and her confinement to the house. Yet older interpretations lingered on, and it was generally believed that a man could beat his wife, although not in a violent or cruel manner – not with a stick thicker than his thumb.

But a wife was not without legal protection against her husband; she had two means of acting legally against him in her own defence. She could prosecute her husband for assault and battery or for threatening or attempting to do her grievous bodily harm; or she could, by a process called swearing the peace, apply to a court for an order binding her husband to keep the peace if he had subjected her to bodily injury, imprisonment, or cruelty. These were long the only cases in which a wife was allowed to give evidence in court against her husband. Not until 1891, in the famous case of *R* v *Jackson*, did the Supreme Court finally rule that a husband had no right to coerce his wife or confine her against her will. In this case a man whose wife had left him seized her forcibly in the street one day and carried her off to his house, where he locked her in; her friends then successfully brought habeas corpus proceedings against him. Commenting on the court's decision, a contemporary periodical declared, 'One fine morning last month marriage in England was suddenly abolished.'[5]

The husband's guardianship of his wife had implications not only for her personal well-being and freedom but for her treatment under the criminal law as well. For example, a married woman who committed any but the most serious crimes – murder and treason – in the presence of her husband was presumed to be acting under his coercion and this could be pleaded in her defence. Not until 1925 was this presumption of marital coercion abolished. (It was never presumed that a man who committed a crime in his wife's presence was coerced by her.) As another example, a husband could be made an accessory after the fact to a felony committed by his wife, the presumption being that he might well have connived at her offence; but generally a wife did not become an accessory after the fact to her husband's felony, for she was considered not as having aided and abetted a criminal but as having received and helped her husband as any dutiful wife should do.

While the law recognized the husband as both the legal representative and the moral guardian of his wife, it also presumed him to be the family breadwinner, responsible for maintaining his wife and children. This being the presumption, it seemed only natural and just that the law should give the husband ownership or control of his wife's property to help him meet his obligations to his family. However, the law failed to provide any effective way of compelling a husband to meet his financial responsibilities for his family if he shirked them. His wife could not, of course, charge him with non-support, for legally they were one person and could not sue each other.

There were only two indirect and cumbersome means whereby a wife could try to compel her husband to support her. The first such means was for her to invoke the law of agency and pledge her husband's credit with tradesmen for the supply of necessaries. But tradesmen were understandably loath to supply a married woman when this might involve them in a lawsuit with her husband, who could rebut the presumption of her agency. Moreover, obtaining supplies on credit was probably a practice more prevalent among the prosperous classes of the community than the poorer classes. The second means was for a wife to appeal to the provisions of the Poor Law. As early as 1601 the Poor Law had recognized the responsibility of parents to support their children so that they did not become charges on the parish, but it did not recognize a husband's liability to support his wife until 1834. The Poor Relief Act of that year provided that relief given to a married woman by the Poor Law guardians should be considered a loan which the guardians could recover from the husband. An amending act of 1868 provided that when a married woman required relief, the guardians might apply to the local magistrates, who in turn could order the husband to pay a reasonable amount weekly or otherwise for his wife's maintenance, if he failed to show good cause why he should not support her. However, the legal initiative rested not with the wife but with the Poor Law guardians, who might refuse to act, in which event a woman had no recourse.

A woman might try to support herself and her children if her husband did not do so, or to supplement the support that he did provide, but her way was beset with legal problems, whether she worked on her own account or worked for others. As has been seen, it was difficult for a married woman to carry on her own business because of her contractual incapacity under the law. A husband was naturally reluctant to agree to his wife's trading separately when this meant that he could not profit from the business but was legally responsible for it, while tradesmen were hesitant to do business with a woman who was legally not independent but merely acting as her husband's agent. As for the married woman who worked at some occupation for a salary or wages, her earnings were personal property and as such were the property of her husband, who could dispose of the money however he pleased.

The problem of enforcing a wife's right to maintenance by her husband was particularly acute when the marriage had ended, in effect but not legally, whether by mutual agreement of the parties to separate or by the desertion of one by the other. A special problem in this connection was that separation of husband and wife, even when a husband deserted his wife, did not end his common-law rights in her property. He still controlled and received the income from her real property, her chattels real, and her choses in action, and still was the absolute owner of her personal property. In such a case a wife had several courses open to her, none of them very effective or desirable.

A woman might reach an agreement with her husband that they would live apart and he would pay her an allowance. But such agreements were long considered to be outside the scope of the common law, for they were equivalent to contracts, and under the law husband and wife could not contract with each other. Consequently a husband's undertaking to pay his wife an allowance could not be legally enforced. Not until a decision by the lord chancellor in a case in 1862 did the common law recognize such separation agreements as binding.

A woman who lived apart from her husband could also invoke the law of agency, pledging his credit for her support. Originally, as has been seen, the law had recognized a wife's right to act as her husband's agent only with his express consent or with his consent implied by the fact that they lived together and she was responsible for the management of their household. But the ruling in a leading case in the early eighteenth century, upheld by later decisions, was that if a wife left her husband for good cause or if he deserted her, so that she was unprovided for or had an inadequate allowance, then she became his agent of necessity, entitled to pledge his credit. Still, difficult problems were likely to arise in these circumstances. In the first place, a woman had to find tradesmen willing to supply her with necessaries at the risk of having to sue her husband to recover debts she had incurred in his name. Then, if it came to a court case for recovery of the money, the husband might successfully rebut the presumption that his wife was acting as his agent of necessity. He could claim that his wife had left him without good cause; that she had committed adultery after their separation; that he had paid her an adequate allowance, or that he had paid her the allowance they had agreed upon, even though it proved inadequate for her needs; that she had other means of support, or that she had earned money while living apart so that she had no need to pledge his credit; that he had warned tradesmen not to give her credit; that the debts she had incurred were extravagant in view of his station in life; and that she had refused his offer to return to cohabitation. In each case the burden of proof rested not on the husband but on the creditor.

A woman deserted by her husband might also seek relief from the ecclesiastical courts. These courts could issue a decree for restitution of conjugal rights on the petition of either a husband or a wife who had been deserted by the other partner to the marriage, provided the desertion was not caused by the petitioner's adultery or cruelty. Such a decree ordered the deserting spouse to return to cohabitation with the petitioner. Originally the penalty for failure to obey such an order was the purely spiritual one of admonition, followed by sterner ecclesiastical measures if need be, but in the early nineteenth century imprisonment by the civil authorities became the penalty. However, imprisonment of her husband was no aid to a wife seeking maintenance from him, and if he returned to cohabitation under threat of imprisonment he was not likely to be well-disposed or generous to her.

As a last resort, a woman deserted by her husband or living apart from him without adequate means of support could apply for poor relief. But, as seen above, the Poor Law guardians might not grant her request for aid or might not apply to the magistrates for an order requiring her husband to contribute to her support, so that she was left without recourse.

Finally, something needs to be said about the law relating to the custody of children. This question, like that of a wife's right to maintenance by her husband, was especially acute in cases of separation of husband and wife. The common law on this matter is easily summed up: the father had the absolute right to custody of the children; the mother had no rights at all. If a father took his children away from the mother against her will, he did so with impunity. If a mother kept her children from their father, he could enforce his right to possession of them through habeas corpus proceedings in a court of common law, which would take no account of the fact that the father's character was bad and the mother's unblemished. This legal rule resulted perhaps not from the law's blindness to the fact that children had two parents and not merely one, but from the fact that married women had no property legally under their control and thus no practical means of supporting their children. At the same time a father's only legal responsibility for the support of his children, as for the support of his wife, was the so-called Poor Law obligation not to allow them to become charges on the parish. Only in the case of an illegitimate child did a mother have the unquestioned legal right to custody. She was also legally responsible for supporting the child, although several acts passed during the nineteenth century attempted to compel the putative father to contribute to the child's support.

The common law may have served well the needs and interests of a patriarchal society dominated by the noble classes such as existed in medieval times when land was the most important kind of property. In those times married women enjoyed substantial legal protection with respect to property. If a wife surrendered to her husband management of her land, at least she must agree to any alienation of it. If she died before her husband, her land passed not to him but to her legal heirs. If she was left a widow, her real property reverted to her control, and she enjoyed a life interest in part of her husband's lands as well. When personal property was of relatively little importance compared with land, and when it was produced or used by the family or household functioning as an economic unit rather than by individuals, perhaps it mattered little in practice that married women could not legally own such property.

But medieval times were long past, and the common law did not serve well the needs and interests of a country where enormous economic and social changes had taken place over the centuries. In particular, it did not serve well the needs and interests of married women, whose position, especially with respect to property, had been drastically altered.

In the first place, as conditions of landholding changed, the law of real property had been amended, but not for the benefit of married women. With the ending of land tenure in exchange for military service by the seventeenth century and with the decline of the medieval peasant communities, the original practical reason for a husband's management of his wife's land had disappeared, but the law still recognized his control. Freedom of testation with respect to land replaced the medieval rules of hereditary succession and primogeniture, but a married woman still could not legally devise her real property by will. A widow's protection through her right of dower in her husband's lands had been gradually whittled away and in the early nineteenth century was at last abolished, but a husband still retained his right by the 'curtesy' to a life interest in his deceased wife's lands.

Second, with the passage of time new forms of wealth had appeared that did not fit neatly into the old legal categories of real and personal property. To these new kinds of property were applied some of the rules relating to land and some of the rules applying to personal chattels, with the result that the common law of property became ever more complicated, unintelligible to lay people and confusing even to lawyers. By the nineteenth century these new forms of property, rather than land as in medieval times, were most likely to comprise the possessions of wealthy women. Many of these women came from those new classes of society whose wealth derived not from land but from industry and trade, and therefore they did not fit into the hierarchical structure of medieval society. At the same time the old landed classes, in making provision for their children, usually preferred to bestow upon their sons real property and the responsibility for its management, while to their daughters they gave more easily manageable forms of property, such as leasehold land and investments of monies in government funds and joint-stock companies. Under the legal rules applied to them, such forms of property belonging to a woman passed into the absolute control of her husband during his lifetime, although he could not make a will disposing of them after his death.

Finally, personal property had increased tremendously in amount and value over the centuries, and was now totally different in nature from the simple personal chattels recognized by the medieval common law. This change resulted as the agrarian society of the middle ages, with its small-scale, family-based commercial and industrial enterprises, gave way before a modern industrialized society. The growth of large-scale business ventures, especially the rise of factory industry in the later eighteenth and nineteenth centuries, enormously increased the country's wealth while breaking down the traditional organization of trade and industry. Men, and women as well, went out to work in factories, shops, and offices, so that a great proportion of personal property now consisted of the money paid as salaries and wages to those who were employed outside the home. Such property, when acquired by a married woman, belonged legally not to her but to her husband, who as the absolute owner could use and dispose of it however he pleased, both during his lifetime and by will after his death.

To the feminists of nineteenth-century England the common law relating to the property of married women was one of the most basic, if not the most basic, of all the disabilities under which women suffered. By depriving married women of property the law deprived them of legal existence, of the rights and responsibilities of other citizens, and thus of self-respect. Since they had no property under their control, married women could not enter into contracts, nor could they sue and be sued. They could not carry on a business or trade, or could do so only with great difficulty. Married women could not be held liable for their actions, their husbands being legally responsible instead. Here the law might be as unjust to men as to women, for husbands were liable for their wives' actions whether or not they had obtained property from them. From this it followed naturally that married women were subject to their husbands' control of their persons as well as their property. In short, the law placed married women in the same category with criminals, lunatics, and minors as being legally incompetent and irresponsible.

The practical hardships that married women suffered under the law were more serious than any psychological injury. Since men gained legal ownership or at least control of their wives' property, it naturally occurred to the more unscrupulous that they should marry a woman of wealth, or at least an able and industrious woman who could earn a living for them or help them to earn a living. The law assumed that husbands supported their wives and children, and this assumption seemed to justify the legal rule that husbands owned or controlled their wives' property. If it was true that most men did support their families, it was equally true that some men could not or would not do so. In many instances, especially among the lower classes, families were as much dependent upon the property, particularly the earnings, of the wife as upon the husband's, and sometimes the work of the wife and children furnished the whole of the family's income. But whatever the circumstances, the husband remained legally the owner or custodian of the family property, and too many sad cases showed that he could use this property, including that brought to him by his wife, in any way he chose, that he could leave his wife and children penniless and dependent upon the charity of relatives and friends or upon the colder charity of the workhouse, if, indeed, they could obtain even that.

Such facts justified the feminist claim that marriage, or at least the married women's property law, reduced women to a state of 'virtual slavery.'

3

'The Guardian of the
Weak and Unprotected'
Equity and
Married Women

To describe the common law relating to the property of married women is to give only a part (although by far the larger part) of the picture of the position of wives with respect to property. To correct the omissions and injustices of the common law, there had developed over the centuries the rival system of equity. Under the common law, so feminists maintained, married women were little better than their husbands' slaves. In equity, married women enjoyed a special status with property rights not only equal but in some ways superior to the rights of their husbands and of unmarried women.

Both the common law and equity proceeded upon the assumption that married women needed protection. The common law regarded a woman's husband as her guardian, under whose 'wing, protection and cover' she lived, moved, and had no legal being. But equity, generally considered to be 'the guardian of the weak and unprotected, such as married women, infants and lunatics,' tended to view a woman's husband as 'the enemy,' and against his 'exorbitant common-law rights the Court of Chancery waged constant war.'[1] As a result, the rules of equity relating to married women's property were diametrically opposed to the rules of the common law.

One might argue that if the common-law rules of the identity of husband and wife reflected the sacramental view of marriage held in medieval times, then the opposite view of husband and wife in equity resulted from the breakdown of the doctrines and power of the Church in the Reformation and post-Reformation ages. After the marital misadventures of Henry VIII and, in particular, after the more radical Protestant sects began to claim that marriage was not a sacrament at all but merely a civil contract, it was increasingly difficult to maintain that marriage was both a physical and a spiritual union of two persons sanctified by the Church, a union which the law should recognize in secular matters.

A more persuasive argument as to the origin of the equitable assumptions respecting husband and wife is that, just as the common law reflected the economic and social realities of the medieval period during which it developed, so

equity reflected the changed realities of a time when the structure of the medieval society and economy began to crumble. The common law had always
recognized an owner's right to dispose of personal property, and as conditions of
landholding changed, with the abrogation of military land tenure and the legal
recognition of testation with respect to land, the general rule of the law came to
be freedom of disposition of all property, real as well as personal. The landed
classes were alarmed, for freedom to dispose of property implied the dangerous
ability of both sons and daughters to squander the family wealth if their actions
could not somehow be controlled. At the same time there had appeared important new classes of society whose wealth, derived not from land but from commerce and industry, did not fit comfortably within the legal categories of real
and personal property. These classes, too, were concerned to find protection for
their property to prevent its being wasted by sons and daughters alike. And both
the old landed aristocracy and the new aristocracy of the business world felt
acutely the special need to protect the property of their daughters from the
common-law rights of husbands, and to ensure that if there were no children of a
marriage the property would not pass to their daughters' husbands but would
return to their own families. It was in these circumstances that the wealthy
classes turned to equity for the protection of their property that they could not
find under the common law.

To meet the needs of the propertied classes, equity developed the trust settlement of property. Originally trusts were matters of private arrangement, and
they remained unrecognized by the common law and unenforceable in the common-law courts. By the early sixteenth century the form of trusts called 'uses'
had developed, enabling landholders not only to avoid paying feudal dues to the
crown but also to make provision for their wives and children after their death.
In such a case a man of property would convey land to a friend as trustee, to
hold it for the benefit of his widow and children. The common-law courts looked
only at who was named the new owner of the land (that is, the friend-trustee)
and did not recognize that the surviving wife and children had any interest in
the property. But early lord chancellors, as 'keepers of the king's conscience,'
took upon themselves the enforcement of trusts, since otherwise there would
have been no protection for wives and children against the wrongdoing of trustees. The common-law judges acquiesced in the development of equitable trusts,
coming to regard settled property as merely a chose in action and therefore not
legally property at all – that is, neither real nor personal property. (However, as
has been seen, the common law eventually recognized certain choses in action as
property, intermediate between real and personal property.) The Statute of Uses
of 1535 effectively barred the courts of equity from enforcing this early form of
trusts, at least when they were used to avoid payment of feudal dues to the

crown. Yet trusts continued, for the Statute of Uses specifically allowed a woman to surrender her dower right in her intended husband's land in exchange for his settlement upon her of a jointure, which was a freehold estate secured to a woman for her life following the death of her husband.

It was in the seventeenth century that the great mass of the equitable doctrines and procedures relating to trust property developed. This was a time of troubles for the propertied classes. In the midst of religious and political revolution lives might be lost, and property as well, forfeited by the losers in internecine struggles unless it could be safeguarded by equity. Feudal dues to the crown – and the crown itself, for a time – were abolished, and by this time the modern form of trust, the 'use upon a use,' had developed and was enforced by the courts of equity. In particular, a device originally used by landholders to avoid feudal dues and to provide for their widows and orphans was adapted to secure property to married women.

In practice the Court of Chancery allowed the creation of a special category of property, the so-called separate property or separate estate of married women. At law a married woman could not own property, but in equity property could be settled upon her for her use under the management of a trustee who was responsible to the court for carrying out the terms of the trust. At first it was necessary to prove to the court's satisfaction that there was good reason for the creation of a trust, as, for example, that the husband was a wastrel or that the woman was separated from her husband. But soon equity came to accept without inquiry any trust created for a married woman. The separate property created by the trust would be protected by the Court of Chancery against a woman's husband and all other persons according to the wishes of the donor. Interestingly, a married woman's separate property in equity existed only during her marriage, for its existence was due to the need to protect it against her husband's common-law rights.

Separate property in equity could be of any kind – that is, property which at law would be categorized as real property, personal property, chattels real, and choses in action – and it could be created at any time by any person who was of full age and sound mind. Both before and after a woman's marriage she, her relatives, and her friends could settle property upon her for her separate use. In the seventeenth century the Court of Chancery applied the general rule that a man must consent to the settlement of property upon his wife – just as, at law, a man must know of and agree to his future wife's disposition of her property – but gradually this rule was dropped. Also, a man could create separate property for his future wife, as by the settlement of a jointure upon her in return for her surrender of her right of dower in his lands. Likewise after marriage a man could bestow separate property upon his wife, an act impossible under the common law, which held that husband and wife, being one person, could not make gifts to one another.

Separate property could be created in several ways. The usual way was the drawing up of a written instrument setting forth the terms of the trust, either a deed or will disposing of property or a marriage settlement, a contract negotiated between the parties to a marriage or their families before the marriage took place. Such a contract was enforceable only in the courts of equity, for the common law, holding that husband and wife could not contract with each other, in effect voided contracts made by a man and woman who later married. Frequently the document creating a woman's separate estate in equity used some set form of words to describe the property, as, for example, that it was 'for her sole and separate use and benefit, independently and exclusively of the said [husband], and without being in anywise subject to his debts, control, interference or engagements.' No special form was required, however, and the obvious intention of the donor would suffice to create separate property. Usually the document specifically named a trustee of the separate property, but the Court of Chancery would validate the trust even if this was not done. In such a case the court recognized the husband as trustee for his wife, since under the common law the property would have been his to control, but he was required to deal with the property according to the terms of the trust and not treat it as being his own.

Separate property in equity could also be created otherwise than by a written instrument. This could be done by a merely verbal agreement between husband and wife, or by the husband's simply acquiescing in his wife's treating certain property as her separate property. In both cases the husband was considered as having constituted himself the trustee for the separate property thus created.

Separate property could also be created by operation of the rule known as a wife's equity to a settlement. While a husband had the unquestioned right to reduce into possession his wife's legal choses in action by taking appropriate action in the common-law courts if necessary, he could gain possession of his wife's equitable choses in action only by application to the Court of Chancery. Equitable choses in action included, for example, monies in the hands of a wife's trustee, stocks standing in the name of a trustee for a wife's benefit, legacies left to a wife but not yet paid her by the executor of a will, and property coming to her from the estate of an intestate but still unpaid by the administrator of the estate. Acting upon the principle that 'he who seeks equity must do equity,' the Court of Chancery since the seventeenth century had held that the husband would be allowed the property in question only if he settled part of it upon his wife and children. In such cases the court examined the wife separately from her husband to determine her wishes with regard to the property. If she agreed, her husband could take all of it. If she insisted upon her equity to a settlement, usually one-half of the property or any lesser amount she agreed to take was settled upon her and her children and the remainder was paid to the husband. Still, the court could order more than half the property or even the whole of it to be settled upon the wife and children. Further, even if her husband did not apply to the court to obtain her property, a wife could apply to have it settled upon herself. In practice, however, a wife seldom asserted her right to a settlement except to protect the property in question against her husband's creditors.

Still, there were occasions when a wife's equity to a settlement did not obtain. If a woman left her husband without cause such as his physical ill-treatment of her, or was guilty of adultery, she forfeited her right. She had no claim if her husband had settled property upon her before marriage in the expectation of receiving property from her after marriage. If the property in question was worth less than £200 in total value or less than £10 in annual value, it was given to the husband as a matter of course and without his wife's consent, unless he was insolvent. Finally, if a trustee, an executor, or an administrator had already paid the money in question to the husband without advising the wife of her right to a settlement, she could not claim it.

The Court of Chancery also recognized as separate property one special category of goods. This category included wedding presents given to a woman and articles such as clothing and jewellery given her by a third person which, if given her by her husband, would have been considered by the common law as paraphernalia (and which he could dispose of freely during his lifetime but not by will after his death). A married woman had no legal right during her husband's lifetime to articles of a personal nature he had given her, but equity would ensure her possession of such gifts from friends and lovers!

The rights a married woman enjoyed with respect to her separate property varied, depending upon the way that property had been created. A written instrument settling property upon a woman often stated specifically what she could and could not do. For example, she might be expressly allowed to dispose during her lifetime of real property settled upon her or expressly barred from doing so, or she might be allowed or denied the right to dispose of her separate property by will, and so on.

One special restriction upon a woman's rights over her separate property, a restriction which was commonly applied, was the restraint on anticipation or restraint on alienation. In such cases the written instrument might state that 'the said [wife] shall not have power to dispose of or affect the same [property], or any part thereof, by any sale, mortgage, or charge, or otherwise in the way of antici-pation,' or it might simply describe the property settled as being 'without power of anticipation.' No special words were required, and the clear intention of the settlor of the property sufficed to enforce the restraint. In practice it meant that a woman could not dispose of her separate property, nor could she anticipate the income from this property by charging it with debts.

The original purpose of the restraint on anticipation, like all the equitable rules relating to separate property, was to protect a woman's property against her husband. Lord Thurlow, one of the great reforming lord chancellors of the eighteenth century, had invented the device when, acting as trustee for a young heiress, he maintained that if she were able to dispose of her separate property freely her husband could, in his words, 'kiss or kick her out of it.' That is, for her own protection a woman must not be allowed to sell her separate property and give the proceeds to her husband, or to make her property chargeable for his debts. But by the mid-nineteenth century the restraint had come to serve an altogether different purpose. The restraint was then usually included in the settlement of property upon a woman only when her husband was engaged in trade, in order to secure the property and the income from it for the family, free from the claims of the husband's creditors, especially in the case of his bankruptcy.

The rule relating to the restraint on anticipation was first amended in 1881. The Conveyancing and Law of Property Act of that year allowed the High Court of Justice to remove the restraint on a woman's separate property when she consented to this and when the removal was apparently in her best interests. The argument used to justify this reform was that the restraint was designed to protect a woman's property against loss, not to prevent her from using this property to the best advantage, as, for example, by selling it and using the proceeds to make more lucrative investments.

It is interesting that the restraint on anticipation operated only during marriage, for it applied only to separate property, which existed only during marriage. That is, the restraint did not operate while a woman was single or widowed, although if she remarried the restraint came into effect again. Also the restraint did not prevent a woman from making a will disposing of her separate property, for this disposition would take effect only when the marriage was terminated by her death.

A married woman might enjoy unrestricted rights with respect to her separate property. The written instrument creating this property might contain no provisions restricting her rights, and no restrictions applied to separate property which was created otherwise than by a written instrument. In that case, a married woman had unlimited powers, for her trustee was bound to deal with her separate property according to her directions.

If no restrictions were placed upon her, a married woman could use and dispose of her separate property however she chose. She received the income from the property free from common-law liabilities – that is, free from her husband's rights and the claims of his creditors. She could alienate her real property by a 'deed unacknowledged,' whereas under the common law she could do so only with her husband's consent and jointly with him by a 'deed acknowledged.' She could give away or sell her personal property, which the common law would have considered to be her husband's absolutely. She could dispose freely of her chattels real and equitable choses in action, which under the common law would have been under her husband's control during marriage, although he could not make a will disposing of them.

At the same time a married woman with unrestricted rights over her separate property enjoyed a contractual capacity impossible for wives whose property came under the operation of the common law. She could make binding contracts, a right which carried with it the ability to sue and be sued in equity with respect to these contracts. (More precisely, her trustee sued or was sued in her stead.) She could lend money out of her separate property and incur debts which had to be satisfied by that property. Using her separate property she could carry on a business independent of her husband and free from his claims and those of his creditors, and she was liable for the satisfaction of her own business contracts. Equity even recognized that a married woman could contract with her husband (for example, by lending him money from her separate estate) and could sue and be sued by him. In addition, equity, unlike the common law, held that contracts made by a man and woman who later married were not void but valid.

Finally, a married woman with unrestricted rights over her separate property could dispose of it freely by will. This, too, was in striking contrast to the common-law rule that a married woman could make no will devising her real property and could bequeath her personal property, chattels real, and choses in action by will only with her husband's consent.

When a married woman made no will disposing of her separate property, the statutory rules relating to the property of intestates came into operation. This was so because separate property, created to protect a woman from her husband during marriage, ceased to exist when the marriage ended. In such cases a woman's real property passed to her legal heirs, subject to her husband's right by the curtesy to a life interest in it (although this point, involving property held in trust, was not finally settled in the husband's favour until 1877). In like manner equity long rejected a wife's right to dower out of her husband's trust estates, but this right was at last recognized by the Dower Act of 1833. As for the woman's personal property, chattels real, and choses in action, these passed into the absolute possession of her husband.

The provisions of equity also contrasted with those of the common law in their effect on husbands and wives who separated. Since the seventeenth century the courts of equity had recognized and enforced deeds of separation which were agreed to by husbands and wives who parted by mutual consent. Such deeds usually stipulated that the husband would provide a separate maintenance for his wife, and this maintenance constituted her separate property in equity, vested for her benefit in trustees who agreed to release the husband from his common-law liabilities for his wife's debts. As has been seen, it was not until 1862 that the common law came to recognize such deeds of separation.

Also, since the seventeenth century the Court of Chancery had assumed jurisdiction to order a husband to pay maintenance to the wife whom he had deserted. Here equity supplemented the jurisdiction of the ecclesiastical courts, which in cases of desertion could merely order the deserting spouse to return to cohabitation. However, applications by deserted wives to the Court of Chancery were uncommon, because the slowness and costliness of the proceedings limited their use to women of the wealthy classes.

Finally, something should be said about the equitable rules relating to the custody of children. While the common law always recognized the absolute right of the father to custody, equity proceeded upon the principle that the primary consideration in every case was the welfare of the child. Upon the petition of the mother or a third party, the courts of equity would refuse a father custody on several grounds, including the unfitness of his character and conduct and his refusal or inability to support the child. In such cases the courts appointed some other person to act as guardian, and restrained the father from interfering. In theory the jurisdiction of the courts in matters of custody was unlimited. In practice this jurisdiction could be exercised only when a child was independently possessed of property, for otherwise the courts had no way of enforcing their orders by directions regarding that property. But by the mid-nineteenth century the settlement of little more than a nominal amount of property upon a child would enable the courts of equity to exercise jurisdiction.

Clearly the position of married women with separate property in equity was greatly superior to that of women who came under the provisions of the common law. At nearly every point where the law discriminated against wives, equity afforded them relief, with the result that the legal rules and the equitable rules applying to married women's property stood in startling contrast to each other.

But however substantial the relief afforded by equity to married women, the equitable provisions relating to their property were far from perfect, and were open to valid criticism on several important points. A married woman with separate property in equity did not have the same proprietary status as a man or an unmarried woman. Rather, she enjoyed a special status, having rights with respect to certain property only, and she escaped some of the liabilities attaching to property generally. As one lawyer expressed it, 'married women ... are allowed in Chancery the benefit, without the responsibility, of property.'[2]

This special status of married women with separate property in equity is illustrated by their peculiar contractual capacity. Some judges referred to a married woman's contracts in equity as 'engagements,' to indicate that they were not true contracts. In equity, as at law, a married woman could not make contracts binding herself personally; she could make only contracts binding her separate property in equity. For example, if a married woman incurred debts larger than could be paid out of her separate property, she was not liable with respect to any other property. Also, judicial decisions in 1881 and 1887 on two long-disputed points made it clear that a married woman's contracts in equity were void if she had no separate property at the time of contracting, and that her contracts bound only the separate property she had at the time of contracting and not that she acquired afterward. For example, a married woman with no separate property might incur a debt of, say, £100, and the fact that she later acquired separate property to the value of £100 or even £1,000 would not make her liable to repay the debt. A woman with separate property valued at £50 might become indebted to the amount of £100, and if she later acquired an additional £50 or more in separate property she was still liable to repay only £50 and not £100. Finally, no contract made by a married woman with respect to her separate property was valid if the property was subject to the restraint on anticipation. In any case arising with respect to a married woman's contracts, the burden of proof lay not upon her but upon the other party to the contract, who must show conclusively that she had separate property unrestrained and sufficient in amount to meet her obligations. Clearly, in these circumstances a married woman's creditors might well find themselves defeated.

As a married woman's contractual capacity in equity was limited and peculiar, so too was her testamentary capacity. A woman could make a will disposing only of her separate property and not of other property. Her will was not valid if she had no separate property when it was drawn up, and her will bound only the separate property she had at the time of testation and not that which she acquired afterward. That is, the whole of a woman's separate property, if she had had none when she made her will, or that separate property which she had acquired after drawing up her will, passed not to those whom she designated as her heirs in the will but to her legal heirs under the rules applying to the property of intestates.

Another major criticism of equity was that a married woman's possession of separate property did not free her husband from his responsibilities as her legal representative. A woman's separate property, unless it was subject to the restraint on anticipation, was liable for the satisfaction of her antenuptial obligations. However, her husband was liable for her debts incurred and her contracts entered into after marriage in so far as these did not bind her separate property, and contemporaries made many disparaging remarks about those women who, to evade responsibility for their actions, claimed that they had been acting as their husbands' agents in incurring financial obligations and that they had not intended these obligations to bind their separate property. Still, in any case arising with respect to a married woman's obligations, the jury, in deciding whether and to what extent she had bound her husband in her capacity as his agent, would take into consideration the fact that she had separate property. A husband was also responsible for torts not related to her separate property that his wife committed during marriage, at least until a ruling in 1875 by Sir George Jessel, master of the rolls, that a woman's separate property was liable for all her torts.

A man likewise remained responsible for the support of his family even when his wife had separate property. A woman might choose to let her husband receive and use her separate property for the support of their family, in which case she was considered to have given it to him absolutely and irrevocably. But she did not have to do this, for she was under no equitable obligation to support her husband and children and to contribute to household expenses out of her separate property.

Finally, by far the most damning criticism of equity was that the protection it afforded with respect to married women's property was accessible only to wealthy women. It was completely impracticable to tie up small sums of money or even small fortunes of a few hundred pounds in trust settlements. Also, the proceedings in the courts of equity were very expensive. For example, fees for drawing up a marriage settlement usually amounted to well over £100, and this was but one of the expenses involved. In these circumstances, according to one estimate, marriage settlements in equity applied to only one-tenth of the marriages in the country.[3]

To the feminists of Victorian times, the equitable rules relating to married women's property were naturally much more acceptable than were the rules of the common law. The law deprived married women of property, and thus deprived them of the rights and responsibilities of other citizens and subjected them to serious practical hardships. Equity allowed married women to have property, and thus ensured their independence and freedom of action. Under the law married women could have no legal existence separate from the husbands who controlled their property. In equity married women had an identity separate from their husbands because they controlled property.

At the same time feminists criticized the equitable rules applying to married women's property for two important reasons. First, as has been seen, equity did not recognize married women as having the same proprietary rights as other citizens, but accorded them special rights over certain property only. The anomalous result was that married women with separate property in equity enjoyed the rights but might escape the responsibilities attaching to property generally. In other words, equity failed to meet the feminist criterion of excellence – that all women should have rights and responsibilities equal to those of men. The feminists' second major criticism of equity, and by far the more serious, was that, as seen above, the relief it afforded from the provisions of the common law was not available to women who were not wealthy. The great majority of women in the country did not have property sufficient in amount and suitable in nature to be settled upon them as their separate property through the costly proceedings of the courts of equity. As A.V. Dicey summed up the situation, 'There came ... to be not in theory but in fact one law for the rich and another for the poor. The daughters of the rich enjoyed, for the most part, the considerate protection of equity, the daughters of the poor suffered under the severity and injustice of the common law.'[4]

When feminists denounced the common law and criticized equity, and called for thoroughgoing reform of the married women's property law, they had a large and sympathetic audience. This was so not because most people agreed with feminist demands for equality for women, but because legal reform generally was the order of the day and the Victorian conscience was troubled by the sufferings of women under the law as it then existed. Many reformers who were concerned about the state of English jurisprudence could see the reasonableness of feminist arguments for ending the glaring contrasts and discrepancies between the provisions of the common law and equity relating to married women's property. Indeed, no better example could be found of the contradictions and confusions which were characteristic of English jurisprudence at the time and against which reformers inveighed, and no better proof existed of the crying need for general reform. At the same time many more people could agree with the feminists about the intolerable injustice of the existence, in fact if not in theory, of 'one law for the rich and another for the poor,' and could accept the plea that poor women who suffered under one body of law should be granted protection similar to that enjoyed by wealthy women under a completely different body of law. So it was that in the 1850s the first campaign to win reform of the married women's property law began.

4

'The Germs of an Effective Movement'
Feminism in the 1850s

The question of why movements for social reform arise when they do and why they succeed or fail is perennially fascinating to historians. They happily construct models and write equations to subsume and give coherence to the particular historical data at their disposal, and to serve as a key to the understanding of social reform movements in general. To judge by the beginnings of feminism as an organized movement in England in the 1850s, the following seem to be necessary for the appearance and success of reform movements: economic discontent; political unrest, arising from such developments as the discrediting of the government in power or the emergence of a particular problem to be solved through the political process; the presence of leading personalities to voice economic and political discontents, to educate and to arouse the conscience of the public about the reform desired, and to present a philosophy of change; and some effective organization or machinery to push the reform through the appropriate channels. All of these parts of the model, all of these factors in the equation, were present in the England of the 1850s to account for the rise of a feminist movement which had as its first priority reform of the married women's property law.

When one speaks of economic discontent in connection with the rise of feminism in the fifties, this does not mean economic depression. The first long, hard phase of industrialization was past. The 'hungry forties' were over. The long campaign to win repeal of the Corn Laws had succeeded, and Chartism, after a last flare-up in 1848, had disappeared. The country was entering a period of enormous economic prosperity which was to continue almost without interruption till the onset of the Great Depression in the seventies. The beginning of this grand new day was aptly symbolized by the opening in 1851 of the Great Exhibition at the marvellous Crystal Palace in London.

One can argue that this very real economic prosperity fuelled feminist discontent with the legal position of women. The common law affecting women had not changed, but the economic conditions of the society within which the law operated had been dramatically altered with the accelerating pace of industrialization. In short, many more women than ever before felt the severe burden of disabilities placed upon women by the law.

In his classic study of reform of the married women's property law, A.V. Dicey maintained that this reform in the later nineteenth century was prompted by the great and obvious increase in the number of wage-earning wives. In the earlier nineteenth century, according to Dicey, 'The daughters of the wealthy were ... protected under the rules of equity in the enjoyment of their separate property. The daughters of working men possessed little property of their own.' By the mid-nineteenth century this was no longer true. The daughters of the wealthy were still protected by equity, but now many other women worked outside the home and so had property of their own. Yet under the common law this property was not secured to them and protected against their husbands' control. Given the imperfect nature of the census statistics of the earlier nineteenth century, it is impossible to trace with accuracy the growth in the numbers of married working women in the country and thus to prove Dicey's contention. We do know that by 1851 there were in the country well over three-quarters of a million married women at work, and that they represented nearly one-fourth of all working women. These working wives were mostly women of the lower classes, but there were among them a relatively small but growing number of middle-class women; these women, Dicey suggested, being better educated and more vocal than their poorer sisters, had 'the means of making known to the public through the press every case of injustice done to any one of them.'[1] It was in these circumstances that the common law, which clearly did not serve the interests of the large numbers of married women at work in a modern industrialized society, came under forceful attack.

The decade of the 1850s cannot be described as a period of grave political unrest any more than it can be described as a time of economic depression. There was nothing at all comparable with the unrest of the period which culminated in passage of the great Reform Bill of 1832, or with that which ended with passage of the second Reform Bill of 1867. Still, two political developments of the fifties bore directly upon the rise of feminism at this time.

The first of these was the Crimean War. In 1853 Lord Aberdeen's coalition government, carried away by its own and the public's russophobia, lurched into this fiasco. The revelations of its disastrous mishandling of the war completely discredited Aberdeen's ministry and also, if only temporarily, discredited aristocratic government in general. In the midst of public and parliamentary furore, the government fell, to be replaced by a new Whig ministry under Lord

Palmerston. Only two heroic figures emerged from this military misadventure. One was the common British soldier, courageous and uncomplaining in the face of ghastly conditions. The other was Florence Nightingale, who was rewarded for her magnificent efforts in the soldiers' behalf by the country's idolatry. She was the first truly national heroine since Good Queen Bess, and a woman second only to Queen Victoria herself in public esteem – if, indeed, she was second.

Miss Nightingale could hardly be called a feminist. She had a low opinion of women in general, partly because of the agonies she had had to endure at the hands of her mother and sister before she broke away to live her own life and forge her own career, free from domestic and conventional trammels. Still, Miss Nightingale's work made nonsense of claims that woman's place was in the home and that she must be cherished there and carefully protected from the outside world, and the force of her example upon women themselves and upon public opinion generally was enormous, if immeasurable.

The second important political development of the 1850s which bore upon the rise of feminism was the increasing interest of the time in legal reform. It was in the fifties that an important royal commission was appointed to study the procedure of the common-law courts. Its recommendation of a greater fusion of the common law and equity led immediately to passage of a series of acts designed to bring into greater harmony the operations of the courts of common law and of equity, and foreshadowed the provisions of the Judicature Act of 1873. It was also in the fifties that another royal commission was appointed to study the matter of reform of the divorce law. In 1854, and again in 1856 and 1857, Lord Cranworth, the lord chancellor, introduced in parliament bills based upon the commission's recommendations. These legal questions had obvious and important bearings upon the wider question of the position of women. The state of the married women's property law was excellent proof of the need to reconcile the contradictory provisions of the common law and equity. Even more significant at the time, the question of divorce raised important questions about the nature of marriage and the rights of married women.

It was during the debates on divorce-law reform that there flashed again before the public eye the figure of a woman who had been famous, even notorious, for more than twenty years – Caroline Sheridan Norton. Mrs Norton was no feminist. Long after this period she denounced the 'wild and stupid theories' of equal rights for women, declaring, 'I, for one (I, with millions more), believe in the natural superiority of man as I do in the existence of God.'[2] But Mrs Norton's life story was a moving account of a married woman's sufferings under the English law, and her own experience drove her to seek legal reforms advocated by avowed feminists. Moreover, she was in a position to be heard and heeded when she demanded reforms. She was not the sort of woman who could be overlooked, and indeed she had no intention of being overlooked.

A granddaughter of the renowned dramatist and Whig statesman Richard Brinsley Sheridan, Mrs Norton belonged to a family that 'moved on the fringes of society, showy and impoverished, and surrounded always by a faint aura of scandal.'[3] Her father, who had obtained a civil service post through family connections, died when she was only eight, leaving his wife desperately concerned to see their seven children prosperously settled for life. By all accounts Caroline Sheridan was one of the most beautiful women of her day, famed for her luxuriant black hair and luminous black eyes and for her voluptuous figure – 'that superb lump of flesh,' as one admirer described her rather inelegantly. She was as charming as she was beautiful – intelligent, witty, high-spirited, and possessed of considerable literary and musical talent. She and her two equally beautiful and charming sisters were nicknamed 'the three Graces' by London society, to which they had entrée through their grandfather's friends. The eldest sister married the heir of the earl of Dufferin and the youngest married the future duke of Somerset, while a brother eloped with a Scottish heiress. In 1827 Caroline herself was married at the age of nineteen to the younger brother and heir of Lord Grantley, George Norton, a lawyer who had been elected to parliament the year before as member for Guildford. They took a small house in Westminster which quickly became a favourite resort for many leading figures in the political and artistic circles of the time. Mrs Norton became the subject of much gossip and criticism, for she obviously relished the company and attentions of men and collected crowds of admirers.

She was not only the hostess of a celebrated salon but also a celebrity in her own right. Since childhood she had yearned to be a writer, and now she turned to literary work to bring her both the public acclaim she craved and the income she badly needed, since financially her husband had great expectations but little else. Her first long poetic work, *The Sorrows of Rosalie*, published anonymously in 1829, sold well and was followed the next year by another, *The Undying One*, which appeared under her name and soon went into a second edition. Later Mrs Norton would produce four more volumes of poetry, one of which inspired an enthusiastic reviewer to hail her as 'the Byron of modern poetesses,' first among the ten greatest English women writers of poetry. (Elizabeth Barrett placed second.) In 1831 Mrs Norton's play *The Gypsy Father* was produced at Covent Garden, and four years later she published her first novel, *The Wife and Woman's Reward*, which was to be followed by three others. She also contributed innumerable articles, stories, short poems, and pieces of criticism to various magazines, and wrote for publication the words and music of many songs. Besides all this creative work, Mrs Norton also edited at different times several fashionable women's magazines and gift annuals, including *La Belle Assemblée and Court Magazine* and the *Keepsake*. In short, she was one of the most famous literary figures of her day.

Unfortunately, despite her glittering social and literary success, Mrs Norton's marriage was a disastrously unhappy one. Her husband, a dull and stodgy Tory, was completely mismatched with his brilliantly attractive and thoroughly Whig wife. He was jealous, mean-spirited, vindictive, and liable to sudden fits of physical violence. Even Mrs Norton's enemies had nothing good to say about her husband.

In 1836 a series of misfortunes befell Mrs Norton. One day while she was out of the house, her husband abducted their three small sons and thereafter refused to let her see them or even know their whereabouts. Then, while his wife was away on a visit to her brother, Norton advertised in all the daily papers that she had left him and that he would therefore not be liable for her debts. Meanwhile he retained possession of her personal effects – clothing, jewellery, books, and papers – which legally were his property and not hers. Finally, Norton brought an action for criminal conversation against Lord Melbourne, then prime minister, charging him with adultery with Mrs Norton.

The question of the innocence of Melbourne and Mrs Norton, which both stoutly maintained till the end of their lives, was hotly debated at the time and has been since. Certainly their intimate friendship had given rise to much gossip, and Norton's legal action could be considered as the necessary first step taken by a wronged husband in order to obtain a divorce by private act of parliament. But many people believed that the action was a cruel attempt by Norton, who was financially hard-pressed, to win substantial damages, and was also part of a low Tory plot to discredit the head of the Whig government.

The trial was the sensation of the day. Melbourne did not appear in court, merely submitting a deposition asserting his innocence. Mrs Norton, a legal non-person like all married women, could not appear in her own defence. To win his case, Norton had to prove both his wife's adultery and his own ignorance of the fact, since his knowledge of it would be taken as evidence of his condonation. He had obviously known about and even encouraged his wife's friendship with Melbourne, through whose good offices he himself, after losing his seat in parliament at the election of 1830, had obtained a judgeship in the Metropolitan Police Courts, a position he held until a few years before his death. His case rested entirely upon a few notes written by Melbourne to Mrs Norton appointing times when he would call upon her, and the testimony of former servants in the Norton household who did not make a good impression in the witness box. The jury returned a verdict of not guilty without even leaving the courtroom to deliberate.

As the law then stood, divorce was impossible for the Nortons. His action for criminal conversation having failed, Norton had no grounds for divorce either in the ecclesiastical courts or in parliament, and the fact that his wife had left him briefly the year before, only to return to him in response to his imploring letters, would be considered evidence that she had forgiven his cruelties, which she therefore could not plead as grounds for divorce. Now, her reputation sullied by the scandal of the Melbourne trial, despite the verdict of innocence, and bound without legal recourse to a man whom she despised, Mrs Norton began a new life in a strange no-woman's-land. Women like her, separated from their husbands, had none of the protection that marriage supposedly afforded, yet suffered under all the disabilities that the law imposed upon married women.

Mrs Norton now began her first campaign to win reform of the law. A devoted mother, she was driven frantic by separation from her children, but her husband had been well within his legal rights in removing them from her and refusing her access to them. To arouse interest in the question, she published in 1837, privately and at her own expense, a pamphlet entitled *The Natural Claim of a Mother to the Custody of Her Children as Affected by the Common Law Right of the Father*. This was followed the next year by two more pamphlets, *The Case of the Hon. Mrs. Norton*, published anonymously, and *A Plain Letter to the Lord Chancellor on the Law of Custody of Infants*, published under a pseudonym.

In parliament the cause of reform was taken up by Mrs Norton's friends Lord Lyndhurst and Serjeant-at-law Thomas Noon Talfourd. Lyndhurst, a handsome, urbane, and popular figure in fashionable society, was one of the most distinguished jurists of his time. He had already served twice as lord chancellor in Tory governments and would serve in that office a third time. (Lyndhurst was Dickens's model for the lord chancellor in *Bleak House*, a novel which understandably infuriated him.)[4] A prominent lawyer who was later to be appointed a justice of the Court of Common Pleas, Talfourd was equally well known as a writer of essays and successful plays. His experience in his own legal practice had convinced him of the cruelty of the law relating to custody and of the need to amend it. Meanwhile Mrs Norton's enemies were declaring that she wanted custody of her children only so that she could present a façade of respectability to society, and the Tory *British and Foreign Review* implied that her relations with Talfourd were something more than friendly consultations about a reform bill. As a married woman Mrs Norton could not sue the paper for libel – her husband would have had to sue in her stead, and the damages collected would have been his property – but she defended herself and relieved her feelings in a letter written to the liberal *Examiner* and later reprinted in *The Times*.

In 1839 the Infant Custody Bill became law. It provided that a mother whose children were in the care of their father or a person chosen by him, or of a guardian appointed by the father to serve after his own death, could apply to the Court of Chancery for relief. If the children were under the age of seven, the court could deliver them to the mother until they reached that age; if they were older, the mother could obtain a court order allowing her to visit them at stated times. However, no woman was to benefit from the act if she was guilty of adultery, proved either by sentence of the ecclesiastical courts or by judgment in an action for criminal conversation brought by her husband in the common-law courts.

This act, passed largely through Mrs Norton's efforts, was the first in a series of nineteenth-century statutes amending the common law relating to the custody of children. The Custody of Infants Act of 1873 extended the relief granted to mothers by the act of 1839 in two ways: by empowering the Court of Chancery to give a mother custody of children up to the age of sixteen, rather than seven, and by removing the bar to relief for a mother against whom adultery had been proved. The act also provided that no separation deed made by husband and wife and giving to the latter custody of their children would be held to be invalid, although the court could invalidate the deed and deprive the mother of custody if this seemed to be in the best interests of the child. The Guardianship of Infants Act of 1886 provided that on the father's death, the mother was to be guardian of their children, either alone when the father had appointed no guardian, or jointly with the guardian appointed by the father. But the act's most important provision in effect gave the court full jurisdiction to override entirely the father's common-law rights of custody: on the mother's application the court could make any order it thought fit respecting custody, having regard to the welfare of the children, the conduct of the parents, and the wishes of the mother as well as those of the father. Still, full equality for women did not come until the twentieth century. The Guardianship of Infants Act of 1925 provided generally, as equity had always held, that the welfare of the child was the paramount consideration, and provided specifically that a mother as well as a father could appoint a guardian to act jointly with the surviving parent. The Guardianship of Minors Act of 1973 provided that mothers should have the same rights as the law had previously allowed fathers.

After passage of the act of 1839 Mrs Norton began preparing a petition to the lord chancellor requesting custody of her children. The case never came to a hearing, however, for she and her husband reached a compromise whereby their children lived part of the time with her. Three years after this, while staying with his father, the Nortons' youngest son died of injuries resulting from a fall from his pony, and Mrs Norton bitterly blamed her husband's neglect and carelessness for this fatal accident.

In addition to worry over her children, Mrs Norton was plagued by financial difficulties. She had only a small amount of property secured to her by her marriage settlement, her mother having been misinformed about Norton's real financial situation at the time the settlement was drawn up. Her personal property, including the small sum she received annually from her dead father's pension and her earnings, belonged legally to her husband. After his failure in the Melbourne trial, Norton offered her an allowance of £300 a year out of his own annual resources of £3,000 – his salary and the income from estates he had recently inherited from a cousin – but he soon refused to pay. In 1838 he was sued by some of his wife's creditors for debts she had incurred, and he was forced to pay.

Matters drifted for years. Mrs Norton lived on the allowance from her husband, when she could obtain it, and on her earnings from her writing. She also received financial help from Melbourne, who died in 1848 leaving instructions in connection with his will that aid to her should be continued. In that year the Nortons almost reached agreement on a formal deed of separation. Mrs Norton was to allow her husband to raise money by a mortgage on the trust property secured to her by her marriage settlement, while he was to pay her an annual allowance of £500 and his liability for her debts was to be restricted. But the deed never became legally binding, for the person Mrs Norton had chosen as her trustee refused to act for her, believing the terms to be too unfavourable to her. When Mrs Norton's mother died three years later, her husband inherited a life interest in the property which came to her from her father and which had not been secured to her, while she herself inherited from her mother a life income of £480 annually which was secured to her. Norton then proposed to reduce the allowance he paid his wife. She refused to agree to this, but to no avail. When she tried to draw her allowance, the bank did not honour her cheques, and Norton refused to discuss the matter. Soon he was sued again by a creditor seeking to collect a debt which his wife had incurred.

The trial of this case in 1853 was more dramatic if less sensational than the Melbourne trial seventeen years before. Norton appeared as the defendant, while his wife also appeared, subpoenaed as a witness. Norton argued that the deed of separation drawn up in 1848 was not legally binding, which was true, and added that he had stipulated at the time that his wife swear that she had never received money from Melbourne. Mrs Norton spoke well in reply, to the applause of the crowded courtroom. She reasserted her innocence with regard to Melbourne, who, she said, had aided her only because of all she had suffered from her friendship with him. As it turned out, Mrs Norton's creditor lost his case, on the technical ground that her debt had been incurred before her husband stopped payment of her allowance. To more applause, she declared of the verdict, 'I do not ask for my rights. I have no rights; I have only wrongs.' Furious, her husband leapt up to harangue her, the judge, and all others present, accusing her of gross falsehoods and much else.

Thereafter the Nortons' quarrel raged in print. Mrs Norton wrote a letter to *The Times* pointing out the flaws in her husband's charges against her. For one, he had stopped payment of her allowance before he examined her bankbook, which her bankers had delivered to him and which would have revealed payments made to her by Melbourne and his family. Norton was apparently infuriated when he discovered by examining her bankbook that his wife had more money than he thought. He in turn wrote to *The Times*, asserting his belief in his wife's guilt in the Melbourne affair and accusing her of taking advantage of a wife's legal non-existence to plague him with debts and litigation. He continued to refuse payment of her allowance, and her financial situation became desperate.

Again Mrs Norton turned to polemical pamphleteering. In 1854 she published at her own expense for private distribution *English Laws for Women in the Nineteenth Century*. This related the story, as it might have been told in court, with evidence to support her every statement, of how she had 'learned the English law piecemeal by suffering under it.' 'My husband,' she said, 'is a lawyer; and he has taught it to me by exercising over my tormented and restless life every quirk and quibble of its tyranny ...' Soon after, the lord chancellor introduced in parliament the first measure brought in to reform the divorce law, and in 1855 Mrs Norton published *A Letter to the Queen on Lord Cranworth's Marriage and Divorce Bill*. Once more she related her sufferings under the law, and discussed the merits of the bill in question. Dwelling upon the point that her interest in the bill was not merely a selfish one, Mrs Norton wrote:

My husband has taught me, by subpoenaing my publishers to account for my earnings, that my gift of writing was not meant for the purposes to which I have hitherto applied it ... It was meant to enable me to rouse the hearts of others to examine into all the gross injustice of these laws, to ask the nation of gallant gentlemen whose countrywoman I am, for once to hear a woman's pleading on the subject ... I deny that this is my personal cause – it is the cause of all the women of England ... Meanwhile my husband has a legal lien on the copyright of my works. Let him claim the copyright of this!

Of this pamphlet Lord Brougham, no friend of Mrs Norton's, said, 'It is as clever a thing as ever was written, and it has produced a great good. I feel certain that the Law of Divorce will be much amended, and she has greatly contributed to it.'[5] The divorce law was greatly amended in 1857. But before that, Norton had resumed payment of his wife's allowance, although still quibbling about the amount, for otherwise the newly created Divorce Court might well have compelled him to pay.

During the years that followed, Mrs Norton still had to work hard to support herself and help her two sons. Her last long poetic work and two last novels appeared, but most of her writing was simply hack work for magazines. Her husband died at last in 1875, and Mrs Norton grumbled that having lived so long, he might have obliged her by outliving his brother and so making her Lady Grantley. Two years later she married an old friend, Sir William Stirling-Maxwell, but only three months after her marriage her 'tormented and restless life' ended.

The career of Caroline Norton is sometimes credited with having inspired the first public work for women's causes of Barbara Leigh Smith, a young woman who was to play an important part in the early feminist movement in England, and who may indeed be called the real founder of that movement. Like Mrs Norton, Miss Leigh Smith was in a position to make her views known; but unlike her, she was a Radical and a feminist born and bred. Her grandfather and father alike were wealthy Radical MPs of Unitarian persuasion, the former well known for his part in the campaigns to abolish slavery and religious disabilities and to win parliamentary reform, the latter for his work for repeal of the Corn Laws. So unconventional were her father's views that he neglected to marry the young milliner's apprentice whom he took under his protection and who bore him five children before her early death of tuberculosis. As a consequence the Leigh Smith household was referred to by relatives and friends as the 'tabooed family,' but it was a very happy one. Benjamin Leigh Smith treated his children equally, not favouring his two sons over his three daughters. He provided them all with the best education he could obtain for them from private tutors; he gave each of them an annual allowance of £300 on their coming of age; and when he died in 1860 his handsome fortune was divided equally among them. As the eldest child, Barbara enjoyed an especially close relationship with her doting father. She entered eagerly into his various philanthropic and reform projects, and acted as his hostess at their London home in Blandford Square, which was a favourite meeting place for English reformers and for liberal exiles of all nationalities from the continent.

Bred in such an atmosphere, Barbara Leigh Smith was 'one of the cracked people of the world,' as she once called herself, saying, 'I like to herd with the cracked ... queer Americans, democrats, socialists, artists, poor devils or angels; and am never happy in an English genteel family life.'[6] Being financially secure, she could afford to be unconventional. She was able to study art and develop her talent, and achieved considerable renown as a painter. She was also able to take up practical work for women's rights, a cause to which she was drawn for personal as well as ideological reasons.

Tall and amply proportioned (her friend Dante Rossetti called her fat), with vivid colouring and abundant red-gold hair, Miss Leigh Smith was a figure out of a Titian painting. She was also blessed with excellent health, high spirits, and a great zest for life. With these attributes and wealth as well, she did not lack admirers. But the thought of a conventional marriage with all its attendant legal disabilities and the prospect of losing her independence appalled her. At this time she was even contemplating an extramarital liaison with the publisher John Chapman, a handsome but feckless man who was already married and a father, and who, in the midst of his perennial money troubles, was perhaps as much attracted by her financial assets as by her personal charms. When she confided her plans to her father, he promptly put an end to the affair – love without marriage was all very well for him but not for his daughter!

It was in these circumstances, and in the midst of revived public interest in the troubles of Caroline Norton, that Miss Leigh Smith published her first work. Brought out by Chapman in 1854, it was a little book called *A Brief Summary, in Plain Language, of the Most Important Laws Concerning Women, Together with a Few Observations Thereon*. The title aptly described the contents. Here was no impassioned and rhetorical plea for women's rights, but a clear and concise description of the existing laws. The book attracted considerable public attention and press comment, and early in 1856 a second edition appeared.

To capitalize on the interest thus aroused, Miss Leigh Smith formed a committee, composed mostly of her close personal friends, who were dedicated to work for reform of the laws affecting women, and who set as their first goal reform of the married women's property law. The appearance of this committee is an important and noteworthy event, for this was the first organized group of women in England to discuss and promote women's rights. It marked, in short, the beginning of an organized feminist movement.

Heading the committee with Miss Leigh Smith was another young woman, Bessie Rayner Parkes, who had been her intimate friend since their girlhood and who continued active in the feminist movement for several years. She, too, was from a background that was Unitarian in religion and Radical in politics – a proud descendant of the great Unitarian philosopher, scientist, and Radical politician Joseph Priestley (the friend and mentor of Jeremy Bentham) and daughter of the Radical lawyer Joseph Parkes, who for decades was an intimate of Whig reform circles. A great lover of literature, Miss Parkes published several volumes of poems, the first in 1852. She also wrote two works on women's questions, *Remarks on the Education of Girls*, published anonymously in 1854, and *Essays on Woman's Work*, published in 1866. In 1858 she became co-editor of the *English Woman's Journal*, founded in that year by this same circle of feminists to serve as organ of the women's movement, and she contributed numerous articles and

some poems to its pages. She was also active in the work of the Society for
Promoting the Employment of Women, organized in connection with the *Journal* in 1859, and in that of the Female Middle Class Emigration Society, founded
three years later. She astounded and dismayed her friends, who felt she was
deserting the cause, by her conversion to Catholicism in 1864 and by her marriage three years later to a Frenchman, Louis Belloc, the invalid son of the
distinguished artist Hilaire Belloc. Her married life was idyllically happy but
tragically brief; in 1872 she was left a widow with two small children to care
for – a daughter Marie, afterward Mrs Frederic Lowndes, a talented journalist
and novelist, and a son Hilaire, later the distinguished man of letters, political
thinker and sometime MP, and champion of the Catholic Church.[7]

Acting as secretary of the women's committee was Mary Howitt, an older
woman who had been Miss Leigh Smith's friend since her childhood. Mrs Howitt's name is little known today, but she and her husband William were among
the most prolific and popular writers of their time, and both received civil list
pensions from the government in recognition of their literary contributions.
They came from rather humble backgrounds, Mary the daughter of a land surveyor, William the son of a farmer who apprenticed him to a carpenter. Both
rebelled against their narrow Quaker upbringing and after fifteen years of marriage, mostly spent in Nottingham, where William ran a druggist's shop, they
moved to London, determined to find their livelihood and indulge their love of
literature by writing. Both singly and in collaboration they turned out innumerable works of all kinds – popular histories, travel stories, descriptions of nature,
books for children, novels, poems, articles for various newspapers and magazines, and translations, including the first English editions of the works of Hans
Christian Andersen and of the Swedish feminist Frederika Bremer.

The Howitts were also well known as reformers. In middle life they were
plagued by religious doubts, drifting toward Unitarianism, toying with spiritualism, and Mrs Howitt, like her young friend Bessie Parkes, was to end her long
life within the Catholic fold. But the Howitts never lost the sober outlook of
their Quaker background, and for them the purpose of literature and of life itself
was to instruct and to uplift. Much that they wrote was of a moralizing and
didactic nature, and their own periodical, *Howitt's Journal of Literature and Popular Progress*, a venture into cheap journalism for the masses, was a praiseworthy if
short-lived attempt to improve the morals and the status of the working classes.
The antislavery campaign, the campaign to repeal the Corn Laws, the movement for parliamentary reform, the co-operative movement among workers – all
these and many other reforms engaged the Howitts' pens and personal energies.
Feminism was certain to be of special interest to them, for the equality of the
sexes in the ministry of Christ was one of the basic principles of the Quakers,

and the Howitts' own lives were a fine practical example of a completely happy marriage and a phenomenally successful working partnership. Mary Howitt enthusiastically supported her young friend Barbara Leigh Smith in her plans to petition parliament for reform of the married women's property law, just as she later supported her in establishing the *English Woman's Journal* and in beginning the women's suffrage movement.

The Howitts' elder daughter Anna Mary was also a member of the women's committee. Family ties and their mutual love of art made her a special friend of Barbara Leigh Smith. Miss Howitt had studied for two years in Germany with the famous painter Ludwig von Kaulbach, and her delightful letters describing her experiences, published first in the *Athenaeum, Household Words*, and *The Lady's Companion*, were later collected and published with great success under the title *An Art Student in Munich*. Like Miss Leigh Smith, she was an enthusiastic admirer and personal friend of Dante Rossetti and other members of the pre-Raphaelite brotherhood, who encouraged her in her work. The two young women actively promoted Rossetti's marriage to Elizabeth Siddal, a marriage that was to end tragically when 'Lizzie' took a fatal overdose of laudanum. However, Miss Howitt's career in art did not prosper. Sensitive and diffident, she was completely crushed by a cruel letter of criticism from Ruskin, whose opinion she had requested on an oil painting which she considered her great work, a depiction of Boadicea brooding over her wrongs (for which her friend Barbara had served as model). For a time her family feared for her mental stability, especially as she refused to paint or write except under the direction of the spirits in which she believed. She found security and happiness at last after her marriage in 1859 to her childhood friend Alaric Alfred Watts, the son and biographer of Alaric Alexander Watts, who was a minor poet and a learned but financially unsuccessful literary editor.

Another young artist who was involved in the work of the women's committee was Eliza Fox, the daughter of a famous father. William Johnson Fox was prominent for years as minister of the Unitarian chapel in South Place, London, but was best known for his journalistic work in the cause of social reforms that ranged from repeal of the Corn Laws to equal rights for women. Under his editorship in the early 1830s, the Unitarian *Monthly Repository* had become an important Radical organ and boasted among its contributors the young John Stuart Mill. After the *Repository*'s demise, Fox wrote frequently for a number of other sympathetic periodicals and newspapers, including Mill's *Westminster Review* and the liberal *Daily News*. He also served the cause of reform in parliament as member for Oldham from 1847 to 1862. Fox was unfortunate in his marriage, and to the consternation of many of his friends and members of his congregation, he separated from his uncongenial wife and set up another household with Eliza Flower, a beautiful young woman of great musical talent for whom he had acted as guardian since her father's death. Fox's daughter Eliza, known affectionately to relatives and friends as 'Tottie,' and one of her two brothers were members of the new and unconventional household. Eliza Fox had first aspired to a career on the stage, but was discouraged in this project by her father and his friend Macready, the renowned actor-manager. She then began the study of painting, and her works later won her a considerable reputation. In Rome, where she went to continue her studies, she met the gifted young artist Frederick Lee Bridell, and in 1859 they were married. Thereafter she styled herself Mrs Bridell Fox. The marriage was a happy one but brief, for Bridell died of tuberculosis only four years later.

Like her friend Mary Howitt, Anna Murphy Jameson was a celebrated public figure who took an active interest in the work of her younger feminist friends and contributed significantly to the early women's movement. Mrs Jameson had been a fixture on the literary scene for nearly thirty years, the author of a variety of popular works, including an especially acclaimed study of Shakespeare's heroines. The daughter of an artist and herself a great lover of art, she secured her reputation in her own day and for many years to come with a series of works known collectively as *Sacred and Legendary Art*, the first two volumes of which appeared in 1848 and the last after her death in 1860.

Mrs Jameson had become a convinced feminist as a result of her own experiences in life. On a less grandiose scale her story was like that of Caroline Norton – the story of an unhappily married woman forced to make her own way in the world alone. Anna Murphy began her working life as a governess at the age of sixteen, and although her employers do not seem to have been difficult or disagreeable, she later wrote bitterly of the lot of governesses. Understandably she was interested in better education and wider employment opportunities for women. In 1825 she married Robert Jameson, a lawyer, but after only four years together they parted. Jameson then obtained judicial appointments in the colonies and went off alone, first to Dominica and later to Canada, leaving his wife to shift for herself. At his urging, in an attempt to patch things up between them, she joined him briefly in Toronto, where she spent a miserable winter before returning to England for good. They had agreed to a formal deed of separation under which Jameson was to pay her an annual allowance of £300, and his payments to her continued until his retirement from the bench in 1849. Thereafter well-placed friends obtained for her, in recognition of her literary work, a government pension which brought her £100 a year. Jameson died in 1854, and to her consternation his wife learned that he had left her nothing; all of his considerable property went to a clergyman of Toronto who had befriended him. Like most of her earlier life, Mrs Jameson's later years were spent in a struggle to support not only herself but also her aged parents and her four younger sisters.

Elizabeth Sturch Reid, like her friend Mrs Jameson, was another among the older generation of feminists who, together with her sister, took an active interest in the work of Miss Leigh Smith's little committee. The daughter of a wealthy London ironmonger, she was left a widow in 1822, after only one year of marriage to Dr John Reid, who had enjoyed a certain renown as a specialist in nervous diseases. Her husband's death and that of her parents left Mrs Reid independent in financially comfortable circumstances. Her claim to fame as a feminist rests on the fact that she was the founder and a great benefactress of Bedford College for Women, which opened its doors to students in 1849 and was later included among the constituent colleges of the reorganized University of London. Mrs Reid's interest in providing a place of higher education for women sprang from her conviction that the mental and moral education of women would benefit society as a whole. As she said, 'We shall never have better Men till men have better Mothers.' Apparently she had two reasons for establishing another college for women in addition to Queen's College, which had begun operations in 1848. First, as an enthusiastic Unitarian, she wanted an institution that was strictly non-denominational in character, unlike Queen's with its close ties to the Anglican King's College. Bedford was therefore affiliated with the non-denominational University College. Second, she wanted to include women on the governing body of the college, again unlike Queen's, where only men were members of the college council. Among the women serving on the council of Bedford College was Mrs Reid's great friend Julia Smith, the favourite aunt of Barbara Leigh Smith, both of whom attended the earliest classes at the college.

However talented, energetic, and dedicated the members of the married women's property committee might be – and they were all of these – they could have achieved little or nothing if they had not won the sympathetic attention and practical support of a number of prominent men who were in an excellent position to help publicize their demands and press their claims in parliament. Pre-eminent among these were Lord Brougham and Matthew Davenport Hill, both of them well known to Barbara Leigh Smith as friends of her father and fellow workers with him in various reform projects.

Henry, Lord Brougham, one of the most colourful and commanding personalities of his time, had had a long and distinguished if turbulent career in politics, and his name had become almost a synonym for reform.[8] As a young Scots lawyer he had been associated with the brilliant intellectual circle connected with the *Edinburgh Review*, which was dedicated to promoting reform in all fields. For twenty years after his election to parliament in 1810 he was the undisputed leader of the Whigs in the House of Commons. In 1830 he became lord chancellor in Lord Grey's Whig government, piloting through the upper house the great Reform Bill of 1832 and other important measures, and beginning the long-overdue reform of the Court of Chancery. But however brilliant he was, Brougham was also ambitious, arrogant, and domineering, and afflicted with fits of depression that verged upon insanity, all of which made him a difficult and eventually an impossible colleague. Excluded from the ministry of Lord Melbourne in 1834 (he believed Caroline Norton was partly responsible for this), he was for years a political Ishmael, and he never again held government office. But now, in old age, Brougham had at last attained serenity and peace of mind. Quiet and reasonable, warm and kindly, he was a revered figure in the House of Lords, and his prestige and popularity with the public were enormous.

Three fields of activity chiefly occupied Brougham during his long career – the abolition of slavery, the advancement of popular education, and legal reform – and in each of these he was keenly aware of the significant role that women could play. The first important measure Brougham introduced in parliament was a bill to abolish slavery, and he urged the enlistment of women in the antislavery campaign by appeals to them to consider the degraded condition of women slaves. They responded enthusiastically; dozens of abolition societies sprang up all over the country, and victory was won at last in 1833. Brougham's many ventures in the field of education included the founding of the Society for the Diffusion of Useful Knowledge. He himself wrote several of the popular treatises published by the society, and he enlisted in this work the talents of women such as Mary Somerville, the celebrated and largely self-taught mathematician and astronomer for whom Somerville Hall, Oxford, was later named. To further the cause of legal reform Brougham founded in 1844 the Society for Promoting the Amendment of the Law, usually called simply the Law Amendment Society, and served for years as its president. The society included many of the most eminent men of the time, among them important members of parliament of all political persuasions who promoted the enactment of specific reforms which the society sponsored. Within parliament Brougham himself was credited with having introduced or inspired more than a hundred important measures, and the last of these which he introduced was an amendment to the law relating to married women's property.

Matthew Davenport Hill was a great friend of Brougham and was associated with him in many of his reform undertakings. Despite his rather humble origins as a schoolmaster's son and his lack of powerful connections, Hill had earned a fine reputation at the bar. He was famous chiefly for his part in cases involving questions of civil and religious liberties, such as his defence of, among others,

Major John Cartwright, the Rebecca rioters, and Daniel O'Connell. (His brother, Rowland Hill, was to win an even greater reputation as a postal reformer and father of the penny post.) In 1839 Hill became recorder of Birmingham, and in 1851 commissioner of bankrupts for the Bristol district. His experience on the bench at Birmingham and his friendship with Mary Carpenter of Bristol turned his interest in his later years to reform of the criminal law and better treatment for prisoners, especially juvenile offenders, and on these subjects he became an acknowledged expert.

Hill was a lifelong supporter of women's rights. In 1832, as a successful parliamentary candidate at Hull, he had spoken in favour of women's suffrage and had always taken care that special places for women be provided at his campaign meetings. (Two years later Hill lost his seat in parliament, and despite repeated invitations from other constituencies to represent them, he never again stood for election, largely because of his delicate health.) As a popular lecturer on a variety of subjects in later life, Hill likewise spoke out for women's rights. He called attention to the great loss that society suffered 'by preventing women from taking a more important part than is accorded to them in its affairs,' adding that the 'right limits of the employment of that talent [of women] it is impossible to predict, so much has the prejudice arising from unequal laws, and restrictive usages, operated to prevent its free development.'[9] Hill's own daughters, Florence and Rosamond, took a prominent part in society's affairs – the former active in the campaign to reform the nursing in workhouses, the latter serving for many years as a member of the London school board.

It was Hill who brought Barbara Leigh Smith's *Brief Summary* to the attention of the Law Amendment Society, which he had helped to organize and in which he was a very active member. Miss Leigh Smith had turned to Hill for expert legal advice in the preparation of her work, and he had declared himself 'ready at all times' to help her in her 'good undertakings (and they seem all to be good), to the best of my power.'[10] About the same time a paper on the subject of the married women's property law was presented to the society by another member. So induced to investigate the matter thoroughly, the society referred the subject of property-law reform to its Personal Laws Committee.

This committee was presided over by a man who was much less famous than Brougham and Hill but was to become more important than they in actively fighting for the women's cause – Sir Thomas Erskine Perry. Perry was known for his interest in Indian affairs rather than domestic reforms, although from his youth he had been an ardent liberal and had championed the Reform Bill of 1832. He had been called to the bar and had worked as a law reporter for several years before obtaining an appointment to the Supreme Court of Bombay. There he served with distinction for twelve years, rising to the position of chief justice, and he later recalled that his experience on the bench had brought forcefully to his attention the state of the married women's property law and the need for its reform. Perry returned to England in 1852, and two years later was elected to parliament as member for Devonport. He gave up his seat in 1859, when he was appointed a member of the new Council for India, created by the act of the previous year which transferred the government of India from the East India Company to the crown, and he held this position till shortly before his death in 1882.[11]

Early in 1856 the Personal Laws Committee of the Law Amendment Society completed its report. Having set forth in detail the differences between the common law and equity, the report concluded that the existence of 'two different sets of courts [which] dispense diametrically opposite rules, and, in point of fact, two distinct codes' was 'most discreditable to our system of laws,' for which no 'claim for principle' could be made. Further, 'the operation of the law is even more reprehensible than its want of scientific character and uniformity,' for 'the rich are enabled, in many cases, to avoid the harshness of the common law, from which the middle classes, and those too poor to encounter the expenses of the courts of equity, are unable to escape.' The report concluded firmly that it was the duty of parliament to amend the existing law, 'to introduce one uniform rule, based on general principles, which shall keep in view all the relations of the married state, be applicable to all classes, and be administered by all courts of justice, whether of law or equity.'[12]

Meanwhile, in 1855 Miss Leigh Smith's committee had begun a country-wide campaign to win reform of the married women's property law. This campaign was of the greatest significance for, as Bessie Parkes later wrote, 'people interested in the question were brought into communication in all parts of the kingdom, and the germs of an effective [women's] movement were scattered far and wide.'[13]

One purpose of the campaign was to bring to light evidence of the sufferings of married women under the existing law. There was then little public knowledge of the lives of women. Aside from the fact that the whole weight of public opinion was against their complaining, women had no effective means of voicing their grievances except, as during this particular campaign, by attending and testifying at public meetings or by writing letters to sympathetic correspondents. Mrs Norton's case was famous – she herself had made it so – but now a mass of evidence was accumulated showing that sufferings such as hers occurred every day and in all ranks of society, as just a few examples from among those collected will prove.[14]

A young woman, the daughter of a journeyman carpenter, worked as a cook and had saved a considerable sum of money. She was courted by a man who posed to her and her father as a successful doctor. After their marriage it was discovered that the husband was actually a former footman who had learned of her savings, which he quickly squandered.

A young lady of fortune whose parents were dead married a poor but apparently respectable man who had risen from humble origins to become chief manager of his master's business. At the time of the marriage he agreed to the settlement of several hundred pounds upon his wife, with the understanding that he was to invest the rest of her property in a business of his own. Soon afterward he disappeared, and her property with him. At the same time his master's wife and one of his children and a considerable portion of his plate and other possessions also disappeared. It turned out that there had long been suspicions of the husband's intimacy with his master's wife, and that he had married only in order to obtain money so that they could go off together to Australia.

A poor woman who had been deserted by her husband was set up in business as a laundress by some friends. She prospered enough to support herself and her children, and also to put away in a savings bank a comfortable sum to provide for her old age. Her husband heard of this and went to the bank to demand that her money be paid to him. The woman found herself penniless, the savings of years gone.

A lady was deserted by her husband, who went off with another woman to Australia to seek his fortune in the gold fields. She opened a school in order to support herself, but her husband, having failed in his venture, returned to England and seized all her property.

A woman was cruelly treated by her husband, who at last was convicted by a court of assault upon her. Meanwhile her father died, leaving her considerable property. But the husband was the legal owner, and since he was a convicted felon the property was forfeited to the crown.

A woman who had inherited property from her father married without having it settled upon her, since she trusted her husband and also lacked knowledge of financial matters. Soon afterward her husband died without having made a will, and half of her property went to his heir-at-law, a nephew, so that she was left in very straitened circumstances.

A woman whose husband had failed in business set up a fashionable millinery establishment with the aid of friends. So successful was the venture that she made a considerable fortune and retired from business to live on the proceeds of her savings. Meanwhile her husband did not work, and she supported him. When he died, he left a will bequeathing her property to his illegitimate children, so that she was left penniless and had to become a milliner again.

To publicize these findings about practical grievances and to present the philosophical arguments in favour of reform of the property law, the women's committee found an especially effective spokeswoman in the person of Caroline Frances Cornwallis. The daughter of a clergyman, Miss Cornwallis was a woman of distinguished intellect who through her own unguided studies had acquired immense knowledge of a great variety of subjects – Latin, Greek, Hebrew, German, philosophy and theology, natural science, history, and law. She edited the widely read series entitled *Small Books on Great Subjects* and wrote several of the twenty-two volumes, which began to appear in 1842 and included works on Greek philosophy, theology, geology, chemistry, and criminal law. Miss Cornwallis was an ardent advocate of higher education for women and of removal of their legal disabilities. Now she contributed to the *Westminster Review* two lengthy, closely reasoned, lucidly written articles which forcefully presented the case for reform – 'The Property of Married Women,' published in 1856, and 'Capabilities and Disabilities of Women,' which appeared the following year. Her presentation foreshadowed the great debate on reform that would not come till a decade later.[15]

First, Miss Cornwallis pointed out the necessity of ongoing reform of the law. Early law generally, she said, was adapted to 'a state of semi-barbarism,' when the chief need was to crush violence and maintain order, and when physical strength was the best claim to authority. The common law relating to married women was an excellent illustration of this; it obviously descended from 'barbarous times' when women were at the mercy of those rich enough to buy or strong enough to seize them, and their position relative to their husbands was precisely that of bondwomen to masters. Like slaves of old, wives could not possess property, sue or be sued, or testify in court; instead of civil rights, including the right to own property, they received merely food, clothing, and lodging. It was for a later, more advanced age, said Miss Cornwallis, to 'eliminate from its rough unwritten common law the dicta and customs of unlettered law givers in an uncivilized age.' But, she added, reform had been carried through only slowly in England, where 'the great principles of social law' were still hardly accepted or acted upon.

What were the 'great principles of social law'? The first of these was that law must rest upon the 'inalienable rights' of every human being, which, according to the great Blackstone, were the rights of personal security, personal liberty, and private property. 'When these rights are withheld,' Miss Cornwallis declared, 'a wrong is committed.' The true purpose of law was 'to accomplish, by peaceable means, that defence of inalienable rights which would otherwise be attempted by more violent methods,' and these great 'human rights' could justly be abridged only so much as was necessary to 'place all, whether strong or weak, upon an equal footing of security.' How, then, could there be any justification of the legal position of married women, of the fact that, as Blackstone also said, the legal existence of women was suspended during marriage? What crime had a woman committed by marrying that she was 'instantly deprived of all civil rights, which in most countries is considered as the punishment of felony'? Surely, too, social law should protect the weak against the strong, not 'give up the weaker, bound hand and foot, into the power of the stronger.'

To those who would argue that liberating women by changing the marriage laws would lead to the dissolution of marriage ties, the desecration of homes, and all uncleanliness, Miss Cornwallis replied disdainfully. Were mothers, sisters, and daughters who asked for their birthright as free citizens to be told that they were 'unfit for exercising it'? Was it true that if they were not 'bound by no less a penalty than the loss of all personal identity, they would render asunder all the dearest affections of the human heart'? Were women really 'so little observant of Christian duties, or so little influenced by human feeling' that they would 'at once abandon their best hopes, both here and hereafter, and defy both God and man in their licentious madness'?

On the contrary, Miss Cornwallis maintained, the true ends of marriage were actually subverted by the existing laws. The purpose of marriage, she said, was surely the nurture and education of children but also, and above all, 'the mutual incitement to all good and noble deeds, the disinterested affection, the support in sickness and sorrow [which] render the union a spiritualized and holy inter-course.' These objects, she continued, were 'the free growth of a noble nature cultivated to its highest point, so that all its impulses are controlled and bal-anced by the rational will.' But, she asked, 'have we ever found that the best mode of cultivating the higher virtues was to take away, as far as the law can do it, all the common rights of our nature, and to leave the individual in a state of utter subjection?' Surely 'equality of rights' rather than subjection was 'most conducive to happiness,' as it was 'most befitting rational and responsible beings who have separate duties to perform.'

Miss Cornwallis went on to show in detail how the existing laws degraded women. Among those of the lower classes 'all the energies of honest industry' had been crushed out by the laws, which thus 'poisoned society at its very source' and left women 'heartless, vicious, and reckless.' Why should a woman work and save, when her husband could take away all her money? 'What she earns she will think she had better enjoy at once, and too often the enjoyment of the overtasked wife will be found at the gin-shop.' As for women of the middle and upper classes, the existing laws had a baneful influence upon the sort of education they received. Parents were naturally guided in determining their children's education by their likely future careers, and thought it needless to teach them what would be useless to them. Now daughters would marry and, together with their property, be taken care of by their husbands. What they needed, therefore, were 'showy accomplishments' to attract potential husbands, not 'solid acquirements' that would enable them to find employment and manage property. Also, parents, being anxious to 'marry off' their daughters and knowing that young women of independent spirit might hesitate to marry when this meant their loss of legal existence, encouraged their daughters to be dependent, to believe it 'unfeminine' to have strong opinions and indelicate to know about public affairs. As a result these women tended to become frivolous and ornamental creatures who could not win the respect of their husbands or sons because of 'their ignorance of things which men know because they have been taught, and which women do not know because they have not been taught.'

The evil effects of the marriage laws could be seen, said Miss Cornwallis, not only in the circle of family life but also on the wider stage of public life. The experience of Europe in the past three years – that is, the Crimean War – furnished evidence of what befell a nation that was careless of the civil rights of women: 'our present lack of accomplished statesmen and legislators may be traced back to the unequalled barbarism of ancestral laws which have retained the mothers of the nation in a degraded position.'

At the same time the Crimean War had furnished, in the person of Florence Nightingale, a shining example of what liberated women could achieve. 'Must we,' Miss Cornwallis demanded, 'lose another army by mismanagement ere we shall acknowledge the administrative skill of women, or emancipate them from the eternal tutelage in which the law insists on holding them?' It was, she maintained, 'a suicidal act' to 'tie the hands of half of mankind.' The nation could not afford 'to lose the labour of earnest workers, because an ill-founded prejudice has deemed women unfit for affairs.'

Among much else she had to say about the marriage laws, Miss Cornwallis's grand theme as to what reform of these laws would accomplish emerged clearly: 'Public opinion needs to have a better tone given to it; women themselves need to be taught to use the rights which God has given them for the advantage of society generally; and both men and women ought to learn ... that woman was not made to be either a plaything or a slave, but that her noble endowments, fine tact and intellectual power were given her for better purposes than they usually have been employed in.'

This theme was being taken up by others, perhaps most notably by Anna Jameson. In 1855, in the hospitable drawing-room of Elizabeth Reid, Mrs Jameson presented a lecture on 'Sisters of Charity Abroad and at Home,' and the following year another on 'The Communion of Labour,' both of which were later published. Appealing, like Caroline Cornwallis, to the example of Florence Nightingale, Mrs Jameson declared that there existed 'at the core of our social condition a great mistake to be corrected, and a great want supplied ... men and women must learn to understand each other, and work together for the common good ... in the most comprehensive sense of the word, we need Sisters of Charity everywhere.' For Mrs Jameson and Miss Cornwallis, as for so many other early feminists, women's right to be free entailed their duty to serve and to uplift, and their words gained a wide and sympathetic hearing.

In addition to collecting evidence of the sufferings of women under the existing marriage laws and presenting the philosophical arguments for reform of the laws, Barbara Leigh Smith's little committee had also undertaken the arduous task of circulating throughout the country petitions to parliament requesting reform. This drive was a great success, for in the space of a few months more than seventy petitions with over 26,000 signatures were gathered for presentation to parliament. In London alone the petition drafted by Miss Leigh Smith had more than 3,000 signatures. Of this work Anna Mary Howitt reported to her sister, 'Various little incidents of interest have occurred, such as a very old lady on her death-bed, who asked to be allowed to put her name to the petition, and thus wrote her signature for the last time.'[16]

It was fortunate that Mary Howitt was the nominal head of the petition campaign in London. Not only was her prestige so great that her advocacy of property-law reform would be certain to impress the public, but also, in obtaining leading signatures on the petition, she was guided by the belief that it was 'most needful to have an eye to the moral status of the persons supporting this movement.'[17] These persons should be either women who were happily married, like Mrs Howitt herself, or well-known single women, for neither of these classes of women could then be said to have a personal or selfish interest in the reform they advocated. Women such as Mrs Norton would definitely not be included. As the result of Mrs Howitt's efforts, the sixteen signatures that headed the petition together with the names of eight of the committee members were those of women whose respectability no less than their celebrity would be certain to win favourable public attention to the cause.

Perhaps the most glittering of all the names affixed to the petition was that of Elizabeth Barrett Browning. For more than a decade she had been acclaimed as England's greatest poetess. Also, she was famous as a real-life romantic heroine – one who had escaped the clutches of a despotic father and the confines of a deadly sickroom to find love and life itself by running away to Italy with the poet who adored her. In the summer of 1855 the Brownings were in England for a visit. Perhaps it was Anna Jameson who approached Mrs Browning for her signature on the petition. Years before, Mrs Jameson had sought the acquaintance of Miss Barrett, as she then was, and had become one of the handful of persons besides members of the family who were allowed admittance to her sickroom. She was one of the few people to be informed of her friend's plans to elope with Browning, although the letter telling her of the elopement miscarried, and only by accident did she meet the newly married pair in Paris. Then, in her characteristically affectionate and managing fashion, she took them under her wing and travelled southward with them to Pisa. Both the Brownings remained devoted to her all her life. Or perhaps Mrs Browning gave her signature at the request of Eliza Fox, with whom she exchanged affectionate letters. Browning called William Johnson Fox his 'literary father,' and always remembered gratefully his encouragement of his own early poetic attempts and his aid in finding a publisher. Later, when Eliza Fox was married in Rome, Browning gave her away in her father's place and at his request.

Certainly it was not disenchantment with her own marriage that awakened Mrs Browning's interest in the women's movement. Once, before her marriage, she had professed herself generally sceptical about the married state, saying that she would choose 'absolute contentment with single life as the alternative to the great majority of marriages.' But in the first year of her marriage she wrote to Mrs Jameson, 'Women generally *lose* by marriage, but I have gained the world by mine.' And shortly before her death she wrote to another friend, 'For me, if I have attained anything of force or freedom by living near the oak, the better for me. But,' she added, 'I hope you don't think that I mimic him or lose my individuality.'[18]

Despite her ill health and her isolation from the world of affairs, first in her sickroom in London and then as an expatriate in Italy, Mrs Browning had a lively social conscience and lent her poetic talents to various reform movements – the anti-Corn Law campaign in England, the antislavery crusade in the United States, the cause of Italian liberation, and the movement for women's rights. In particular, her project in 1855 was one she had had in mind for years – a long verse novel telling the story of an emancipated woman and dealing with the great social evil of prostitution. When it was published the following year, *Aurora Leigh* was an immediate sensation, and a second and a third edition quickly followed the first. Of this reception Mrs Browning wrote from Italy:

I am assured ... by a friend ... that the 'mamas of England' in a body refuse to let their daughters read it. Still, the daughters emancipate themselves and *do* ... the number of *young* women, not merely 'the strong-minded' as a sect, but pretty, affluent, happy women, surrounded by all the temptations of English respectability, that cover it with the most extravagant praises is surprising to me, who was not prepared for that particular kind of welcome.[19]

Also signing the petition were Mrs Browning's sister-in-law Sarianna and her great friend Isabella (Isa) Blagden. Miss Browning was a bright, cheerful, commonsensical woman who never married. Instead she devoted her life to the care of three successive generations of Browning men – her ineffectual father, her widowed brother, and her nephew Pen. Miss Blagden, who lived an expatriate's life in Florence, had some little reputation as a writer of novels and poetry. However, she is chiefly remembered today for her unfailing hospitality and kindness to English travellers and fellow exiles in Italy, and for her warm friendship with many notables of the time, pre-eminent among them the Brownings.

Another signature which Mrs Howitt had been anxious to obtain was that of Elizabeth Stevenson Gaskell. From one point of view Mrs Gaskell could be seen as the perfect Victorian matron, the acme of respectability. A handsome woman who prided herself on her fashionable dress, she was the devoted wife of a distinguished Unitarian minister and college professor in Manchester, the doting mother of four conventionally educated daughters, a charming hostess whose home was always open to a constant stream of appreciative visitors, and a socially conscious, active supporter of good works among the poorer classes in her city. At the same time Mrs Gaskell was one of the most distinguished writers of her day, and her works continue to receive critical acclaim today. She had turned to writing as a relief from the burden of grief that followed the death of her only son in infancy. The Howitts encouraged her first literary efforts and published her earliest stories in *Howitt's Journal*. Her first novel, *Mary Barton*, published anonymously in 1848, was an immediate sensation, and was followed by six others over the next fifteen years. Mrs Gaskell was also the first and official biographer of Charlotte Brontë, whose friendship she had assiduously cultivated.

Despite her reputation in the literary world, Mrs Gaskell was no feminist. She confessed to enjoying inordinately the company and admiration of men – 'I believe, we've a mutual attraction of which Satan is the originator,' she once wrote to a friend – and to preferring men's good sense and judgment to those of women, who were 'at best angelic geese.'[20] She stoutly maintained that a woman's true role was that of wife and mother, and that she herself was much fonder of her domestic duties than of her literary labours. Still, Mrs Gaskell was acutely aware of the many problems women faced, and dealt with some of these in her fiction. For example, her third novel, *Ruth* (1853), presented with great sympathy the story of a fallen woman who bore a child out of wedlock. To her discomfiture, many critics condemned her for treating such a subject, and at least one London circulating library withdrew the work as being unfit for family reading.

It is rather surprising that Mrs Gaskell did not develop marked feminist sympathies, at least where the married women's property law was concerned. In 1850 she wrote to her young friend Eliza Fox that for her story 'Lizzie Leigh,' which like her novel *Ruth* told the story of a fallen woman, she had received from *Household Words* the sum of £20, adding, 'William [her husband] has composedly buttoned it up in his pocket. He has promised I may have some for the Refuge [for women].' The next year she was writing to her publisher about payment for another story: 'Mr. Gaskell sends me word that he has received the 50 £ quite safely; now I don't know if he is to acknowledge it or if I am, but I fancy you will like a double acknowledgment better than none at all.'[21] Obviously her husband had again appropriated her earnings. When Eliza Fox wrote to her early in 1856 requesting her signature on the married women's property petition, Mrs Gaskell replied:

I don't think it is very definite, and *pointed*; or that it will do much good ... a husband can coax, wheedle, beat or tyrannize his wife out of something and no law whatever will help this that I see. (Mr Gaskell begs Mr Fox to draw up a bill for the protection of *husbands* against wives who will spend all their earnings.) However our sex is badly enough used and legislated *against*, there's no doubt of *that* – so though I don't see the definite end proposed by these petitions I'll sign.[22]

Another woman of towering reputation whose name appeared upon the petition was the famous Radical, Harriet Martineau. Like her friend Anna Jameson, Miss Martineau had been a fixture on the literary scene for many years. Daughter of a prominent Unitarian family of textile manufacturers of Norwich, and sister of the distinguished theologian Dr James Martineau, she had begun writing in hopes of earning money after her father suffered severe business losses, and with the encouragement of W.J. Fox she became a contributor to the *Monthly Repository*. Her series of tales entitled *Illustrations of Political Economy*, published in 1831, caught the public's fancy and instantly brought her wide acclaim. This was followed by a series of tales illustrating the proper principles of the Poor Law and the treatment of paupers, a series commissioned by Lord Brougham for publication by the Society for the Diffusion of Useful Knowledge. These works established Miss Martineau's reputation as an 'instructor of the people,' as one friend put it, in all manner of subjects, from foreign policy to farm management. Among her many later works were two studies of life and society in America, inspired by her extended visit to the United States, where she was treated like visiting royalty; a work on comparative religion suggested by a later visit to Egypt and Palestine; an instructive guide for female domestic servants; another book of instruction on the education of children; a study of the American abolitionist movement, which she heartily supported; two novels, one of them based on the career of Toussaint l'Ouverture, the black liberator of Haiti; and a fine history of the earlier nineteenth century. In her later years Miss

Martineau turned increasingly to journalistic work as a forum for the presentation of her views, contributing articles to many leading periodicals and writing frequent leaders for the liberal *Daily News*. To be sure, Miss Martineau could startle and offend both her reading public and her personal friends, among whom two of the most loyal were Elizabeth Reid and Julia Smith – as by her announcement of her miraculous resurrection through the powers of mesmerism from what she had been convinced was her deathbed, and by her public repudiation of Christianity and hearty acceptance of agnosticism. But she could not be overlooked, for she was one of the best known and most influential writers of her day.

Miss Martineau was a staunch feminist. She wrote, she said, because she wanted to have some impact upon political life, and literary work was the only means whereby women could have such an influence. Her very first contribution to the *Monthly Repository* dealt with women writers on divinity, and another early article in the *Repository* treated the question of the proper education of women, which, she maintained, should prepare them, married and unmarried alike, 'to transform narrow, selfish charity into intelligent benevolence aimed at the permanent improvement of mankind.'[23] To Miss Martineau, one of the great violations of the democratic principles which she advocated and which she had observed in practice in America was the lack of women's suffrage. In the later 1830s she was enthusiastically involved in the 'Women's Friend scheme,' as she called it, a project to establish and edit a journal devoted to women's causes. This particular plan came to nought, but she was always ready to do anything she could to improve the position of women. For example, in 1859 she published *England and Her Soldiers*, a work about the Crimean War which was based on information privately communicated to her by Florence Nightingale, one of her heroines, and she agitated for army and nursing reforms both through her writings and through her own political connections. Also in 1859 she published in the *Edinburgh Review* an important article on 'Female Industry,' which dealt with the problems of working women and inspired the founding of the Society for Promoting the Employment of Women. Now she signed the married women's property petition, sent to her by her old friend W.J. Fox or by his daughter Eliza, 'remarking wittily that there is joy in the spectacle of all sorts and conditions of men trying to explain their attitude toward wife beating!'[24]

Another name from the world of literature which was placed upon the women's petition was that of Mary Cowden Clarke. Like Mary Howitt, she is little known today but in her own time she enjoyed an international reputation. She was a daughter of the distinguished musician and music publisher Vincent Novello, whose large family, affectionately close-knit and highly talented, were on terms of intimate friendship with many persons who were famous in artistic and literary circles. Mary's sister Cecilia, who had a successful career as an actress, married the dramatist Thomas James Serle, and her sister Clara, later Countess Gigliucci, was one of the finest singers of the time. Mary herself worked first as a governess but soon gave up her post because of ill health. In 1828 she married Charles Cowden Clarke, long an intimate friend of the family. He had begun work as a teacher in his father's school at Enfield, where he discovered and encouraged the poetic talent of the young John Keats, who was a pupil there. Later he entered the publishing business, first in partnership with Leigh Hunt's brother John and then in the firm of his father-in-law. He also wrote for a number of papers, including Hunt's *Tatler* and the liberal *Examiner*. Literature was his great love. His two works, *Tales from Chaucer* and *The Riches of Chaucer*, published in the 1830s, helped to popularize the great medieval writer, and for more than twenty years he was a popular lecturer to mechanics' institutes on various literary topics. Mrs Cowden Clarke also devoted herself to literature, and gained a modest though substantial reputation for her novels and miscellaneous pieces. Her major work was the first *Complete Concordance to Shake-speare*, begun the year after her marriage but not published until 1845. The fact that this herculean work had been accomplished by an unassuming young married woman caught the public imagination, and the work itself, which was not superseded for decades, immediately established her reputation as a Shakespeare scholar. It led to invitations to her to undertake a revised edition of Shakespeare's works, which was published in 1859-60, and an annotated version of Shakespeare's plays, which she and her husband completed in 1868.

The Cowden Clarkes were progressive in outlook and ardently feminist. Asked once whether they were Whig or Tory, Mary declared, 'Neither, my dear sir; stauch Liberals!' For his part Charles denounced the 'favourite cant phrase in Noodledom ... about "strong-minded women," which seems to preclude the possibility of strength in co-existence with gentleness of feeling and softness of manner. As "strong-minded women" are frequently spoken of, one would think a "strong-minded woman" must necessarily have the figure of a horse-guard, the swag of a drayman, and the sensibility of a carcase-butcher.'[25] The Cowden Clarkes were active in the organization and work of the Anti-Corn Law League, in which they became interested through their great friend Leigh Hunt. For a time they were the next-door neighbours in Bayswater of W.J. Fox and Eliza Flower, and spent many happy hours in their company, apparently unconcerned about the irregular nature of their household.

In the midst of her scholarly labours Mary Cowden Clarke also devoted herself to the education and elevation of the women of her time through the medium of literature and history. In a series of portraits of Shakespeare's women characters published in *The Ladies' Companion* in 1849-50, she maintained that of all male writers Shakespeare saw most deeply into the female heart, asserting women's rights while admonishing their failings and errors, and she urged women to learn the lessons Shakespeare teaches: 'note her capabilities, to improve them; her powers, to enlarge them; her faculties, to cultivate them; her sentiments, to refine them; her passions, to regulate them; her ideas, to elevate them; her sense and judgment, to strengthen them; her virtues, to cherish them; her defects, to amend them; her vices, to check, eradicate, and destroy them.' To the same journal she contributed in 1851-3 a series called 'The Women of the Writers,' a study of the heroines of great writers such as Chaucer, Cervantes, Spenser, and Richardson, and likewise held these up as models for Victorian women to emulate. In 1858 there appeared her *World-Noted Women, or Types of Womanly Attributes of All Lands and Ages*, a study of fifteen famous women from Sappho, Aspasia, and Cleopatra to Florence Nightingale. Mrs Cowden Clarke's own life as well as her writings was an inspiration to women. Again like Mary Howitt, she provided an ideal model of Victorian womanhood – a thoroughly happy wife who enjoyed an outstandingly successful intellectual partnership with her husband.

Also signing the petition was Jane Webb Loudon, who like Mary Cowden Clarke was quite famous as a writer in her own time, although now she is forgotten. She had turned to writing in order to earn her own living after her father's death, and her first work, *The Mummy, A Tale of the Twenty-second Century*, published in 1827 when she was only twenty, brought her to the attention of John Claudius Loudon, who printed a favourable notice of it in one of his journals. Three years later they were married. Loudon was already well known as a landscape gardener and a writer on horticultural subjects, and at one time he was editor of no fewer than five periodicals dealing with gardening, natural history, and architecture. It was in his *Magazine of Natural History* that John Ruskin made his first appearance in print in 1834. The Loudons were neighbours and great friends of the Cowden Clarkes. Their evening parties, inspired by their daughter Agnes, often took the form of amateur theatricals, in which they all delighted. One amateur performance of Sheridan's *The Rivals* which they arranged featured Mary Cowden Clarke as Mrs Malaprop. This soon led to her introduction to Dickens and her appearance as Dame Quickly in his amateur company's production of Shakespeare's *Merry Wives of Windsor*, the cast including John Forster, Mark Lemon, George Henry Lewes, and George Cruikshank, with the proceeds going to the preservation of Shakespeare's birthplace at Stratford.

Throughout their married life Mrs Loudon was indeed a helpmeet to her husband, who was crippled and suffered chronic ill health, and was plunged so deeply into debt by two of his publishing ventures that he had to struggle desperately to pay off his creditors. Mrs Loudon often accompanied her husband on the travels connected with his landscape gardening, and she served as his amanuensis. She also continued her own career as a writer, producing chiefly botanical works of a popular character. The most successful of these, *The Ladies' Companion to the Flower Garden*, sold thousands of copies when it was first published in 1841 and eventually went through nine editions. However, two ladies' gardening magazines which she launched, the first in 1842 and the second a decade later, did not succeed. In 1843 Loudon died, literally on his feet, at work, supported by his wife. Mrs Loudon, who received a civil list pension of £100 a year after her husband's death, continued her literary career until her own death in 1858, publishing numerous works of her own and also new editions of her husband's works. She knew, if any woman did, the labour and heartache involved for a wife who must help support a family and also meet a husband's financial obligations.

Another famous woman in the literary world who signed the married women's property petition was Geraldine Jewsbury. A native of Manchester, and a neighbour and friend there of the Gaskells, Miss Jewsbury managed the household of her widowed father and then the establishment of her older brother until his marriage, and she was known as an excellent housekeeper and a gracious hostess. In 1854 she moved to London, to be near her adored friend Jane Welsh Carlyle and to continue her literary career. She had first blazed before the public eye in 1845, when her novel *Zoe* was published, scandalizing and titillating with its descriptions of romantic passion, descriptions not based on personal experience but drawn entirely from the author's lively imagination. Six more novels followed *Zoe*, the last appearing in 1859. Thereafter Miss Jewsbury worked chiefly as literary critic for the *Athenaeum*, and contributed occasional articles to it and other periodicals.

Geraldine Jewsbury was a strange amalgam of romantic nonsense and practical good sense. On the one hand, as Mrs Carlyle said, her 'besetting weakness by nature,' which her trade as a novelist aggravated, was 'the desire of feeling and producing violent emotions,' and she was always seeking some grand passion to fill her life. She never found one, or rather, those she herself felt were not requited. On the other hand, Miss Jewsbury saw clearly that many of the marriages around her, pre-eminently that of the Carlyles, were hardly romantic idylls, and that most men, if they were not selfish boors, were certainly not heroes. As she once wrote, 'We [women] desire nothing better than to obey one wiser and stronger than ourselves ... It is not women who fail in docility but the men who are not high enough to rule.' Her own life was, by necessity if not by choice, that of an emancipated woman. 'I used to cry to be carried, indeed I have had a great taste for it all my life,' she once said, 'but I have been made to find my own feet.' In some of her novels, as in her own life, she championed women's right to develop and use their talents freely, and in letters to Mrs Carlyle she poured out her thoughts on the position and nature of women. 'We only want to be let alone,' she said, 'and then we shall neither be "strong-minded" women nor yet dolls.' She looked hopefully to future generations of women who would be very different from the women of her own day, because they would not have 'their manners and characters flavoured with certain qualities, or shadows of qualities, just to the point which may make them fancied as wives,' but would have 'a genuine, normal life of their own to lead ... able to be friends and companions [to men] in a way they cannot be now ... able to associate with men, and make friends of them, without being reduced by their position to see them as lovers or husbands.'[26] In writing so, Miss Jewsbury, consciously or not, was criticizing not only other women of her time but herself as well.

Mrs Carlyle, too, added her signature to the married women's property petition, an unusual and uncharacteristic thing for her to do, as she never took part in public affairs. A few years after this she wrote to a friend of having been disturbed by an early morning caller who at first she feared 'might be some "good lady" with a petition, a sort of people I cannot abide.' But however retired from the affairs of the world, Mrs Carlyle was well known, not only to the public in her 'character of Lion's Wife,' as she called it, but also to a wide social circle in London as a remarkable person in her own right, sympathetic, witty, and highly intelligent.[27] Miss Jewsbury was only one of many people who had called to worship at Thomas Carlyle's shrine but stayed to worship at his wife's.

The precocious and spoiled only child of an affluent Scots doctor, Jane Welsh had chosen to devote her life to her husband, whom she considered a genius to be nurtured if also rather a rough diamond. She had had fair warning of what her life with him would be, for before their marriage Carlyle wrote to her:

The Man should bear rule in the house and not the Woman. This is an eternal axiom, the Law of Nature ... which no mortal departs from unpunished ... I must not and I cannot live in a house of which I am not head ... it is the nature of a man that if he be controlled by anything but his own reason, he feels himself degraded; and incited, be it justly or not, to rebellion and discord. It is the nature of a woman again (for she is essentially *passive* not *active*) to cling to the man for support and direction; to comply with his humours, and feel pleasure in doing so, simply because they are his; to reverence while she loves him, to conquer him not by her force but her weakness, and perhaps ... after all to command him by obeying him.[28]

Mrs Carlyle followed her husband's prescription for marriage, managing their household efficiently and with true Scots economy, and catering to his every whim, but not always with good grace. 'For,' as she wrote to a friend, 'in spite of the honestest efforts to annihilate my *I-ety*, or merge it in what the world doubtless considers my better half, I still find myself a self-subsisting, and alas! self-seeking *me*.' Carlyle himself seems to have found his own prescription not entirely palatable, for of his wife he once wrote to his brother, 'I tell her many times there is *much* for her to do if she were trained to it; her whole sex to deliver from the bondage of frivolity, dollhood and imbecility, into the freedom of valour and womanhood.' And to Jane herself he later wrote, 'My prayer is, and always has been, that you would rouse up the fine faculties that *are* yours into some course of real work which you felt to be worthy of them and you.'[29] Apparently the Sage of Chelsea could not realize that the role of passivity and submission which he, like many other Victorian husbands, demanded of his wife was hardly calculated to train her to be a free and valorous woman, or to encourage her to take up some real and worthy course of work.

Mrs Carlyle never found her mission to fulfil – aside, that is, from catering to her husband, cultivating her friendships, and writing the multitude of letters which have helped to keep her reputation alive. Beyond this there was nothing to fill her life, and as the years passed she suffered increasingly from ill health and from fits of depression which caused her to fear for her sanity. In particular, she suffered for years from morbid jealousy of Carlyle's slavish if platonic devotion to Lady Harriet Baring, afterward Lady Ashburton, the brilliant centre of a circle of brilliant men, whose company Carlyle constantly sought in preference to his wife's. The journal she kept in the years 1855-6 to relieve her feelings makes sad and terrible reading. In 1855 Mrs Carlyle presented to her husband a paper entitled 'Budget of a *Femme incomprise*,' a symptom of a much deeper problem than financial matters. In it she explained in great detail that their cost of living had risen exactly £29 11s. 8d., asked that this amount be paid to her in quarterly instalments, and declared:

When you tell me '*I pester your life out about money*' – that '*your soul is sick with hearing about it*' – that '*I had better make the money I have serve*' – '*at all rates, hang it, let you alone of it*' – all that I call perfectly unfair, the reverse of kind, and tending to nothing but disagreement. If I were greedy or extravagant or a bad manager, you would be justified in 'staving me off' with loud words; but you cannot say that of me (whatever else) – cannot think it of me ... through six and twenty years I have kept house for you at more or less cost according to given circumstances, but always on less than it costs the generality of people living in the same style ... Mercy! to think there are women – your friend Lady A for example ... who spend not merely the additional pounds I must make such pother about, but four times my whole income on the ball of one night – and none the worse for it nor anyone the better.[30]

Carlyle gave in at once, as he often did when his wife was sufficiently aroused, writing at the bottom of her paper, 'Excellent, my dear clever Goody, thriftiest, wittiest, and cleverest of women ... thy £30 more shall be granted, thy bits of debt paid, and thy will be done.' It was in these circumstances that Mrs Carlyle put her name to the married women's property petition.

Like Mrs Carlyle, Mary Clarke Mohl, who also signed the women's petition, was known not for her own achievements in the arts but for her personal connections with the great figures of her time. Born in England, Mary Clarke grew up and was educated in France, where she always made her home. In middle life she married Julius Mohl, the German-born professor of Persian at the Collège de France, a member of the French Academy, and one of Europe's most distinguished Orientalists. Madame Mohl had always consciously modelled her career on that of her adored older friend Madame Récamier, whose biography she wrote. For forty years, both before and after her marriage, her salon in Paris was an internationally famed centre of hospitality and brilliant conversation where the leading political and intellectual figures of the day gathered. A distinguished German scientist who was a great admirer of Madame Mohl recalled of her, 'We none of us looked upon her as a woman: we met her on equal terms, as if she had been a man; she was more like a man. Her mind was essentially masculine; it had that quality of looking at every side of a subject that you seldom meet in a woman, and she never expected compliments. This set men very much at ease with her; one could talk to her without any effort to make oneself agreeable.'[31]

Madame Mohl had no very high opinion of her sex in general. She frankly preferred masculine to feminine company, and was frequently heard to declare, 'I can't abide women.' She felt that most women were silly and uninteresting, and this through their own fault. 'Why don't they talk about interesting things? Why don't they use their brains?' she demanded. 'Why don't they exercise their brains as they do their fingers and their legs, sewing and playing [the piano] and dancing? Why don't they read?' In short, why were they not like her? At the same time Madame Mohl attributed to masculine attitudes the social inferiority of women, or at least of women in England compared with those in France. According to her, Englishmen cared chiefly for beauty and virtue in women and wanted not wives who could shine in society but decorative wives who could nurse them and brew them comforting cups of tea. In England, if a man went out to his club, he expected his wife to sit at home alone awaiting his return, not to have callers in to amuse her. As a result, she said, Englishmen patronized women, talking to them merely to be nice to them and not because they enjoyed what women had to say. To a Frenchman, a woman's 'nursing capacities and her coffee are not so interesting as her companionable qualities,' for 'not only will her *esprit* amuse him when they are alone, but it will also make his house the resort of an agreeable circle.' As a result, Frenchmen conversed with women for their own pleasure.[32]

Holding such views on women generally, Madame Mohl earnestly sympathized with those who rose above what she considered to be the general mediocrity of their sex, and she took a keen interest in the aspirations and activities of those women who sought to raise others from the level of dependence and silliness which she deplored. Among her many women friends in England, with whom she exchanged letters and visits, were Florence Nightingale, to whom she was always 'dear Clarkey,' Anna Jameson, and Elizabeth Gaskell. Perhaps it was at Mrs Jameson's request, or at that of her younger friend Bessie Parkes, that Madame Mohl now signed the women's petition as a gesture in the good cause of improving the position of women.

Also signing the petition was Amelia Blandford Edwards, a young woman who was just beginning a highly successful career as a writer, although her chief contribution was to be in the field of archaeology rather than literature. Educated at home, chiefly by her mother, Miss Edwards early displayed remarkable talent for music, literature, and art. When forced by straitened family finances to earn her own living, she began work as a church organist and teacher of music and also contributed articles, stories, and drama and art criticism to several leading periodicals, including *Chambers's Journal* and the *Saturday Review*. In 1855, at the age of twenty-four, she published her first novel, *My Brother's Wife*, which was to be followed by seven other novels, two works of history, and three volumes of poetry. The financial success of her literary work enabled her to indulge her passion for travel, which furnished material for four more books and brought her to the turning-point in her career. In 1877, after an extended visit to Egypt, she published the work entitled *A Thousand Miles up the Nile*, which was the best and most comprehensive account of the archaeology and art of ancient Egypt that had appeared till that time. Thereafter Miss Edwards abandoned her other activities to devote herself to Egyptology. She helped to found, under the sponsorship of the British Museum, the Egypt Exploration Fund, which she served as honorary secretary; she published many articles in European and American journals; and she lectured widely, including a lecture tour in the United States. Her international reputation as a scholar brought her honorary degrees from a number of universities. When she died in 1892, her valuable collection on Egyptology went to University College, London, together with enough money to establish the first chair of Egyptology in England.

Another name appearing on the women's petition was that of Anna Blackwell, who had some claim to literary fame although she was best known as the eldest

member of a famous family of feminists, a family native to England but trans-
planted in the 1830s to the United States. Her brothers Henry and Samuel
played important parts in the antislavery movement and in the early women's
movement in America; Henry married the veteran abolitionist and feminist
Lucy Stone, while Samuel Blackwell married Lucy's friend Antoinette Brown,
another early feminist who was the first woman to be ordained a minister. Better
known in England was Anna's younger sister Elizabeth Blackwell, the first
woman doctor of modern times, whose example in entering the medical profession was followed by another sister, Emily. Both Elizabeth and Emily Blackwell
obtained their medical education in the United States despite many obstacles,
and then continued their studies abroad before returning home to practise in
New York City. There Elizabeth Blackwell established a dispensary out of
which developed the New York Infirmary for Women and Children, a hospital
staffed and run by women doctors, and also founded a medical school to train
women doctors. While studying in England in 1849, Elizabeth Blackwell had
been sought out by Barbara Leigh Smith and Bessie Parkes and welcomed to
their circle of relatives and friends. Ten years later, at the special request of these
friends, Dr Blackwell returned to England to deliver a series of lectures to
women, designed to stimulate interest in opening the medical profession to
women there. One of her converts was Elizabeth Garrett, who was to be the first
woman to qualify as a doctor in England. A decade after this, Dr Blackwell
returned to England to settle permanently, practising medicine, serving as professor of gynaecology at the newly founded London School of Medicine for
Women, and writing various works on medical and moral questions.

Anna Blackwell herself, like her more famous sisters after her, began her
working life as a teacher, but soon turned to literary work as a life career. She
wrote articles and stories for various American papers and periodicals and, being
an accomplished linguist, undertook works of translation as well. Among these
was a translation of George Sand's *Jacques*, which appeared in 1847, dismaying
her family because of its frank advocacy of free love, a doctrine which Miss
Blackwell embraced in theory although not, apparently, in practice. She also
espoused such causes as mesmerism, vegetarianism, spiritualism, and socialism,
and as a result of her interest in communal living spent a brief time at Brook
Farm and also visited a number of other utopian communities. In 1848 Miss
Blackwell sailed for Europe, having been offered a substantial salary and travelling expenses for undertaking an English translation of the complete works of
her mentor, the French socialist Fourier. The next year she settled in Paris,
where her sister Elizabeth was then studying. She was to spend many years in
France before retiring to England to live near Elizabeth. In addition to her

translations, Anna Blackwell produced a volume of poems which was highly praised and several works on spiritualism, but she earned her living chiefly by her work as a foreign correspondent for several papers, including Horace Greeley's *Tribune* and the *English Woman's Journal*, to which she contributed an account of her sister Elizabeth's career to inspire readers.

The greatest of the writers who signed the married women's property petition, although for obvious reasons her name did not appear among the leading signatures, was Marian Evans, not yet known to fame as George Eliot. Barbara Leigh Smith had been her intimate friend for several years, introduced to her first by Bessie Parkes, whose father had commissioned Miss Evans's translation of Strauss's *Leben Jesu*. It was to her friend Barbara that Miss Evans turned for advice and support before her decision in 1854 to enter into the extramarital liaison with George Henry Lewes which long placed her beyond the pale of respectable society. Lewes could not obtain a divorce from his unfaithful wife, for he had accepted as his own son the first of several children whom she bore to his friend and literary colleague Thornton Hunt, and this fact would be legally construed as evidence of his condonation of her adultery. In turn, Miss Evans sympathized deeply with her friend in her infatuation with John Chapman; Miss Evans herself had nearly succumbed to Chapman's charms while boarding in his household during her work with him as assistant editor of the *Westminster Review*. A few years after this, Miss Leigh Smith – by then Madame Bodichon – was the first person to guess the identity of the anonymous author of the sensational best-seller *Adam Bede*; she had not even read the novel, merely some extracts in press reviews, but with amazing intuition she leapt to the conclusion that only her friend Marian Evans could have written it. Later still, she served as the model for George Eliot's *Romola*.

Marian Evans – or Mrs Lewes, as she always insisted upon being called – took a keen interest in her friend's campaign to win reform of the married women's property law. In addition to signing the petition herself, she recommended support of it to other friends, saying that this reform, which would 'help to raise the position and character of women,' was but 'one round of a long ladder stretching far beyond our lives.' Also, she and Lewes probably were the ones who suggested a revision in Miss Leigh Smith's petition as originally drafted to include a paragraph stating that parts of the law bore unjustly on the husband as well as the wife, such as his legal responsibility for her debts contracted before marriage 'even although he may have no fortune with her,' and the wife's 'too unlimited power' of contracting debts in the name of her husband, who was legally responsible for them.[33] Lewes never failed to support his wife's ménage after his separation from her, and it is indeed ironic that some of the fabulous earnings of

George Eliot, who always considered herself morally although not legally married, should have gone to maintain Lewes's legal but unfaithful wife and her illegitimate children.

The name of another great celebrity to be added to the petition was that of the American-born actress Charlotte Cushman, who was at the time the toast of the English theatrical world. Tracing her ancestry back to the Puritans of *Mayflower* times, Miss Cushman was the daughter of a Boston merchant whose reverses in business forced her to earn her own living, and she had enjoyed substantial if not spectacular success upon the American stage for ten years before she sailed in 1845 for England, to try her luck there. Appearing in London first in Milman's tragedy *Fazio* and then in a number of Shakespearean productions, she won tremendous acclaim and was courted by the fashionable world. By all accounts Miss Cushman, tall, strong-framed, and deep-voiced, was a commanding figure who thrilled her audiences by her intellectual appreciation of the roles she played no less than by the depth of feeling, vividness, and power of her execution. To be sure, some criticized her for portraying not only such traditional female starring roles as Lady Macbeth and Rosalind but masculine roles as well – Hamlet, Romeo, Cardinal Wolsey, and others – and for affecting masculine-style dress offstage. One of Miss Cushman's earliest friends in England was Geraldine Jewsbury, who introduced her to Jane Carlyle, Anna Jameson, and other friends and notables, and portrayed her as the actress Bianca in her novel *The Half-Sisters*, published in 1848. Another early friend, who also gave Miss Cushman introductions in the fashionable world, was Mary Howitt, whose straiter-laced sister was rather shocked by her friendship with 'stage-girls,' as she called them. In 1849 Miss Cushman returned to the United States in triumph to undertake a series of highly successful tours. Three years later she was again in England, living in London and acting both there and in the provinces amidst a continuing chorus of praise. Later still she settled in Rome, where she maintained her principal residence until her final return in 1870 to the United States, where she died six years later, having continued to work almost until the end, appearing on the stage and presenting dramatic readings of poetry and plays. In her own time she was acclaimed as the greatest actress the United States had ever produced, and as one of the greatest living Americans. She was also one of the wealthiest, having accumulated a handsome fortune in the course of her career.

An intimate associate of Charlotte Cushman's who also signed the women's petition was Matilda Mary Hays. Miss Hays had presented herself to the great actress during her tour of the English provinces in 1849, an eager pupil who yearned for a career in the theatre. Miss Cushman's younger sister Susan had recently married and retired from the stage, where she had played Juliet to

Charlotte's Romeo, and Miss Hays was accepted as her replacement. Within a few months she made a successful debut with Miss Cushman and then toured with her in England and the United States. But soon it became apparent that she lacked the stamina and determination to pursue a theatrical career. Meanwhile, the friendship between the two actresses had ripened into a deep attachment – Elizabeth Barrett Browning called it a 'female marriage' – and they agreed to continue living together, in London and then in Rome, while Miss Hays, who gave up acting, turned to literature, translating some of the novels of George Sand. The two finally parted in 1856, when Miss Hays returned to London after accepting an invitation from Bessie Parkes to become co-editor with her of the *English Woman's Journal*. Of the two women's editorial work George Eliot wrote to a friend, 'Bessie has talent and real ardour for all goodness, but I fear Miss Hayes [sic] has been chosen on the charitable ground that she had nothing else to do in the world. There is something more piteous almost than soapless poverty in this application of feminine incapacity to Literature.'[34] Later Miss Hays also served as co-manager of the Victoria Press, an undertaking sponsored by the Society for Promoting the Employment of Women to train women as printers. She soon formed an ardent friendship with Theodosia, Dowager Lady Monson, who like her friend Anna Jameson was interested in the feminist projects of younger women, and spent many years as her companion.

Another figure from the world of the theatre who signed the women's petition was Mary Anne Lacy Lovell. The daughter of a theatrical family, she had begun her career as an actress in 1818, when she was only fifteen, and she enjoyed considerable success for a number of years before retiring from the stage upon her marriage to George William Lovell. Lovell was a popular playwright whose works were eagerly sought by such theatrical luminaries as William Macready, Charles Kemble, and Charles Kean. Mrs Lovell, too, turned to writing for the theatre, and her plays *Ingomar the Barbarian* and *The Beginning and the End* were successfully produced in the 1850s.

The last of the leading signatures on the married women's property petition was that of the Honourable Julia Maynard. She was the fourth and youngest daughter of Henry, Viscount Maynard, whose honours became extinct on the death of his only son without a male heir in 1865. Julia Maynard herself died unmarried three years later. Interestingly, she was the only member of a noble family whose name was among the leading signatures on the petition. Perhaps her support was solicited chiefly because of her family's position, for apparently she herself took no active part in the feminist movement.

On 14 March 1856 the petition of the married women's property committee, popularly known as 'the petition of Elizabeth Barrett Browning, Anna Jameson,

Mrs Howitt, Mrs Gaskell, etc,' was presented in parliament, by Lord Brougham
in the upper House and by Sir Erskine Perry in the Commons (see appendix 1).
The petition, which had been signed by women only, was said when unrolled 'to
have reached the length of the House of Commons, and to have created a sensation.' As Anna Mary Howitt reported the occasion to her sister, Brougham
'made a capital little speech ... paying Mrs. Jameson and our mother each a very
nice compliment, to which there was a "Hear, hear,"' while Perry said that 'contrary to his expectation, the petition was received very respectfully ... without a
sneer or a smile.'[35]

The petition pointed out that

the law expresses the necessity of an age, when the man was the only money-getting
agent; but ... since the custom of the country has greatly changed in this respect the
position of the female sex ... since modern civilisation, in indefinitely extending the
sphere of occupation for women, has in some measure broken down their pecuniary
dependence upon men, it is time that legal protection be thrown over the produce of
their labour, and that in entering the state of marriage, they no longer pass from freedom into the condition of a slave, all whose earnings belong to his master and not to
himself.

The matter of legal protection for women's earnings 'might once have been
deemed for the middle and upper ranks, a comparatively theoretical question,'
said the petition, 'but is so no longer, since married women of education are
entering on every side the fields of literature and art to increase the family
income by such exertions.' The names of the distinguished women who signed
the petition amply proved this point. At the same time women of the lower
classes were widely employed in factory work and in 'other multifarious occupations.' Therefore the protection of married women's property 'must be recognized by all as of practical importance.'

It was true that marriage settlements might protect some wives of the
wealthier classes, 'proving that few parents are willing entirely to entrust the
welfare of their offspring to the irresponsible power of the husband.' But trustees
of marriage settlements might prove 'dishonest or unwise,' the courts of equity
might 'fail in adjusting differences which concern the most intimate and delicate
relations of life,' and in general, 'legal devices, patched upon a law which is
radically unjust can only work clumsily.' How 'real is the injury inflicted' by the
law upon those who could not escape its operation by means of the expensive
and unsatisfactory provisions of equity was proved by 'well known cases of hardship suffered by women of station, and also by professional women earning large
incomes by pursuit of the arts.' Even greater was the injury inflicted by the law

upon a woman of the lower classes, for 'the education of the husband and the habits of his associates offer no moral guarantee for tender consideration of a wife,' and she had no legal protection of her earnings against 'the robbery' of her husband, no protection against 'the selfishness of a drunken father, who wrings from a mother her children's daily bread.' In short, said the petition, in view of the large numbers of married women at work and the lack of legal protection for their property, what was needed here as in other areas of the law was 'a clearance of the ground' by thoroughgoing reform.

To attract still wider attention to the question of reform after the presentation of the women's petition in parliament, the Law Amendment Society sponsored a large public meeting in London on 31 May. The society's journal recorded the presence of 'a large number of ladies,' including Mrs Jameson, Mrs Howitt, and 'many other lady authors.' Sir John Pakington, the secretary for war, who presided in Lord Brougham's absence because of illness, expressed gratification at their attendance, saying that it was important to have women's opinions and feelings about the proposed reform. Sir Erskine Perry moved a resolution declaring that the rules of the common law relating to married women's property were 'unjust in principle and injurious in their operation,' that the principles of equity were 'in accordance with the requirements of the age and in conformity with the opinions and usages of the wealthier and better classes of society,' and that 'the conflict between law and equity on the subject ought to be terminated by a general law based on the principles of equity which should apply to all classes.' The resolution was seconded by Matthew Davenport Hill, supported in speeches by several other notables, and carried unanimously.[36]

Now, in the early summer of 1856, the stage was set for action in parliament to win reform of the married women's property law. Barbara Leigh Smith's little committee had done their work well. They had collected evidence of the hardships suffered by women under the law and had publicized their findings. They had enlisted the power of the press in stating their case for reform. They had, through the petition campaign, gathered proof of the widespread support for reform by the women of the country, including some of the most distinguished women of their time. Most important of all, they had won the sympathy and the powerful practical support of the Law Amendment Society, whose members would fight the women's battle in parliament to enact legislation embodying the reform which held first place among all the legal reforms advocated by feminists.

5

'The Wind Out of Our Sails'
Property-Law Reform
and Reform of the
Divorce Law

In June 1856, Sir Erskine Perry presented for debate in the House of Commons the same resolution that had been approved at the public meeting sponsored by the Law Amendment Society ten days earlier. His object, Perry said, was to elicit the opinion of the House as to 'which of two principles was the sound one' – the principle of the common law or that of equity – and its opinion as to whether the conflict between the two, which meant in practice one law for the rich and another for the poor, should continue. In doing so, he did not want to 'assert a new principle of woman's social position,' for he himself believed that the 'fitting place for woman was not to be engaged in a struggle with man for her bread ... [but] enshrined in her own home, however humble, a place of light and joy to her husband.' He wanted merely to 'correct a practical grievance,' for there were many cases of hardship arising under the law, cases of husbands taking their wives' property and leaving them to live in adultery with other women, of brutal husbands wresting away the earnings of their hard-working wives. That women desired this reform, Perry said, was shown by the petition which he had presented earlier and which included the names of many women 'who had made the present epoch remarkable in the annals of literature.'[1]

Perry's resolution enjoyed substantial support. It was seconded by Lord Stanley, son and heir of the former prime minister Lord Derby. Stanley, who had served in his father's government and would hold office under him again before leaving the Conservative party to join the Liberals, was known as an ardent advocate of many social reforms. In the ensuing debate W.J. Fox and several others also spoke forcefully in favour of the resolution.

Leading the opposition to the resolution, as Perry later recalled, were some of the most distinguished lawyers in the House.[2] Among them was Richard Malins (later Sir Richard), Conservative member for Wallingford from 1852 to 1865, who had built up a very successful practice in the courts of equity and had been appointed a queen's counsel. He trained numerous pupils in his chambers, the most eminent among them being Hugh McCalmont Cairns, the future lord chancellor. In 1866 Malins was appointed vice-chancellor, a position he was to hold for fifteen years. Now Malins declared that if Perry proposed to 'set up a separate establishment in every house,' he would oppose this to the utmost as being 'contrary not only to the law of England, but to the law of God.' The English law, he said, was founded upon 'the soundest principle ... that when a man and woman married they became one, and that their property ought not, therefore, to be separated.' He added, interestingly in view of his own practice and experience, that he was not sure that in this respect equity 'had not proved detrimental to the best interests of society.'

Another of Perry's distinguished legal opponents was Thomas Chambers (later Sir Thomas). He had long had a lucrative practice in the common-law courts, and afterward was to serve as common serjeant and as recorder of London. He was the Liberal member for Hertfordshire from 1852 until 1857; in 1865 he returned to parliament as member for Marylebone and held this seat for twenty years. Referring to the practical aspects of the reform proposed in Perry's resolution, Chambers maintained that whatever grievances might exist, they could not compare with 'the mischiefs that would follow from the assertion of the vicious principle' of the resolution.

Yet another distinguished lawyer opposed to Perry was John George Phillimore, who was reader in constitutional law and legal history at the inns of court and the author of several works on jurisprudence, and who served as Liberal member for Leominster from 1852 to 1857. He suggested now that something might be done by the Divorce Bill then before the Lords to remedy practical grievances, but he trusted that parliament would maintain unbroken the principle of 'the identity of interest between husband and wife,' for nothing could be 'more frightful than to teach wives that their interests were on one side, and those of their husbands on the other.' Phillimore concluded grimly, 'When people talked of the sufferings which the law caused women, what could be more natural, what more desirable for women to know than that, if they acted foolishly and contracted imprudent marriages, they must bear the consequences?'

Judged by the statements of the two law officers of the crown, Palmerston's government was divided in opinion on property-law reform. The solicitor general, Sir Richard Bethell, thought Perry's resolution lacked clarity. Like Malins, he questioned whether equity's recognition of the separate interests of married women had not been carried too far, and like Phillimore, he suggested that when the Divorce Bill came down from the Lords it might include a provision protecting the property of deserted wives. Perry's resolution was cordially approved by the attorney general, Sir Alexander Cockburn, a brilliant Scots advocate who was soon to be appointed chief justice of the Court of Common Pleas and then chief justice of the Queen's Bench, hailed as 'the greatest of the Chief Justices ... during this period.' Cockburn viewed the matter as only part of a larger question, that of making the common law consistent with equity – that is, consistent with 'reason, justice and common sense.' He said that he had conferred with the lord chancellor, who agreed with him that it was time to amend the law, and added that the government's legal authorities would attend to the matter during the parliamentary recess so that in the next session a comprehensive and satisfactory measure could be brought in. Meanwhile, he urged Perry not to press the House to adopt an abstract resolution, a course which would make it 'neither more nor less than a debating society,' but to introduce legislation instead.[3]

So confronted, Perry withdrew his resolution. He expressed confidence in Cockburn's good intentions, but added significantly that Bethell's remarks made him fear that 'years might elapse before a satisfactory marriage law will be carried out.'[4]

In 1857 legislation to reform the married women's property law finally came before parliament. In February Lord Brougham introduced a bill which, he said, embodied the principles approved by the Law Amendment Society under the inspiration of Matthew Davenport Hill.[5] At the same time Brougham moved three resolutions for debate. The first declared that the state of the law imperiously demanded reform. The second stated that a married woman should be in the same position as an unmarried woman with respect to property. Brougham admitted that some might think this proposed change too great, but he added that 'no good proposal for amending the law ever was made in vain, because how hopeless soever of acceptance it might at first seem to be, yet in the end it was sure to produce good fruits.' He likened his present proposal to the beginning of the long campaigns to abolish slavery and to reform the civil and criminal law, campaigns in which, he added with characteristic immodesty, he had played a prominent part. The third resolution stated that until reform of the married women's property law could be carried through, a wife should be given easy and speedy access to a court in order to secure protection for her property. Presumably this resolution was designed to commit the Lords to include such a provision in the Divorce Bill they had been considering.

After Brougham's speech, brief congratulatory remarks were made by Lord Campbell, chief justice of the Court of Queen's Bench and afterward lord chancellor, and by Lord Granville, the distinguished statesman who was then serving as lord president of the Council and government leader of the Lords. Debate on the resolutions was then adjourned, and Brougham's bill was read a first time. It proceeded no further, for soon afterward Palmerston was defeated in a vote on his foreign policy, and the government resigned. Twelve years were to elapse before the Lords again took up the question of reform of the married women's property law.

The general election of 1857 was a resounding popular victory for Palmerston, and the Whigs returned to office with an increased majority. In May, shortly after the new parliament assembled, Sir Erskine Perry introduced in the Commons a Married Women's Property Bill different from Brougham's measure, which had been amended and altered by the committee of the Law Amendment Society over which Perry presided.[6] Simple and clear in its provisions, Perry's bill did not interfere with the right to make marriage settlements in equity, but it provided that in all other cases married women would be as capable as unmarried women of acquiring, holding, dealing with, and disposing of property both real and personal. Specifically, they and not their husbands would be liable for all debts they incurred and all torts they committed both before and after marriage. They would be able to make binding contracts and to sue and be sued. They would be able to dispose of their property freely during their lifetime, and to dispose of it by will or, if they died intestate, the same principles of distribution would apply to their property as applied to that of their husbands.

In introducing his bill, Perry expressed regret that the government had not taken up the matter of reform, as Cockburn had indicated during the last session that it would do. He pointed out that the bill was sponsored by the Law Amendment Society, which included distinguished members on both sides of the House, that it had been approved by government draftsmen, and that popular support for it was evidenced by the petitions he had presented in parliament the year before. In contrast, Perry claimed, there was no popular demand for passage of the Divorce Bill then before the Lords, and he believed that if his Married Women's Property Bill were passed, there would be no demand or necessity for easier divorce, which he felt would lead to 'the corruption of morals.' The Commons would soon be considering the Divorce Bill, now amended by the Lords so as to protect the property interests of married women; if the Commons did not approve this bill, his own measure would be necessary, and for this reason he refused to withdraw it, although he admitted that he had no real expectation of its passing during that session.[7]

The members who spoke on the introduction of Perry's bill and in the debates on the second reading two months later were almost evenly divided in opinion. The co-sponsor of Perry's bill and his staunchest supporter was Richard Monckton Milnes. Milnes had a long career in parliament, serving in the Commons as member for Pontefract for a quarter of a century before his elevation to the peerage as Baron Houghton in 1863, but to his great disappointment high political office eluded him. A poet of some talent and reputation, Milnes was best known as a widely travelled, cosmopolitan leader of society, whose wit and charm made him as popular in foreign capitals as in London. He once boasted that he had known every person worth knowing in the Europe of his day with the single exception of Goethe. His glittering social life rather obscured for all but his most intimate friends his very solid virtues – a keen intelligence, a genuinely humane and tolerant nature, and a tender conscience alive to the sufferings in the world about him. In parliament his special interests included passage of the Factory Acts and the establishment of reformatories for youthful offenders against the law. It is some measure of Milnes's worth that that woman of genius Florence Nightingale adored him and would have married him but for her long-delayed decision that only in a celibate life of service could she fulfil the mission to which she believed God had called her. (Later Milnes was very happily married to another woman.) Next to Milnes, Perry's chief supporter was Henry Drummond, the independent-minded member for West Surrey, who was something of a religious crank and long a remarkable if rather ludicrous figure in the House.[8]

In opposition to the bill stood Richard Malins, who reiterated the opinions he had expressed the previous year. (His former colleagues in opposition, Thomas Chambers and J.G. Phillimore, had been defeated in the election of 1857.) But the voice now most vehemently raised in opposition was that of Alexander James Beresford-Hope, who had just been elected to parliament as Conservative member for Maidstone, a seat he had held earlier for eleven years, and who would later represent Stoke-upon-Trent and then the University of Cambridge. Devotion to the Established Church was the ruling passion of his life. An authority on ecclesiastical architecture, he used part of his large fortune to build and restore churches; a High Churchman, he interested himself in Church ritual and hymnody; and as a member of the Commons he opposed all measures that he believed threatened the position and privileges of the Church, such as the proposed abolition of Church rates and disestablishment of the Church in Ireland. Beresford-Hope was also a writer with a keen interest in journalistic work, and in 1855 he had helped to found the *Saturday Review*, which proved an immediate success with its witty and well-written articles and which was always known for its slashing High Toryism and its virulent anti-feminism.[9]

Beresford-Hope denounced 'the rather extravagant demands of the large and manly body of "strong-minded women"' for whom Perry spoke, and the whole question of 'abstract women's rights which were sometimes advocated by young ladies in pamphlets, and further developed ... in the pages of *Aurora Leigh*.' While he admitted that the law should be amended, he maintained that parliament must 'steadfastly resist the breaking down of the distinguishing characteristics of Englishmen – love of home, the purity of husband and wife, and the union of one family.' The *Saturday Review* echoed these sentiments, denouncing the 'perfect rage for Acts of Parliament to redress all the little social and domestic miseries of human life,' and declaring that 'so long as the petticoat rebellion was confined to a mistaken petition of a few literary ladies whose peculiar talents had placed them in a rather anomalous position, we really had not the heart to say anything about it.' But now, the *Review* continued, the proposals of the Law Amendment Society 'set at defiance the experience of every country in Christendom and the common sense of mankind' and were enough 'to remove the whole discussion from the region of reality to that of burlesque.' Hardships under the existing law were not numerous or brutal enough to justify the proposed 'revolutionizing' of society and, the *Review* concluded, 'there is besides a smack of selfish independence about it which rather jars with poetical notions of wedlock.' Presumably no smack of selfish independence and no jarring of poetical notions were involved in men's insistence on having their wives' property as well as their own.[10]

Monckton Milnes called Beresford-Hope to task for treating a serious matter in a jesting spirit. He also pointed out that it hardly became his opponent to sneer at 'strong-minded women' for 'if the public prints were to be believed no Member of the House was more indebted for the honourable position he now occupied to the influence of the sex whose interests this Bill would protect.'[11] This was a reference to Beresford-Hope's powerful political connections through his wife, Lady Mildred Cecil, eldest daughter of the Marquis of Salisbury and sister of the future prime minister who was for many years a celebrated leader of London society.

More serious than Beresford-Hope's tirades was the opposition of Sir Richard Bethell, who had now succeeded Cockburn as attorney general. While not opposing the introduction of Perry's bill and even favouring discussion of it in view of the impending debates on the Divorce Bill, Bethell warned that this was no ordinary scheme of legal reform, for it 'must involve a material change in the social and political institutions of a nation.' Like Beresford-Hope, Bethell believed that the bill would tend to 'the placing of the women of England in a "strong-minded and independent position," which so few chose for themselves,' and that such a position, rendering them 'accountable for every thing which they might say or do,' was not one which 'the best and most amiable women of England were anxious to occupy.'[12]

Despite this opposition, Perry's bill was approved in the vote on the second reading by the comfortable majority of 120 to 65. Then, however, it dropped from sight. As Perry recalled years later, and as he had feared at the time would happen, the Divorce Bill 'took the wind out of our sails.'[13]

An account of the divorce law, like an account of the law relating to married women's property, reveals the confusion that characterized English jurisprudence in the mid-nineteenth century, a result of the survival of medieval institutions in an age when new ideas had won acceptance and other institutions had developed.[14] As the law then stood, a divorce could be obtained from either of two tribunals, which followed different procedures and afforded different remedies and in both of which the cost of proceedings was so high as to place relief beyond the reach of all but the wealthiest classes. Thus, reform of the divorce law, like reform of the married women's property law, was but a part of the wider movement of legal reform which had as its goals to harmonize conflicting legal systems and to rationalize and modernize the country's judicial machinery.

Since the middle ages the Church had exercised exclusive jurisdiction over matrimonial causes, for marriage was regarded as a sacrament, and all questions relating to it were governed by the canon law administered in the bishops' courts. In these courts two kinds of divorce could be obtained. One was a divorce *a vinculo matrimonii* (from the bonds of matrimony), which was awarded on the petition of either husband or wife on the ground that the marriage was null and void because of some defect relating to it and existing from its beginning – consanguinity or blood relationship, affinity or relationship by marriage, physical incompetence, and insanity. Such a divorce, declaring a marriage invalid, enabled the parties to marry again, but it rendered their children illegitimate. The other remedy was divorce *a mensa et thoro* (from bed and board), which could be granted on the petition of either husband or wife on three grounds – adultery, sodomy, or cruelty, usually narrowly interpreted as meaning physical violence. This kind of divorce did not dissolve a marriage and enable the parties to marry again, but merely relieved them of the legal and religious obligation of cohabitation. In both kinds of cases the ecclesiastical courts did not follow the common-law rule that a woman could not testify against her husband, for matrimonial causes obviously could not be decided if wives were barred from giving evidence.

Divorce by the ecclesiastical courts was subject to valid criticism on a number of important points. The most general criticism was that it was anomalous and unfair for the Church to have exclusive jurisdiction over matrimonial causes in an age when so large a proportion of the population were not even nominal members of the Church, and when the state recognized marriages not solemnized by the Church but by Nonconformist ministers and also marriages contracted through civil proceedings.

A problem of particular importance to women was that of property rights in cases of ecclesiastical divorce. Since it dissolved a marriage, a divorce *a vinculo matrimonii* ended the rights husband and wife had in each other's property. But in the case of a divorce *a mensa et thoro*, the marriage remained valid and the wife did not regain the rights over property enjoyed by an unmarried woman; her husband retained his common-law rights over her property instead. To be sure, the ecclesiastical courts would grant the woman alimony, ordering her husband to pay an annual sum for her maintenance. The amount of alimony was set as a proportion of the parties' joint income if the wife had separate property in equity, or otherwise as a proportion of the husband's income, usually one-third, although it might be as much as one-half if his conduct had been especially bad or if the bulk of his fortune had come to him from his wife. The amount of alimony could be varied periodically because of the changed circumstances of the parties. Still, alimony was not a legal debt – that is, a debt which could be collected through proceedings in the common-law courts – and the ecclesiastical courts could enforce payments by the husband only by ecclesiastical censure, until an act of 1813 added the penalty of imprisonment. Also, alimony was payable only during the husband's lifetime and was not payable out of his estate after his death, since the ecclesiastical courts had power only over his person and not over his property. Finally, the ecclesiastical courts never granted alimony to a wife guilty of adultery, regarding her offence as so heinous that she forfeited all right to her husband's protection and support.

Another problem related to the ecclesiastical courts' divorce *a mensa et thoro* was that the grounds recognized for such a divorce were very narrow. In particular, desertion was not recognized, and the only remedy obtainable from the ecclesiastical courts was a decree for restitution of conjugal rights – that is, an order to return to cohabitation, with a penalty of imprisonment for non-compliance.

Yet another criticism of ecclesiastical divorce was that the cost of the proceedings was very high. In the 1850s it was estimated that an uncontested divorce *a mensa et thoro* cost between £300 and £500, while if the divorce was contested the cost might run into thousands of pounds. (A woman's legal expenses in a matrimonial cause were considered 'necessaries' for which her husband was liable.)

By far the most popular criticism of the ecclesiastical law was that while a divorce *a vinculo matrimonii* enabled the parties to marry again, a divorce *a mensa et thoro* did not. There is some evidence that during the later sixteenth century, as a result of the upheaval caused by the Reformation, the ecclesiastical courts granted divorces *a vinculo matrimonii*, allowing the parties to marry again, on grounds other than that of some defect which rendered the marriage void from the beginning. But in a famous case in 1602 the Court of Star Chamber ruled that a valid marriage could not be dissolved.

Still, the desire to obtain absolute divorces with the right of remarriage could not be gainsaid, and in the later seventeenth century there arose the practice of obtaining a divorce *a vinculo matrimonii*, on the ground of adultery, by private act of parliament, a practice based on the constitutional omnicompetence of parliament which was one result of the Reformation. Two legal steps were necessary before a divorce could be obtained through parliament. First, a divorce *a mensa et thoro* must be obtained from the ecclesiastical courts. Second, if it was the husband seeking the parliamentary divorce, he must charge another man with criminal conversation – that is, adultery – with his wife, either in the ecclesiastical courts or in the common-law courts. After these initial steps a divorce bill could be introduced in the House of Lords, where the bishops had charge of it and where a clause was invariably inserted (only to be struck out later) providing that the petitioner would not marry again during the other party's lifetime. After approval by the Lords, a divorce bill almost automatically passed through the Commons and received the royal assent.

There were obvious advantages in obtaining a divorce by act of parliament rather than in the ecclesiastical courts. In the first place, the parties were free to marry again – indeed, this was the reason why divorce by act of parliament developed. Also, a parliamentary divorce, unlike a divorce *a vinculo matrimonii* in the ecclesiastical courts, seldom bastardized the children of the marriage except in a very clear case. Finally, a parliamentary divorce settled questions of property between husband and wife. Since the marriage was dissolved, the legal rights of each in the property of the other were ended. Also, divorce bills passed by parliament always included some financial provision for the wife, usually a provision arranged previously between her and her husband. The provision commonly consisted of the settlement on her of sufficient property to produce an income that would give her a bare subsistence at least. Provision was made for the wife even when she was the guilty party, on the ground that the husband was being granted an extraordinary indulgence and that even an adulterous wife should not be left to starve.

Still, there were serious disadvantages in obtaining a divorce by act of parliament. For one thing, the expense was enormous, estimated in the 1850s as being between £600 and £800. For this reason, and also because of the stigma then attaching to divorced persons, only one or two divorces were granted by parliament each year – 134 in the eighteenth century, and 90 in the nineteenth century (before the reform of 1857). Also, in practice if not in theory, it was nearly impossible for a woman to obtain a divorce through parliament. There were only four recorded cases of women receiving a parliamentary divorce, and in each of these cases the husband's bigamy or incest had been pleaded in addition to his adultery as grounds for the divorce.

Reform of the divorce law was a very difficult undertaking, for it aroused the strongest emotions and also involved the solution of complicated practical problems. The chief opposition to reform came from Churchmen and from laymen of conservative religious and social views. Perhaps they could not prevent the transfer of the Church's jurisdiction in matrimonial causes to a secular court, a transfer that meant creation of an acceptable new court – no easy matter in view of the bewildering variety of secular courts already in existence. But opponents of reform could and did try to prevent any change in the law as it had been administered by the ecclesiastical courts. Their stand led to a debate on the whole question of the nature of marriage. Relying upon their particular interpretation of biblical injunctions, opponents of reform maintained that marriage was a sacrament indissoluble save, perhaps, on the ground of adultery, and that the whole fabric of society would be rended by any tampering with the sanctity of marriage and the home. On the other hand, supporters of reform argued that society was ill served by forcing unhappy couples to remain wedded, and that marriage should be treated as merely a civil contract, dissoluble for reasons other than adultery at the desire of the parties. This debate in turn gave rise to other questions. What should be the grounds for divorce? Should divorce be available to women as well as men, and available on the same grounds? What remedies short of divorce should be made available, especially for women? Finally, should the poorer classes, presumed to be ignorant and prone to immorality, be allowed access to a divorce court equally with the rich, who were presumably better than they intellectually and morally? In effect, should divorce continue to be expensive or should it be cheap? With all these emotion-charged and practical questions parliament had to deal.

The matter of divorce-law reform had now been before parliament for several years. In 1854 Lord Cranworth, the lord chancellor, introduced a Divorce Bill based on the recommendations of the royal commission appointed in 1850, then withdrew it a month later, saying that the government intended to deal during the next session with the whole question of the ecclesiastical courts' jurisdiction. But in 1855 the Aberdeen government came crashing down as a result of its mismanagement of the Crimean War, and the Whigs took office under Lord Palmerston. The next year Lord Cranworth, who had remained lord chancellor, introduced another Divorce Bill, which at the urging of Lord Lyndhurst and Lord Brougham was submitted to a select committee for amendment. The amended bill was finally passed by the Lords despite strenuous opposition to it led by the bishop of Oxford, Samuel Wilberforce, and was sent down to the Commons, where it could not be proceeded with because of the lateness of the session. In 1857 the Lords again passed the Divorce Bill, which they had amended further in committee of the whole, and again sent it to the Commons.[15]

The Divorce Bill came on for its second reading in the lower House on 24 July, nine days after the second reading of Perry's Married Women's Property Bill, and thereafter consumed the time and energies of the Commons. Gladstone was prominent in opposition to the measure, and was supported by Malins and many others in his efforts to amend it substantially if he could not defeat it. The sessions grew long and tempers short. Lord John Manners, for one, voiced exasperation with a government which 'called upon the House to sit, at the end of August, from noon to midnight to consider a question of such vast importance.' But Palmerston was adamant. He had told members earlier that they should not be 'frightened by the names of July and August,' and now he informed them that 'we shall return and sit here day by day, and night by night until this Bill be concluded.' At last, on 21 August, it was concluded and sent back with amendments to the Lords, where it was approved after still more changes. Next day the Commons agreed to the Lords' further amendments, and three days later parliament was prorogued. So the Matrimonial Causes Act of 1857, more commonly called the Divorce Act, became law (20 & 21 Vict., c 85). It represented essentially a victory for the conservatives.[16]

The act transferred jurisdiction in marital matters from the ecclesiastical courts to a new Court of Divorce and Matrimonial Causes. This court was to be presided over by the judge ordinary, who was also to preside over the new Court of Probate, created by legislation of the same year which ended the ecclesiastical courts' jurisdiction in matters relating to wills. Some cases could be decided by the judge ordinary sitting alone, while others must be decided by him together with one or more of the other judges of the court – the lord chancellor, and the chiefs and the senior puisne judges of the three superior common-law courts. Appeal from decisions of the judge ordinary could be made to the full court, whose decisions were final except in cases of divorce petitions, which could be appealed to the House of Lords. The act stipulated that the practice of the new court should conform as nearly as possible to the principles and rules followed by the ecclesiastical courts.

Under the provisions of the act, three of the matrimonial causes previously handled by the ecclesiastical courts continued as before. The old divorce *a vinculo matrimonii*, now called a decree of nullity, continued to be available on the ground of some defect relating to the marriage and existing from the time of marriage. It continues, in amended form, today. Second, a decree for restitution of conjugal rights, an order to return to cohabitation, could still be obtained. This decree was abolished in 1970. Finally, a decree for suppression of jactitation of marriage was still available. This rarely used decree, designed to prevent false boasting of a marriage which did not exist, lingered on till the mid-twentieth century.

In addition to continuing these familiar causes, the act of 1857 introduced the new decree of judicial separation. This decree, which replaced the divorce *a mensa et thoro* previously granted by the ecclesiastical courts, could be obtained by either husband or wife on the grounds the ecclesiastical courts had recognized, to which was now added desertion without cause for two years. Not divorce *a mensa et thoro* but a decree for restitution of conjugal rights had been the ecclesiastical courts' remedy in cases of desertion. The new decree of judicial separation had the same effect as the old – that is, the parties were free from the obligation of cohabitation, but they were not free to marry again.

The Divorce Act provided that in the case of a wife who obtained a judicial separation, the court could order the husband to pay her alimony, as the ecclesiastical courts had done before. The court could order this paid to the wife herself or to a trustee for her benefit, and could impose any terms or restrictions it considered expedient. Following the precedent established by the ecclesiastical courts, the Divorce Court generally set alimony at one-third of the husband's income. This 'one-third rule' was cited as the governing precedent as late as 1900, but thereafter the court began to exercise more discretion in the award of alimony. After 1857, as before, the amount of alimony could be varied to meet the changed circumstances of the parties, while a woman's right to receive alimony, being a personal right against her husband, could be enforced only during his lifetime and not against his estate after his death. The Divorce Court also followed the precedent of the ecclesiastical courts in always refusing alimony to an adulterous wife. Further, when a judicial separation was obtained on the ground of the wife's adultery and she was entitled to property, the court was empowered to order settlement of that property or any part of it to be made for the benefit of the husband and children.

In addition to the new decree of judicial separation, the act also introduced the new decree of absolute divorce, essentially a replacement of the divorce *a vinculo matrimonii* previously obtainable by private act of parliament. A husband could petition for an absolute divorce on the ground of his wife's adultery alone. A wife, however, could obtain an absolute divorce only if her husband was guilty of rape, of sodomy or bestiality, or of adultery coupled with some other offence – incest, bigamy, cruelty as it had been defined by the ecclesiastical courts (that is, usually physical violence), and desertion without cause for two years. This decree, dissolving a marriage as it did, enabled the parties to marry again. Clergymen of the Established Church were specifically allowed by the act to officiate at the marriages of divorced persons, with the stipulation that none was required to officiate if he conscientiously objected to doing so.

Here it should be mentioned that the Divorce Act abolished the old common-law action for criminal conversation, which had previously been a prerequisite when a man obtained a divorce by act of parliament. The principal supporter of its abolition was Lord Lyndhurst. In his eighties and confined to a wheelchair, Lyndhurst spoke eloquently during the debates on the Divorce Bill in favour of equal treatment for women. He pointed out that in cases of criminal conversation women had no right to appear in their own defence and could be defamed and their reputations destroyed with impunity. Obviously he had in mind his old friend Caroline Norton, whose writings he quoted in his speeches.

However, what one section of the Divorce Act abolished, another section restored. A man was still allowed to claim damages from an adulterer, either in a petition in the Divorce Court limited to that object or in a petition for divorce or judicial separation; and the court was empowered to direct how the damages were to be paid or applied, and to order the whole or part to be settled for the benefit of the children of the marriage, if any, or for the maintenance of the wife. A wife, however, could not claim damages from an adulteress. The apparent contradiction in the act, the abolition and then the reinstatement of the right of husbands to claim damages, is presumably explained by the fact that the act was merely transferring jurisdiction in such cases from the common-law courts to the new Divorce Court.

The act of 1857 empowered the Divorce Court to do as parliament had done in its passage of divorce bills – to order the husband to pay his wife maintenance, either a gross sum or a sum payable annually for any term not longer than her life. The amount of maintenance was to be decided by the court in view of the wife's fortune, if any, the husband's ability to pay, and the conduct of the parties during the marriage. In practice, until the early years of the twentieth century the court applied the 'one-third rule' in cases of divorce as it did in cases of judicial separation. Maintenance granted to a divorced woman differed from alimony awarded to a woman who obtained a judicial separation in that the amount could not be varied because of the changed circumstances of the parties, and payment could continue beyond her former husband's lifetime, since her right to maintenance was not a personal right against him but a right against the property appropriated for her.

The payment of maintenance was usually secured by the settlement of property upon the wife through proceedings in the Court of Chancery. An amending act of 1859 empowered the Divorce Court to vary the marriage settlements of persons who had been divorced. Another amending act of 1866 provided that when the husband did not have enough property to secure to his wife an annual payment, the court could order him to make monthly or weekly payments to her instead. A further act of 1907 provided that the Divorce Court could order for a wife's benefit both a secured maintenance and periodic payments, and not merely one or the other of these as the Court of Appeal had ruled in a leading case in 1882. Yet another act of 1963 has allowed the court to order payment of a lump sum in lieu of or in addition to periodic payments or a secured maintenance.

At first the Divorce Court, like the ecclesiastical courts before it, disliked the idea of forcing a man to support the wife whom he had divorced because of her adultery. Usually the court would merely order that the damages recovered by the husband from his wife's lover be settled upon her, and these damages were rarely enough to make a very large provision for her. Also, when a wife divorced because of her adultery was entitled to property, the court could order the settlement of that property or any part of it for the benefit of the husband and children. However, a Court of Appeal decision in 1883 pointed out that parliament had always included in divorce bills some provision for adulterous wives and that the Divorce Act of 1857 did not indicate that any different principle should be followed, and by the turn of the century it was a well-established principle in the Divorce Court that even a guilty wife was not to be left to starve.

In addition to providing for the payment of alimony to women who were judicially separated and maintenance to women divorced, the act of 1857 contained a provision of the greatest importance relating to the property rights of such women. Lord Lyndhurst had attacked the Divorce Bill as originally introduced because it did not abolish a husband's common-law rights over his wife's property in cases when they were separated or divorced. As the law stood, he declared, again with Mrs Norton in mind, a woman separated from her husband was

almost in a state of outlawry. She may not enter into a contract or, if she do, she has no means of enforcing it. The law, so far from protecting, oppresses her. She is homeless, helpless, hopeless, and almost destitute of civil rights. She is liable to all manner of injustice, whether by plot or violence. She may be wronged in all possible ways, and her character may be mercilessly defamed; yet she has no redress. She is at the mercy of her enemies. Is that fair? Is that honest? Can it be vindicated upon any principle of justice, or mercy, or of common humanity?[17]

At Lyndhurst's urging the bill was amended by unanimous decision of the select committee of the Lords in 1856 to protect such women.

As finally passed, the Divorce Act provided that any woman who obtained either a judicial separation or a divorce was to have all the rights of an unmarried woman with respect to property she acquired after the separation or divorce. She could dispose of this property freely during her lifetime and also by will, and if she died intestate the same principles of distribution would apply to it as would apply if her husband were dead. She was to be considered an unmarried woman for the purposes of contracts and torts – that is, she would have the right of suing and being sued, and her husband would not be liable on her contracts and torts unless he had failed to pay her alimony or maintenance as directed by the court, in which case he would become liable for necessaries supplied for her use. Further, if husband and wife cohabited again after their judicial separation, any property to which the wife was entitled when cohabitation resumed was to be her separate property, subject to any agreement to the contrary made in writing during the separation.

The act also made provision for the children of parents who were legally separated or divorced or whose marriages were annulled. It provided that the new Divorce Court could make whatever orders it saw fit regarding the custody, support, and education of such children, and could place them under the protection of the Court of Chancery. That is, the court could exercise discretion, and to that extent the old common law which recognized a man's absolute right to possession of his children was abrogated.

Finally, one section of the Divorce Act dealt with the problem of wives deserted by their husbands, specifically granting them protection of their property against their husbands' common-law rights. This provision had been inserted at the instance of Lord St Leonards, the distinguished and respected former lord chancellor. St Leonards hoped by his amendment to prevent what he considered 'a greater evil' – that is, passage of Perry's Married Women's Property Bill, which he believed to be 'a most mischievous one,' certain to 'place the whole marriage law of this country on a different footing and give a wife all the distinct rights of citizenship.' When the Divorce Bill came down to the Commons, Perry had proposed to amend it further by granting protection also to wives who were supporting themselves and whose property was in danger of being seized by their husbands, and Henry Drummond had offered an amendment which would have protected the property of wives who were 'cruelly treated' by their husbands as well as those who were deserted. Malins and others accused Perry of trying in a devious fashion to carry through the principle of his own Married Women's Property Bill, and at the demand of Bethell, the attorney general, Perry withdrew his amendment. Drummond's amendment, which Bethell likewise opposed, was defeated when put to a vote.[18]

The act as finally passed provided that a woman who was deserted by her husband without cause and who was supporting herself by her own industry or property could apply either to a local court or to the Divorce Court for an order to protect against her husband, his creditors, or any person claiming under him any property which she became possessed of or entitled to after her desertion. During the existence of the protection order she was to have the same property rights as an unmarried woman. Moreover, if her husband, his creditor, or anyone else claiming under him seized her property, he was liable to be sued by the wife, who could thereby obtain a sum equal to twice the value of the property seized. (For the act's provisions relating to women's property, see appendix 2.)

The Divorce Act of 1857 was a landmark in the history of English law. Seen in the context of the broad movement for legal reform in the nineteenth century, it was the first major step taken to eliminate conflicting jurisdictions and rival courts. As such, it anticipated the great reform carried through by the Judicature Act of 1873. Seen from the point of view of the nineteenth-century women's movement, the Divorce Act was equally important, for it represented a significant step in the direction of women's emancipation, especially with respect to their property rights. Women who had obtained decrees of judicial separation and divorce under the act's provisions regained the rights over property enjoyed by unmarried women. At the same time the provisions of the act giving the same property rights to wives who were deserted by their husbands as to unmarried women was of the greatest importance in principle if not in practice. As Bethell, the attorney general, noted during the debates in parliament, the law for the first time was giving married women the right to own and control their property.[19]

Still, the Divorce Act was open to attack for a number of its shortcomings. One of these, vehemently denounced by Lord Lyndhurst and others at the time of the act's passage, was its unequal treatment of men and women – the fact that a man could divorce his wife on the ground of her adultery alone, while a woman must prove some offence in addition to her husband's adultery. In rebuttal, Lord Cranworth maintained that a wife could, 'without any loss of caste, and possibly with reference to the interests of her children, or even of her husband,' condone the husband's adultery but that the reverse could not possibly be true, 'for this, among other reasons ... that the adultery of the wife might be the means of palming spurious offspring upon the husband, while the adultery of the husband could have no such effect with regard to the wife.' In addition, it was argued that women's inequality in this respect was already recognized by the law, and that the purpose of the act was not to change the law but merely to change the way it was administered. Not until passage of the Matrimonial Causes Act of 1923 were women as well as men allowed to obtain divorces on the ground of adultery alone.[20]

Another defect of the Divorce Act, so some claimed at the time of its passage and for many years afterward, was its failure to allow divorce for any reason except adultery. For example, W.J. Fox, writing in 1858, declared, 'In Prussia there is no difficulty in obtaining divorce on the ground of incompatibility and without the filthy and immoral requisites demanded by English legislation.' The English law, said Fox, led to cases of collusion in which 'the parties sin for the very purpose of producing evidence,' and he concluded, 'Let the law no longer

THE DIVORCE SHOP.

P<small>RIVATE</small> I<small>NQUIRY</small> A<small>GENT</small>. " WANT A DIVORCE, SIR? CERTAINLY, SIR,—CERTAINLY ! ANY EVIDENCE YOU
MAY REQUIRE READY AT THE SHORTEST POSSIBLE NOTICE ! ! "

reprinted from *Punch* 1890

require the adultery as essential, and there would be an end of the collusion and the adultery too.' Probably few people at that time would have agreed with Fox that 'incompatibility' should be recognized as a ground for divorce, but Lyndhurst, Brougham, and others pointed out that there were grave offences besides adultery that should also be recognized, such as cruelty and desertion.[21]

Demands for divorce on grounds other than adultery met with no success in the Victorian period. Only one concession in this respect was made, by the Matrimonial Causes Act of 1884. This act provided that refusal to obey a decree for restitution of conjugal rights would no longer be punishable by imprisonment but would render the party guilty of desertion. The other spouse could then obtain a decree of judicial separation immediately, rather than waiting for the two years prescribed by the act of 1857. The act of 1884 provided further that if the decree was obtained by the wife and the husband committed adultery after their separation, she could petition for divorce on the ground of his adultery coupled with desertion, even though the desertion might not be of two years' duration. Not until passage of the Matrimonial Causes Act of 1937 were new grounds for divorce added to the old ground of adultery – cruelty, desertion for three years, and incurable insanity.[22]

Finally, the Divorce Act of 1857 was criticized, by Lord Lyndhurst at the time of its passage and by many others afterward, because it did not make proceedings in the Divorce Court cheap. One must accept only with considerable qualification A.V. Dicey's pronouncement that the act 'did away with the iniquity of a law which theoretically prohibited divorce, but in reality conceded to the rich a right denied to the poor.' It is true that proceedings in the new Divorce Court cost no more than proceedings in other superior courts of the time, and this meant that many more people could obtain a divorce after the act of 1857 than could have done so by private act of parliament before its passage. Still, this relief long continued to be so expensive as to be beyond the reach of the poorer classes. As a writer in the cause of divorce-law reform declared shortly before the First World War, 'Here in England we have one law for the rich and another for the poor, for the average cost of a decree is £100; and a case was recently reported in which a woman had saved up twenty years in order to obtain a divorce.' Because of the expensive proceedings involved, and also because of the social stigma still attaching to divorced persons, only a few hundred divorces were granted annually throughout the later nineteenth century – about 500 a year by 1900.[23]

It was doubtless in view of such criticisms of the Divorce Act that, beginning in 1878, a series of laws were passed to provide cheap and speedy relief short of divorce for wives who were cruelly treated or deserted by their husbands.[24] These laws conferred summary jurisdiction in marital matters upon local magistrates' courts, which were empowered to grant separation orders to wives in a number of specified cases. A separation order had all the effects of a decree of judicial separation from the Divorce Court – that is, the wife was relieved of the obligation of cohabitation with her husband, and she regained the property rights of an unmarried woman. The order might also grant her custody of her children. At first she could have custody only of children under the age of ten, but later the age was raised to sixteen.

The grounds upon which separation orders could be obtained became quite broad. One of these grounds was cruelty. The Matrimonial Causes Act of 1878 first defined this as aggravated assault upon the wife, of which the husband had been duly convicted. The Summary Jurisdiction (Married Women) Act of 1895 defined cruelty as any assault by a husband upon his wife for which he was sentenced to pay a fine of more than £5 or to serve a prison term of more than two months. This act also recognized as cruelty any conduct by a husband that forced his wife to leave him and live apart. The Summary Jurisdiction (Separation and Maintenance) Act of 1925 recognized cruelty even in cases when a husband's conduct had not forced his wife to leave him, although a separation order could not be enforced while they were still living together. A second ground for obtaining a separation order was desertion, first recognized as such by the Married Women (Maintenance in Case of Desertion) Act of 1886. A third ground, likewise first recognized by the act of 1886, was the husband's wilful refusal or neglect to maintain his wife. Twentieth-century legislation added still other grounds for obtaining separation orders – habitual drunkenness in 1902, drug addiction and venereal disease in 1925, and adultery in 1937.

In conjunction with separation orders, magistrates' courts could also issue maintenance orders requiring husbands to pay weekly sums for the support of their wives and children. The amount of maintenance was first set at no more than £2 for the wife and 10s. for each child – considerable amounts at the time. These amounts were not increased – to £5 and 30s. respectively – until 1949, when married women were also given the right to take proceedings against their husbands in the High Court of Justice as well as in the local courts for failure to maintain them. At first no maintenance order could be made for the benefit of a wife who was guilty of adultery, but later amendments allowed orders to be made if the husband had connived at or later condoned his wife's action or had conduced to it by his neglect or misconduct. If an order was made, it could be discharged upon the husband's appeal if the wife committed adultery after the order was issued, and some men apparently refused to make payments under the orders in the hope that their wives would be driven to support themselves by prostitution. However, the Summary Jurisdiction (Separation and Maintenance) Act of 1925 provided that the courts could refuse a husband's appeal for discharge of an order on the ground of his wife's adultery if her offence had been caused by his failure to make payments under an order. An act of 1952 provided that men could be sentenced to imprisonment for contempt for failure to make payments under maintenance orders, and another act of 1958 provided that their wages could be attached if they did not pay.

The relief afforded to women of the poorer classes by means of separation orders and maintenance orders was clearly substantial. It was also very popular, judged by the number of orders actually issued by magistrates' courts. In the early years of the twentieth century, for example, while the Divorce Court was receiving an annual average of about 800 petitions for divorces and decrees of nullity, magistrates' courts were issuing well over 7,000 maintenance orders annually. These figures, in turn, suggest how many more people would have sought relief in the Divorce Court rather than in magistrates' courts had its proceedings been equally expeditious and inexpensive.

It was not until the latter half of the twentieth century that divorce became freely available to all classes, and this in turn led to thoroughgoing reform of the divorce law.[25] The Legal Aid and Advice Act of 1949 made legal proceedings, including divorce proceedings, readily accessible to the poorer classes for the first time. As a result, tremendous pressure on the public purse was created by the large number of divorce proceedings that were legally aided – in 1968, 63 per cent of the more than 55,000 divorce petitions filed. This fact, as much as changing social mores and ethical considerations, prompted passage of the Divorce Reform Act of 1969. This act abandoned the old concept of 'matrimonial offences' which must be proved in order to obtain a divorce and which involved sometimes lengthy and always costly adversary proceedings. Instead, the act recognized only one ground for divorce – 'irretrievable breakdown' of marriage. Still, the old concept of guilty and innocent parties lingers on, for of the five 'fact situations' which are taken as evidence of marital breakdown, three correspond to previous matrimonial offences – adultery, cruelty, and desertion. The other, much more controversial, fact situations are separation for two years, with the non-petitioning party agreeing to the divorce, and separation for five years, in which case the non-petitioning party may successfully defeat the petition by proving that divorce would involve grave financial or other hardships for him or, more usually, her.

This sweeping reform was soon followed by further legislation designed to improve the financial provision made for divorced wives – the Matrimonial Proceedings and Property Act of 1970 and the Matrimonial Causes Act of 1973. Under the provisions of these acts all the assets of couples in divorce, separation, and nullity cases are considered as 'matrimonial property' or 'family assets' belonging to them jointly; these assets are pooled and then distributed between the spouses by the presiding judge on the basis of what seems fair and just. The judge is directed to consider the following factors: the spouses' income, earning capacity, property, and other financial resources; their financial needs, obligations, and responsibilities; their standard of living; their age and the duration of their marriage; their physical and mental health; and the contribution made by each to the welfare of the family, including the care of home and children. In general, the parties are to be placed, so far as practicable and having regard to their conduct, in the financial position they would have been in if the marriage had not broken down and if both spouses had properly discharged their financial obligations and responsibilities. Usually the wife receives not half but one-third of the joint assets, as well as such maintenance as is needed for the child or children of the marriage. This 'one-third rule' has been criticized, but it was upheld by the Court of Appeal in a leading case in 1973.

Important as the Divorce Act of 1857 was in the history of nineteenth-century movements for legal reform and for women's emancipation, it was very far from embodying the thoroughgoing reform of the married women's property law which feminists had been demanding – the right of married women to own and control their property as unmarried women did. Discouraged but not daunted, the women of Barbara Leigh Smith's little committee pledged themselves to continue their work for the cause, collecting evidence of the cruelties and injustices arising under the law and promoting petitions to parliament to demonstrate public support for reform.[26]

This first feminist committee soon disbanded, however. Miss Leigh Smith herself was married in the summer of 1857 to Dr Eugène Bodichon, a French surgeon whom she had met a few months earlier during a visit to Algeria. After an extended wedding trip to the United States, they returned to make their home in Algeria, where Madame Bodichon now spent the greater part of each year, devoting her time to her painting and to improving the tone of French colonial society. Fortunately she had found in her husband an ideal partner, someone as unconventional, as wide in sympathies, and as interested in all humanitarian reforms as she herself. Meanwhile, her friends in England turned their energies to other projects, perhaps most notably the founding in 1858 of the *English Woman's Journal* to serve as official organ of the women's movement, and the organization in 1859 of the Society for Promoting the Employment of Women.

Even had the married women's property committee continued in existence, it is doubtful that its efforts would have been successful. The climate of the time was no longer propitious for reform. For one thing, as Perry said, the Divorce Act had taken the wind out of their sails. Before its passage, the cruel hardships suffered under the law by women separated from or deserted by their husbands evoked deeply felt and widespread public sympathy. After its passage, the public generally felt that injured wives were now protected by the law, and asked why uninjured wives should want to own and control their property.

More specifically, the government of the day, having won passage of the Divorce Act, was not disposed to undertake further reform in the interests of women. Palmerston was always more interested in foreign affairs than internal matters, and there was a great deal to engage his attention abroad in the later fifties and early sixties – the Sepoy Mutiny in India, the first confrontation between Sardinia-Piedmont and Austria in Italy, the complications for Britain arising out of the American Civil War, the Anglo-French expedition to Mexico, the Polish rebellion and the question of British relations with Russia, and the dispute over Schleswig-Holstein which foreshadowed a coming confrontation between Austria and Prussia. Certainly Palmerston was not opposed to all domestic reform. It was he, after all, who forced through parliament the Divorce Bill and other reform measures as well. But he was old and past his prime and did not have, had never had, any grand vision of what needed to be done and could be done in the way of domestic reform. In particular, he was uninterested in the great issue of reform of the parliamentary franchise, which in the sixties was again coming to the fore and would again raise the whole question of the rights of women. Queried the year before his death about the future legislative program of his government, Palmerston replied, 'Oh, there is really nothing to be done. We cannot go on adding to the Statute Book *ad infinitum*.'[27] In these circumstances reform of the married women's property law languished for a decade after 1857.

6

'The Peculiar Character of the Modern World' The Setting of the 1860s

> ... what is the peculiar character of the modern world – the difference which chiefly distinguishes modern institutions, modern social ideas, modern life itself, from those of times long past? It is, that human beings are no longer born to their place in life, and chained down by an inexorable bond to the place they are born to, but are free to employ their faculties, and such favourable chances as offer, to achieve the lot which may appear to them most desirable.
>
> JOHN STUART MILL, *The Subjection of Women* 1869[1]

The death of Lord Palmerston in 1865 is often cited by historians as marking the end of an era in English history and the beginning of a great new age of domestic reform. Within three years of Palmerston's death the political scene had changed dramatically. Lord John Russell, who succeeded him as prime minister, was determined to carry a Reform Bill through parliament, but was defeated on that issue a few months later. It was the minority government of Lord Derby, with Disraeli its moving spirit, that carried through the great Reform Bill of 1867, a bill which was considerably more radical than the one Russell had proposed and which committed Britain to political democracy and all its consequences.

Soon after passage of the Reform Bill Derby resigned because of ill health and Disraeli became prime minister, while the ageing Russell gave up leadership of his party to Gladstone. The accession of Disraeli and Gladstone to political supremacy marked the passing from the scene of the older generation of statesmen. For the first time the leaders of both great parties were men born in the nineteenth century. More important, they represented a new kind of statesman, for neither was of noble birth and each had risen by sheer ability to the top. Gladstone sprang from the wealthy, thrusting business classes of Liverpool, and his position of leadership symbolized the ever-increasing importance of these classes in the country's economic and political life. Even more than Gladstone, Disraeli was a self-made man – a baptized Jew, known in his youth chiefly for his talent as a novelist and his foppish and flamboyant dress, he seemed a strange person indeed to have become leader of the aristocratic Tories.

The supremacy of Gladstone and Disraeli also marked the beginning of a new day in political organization, a beginning symbolized by the tendency for the old party labels of Tory and Whig to be replaced by the newer labels of Conservative and Liberal. A long period of political confusion characterized by shifting ideological and factional groupings and unstable ministries came to an end. There followed a period which saw the development of broadly based political parties in the modern sense, each with its formally structured organization and its program of appeals to the widening electorate, and each having the comforting assurance that success at an election would almost certainly mean several years of uninterrupted enjoyment of power.

The general election held late in 1868 was the first in which the newly enlarged electorate created by the Reform Bill took part. Simply put, the Reform Bill gave the vote to urban workingmen, and increased the electorate by more than a million voters. The Conservatives under Disraeli, who claimed to have 'dished the Whigs' by passing the bill, hoped for great things. Instead, the result was a smashing victory for Gladstone's Liberals, who won over half a million more votes than their rivals and a majority of 112 seats in the House of Commons. Disraeli resigned without meeting the new parliament, setting the precedent followed ever since – that a defeated party leader automatically gives way as prime minister to the leader of the victorious opposition. In December Gladstone formed his first and greatest ministry – the ministry whose many accomplishments included disestablishment of the Church in Ireland and passage of the first Irish Land Act, creation of a national system of popular elementary education, reform of the army and the civil service, reorganization of the country's public health services, passage of the great Judicature Act restructuring the country's superior courts, and the first real reform of the married women's property law.

The year 1865 marked the dawn of a new day in the history of English women, as in the history of politics. In that year John Stuart Mill, considered by many to be the greatest liberal philosopher of the nineteenth century, won election to parliament from the important constituency of Westminster. Mill's commanding figure dominated this period of the women's movement, and his support and reputation sustained the movement for years to come. During his campaign Mill publicized his conviction, already set forth clearly in his writings, that women were entitled to representation in parliament on the same terms as men. Later he claimed, mistakenly, 'It was the first time, doubtless, that such a doctrine had ever been mentioned to English electors; and the fact that I was elected after proposing it, gave the start to the movement ... in favour of women's suffrage.'[2]

Mill's belief in women's right to vote was only one aspect of his views of the position of women generally and of the relations between the sexes, and these views in turn were only part of the Radicalism that was his by birth and breeding. Yet his belief in the equality of the sexes might have remained a merely intellectual proposition with him had it not been for the profound influence upon his life of that remarkable woman Harriet Taylor. The two met in 1830 at the home of their mutual friend W.J. Fox. Both were contributors to Fox's *Monthly Repository*, and Harriet Taylor, married and the mother of two sons – her daughter Helen was born the following year – attended Fox's South Place chapel. Mill and Mrs Taylor fell deeply in love, and several years of wretchedness followed their meeting, until they worked out a mode of living whereby the respectable façade of the Taylors' marriage was preserved while Mill and Mrs Taylor were able to spend a great deal of time in each other's company.

Not until 1851, two years after the death of Mrs Taylor's husband, did the couple regularize their unconventional and remarkable partnership by marrying. Shortly beforehand Mill drew up a declaration setting forth his views on marriage:

Being about ... to enter into the marriage relation with the only woman I have ever known, with whom I would have entered into that state; and the whole character of the marriage relation as constituted by law being such as she and I entirely disapprove, for this among other reasons, that it confers upon one of the parties to the contract, legal power and control over the person, property, and freedom of action of the other party, independent of her own wishes and will; I, having no means of legally divesting myself of these odious powers ... feel it my duty to put on record a formal protest against the existing law of marriage, in so far as conferring such powers; and a solemn promise never in any case or under any circumstances to use them. And in the event of marriage between Mrs. Taylor and me I declare it to be my will and intention, and the condition of the engagement between us, that she retains in all respects whatever the same absolute freedom of action and freedom of disposal of herself and of all that does or may at any time belong to her, as if no such marriage had taken place; and I absolutely disclaim and repudiate all pretension to have acquired any *rights* whatever by virtue of such marriage.[3]

Mill's extravagant praise of Harriet Taylor embarrassed many of his contemporaries, and has proved a stumbling-block to Mill scholars ever since. He extolled her penetrating and intuitive intelligence, which enabled her to pierce immediately to the heart of any matter, and the nobility of her character, unselfish and generous, simple and sincere, and passionate in the cause of justice. Theirs, said Mill, was a partnership of 'two persons of cultivated faculties, identical in opinions and purpose,' between whom existed 'that best kind of equality, similarity of powers and capacities with reciprocal superiority in them,' so that each enjoyed 'the luxury of looking up to the other' and 'the pleasure of leading and being led in the path of development.' More specifically, Mill always claimed that his later writings, beginning with the *Principles of Political Economy* (1848), were 'not the work of one mind, but of the fusion of two,' and that his wife's 'genius, as it grew and unfolded itself in thought, continually struck out truths far in advance of me.'[4] Some scholars have taken Mill's statements as he intended them to be taken – as literal truth. Others have seen Mill as a socially naïve and emotionally undeveloped young man, bewitched by an attractive but essentially commonplace woman who somehow kept him in thrall till the end of her days. Whatever the truth of the matter, the fact remains that Mill's life and work would have been far different had he and Harriet Taylor not met over Fox's dinner table.

After his wife's death in 1858 Mill divided his time between Avignon, where she had died and was buried, and London, with his stepdaughter Helen Taylor as his constant companion and amanuensis. 'Surely,' Mill said, 'no one ever before was so fortunate, as, after such a loss as mine, to draw another prize in the lottery of life – another companion, stimulator, adviser, and instructor of the rarest quality.' His work, he now said, must be thought of as 'the product not of one intellect and conscience, but of three, the least considerable of whom, and above all the least original,' he added with his charming modesty, 'is the one whose name is attached to it.' It was at Helen Taylor's suggestion that Mill wrote *The Subjection of Women*, in order to set forth his own and his wife's views on a topic that was so important to them. Mill completed the manuscript in 1861, but decided to delay its publication until the time when he felt it would be most useful.[5] That time came eight years later.

While Mill dominated the women's movement in the sixties, a key role was also played by Barbara Leigh Smith Bodichon, whose activities had been central to the beginnings of the movement a decade earlier. Now, after the first years of her marriage, Madame Bodichon was spending more of her time in England and resuming active work in women's causes. Her family and some of her friends did not understand or quite approve her rather casual attitude toward her husband and her long separations from him. But her marriage, although to her great regret childless, seems to have been a very happy one. Whenever she was in London, Madame Bodichon visited almost daily in Langham Place at the offices

A GENTLEMAN OF INFLUENCE

WISHES TO KNOW WHETHER THERE IS AN ACT OF PARLIAMENT TO PROTECT HIM FROM THIS SORT OF INTIMIDATION.

reprinted from *Punch* 1865

of the *English Woman's Journal* and the Society for Promoting the Employment of Women, inspiring her fellow workers with her vitality and cheerful common sense.

One of Madame Bodichon's great interests at this time was the improvement of women's education, an interest which brought her the personal friendship of Emily Davies and cemented a lifelong partnership between them. Through a chance meeting with Madame Bodichon's family in Algeria, Miss Davies, already a convinced feminist, became acquainted with the women connected with the *English Woman's Journal* and the SPEW. After the death of her clergyman father, she had settled in London, ready to devote herself to work in women's causes. Together she and Madame Bodichon were instrumental in winning the admission of girls to the university local examinations, first at Cambridge in 1863 and later at other universities. Their efforts also helped to persuade the Schools Inquiry Commission, which was appointed in 1864 under the chairmanship of Lord Taunton to study the state of middle-class education, to include a thorough investigation of the condition of girls' education in its activities. Most impressive of all was the work done by Miss Davies and Madame Bodichon in promoting higher education for women, work which led to the founding in 1869 of Girton College, Cambridge. Among their many supporters in this enterprise were John Stuart Mill and Helen Taylor, and at Miss Davies's request Mill drew up the examination in political economy to be taken by the Girton students.[6]

Another of Madame Bodichon's great interests now was women's suffrage. In 1865 a group of about fifty women, calling themselves the Kensington Society, began to meet informally to discuss all subjects relating to the position of women. Besides Madame Bodichon, Miss Davies, and Helen Taylor, the group included many others who were, or were to become, leaders in various undertakings of the women's movement. It was Emily Davies who suggested for the society's discussion the question of whether, and if so how, it was desirable for women to take part in public affairs. Some of them had already taken part, to such an extent that they inspired a cartoon in *Punch*, by parading about Westminster with placards urging the election of Mill to parliament. Miss Davies later reminisced, 'We called it giving Mr Mill our moral support, but there was some suspicion that we might rather be doing him harm, as one of our friends told us he had heard him described as "the man who wants to have girls in Parliament."' Now Madame Bodichon presented a paper before the Kensington Society urging that women be granted the right to vote, and almost all of the members strongly supported her stand.[7]

Early in 1866, when Lord John Russell's Reform Bill was to be brought before parliament, Madame Bodichon sought Mill's advice as to how the women suffragists should proceed. His reply was that if she could obtain a hundred names on a petition asking for women the right to vote, he would present the petition to parliament. As the result, a women's suffrage committee was organized in London, and within a fortnight it had collected 1,499 signatures, including those of some of the most eminent women of the time, the most famous among them Florence Nightingale. (Miss Nightingale was Barbara Bodichon's cousin, but the two seem never to have been friends, perhaps because of the 'tabooed' status of the latter's family.) In June Mill presented to parliament this 'Petition of B.L.S. Bodichon and Others,' as it was known.

The following year more suffrage petitions were presented to parliament, and in May, during the debates on the Reform Bill, Mill moved an amendment which, by substituting in the bill the word 'persons' for 'men,' would have enfranchised women on the same terms as men. His able speech on women's behalf made a great impression, although by no means a universally favourable one. Among the uncomplimentary responses to his speech were those of one member who thanked Mill for 'the pleasant interlude he had interposed to the

MILL'S LOGIC; OR, FRANCHISE FOR FEMALES.
"PRAY CLEAR THE WAY, THERE, FOR THESE—A—PERSONS."

reprinted from *Punch* 1867

grave and somewhat sombre discussions on the subject of Reform,' and of another who said that since the House was anxious to 'proceed to more important business,' Mill should withdraw his amendment, 'which, if pressed to a division, would place many Gentlemen who were great admirers of the fair sex in an embarrassing position.' Yet the amendment mustered a respectable degree of support, 73 votes in favour to 196 opposed. Mill later wrote that his proposal of the amendment, the 'most gratifying' of all his recollections connected with the House of Commons, was 'by far the most important, perhaps the only really important, public service I performed in the capacity of a Member of the Parliament.'[8]

By now women's suffrage committees and societies were springing up all over the country, and were soon to be found in every large city and in many smaller towns as well. Soon a central committee composed of delegates from the provincial societies was organized, and later it united with the London committee. These societies launched a vigorous publicity campaign to win support for their cause. Pamphlets setting forth the women's case were printed and thousands of copies were circulated. Among these were reprints of Madame Bodichon's Kensington Society paper and her paper presented before the Social Science Association congress in Manchester in 1866, and copies of Mill's speech in parliament in 1867. Large public meetings were held throughout the country, and at these meetings women for the first time spoke out in public for their cause. So startling was this sudden appearance of women delivering public speeches on public issues that it called forth rebukes from Queen Victoria herself and from many others lower down the social ladder.

It was in this climate of general reform and renewal, and in the midst of the organization of the women's suffrage movement, that the question of reform of the married women's property law was again brought forward. In a sense Mill was as responsible for this development as he was for the beginning of the suffrage movement. In his speech in parliament in 1867 he had not claimed the franchise for women on the ground that it was an abstract or natural right which all should enjoy. Rather, in true Radical style Mill argued for women's right to vote on utilitarian grounds – women needed the vote in order to protect themselves – and of all the examples he used to prove this point he dwelt most upon the state of the married women's property law. As it stood, Mill said, all that a poor woman had belonged to her husband, who could 'tear it all from her, squander every penny of it in debauchery, leave her to support by her labour herself and her children and ... unless she is judicially separated from him he can pounce down upon her savings, and leave her penniless.' Mill summed up by saying that 'grievances of less magnitude than the law of married women's property, when suffered by parties less inured to passive submission, have provoked revolutions.'[9]

Mill's was a challenging statement of fact and a ringing cry for reform, but organized, practical work was needed if the parliamentary machine was to be set in motion to carry through reform. During the first agitation for reform of the property law in the fifties, this work of pushing for reform by parliament had been undertaken by Barbara Bodichon and her friends in London, but their committee did not survive the failure to win passage of the legislation desired. Now, work for reform was undertaken by another circle of feminists, centred in Manchester. This group organized another, much more effective Married Women's Property Committee, which laboured ceaselessly for more than two years to win in parliament the first, unsatisfactory reform of the law in 1870.

Thereafter its work continued for another twelve years until at last comprehensive reform was won.

The most important woman in this second generation of feminists who reopened the question of property-law reform was Elizabeth Clarke Wolstenholme, afterward Mrs Elmy.[10] Like Emily Davies, her colleague in the cause of women's education, Miss Wolstenholme had arrived at her ardent feminist convictions through 'early and vivid realisation of the unjust disparity of educational and life chances that awaited intellect in one same family, according to difference of sex.' Her older, only brother had a brilliant career at Cambridge, and later became professor of mathematics at the Royal Indian Engineering College. Her own early training was rigidly domestic and unintellectual, and when she was sixteen, after two years spent at a boarding-school, her formal education ended. An orphan, she was unable to persuade her guardians to allow her to attend Bedford College for Women, and she spent the next two or three years in unassisted study and in teaching. Then she became proprietress of a small girls' boarding-school near Manchester, an establishment in which her small inherited capital had been invested on her guardians' advice. Thus, at the same age at which her brother had possessed 'a comfortable and irresponsible competency as a college Fellow,' she was 'left to struggle, virtually unaided, in the responsible and desperately precarious undertaking to which her young enthusiasm had consented, as perhaps the only livelihood honourable to herself and useful to humanity.'

As head of the school near Manchester and later as proprietress of another girls' school at Congleton in Cheshire, Miss Wolstenholme took a very active part in the many efforts being made 'to afford to girls a fuller education and a more pleasant and common-sense training than was then dreamt of' in existing schools. Together with Emily Davies and the great headmistresses Frances Buss and Dorothea Beale, she was invited in 1865 to give evidence before the Schools Inquiry Commission; they and the five other women called were the first women ever examined in person as expert witnesses by a royal commission. Miss Wolstenholme had already organized the Manchester Board of School Mistresses, which suggested the formation of similar associations in other towns. These associations eventually joined to form the North of England Council for Promoting the Higher Education of Women. The council popularized the Oxford and Cambridge local examinations, already opened to girls through the efforts of Emily Davies and Barbara Bodichon; it promoted the system of local lectures, originally for women only, which were delivered by university men and out of which the university extension movement developed; and in 1869 it won the establishment by Cambridge of special higher local examinations for women and opened a residence hall in Cambridge to accommodate some of the women preparing to take these examinations – the nucleus of Newnham College. Miss Wolstenholme also wrote frequently in the cause of women's education, and she was the author, under her pen-name Ellis Ethelmer, of the *Human Flower* series, pioneer works on sex education for children and parents. As Ellis Ethelmer she also published numerous poems, many of them with feminist themes.

Miss Wolstenholme was an early and ardent worker for women's suffrage as for other legal reforms affecting women. In 1865 she helped to organize in Manchester a suffrage committee whose members always prided themselves on the fact that theirs had been the first such committee in the country, although London claimed that honour. Miss Wolstenholme served as the committee's first secretary, and helped to collect signatures on the suffrage petition which John Stuart Mill presented in parliament in 1866. She gave up her school at Congleton in 1872, when she moved to London to act as the women's 'Parliamentary watch-dog.' Years later, when thoroughgoing reform of the married women's property law had been won at last, she took a special interest in the campaign to win further rights for mothers with respect to custody of their children, a campaign which led to passage of the Guardianship of Infants Act of 1886. In 1892 she helped to found and became secretary of the Women's Emancipation Union, which was dedicated to securing 'the political, social, and economic independence of women' by winning for them equality in the central and local government services, in education, in business and industry, and in marriage. Years later, elderly and frail, she joined in the demonstrations before the houses of parliament which signalled the beginning of the militant suffragette movement.

In 1874 Miss Wolstenholme had joined the ranks of married women, becoming the wife of Ben Elmy of Congleton, a minor poet and a firm believer in the equality of the sexes. The story goes that she agreed to regularize her relationship with Elmy only when she was several months pregnant and her friend Ursula Bright persuaded her that she would bring down scandal upon the women's movement by refusing to marry. The wedding was a civil ceremony, in which, said Mrs Elmy – whose only child, Frank, soon afterward appeared – 'no degrading promise of "obedience" is exacted from the wife, but a simple, equal and mutual pledge is given by both parties.'

The second of the women most responsible for reviving the question of property-law reform was Josephine Grey Butler.[11] Mrs Butler's dedication to women's causes was rooted in the liberalism that was hers by birth and breeding and in the mystical religious faith that inspired her life. Her father, member of one of the great old families of the Border country, was a cousin and active supporter of Lord Grey of Reform Bill fame, and his wide sympathies encompassed many other good causes, among them repeal of the Corn Laws, reform of the Poor Law, and above all, the abolition of slavery. As a young girl Josephine

Grey, like other eminent Victorians, underwent a religious crisis. As she recalled it:

Sin seemed to me the law of the world and fate its master. I could not love God who appeared to my foolish and darkened heart to consent to so much which seemed to me cruel and unjust. I asked of the Lord one thing, that He would reveal to me His one, His constant attitude towards His lost world ... the God who answers prayer had mercy on me; He did not deny me my request of His own heart's love for sinners, and when He makes this revelation He does more; He makes the enquiring soul a partaker of His own heart's love for the world.

Thereafter she never wavered in her faith in God's loving presence and in the efficacy of prayer. Her feminism flowed directly from this faith:

Search throughout the Gospel history, and observe His [Christ's] conduct in regard to women, and it will be found that the word liberation expresses, above all others, the act which changed the whole life and character and position of the women dealt with, and which ought to have changed the character of men's treatment of women from that time forward ... it seems to me impossible for anyone candidly to study Christ's whole life and words without seeing that the principle of the perfect equality of all human beings was announced by Him as the basis of social philosophy.

Finally, she was convinced that 'the only condition of our spiritual health is war, unceasing war, against the whole kingdom of Satan, and against all evil things.' To that war she devoted her life.

Josephine Grey was fortunate in her marriage. George Butler, the son of an outstanding headmaster of Harrow, later dean of Peterborough, was himself a distinguished educator and clergyman, who served successively as examiner to the University of Oxford, vice-principal of Cheltenham College, principal of Liverpool College, and canon of Winchester. Of her husband Mrs Butler said, 'The idea of justice to women, of equality between the sexes, and of equality of responsibility for all human beings to the moral law seems to have been instinctive in him. He never needed convincing.' They were in complete agreement that marriage should be 'a perfectly equal union, with absolute freedom on both sides for personal initiative in thought and action and for individual development.' Theirs was not only a supremely happy marriage but also a highly unusual one, for in a curious reversal of the roles expected of husband and wife in Victorian times, Josephine Butler ventured forth into the world, while her husband provided tranquillity and security at home to which she could return for shelter and comfort.

Mrs Butler's first public work was in the cause of women's education and employment. In 1867 she played an important part in the founding of the North of England Council for Promoting the Higher Education of Women, and served as president during the first three years of its existence. The following year she published her first work, a pamphlet entitled *The Education and Employment of Women*. In it she used the census statistics of 1861 to refute the old argument that woman's place was in the home. She pointed out that more than three million women were earning their own living, wholly or in part, and that the miserable wages so many of them received were due partly to their poor education and partly to legal and other restrictions on their employment, and she pleaded for better education for women and the removal of restrictions on their work. Mrs Butler reiterated these themes in the introduction to a volume of essays published in 1869, *Woman's Work and Woman's Culture*, which she edited and which contained articles by her husband and by Elizabeth Wolstenholme, among others.

The year 1869 marked the turning-point in Josephine Butler's life, for it was then that she consented, largely at the urging of Elizabeth Wolstenholme, to become leader of the women's campaign to win repeal of the Contagious Diseases Acts. These three acts were passed without publicity between 1864 and 1869 in an attempt to halt the spread of venereal disease, especially in the armed services. They represented the nearest approach Britain ever made to the continental system of state-regulated prostitution. They provided for the arrest and compulsory medical examination and treatment of those women in the country's chief garrison and port cities whom the police suspected of being prostitutes. Feminists were appalled by the acts' provisions. In the first place, they represented a gross violation of constitutional guarantees of personal liberties, for they allowed the arrest of women merely on suspicion and without formal charges being filed against them, and their detention without trial. Second, the acts were an insult to both God and man, for they were based upon the assumption that sexual purity, although divinely ordained, was impossible for men and that a special class of women must be provided for their enjoyment. Third, by officially stigmatizing women the acts made it very difficult if not impossible for them ever to leave their lives of sin and move into respectable society. Finally, the acts were a glaring example of class legislation, for only the daughters and wives of the poor, not women of the middle and upper classes, were likely to be subjected to them.

Mrs Butler was already well known for her concern for 'fallen women,' and she proved to be the ideal person to head a campaign from which the great majority of 'respectable' women turned away with shudders. Grief-stricken at the accidental death of her only daughter, her fourth and youngest child, Mrs

Butler had resolved, she said, 'to plunge into the heart of some human misery, and to say (as I now knew I could), to afflicted people, "I understand: I too have suffered."' She began by visiting the women in Liverpool's notorious Brownlow Hill workhouse, and soon was taking into her own home women, many of them seduced and abandoned, who had been driven by poverty into lives of prostitution. Later she opened, first in Liverpool and then in Winchester, refuges for such women, many of whom were ill and dying. To her wider, lifelong work of stirring the public conscience and agitating for parliamentary action, Mrs Butler brought a commanding presence and talents of a high order. She was possessed of an extraordinary beauty which did not fade with age, and her appearance of quiet dignity and spiritual strength impressed all who met her. Her voice, low and well modulated, entranced single listeners and large audiences alike. She was also possessed of formidable intelligence. She had had little formal education, but she read widely, acquiring expert knowledge on many subjects, ranging from the history of art and medieval literature to constitutional law, and she spoke several languages fluently. A talented writer, she turned out scores of books and pamphlets, most of them on subjects relating to women but also works of a religious nature and several biographies, including memoirs of her father and husband and a study of the great mystic St Catherine of Siena.

There is no need to recount here the story of Mrs Butler's campaigns, which has been told fully and well elsewhere. It is enough to say that after years of unremitting labour on her part, parliament repealed the Contagious Diseases Acts in 1886, while her efforts also largely inspired a European movement in opposition to both government-regulated prostitution and the white slave trade. Of her work Mrs Butler said in characteristic style: 'God has done me the great favour of allowing me in a manner to be ... the representative of the outcast, of the "woman of the city who was a sinner."'

The third woman who was largely responsible for reviving interest in property-law reform was Emilia Jessie Boucherett, the daughter of a Lincolnshire squire whose family was of French Huguenot origin.[12] A great lover of country life and an enthusiastic rider to hounds, she eventually succeeded to the family's estates, following the deaths of her older, unmarried brother and her older sister Louisa, who was a pioneer in the movement for the boarding out of pauper children. Miss Boucherett had been educated at the school kept by the four daughters of Josiah Wedgwood's partner Thomas Byerley at Avonbank, where Mrs Gaskell had also been a pupil. After her return home, she was, by her own account, 'consuming her soul in solitary desire to help women to better economic conditions,' when by chance she saw a copy of the *English Woman's Journal* in a railway bookstall and bought it, expecting to find in it 'nothing better than the inanities commonly considered fit for women,' but delightedly discover-

ing 'her own unspoken aspirations reflected in its pages.' She lost no time in
going up to London to present herself at the offices of the *Journal*, where 'she
expected to find some rather dowdy old lady.' Instead she saw a 'handsome
young woman, dressed in admirable taste ... Miss [Bessie] Parkes,' who was soon
joined by 'another young lady, also beautifully dressed ... of radiant beauty, with
masses of golden hair ... Barbara Leigh Smith [Bodichon].'

Miss Boucherett entered eagerly into the activities of the ladies of Langham
Place. Her most important project was the organization of the Society for Promoting the Employment of Women, inspired, it is said, by the appearance of
Harriet Martineau's *Edinburgh Review* article of 1859 on the problem of 'redundant women,' that is, the unmarried and unemployed. The society sought to
arouse public opinion to women's need for wider employment. More practically,
it set up a number of pilot projects to train women and find employment for
them in fields of work from which they were then excluded. One of its successful
ventures was establishment of the Victoria Press, a printing business which was
run by women trained by the society and which was soon named Printer and
Publisher in Ordinary to the Queen. Another successful venture was the employment of women as law stationers in several offices established by the society. A
special interest of Miss Boucherett's was the promotion of women's employment
as shop assistants and clerks. To prepare women for such employment she organized special classes which provided a 'solid English education' to younger girls
and training for clerical work to older ones. These classes continued in existence
for nearly forty years, until 1899, by which time they were no longer needed
because of the improvement in education generally and in the education of girls
in particular, and because most schools were providing classes in 'commercial
subjects.'

Miss Boucherett also contributed to the women's movement by her literary
labours. In 1866 she founded as the official feminist organ the *Englishwoman's
Review*, with which the *English Woman's Journal* was amalgamated, and she
served for five years as its editor. She wrote a little book called *Hints on Self Help
for Young Women*, and published numerous pamphlets and articles. She also
encouraged the first literary work of Josephine Butler, who paid a special visit to
London to confer with her about women's education and employment in 1868,
and the following year she contributed an essay to Mrs Butler's volume *Woman's
Work and Woman's Culture*.

During the first agitation for reform of the married women's property law in
the fifties, Barbara Bodichon and her friends had turned for practical support to
the Law Amendment Society, headed by Lord Brougham. Now these younger
feminists sought support from the organization which had developed from the
Law Amendment Society and eventually amalgamated with it. This was the

National Association for the Promotion of Social Science, usually called more simply the Social Science Association, organized in 1857 under the nominal leadership of Lord Brougham, who served as president for seven of its first nine years of existence.[13]

The purpose of the association was to bring together reformers from all parts of the country for the discussion of social problems and the discovery of the natural laws that governed society – that is, the creation of a 'social science.' If the association did not quite discover these social laws, it did provide a remarkable public forum for discussion of some of the most pressing problems of the time and possible solutions of these; and its congresses, held annually in different cities throughout the country, were, in the early years at least, large and impressive assemblies. Brougham invited women to participate in the association's affairs and encouraged them to present papers at the congresses; the *Saturday Review* congratulated him for being the 'first person who has dealt upon this plan with the problem of female loquacity.'[14] Women responded enthusiastically to Brougham's invitation, for they were assured of audiences that were almost invariably sympathetic to their causes. For example, Barbara Bodichon raised the question of women's suffrage at the 1866 Social Science Association congress, and Emily Davies explained her plan for a women's college at the 1868 congress. A number of women's groups, including the Society for Promoting the Employment of Women, were formally affiliated with the association and held their annual meetings in conjunction with its congresses.

More important than the public discussions it sponsored was the association's work as a lobbying group. Its executive council and standing committees studied various problems, proposed remedies, and sometimes drafted specific legislation which was then introduced in parliament by some appropriate member among the large number of MPs who belonged to the association. The association proudly claimed credit for the introduction and passage in parliament of dozens of reform measures, and among these was the first reform of the married women's property law.

An important figure linking the Social Science Association with the revived movement for reform of the married women's property law was George Woodyatt Hastings, who was the real creator of the association, although Lord Brougham was generally credited with being its founder. Hastings, whose father had founded the British Medical Association, was a talented, energetic, and ambitious barrister with a passion for organization. He had early attached himself to the group of reformers associated with Brougham, and served for years as secretary of the Law Amendment Society. Later, as secretary of the Social Science Association, he was its real leader. But while his talents and energies both launched and sustained the association, his arrogant and dictatorial nature contributed in some significant degree to its eventual demise in 1886. By then Hastings had entered parliament as member for Worcestershire, where he lived and was a figure of considerable local importance. His public career ended abruptly in 1892, when he was sentenced to five years' imprisonment for embezzlement of a trust fund and was expelled from the House of Commons.[15]

Before he was sullied by these events, Hastings was an earnest and effective friend of women's causes. In particular he was a great friend of Barbara Bodichon, and during her long absences from London he often made his headquarters at her house in Blandford Square. Perhaps it was at her request that Hastings took up reform of the married women's property law. At the congress of the Social Science Association held in Belfast in 1867, he presented a paper in which he briefly outlined the history of the married women's property law and suggested that reform be carried through in England on the same lines as reform in New York State – that married women be given the same rights as unmarried women with respect to property.[16]

In the fall of 1867 Elizabeth Wolstenholme, Josephine Butler, and Jessie Boucherett began the work of organizing a memorial for presentation to the executive council of the Social Science Association. The memorial, presented in December, requested that the association take up the cause of reform of the married women's property law. It bore more than 300 signatures of persons distinguished in all walks of public life, including some who had signed the first petition to parliament in 1856, among them Mary Howitt and Harriet Martineau. The question was referred to the standing committee of the association's Department of Jurisprudence and Amendment of the Law, which was chaired by Frederic Hill, younger brother of Matthew Davenport Hill. He shared his brother's interest in penal reform, working for several years as an inspector of prisons and publishing a book on crime, and he later served as assistant secretary to the Post Office, where his other brother Rowland Hill had won fame. The Social Science Association's committee, like that of the Law Amendment Society a decade earlier, concluded that the existing law was unjust and should be reformed.[17]

In view of this conclusion the committee proceeded to draft a bill to amend the law, a bill which was substantially the same as that which had been proposed by the Law Amendment Society's committee and introduced in parliament by Sir Erskine Perry in 1857. The bill would not interfere with the right to make marriage settlements in equity, including settlements subject to restraint upon anticipation, although such settlements and restraints were to have no greater force against a wife's creditors than a similar settlement made by a man would have against his creditors. In all other cases married women were to hold all their property free from their husbands' control and obligations, having all the powers of unmarried women to acquire and to alienate property during their lifetime, and to dispose of their property by will; if they died intestate, the same rules would apply to the distribution of their property as applied to that of their husbands, with the exception that their husbands would still be entitled by the curtesy to a life interest in their real property. Married women were likewise to have all the rights of unmarried women to enter into contracts and to sue and be sued, their husbands being no longer liable for their antenuptial debts or for their torts. In any question of ownership of property that arose between husband and wife, either could apply for a decision in the matter to the Court of Chancery or to a county court. The report of the Social Science Association's committee, together with its draft bill, was completed at the end of February 1868. Two months later the bill was introduced in parliament.[18]

As soon as the Married Women's Property Bill came before parliament, the women who had sponsored the memorial to the Social Science Association decided that a special group should be organized to agitate for the bill's passage. Accordingly a general Married Women's Property Committee was formed in April 1868, with a small executive committee centred in Manchester, Elizabeth Wolstenholme and Josephine Butler serving jointly as secretaries. (For members of the executive committee, see appendix 3.) Similar committees were formed in Ireland, one for Belfast and the north and another for Dublin and the south, while another committee worked in Birmingham.[19]

One of the most important members of the Married Women's Property Committee was Lydia Becker, who acted as its first treasurer.[20] Educated almost entirely at home, Miss Becker had an unquenchable thirst for learning, and through wide reading and personal observation she acquired vast knowledge of a variety of subjects, among which botany was her special favourite. Her skill in this field brought her a gold medal, awarded by the Horticultural Society of South Kensington, and this in turn led to some correspondence with Darwin about certain facts she had discovered in her studies and to the publication of a little book she had written called *Botany for Novices*.

Like her friend Elizabeth Wolstenholme, Miss Becker was first drawn into the women's movement by her interest in education. One of her earliest feminist undertakings was the founding in 1867 of a Ladies' Literary Society; the first paper presented before it was one sent in by Darwin. This society, designed to provide comradeship and pleasure in learning, represented Miss Becker's attempt to encourage women to develop their intellectual capabilities at a time when higher education for them was lacking and when the various learned societies refused them membership. In 1870 Miss Becker was elected to the school board of Manchester at the first election held under the provisions of the Education

Act of that year. This act, providing for the creation of a national system of state-supported elementary schools, allowed women both to vote for and to serve upon the local boards responsible for supervising the new schools. One of only four women in the whole country to be elected to school boards in 1870 – Emily Davies and Elizabeth Garrett were also elected at this time – Miss Becker retained her seat until her death in 1890.

Meanwhile, her energies were being increasingly absorbed in work for women's suffrage. Her interest in the subject had first been aroused in 1866, when she heard Barbara Bodichon's paper presented at the Social Science Association congress held that year in Manchester. Soon after, she succeeded Miss Wolstenholme as secretary of the Manchester women's suffrage society, and later became editor of the *Women's Suffrage Journal*, which is an essential source for the history of the movement. In these positions, which she held till the end of her life, Miss Becker became one of the most important suffrage leaders in the country. Her women colleagues paid tribute to her wide sympathies and superb administrative abilities, and her friends in parliament praised her political acumen and her complete mastery of the intricacies of parliamentary procedure. Unfortunately Miss Becker, stout, plain, and bespectacled, was easily ridiculed and caricatured as a feminist battleaxe, and her figure can be seen in many political cartoons of the time, a fact which, as her intimates knew, sorely grieved her.

Another leading figure in the work of the Married Women's Property Committee was Richard Marsden Pankhurst.[21] Indeed, as one of the most important members of the Social Science Association, he had drafted the Married Women's Property Bill which was endorsed by the association and introduced in parliament in 1868. Dr Pankhurst was one of Manchester's most prominent citizens. He had studied at Owens College, where later he was appointed a governor and pioneered in the provision of evening classes and other measures to promote popular education. He had graduated at the University of London and then obtained a doctor of laws degree there, receiving the university's gold medal. After several years of practice as a solicitor, he was called to the bar in 1867. He quickly made a name for himself, handling important legal business for the city of Manchester and taking an active part in social and intellectual life. A fine orator, he was often called upon to be the speaker on important civic occasions, and the newspapers frequently referred to him familiarly as 'our learned doctor.'

But Pankhurst's reputation and his legal practice eventually suffered because of his thoroughgoing Radicalism. The son of a devout Baptist family and himself a former Sunday school teacher, he came to embrace agnosticism and urged disestablishment of the Church and the end of religious disabilities. A convinced republican, he called for the abolition of hereditary aristocracy and the House of Lords as well as abolition of the monarchy. A socialist, member of the Fabian

Society, and great friend of Keir Hardie, he advocated the nationalization of land and other advanced social measures. Finally, he was a dedicated feminist.

In addition to his work on the Married Women's Property Committee, Pankhurst played an important role in the early women's suffrage movement. In 1865 he had helped to organize the women's suffrage committee in Manchester. After passage of the Reform Bill of 1867 he launched a campaign to place upon the voters' registers the names of women who met the new property qualifications for voting, and more than 90 per cent of the eligible women in Manchester sought to be registered. The legal basis of this campaign was the fact that although the Reform Act enfranchised certain qualified 'men,' another act of 1850 provided that words in legislation denoting masculine gender were to be taken as including women unless the contrary was expressly provided. Most of the women who sought registration were refused; some were registered, only to have their names struck off later by the revising barristers, the legal officials responsible for checking voters' lists to see that only those who qualified were registered. Pankhurst then appealed to the Court of Common Pleas against the action of the registrars and revising barristers, but in the leading case of *Chorlton* v *Lings* in 1869, the court held that women were not entitled to exercise any right or privilege unless an act of parliament expressly conferred it on them. The following year a bill drafted by Pankhurst to grant women the parliamentary franchise was introduced in the Commons, and was approved on its second reading by a majority of 33 when the government remained neutral and allowed Liberals to 'vote their conscience.' But then the government, apparently fearful that women, if enfranchised, would vote Conservative rather than Liberal, forced its followers to withdraw their support of the measure, which was killed when the motion for going into committee was defeated by a vote of 220 to 74. Not for years would success for the cause again come so close.

Meanwhile, however, the first victory for women's suffrage had been gained in 1869 under Pankhurst's leadership. A bill to reform the municipal franchise was then before parliament, and Pankhurst drafted an amendment to it which gained government approval and was included in the bill as passed, giving women householders the right to vote in municipal elections. Still, in the leading case of *R* v *Harrald* three years later, the Court of Queen's Bench ruled that married women, even if they qualified as householders, were not entitled to the municipal franchise. The question of whether married women could vote as householders had by then become a matter of importance, for the Married Women's Property Act of 1870 allowed wives the right to hold some property separate from their husbands.

In 1879 Dr Pankhurst, apparently a confirmed bachelor at the age of forty, married the beautiful young Emmeline Goulden, daughter of a prosperous and enthusiastically Liberal cotton manufacturer in Manchester. Mrs Pankhurst later recalled how, at the age of fourteen, together with her mother, she had attended her first suffrage meeting and heard a speech by Lydia Becker, 'a splendid character and a truly eloquent speaker,' and had left the meeting 'a conscious and confirmed suffragist.' In his wife Pankhurst found a vital kindred spirit who quickly developed under his tutelage into a reformer as ardent as he, and their household in Manchester and later in London, where they lived for seven years in order to be at the centre of political life, was a favourite meeting-place for Radicals. However, Pankhurst never entered parliament, being defeated on all three occasions when he presented himself as a candidate – as an independent Liberal at a Manchester by-election in 1883, as a Radical at Rotherhithe in 1885, and as an Independent Labour party candidate at Gorton in 1894. The doctor's wife and daughters – Christabel, Sylvia, and Adela – never forgot his outburst to them after a suffrage meeting at their London home, when he demanded, 'Why don't you *force* us to give you the vote? Why don't you *scratch our eyes out?*' It is a noteworthy fact that Emmeline Pankhurst, who years later was to win world-wide fame as the charismatic leader of the militant suffragette movement, served her feminist apprenticeship as a member of the executive body of the Married Women's Property Committee, onto which she was co-opted at her husband's suggestion.

Another couple who were leading figures in the work of the Manchester Married Women's Property Committee were Jacob Bright and his wife Ursula Mellor.[22] Bright was a younger brother of the great reformer John Bright, who during his long public career, culminating in service in Gladstone's first and second ministries, championed such good causes as repeal of the Corn Laws and free trade generally; the enfranchisement of working men; justice for Ireland, including disestablishment of the Irish Church and land reform; and a peaceful foreign policy, which led him to denounce British involvement in the Crimean War and to plead for good relations with the Union during the American Civil War. The Brights were sons of a typical self-made man of the early industrial age, a devout Quaker who, with the aid of other Friends, learned the textile business and eventually established at Rochdale his own cotton-spinning mill, to which a carpet-printing venture was later added. This elder Jacob Bright, like his sons after him, was a model employer, whose workers turned to him for advice about their personal problems, received money from him to tide them over hard times of unemployment, obtained a raise in wages when they married, and had their children educated in a school which he founded for them. The Bright sons themselves were educated in the best schools then available to Quakers and then returned home to enter the family business, eventually renamed John Bright and Brothers. As John Bright became increasingly involved in public life, his brother Jacob served as chairman of the family firm.

"the Apostle to the Women"

[Jacob Bright]

reprinted from *Vanity Fair* 1877

In 1867 Jacob Bright was elected to parliament as Radical member for Manchester, a position he was to hold, with two brief interruptions, till his retirement in 1895. (John Bright regarded his brother's success as a personal vindication of himself, since he had been defeated at Manchester in 1857 because of his opposition to the Crimean War, although he returned to parliament a few months later when he was elected for Birmingham on the death of one of its members.) Jacob Bright lacked the fine oratorical gifts and the great popular appeal of his brother and was always overshadowed by him – unfortunately, for 'he had all John's fearless and unyielding temper, together with a greater measure of intellectual daring and suppleness.'[23] His career owed much to the support of his wife Ursula, the daughter of a Liverpool merchant and an outstanding woman in Quaker circles. She, it was believed, inspired and guided her husband in his ardent championship of women's causes, and after his death she published a collection of his speeches to preserve his memory.

Jacob and Ursula Bright were certainly best known for their work for feminist reforms. Both served on the executive body of the Married Women's Property Committee throughout its existence. They took an active part in Josephine Butler's campaigns against the Contagious Diseases Acts. Indeed Jacob Bright, together with other Quakers, was the earliest supporter in the Commons of repeal of the acts, which was first debated in 1870 but not carried till 1886. The Brights were also active in the Manchester women's suffrage society, and Jacob Bright was directly responsible for the first parliamentary success of the suffrage cause. It was he who introduced Pankhurst's amendment to the municipal franchise bill of 1869, which was adopted. The next year he introduced the women's suffrage bill drafted by Pankhurst, and this came close to succeeding.

John Bright himself, great reformer though he was, never supported the cause of women's rights. He did vote for Mill's feminist amendment to the Reform Bill of 1867, perhaps wishing to pay a personal tribute to Mill, but thereafter he consistently opposed women's suffrage despite the efforts of his relatives to convert him. Leading them was his favourite sister Priscilla, who had kept house for him and his infant daughter for several years after the early death of his first wife. In 1848 Priscilla Bright became the third wife of Duncan McLaren, a great friend of her brother and the one man, next to Richard Cobden, whom he most often consulted on political questions. To her great sorrow Mrs McLaren was, under the rules then in force, expelled from the Society of Friends for marrying a non-Quaker, but years later, when the society had reformed itself, she was reinstated as a member. Duncan McLaren, a draper of Edinburgh, had become a member of the town council in 1833 and served successively as baillie, treasurer, and provost. In 1865 he was elected to parliament as Liberal member for Edinburgh, a seat he held for sixteen years. So great was his authority on Scots questions that he was sometimes called 'the member for Scotland.' Priscilla McLaren became president of the Edinburgh women's suffrage society when it was organized in 1867, and continued in that position for many years. She was sometimes referred to humorously as 'the best represented woman in the kingdom.' That is, she was represented in parliament by her brothers John and Jacob, by her husband, by her son Charles (later Sir Charles), and by two nephews.[24]

Two of Mrs McLaren's nieces were also interested in women's causes and served on the executive body of the Married Women's Property Committee. Anne and Lilias Ashworth of Bath were the orphaned daughters of Sophia Bright Ashworth, who died soon after their birth. They inherited their mother's striking beauty, and their friend Millicent Garrett Fawcett recalled that on Sundays the fashionable young men of Bath would assemble outside the Quaker meeting-house to see the two sisters enter. Anne Ashworth never played a prominent part in the women's movement, but Lilias, later Mrs Hallett, was one of the most important of the early workers in the suffrage cause, and the Ashworth home was a favourite place of rest and refreshment for the suffragists on their travels about the country.[25]

While the first leaders of the Married Women's Property Committee came from Manchester, the cause of property-law reform attracted supporters from all over the country and especially from London, the centre of political life. Here a very distinguished group lent their names and energies to the committee's work, among them several members of parliament who, often together with their wives, identified themselves with liberal causes generally.

One couple of whom John Stuart Mill expected great things in the way of reform, including women's rights, were the young, wealthy and highly connected Lord and Lady Amberley.[26] They were ardent disciples and intimate friends of Mill, who consented to stand godfather to their younger son, Bertrand Russell. As the son and heir of Lord John Russell, Viscount Amberley was born and bred in the great Whig reform tradition and could be expected to rise to the highest positions in the government, even that of prime minister. He entered parliament in 1866 as member for Nottingham, and delivered his maiden speech during the debates on the Reform Bill of 1867. His beautiful and high-spirited wife, a daughter of the Whig politician Lord Stanley of Alderley, gaily styled herself 'Kate the unconventional,' and prided herself on the fact that to her London 'at-homes' flocked the leading political and intellectual figures of the day.

Unconventional the Amberleys certainly were – dangerously so, according to some. They were referred to as 'the godless couple,' for both had renounced orthodox Christianity and embraced instead a rather vague theism and a very practical humanitarianism. Both were known as democrats and admirers of things American, and in 1867 they embarked on an extended visit to the United States, where they met many persons of note, from the president down, including the veteran feminists Lucretia Mott and Elizabeth Cady Stanton. At home Lady Amberley took an active part in women's causes. She served on the executive body of the Married Women's Property Committee. She had as her personal physician Elizabeth Garrett, and did what she could to forward the progress of women doctors. She helped with the founding of Girton College, although Emily Davies, believing her name to be 'a dangerous one,' refused to have her publicly associated with this work. Lady Amberley's mother, Henrietta, Lady Stanley, was one of Girton's most important benefactresses, although she played no active role in the women's movement until after her husband's death in 1869 for fear of harming his political career. Finally, Lady Amberley was an active suffragist, presiding over the Bristol and West of England women's suffrage society from her country home and speaking in public on the cause, encouraged by Mill, who believed it important that a woman of her high social position should do so. It was a public address given by Lady Amberley at Stroud in 1870 and later published in the *Fortnightly Review* that inspired the queen's tirade against 'this mad, wicked folly of "Women's Rights,"' ending with the observation that Lady Amberley ought to have a good whipping.

Unfortunately the useful careers of the Amberleys were cut tragically short. In 1868 Lord Amberley was defeated in his bid for election to parliament as member for South Devon, after a scurrilous campaign during which his religious views and his advocacy of birth-control measures were denounced as evidence of the blackest immorality. He never again served in parliament but retired to a quiet life in the country, devoting himself to study and writing. In 1874, at the age of thirty-two, Lady Amberley died of diphtheria, as did her little daughter Rachel Lucretia, named for Lucretia Mott. Lord Amberley survived them by only eighteen months.

Another couple known for their sympathies with Mill and Radical causes were Peter Alfred Taylor and his wife Clementia Doughty.[27] Taylor belonged to an old Unitarian family that maintained a connection with W.J. Fox's South Place chapel, and he entered and eventually became a partner in the great firm of silk mercers, Samuel Courtauld and Company, founded by his grandfather. His public life began with work to repeal the Corn Laws, a campaign in which his father took a leading part. In his younger days Taylor's chief interest was Mazzini's cause of Young Italy, and in 1847 he became chairman of the Society of the Friends of Italy. In 1862 he entered parliament as member for Leicester, which he represented till his retirement from public life in 1884. Taylor was also interested in several journalistic enterprises, and from 1873 till 1878 was proprietor of the liberal *Examiner*.

Clementia Taylor, described by friends as a cultivated and charming woman, had met her future husband while she was employed as a governess to his sisters. The Taylors' residence, Aubrey House in Notting Hill, was a favourite meeting-place for a large circle of people interested in reform causes and in literature and the arts. So 'radical' was Mrs Taylor that, like Barbara Bodichon, she cultivated the friendship of that social outcast George Eliot. She served as honorary secretary of the London Society for Women's Suffrage, which boasted Mill as its president. In 1867 this society replaced the original suffrage committee which had been organized the year before to collect signatures on the petition Mill presented in parliament, and which had split apart on the question of tactics. The more conservative members, such as Emily Davies, favoured a non-partisan appeal for support, while others, including Mill and Clementia Taylor, favoured alignment of the group with the Liberal party and particularly with its Radical wing.

Also active in women's causes were Henry and Millicent Garrett Fawcett, who had first met at the London home of Peter and Clementia Taylor and were married in 1867.[28] Blinded in a hunting accident in early manhood but never daunted by his handicap, Fawcett was professor of political economy at Cambridge and a highly respected author. He was also Liberal member of parliament for Brighton, one of the most distinguished of the Radical group that acknowledged Mill as their leader. His special interests were reform of the Indian government, university reform, and the removal of religious disabilities. He rose to become postmaster general in Gladstone's second ministry in 1880 and proved to be one of the most popular men ever to hold that office, concerned to increase his department's services to the public and to improve the working conditions of the department's employees. In particular Fawcett was committed to increasing the employment of women in the Post Office. In 1881 he created the new civil service grade of 'women clerks,' to be recruited by open competitive examinations, and two years later he appointed as medical attendant to the women of the Post Office staff Edith Shove, the first woman doctor to be employed in the central government service. However, Fawcett's relations with Gladstone became strained, perhaps largely because Fawcett stoutly supported women's suffrage, which Gladstone vehemently opposed.

Encouraged by her husband, Millicent Fawcett developed into an important public figure in her own right. Because of his physical handicap, she served as her husband's eyes and hands, reading to him and writing for him, gaining an excellent education in the process and beginning to write works of her own on political economy and the suffrage question. The story goes that winning the vote for women had been assigned to Millicent Garrett as her special task by Emily Davies, the great friend of her older sister Elizabeth, whom Miss Davies always guided and criticized in her efforts to become the first woman doctor in England. With the encouragement of her husband and of Mill, Mrs Fawcett became a frequent and effective speaker in the suffrage cause. After Lydia Becker's death in 1890 she became the acknowledged leader of the suffrage movement, and after victory was won at last in 1918 she was rewarded for her long years of labour in the cause by the title Dame Millicent. Together with her husband she also actively supported the founding of Newnham College, where their daughter Philippa later achieved great distinction, placing above the senior wrangler in the mathematics tripos in 1890 and then joining the teaching staff. It was Millicent Fawcett who recalled that the state of the marriage law had been forcefully brought to her attention when she appeared in court to testify against the thief who had snatched her purse, and heard him charged with stealing property that belonged to her husband. It was natural that she took an active part in the work of the Married Women's Property Committee.

Sir Charles Dilke was another of the promising young men who early won Mill's friendship and was always one of the women's staunchest friends in parliament.[29] After a brilliant career as a student of law at Cambridge, he entered parliament in 1868 as member for the newly created and important constituency of Chelsea, and served briefly as undersecretary at the Foreign Office in Gladstone's first ministry. In 1869 Dilke, as well as Jacob Bright, moved an amendment to the municipal franchise bill to grant women the vote, but Bright's amendment came on for discussion first and was carried. The next year Dilke seconded Bright's bill to grant women the parliamentary vote. Also in 1870 he carried the amendment to the government's Education Bill which provided for the supervision of the new elementary schools by locally elected school boards (for which women could vote and on which they could serve) rather than supervision by committees of the existing boards of Poor Law guardians, as the government had originally proposed.

When the Liberals returned to power in 1880, Dilke became president of the Local Government Board, and in that position he sought to advance the cause of women but found himself increasingly at odds with his antifeminist colleagues in the cabinet. Although his action was of doubtful legality, he appointed several women members of the Metropolitan Asylums Board, which was responsible for supervision of Poor Law institutions in London; but he failed to gain cabinet approval for the appointment of a woman member of the important royal commission of 1884 on the housing of the working classes, and he also failed to win appointment of women as factory inspectors at the Home Office. In 1884 Dilke, together with Henry Fawcett, nearly lost his seat in the cabinet because he abstained in the vote on a Conservative amendment to the Reform Bill of that year that would have given women the parliamentary vote, rather than voting against the amendment together with the rest of the cabinet.

Ironically, it was a woman who destroyed Dilke's political career. In 1885 the sister of his brother's wife accused Dilke, a widower, of adultery, and although the divorce suit brought against her by her husband failed when Dilke was found innocent, the scandal of the case was enough to ruin him. While asserting his own belief in Dilke's innocence, Gladstone refused to include him in his third ministry in 1886, and at the election of that year Dilke lost his parliamentary seat. He gained a wife, however, for his fiancée Emilia, widow of the distinguished Oxford scholar Mark Pattison, insisted on going through with their marriage as planned, despite the scandal. Dilke returned to parliament in 1892 as member for the Forest of Dean but never again held government office, although he continued to do fine work as a private member until his death in 1911.

A respected colleague of Dilke's in parliament was Leonard Henry Courtney, whose wife Catherine (Kate) was a sister of Beatrice Potter Webb.[30] He had had a brilliant career in mathematics at Cambridge, where he became a fellow of St John's College, before deciding to study law. In turn his interest in journalism and in politics and political economy drew him away from legal practice. He joined the staff of *The Times* in 1865, writing hundreds of its leaders over the next sixteen years and also contributing articles to the liberal *Fortnightly Review*, and he occupied the chair of political economy at University College for three years before entering parliament in 1875 as Liberal member for Liskeard. When Gladstone and the Liberals returned to power in 1880, Courtney served successively as undersecretary for the Home Office, undersecretary for the colonies, and secretary of the Treasury, his rapid rise seeming to assure his early entry into the ministry. However, he never attained cabinet rank, for he preferred to sacrifice his prospects to his principles. He resigned from office in 1884 because of his failure to persuade the Liberal government to adopt the principle of proportional representation, which he ardently supported, and two years later he rejected Gladstone's policy of home rule for Ireland and became associated with the Liberal Unionists, although he did serve as chairman of committees and then as deputy speaker of the House until 1892. Later Courtney severed his ties with the Liberal Unionists because of his opposition to the Boer War, and after his elevation to the peerage in 1906 as Baron Courtney of Penwith he often spoke in the House of Lords in favour of Irish home rule, to which cause he had been converted. During his parliamentary career Courtney was one of the women's most dependable friends. An important supporter of women's suffrage, he was also a member of the executive of the Married Women's Property Committee and a member of the governing body of Girton College.

Another couple involved in work for women's causes, both of whom served on the executive of the Married Women's Property Committee, were Arthur Arnold (later Sir Arthur) and his wife Amelia, the only daughter of Captain H.B. Hyde.[31] Originally a surveyor and land agent, Arnold served as government inspector of public works among the distressed mill workers of Lancashire during the cotton famine resulting from the American Civil War, and wrote a history of this period. He also wrote two sensational novels of the sixties, *Ralph* and *Hever Court*. In 1868 Arnold became editor of the new evening paper, *The Echo*, which was one of the earliest and most successful examples of first-class halfpenny journalism, and he continued as editor until the paper was sold in 1875. He also contributed articles to the leading periodicals, some of which were later collected and published under the title *Social Politics*. In 1880 Arnold entered parliament as Radical member for Salford, but he was defeated in his bid for re-election five years later. Thereafter he turned to local politics, serving as alderman and then chairman of the London County Council. After his death in 1902 his wife established in his memory the Sir Arthur Arnold Trust for scholarships at Girton College.

Yet another parliamentary couple who served together on the executive of the Married Women's Property Committee were Frederick Pennington and his wife Margaret, the daughter of Dr John Sharpe, vicar of Doncaster and later canon of York.[32] An East India merchant, Pennington retired from business in 1865. Three years later he unsuccessfully sought election to parliament as member for Surrey, where he was a magistrate. In 1874 Pennington, known as an 'advanced Liberal,' was elected to parliament as member for Stockport, and he held this seat until his retirement from public life eleven years later.

Finally, mention must be made of a couple who were not identified as Radicals or advanced Liberals but who nevertheless played major roles in the women's movement – Russell and Emelia Batten Gurney.[33] The son of a baron of the Court of Exchequer and himself a barrister and queen's counsel, Russell Gurney had become recorder of the City of London in 1857 and had entered parliament in 1865 as Conservative member for Southampton. The year of his election to parliament he was sent out by the Liberal government to investigate the black rebellion in Jamaica and the controversial conduct of Governor Eyre; six years later he was appointed by the Liberal government as a commissioner to settle British and American claims under the provisions of the Treaty of Washington. He also served on a number of important royal commissions and had charge of several important bills in parliament, including the bill to reform the married women's property law.

The devout daughter of a clergyman, Mrs Gurney, together with her husband, played an important part in the work of providing higher education for women and of opening the medical profession to them. At the special request of Emily Davies, who described her as 'heavenly,' she served on the council of Girton College. In 1859 she had helped with the organization of Dr Elizabeth Blackwell's lectures, delivered in London and other cities to encourage women to follow her example in entering the medical profession, and she had advised Elizabeth Garrett in her early career plans. In 1876 Gurney sponsored in parliament the bill which enabled, although it did not require, the country's medical licensing bodies to admit women to their examinations and confer upon them the qualifications entitling them to registration as doctors. The year before this the Gurneys had established a convalescent home for women in Bayswater and here, after her husband's death, Mrs Gurney spent the last eighteen years of her life ministering to the patients.

In addition to these members of parliament and their wives, there were a number of other men and women prominent in the political and social life of London who joined in the work of the Married Women's Property Committee. Among these was Thomas Hare, whose second wife, Eleanora, was a sister of Edward White Benson, archbishop of Canterbury.[34] Hare was a political reformer whose public career spanned more than fifty years. A lawyer, he edited and published a number of authoritative works on leading cases in the courts of equity, in which he practised, and was eventually elected a bencher of the Inner Temple, where he had been a student. He also served as inspector of charities and then as assistant commissioner of charities. Hare wrote a number of works on various reforms he espoused, including relaxation of the Navigation Acts, improved housing for the poor, and reform of local government in London. However, he was best known for his project of devising a system of representation whereby all classes in the kingdom would be fairly, because proportionately, represented in the House of Commons. His two major writings on this subject, published in the later 1850s, inspired a large literature and led to the establishment of various reform societies. The principle of proportional representation was supported enthusiastically, if unsuccessfully, by Mill and others of his Radical persuasion, such as Leonard Courtney.

Also prominent among the London supporters of the Married Women's Property Committee were William Ballantyne Hodgson and his wife Emily, daughter of Sir Joshua Walmsley.[35] Best known as an authority on political economy, Hodgson was one of the most distinguished educators of his day. He was also known for his strong liberal sympathies, although he took little part in politics. He held many important educational posts during his career, acting as secretary to the Mechanics' Institute of Liverpool and then as principal of Chorlton High School in Manchester; lecturing at the Royal Institution in London; becoming an assistant commissioner to the royal commission appointed in 1858 to study elementary education; serving as examiner in political economy to London University and sitting on the council of University College; and finally occupying the first chair of political economy and mercantile law to be established, largely through his efforts, at the University of Edinburgh, where he had been a student as a young man although he did not take a degree. Hodgson frequently attended and spoke at the congresses of the Social Science Association, and he published various works, chiefly on educational subjects but also including a biography of Turgot and a memorial edition of the works of W.J. Fox. The question of women's education was always a subject of great interest and concern to him. While he was working in Liverpool a girls' school was added to the Mechanics' Institute at his urging, and he was appointed its principal. While in Manchester, he agitated for the education of women at the Royal Institution in that city. In London he was a great friend and supporter of Frances Mary Buss, whose North London Collegiate School was the model for the reformed girls' schools that were beginning to be established. Two important lectures which he prepared on the need for reform were published in 1869 under the title *The Education of Girls; and the Employment of Women of the Upper Classes Educationally Considered*.

An important spokeswoman for women's causes in London was Frances Power Cobbe.[36] A lame, stout, serious-minded but high-spirited Irishwoman, Miss Cobbe had dutifully remained at home for years to manage the household of her widowed father. But after his death she had rejected the conventional niche of unmarried sister in her brother's home and set out to make her own way in the world, travelling widely and writing prolifically. Solely through her talent and her winning personality she became a popular figure in the literary and social world of London, where she was a regular staff member of *The Echo* during Arthur Arnold's tenure as editor. She was a theist, a disciple of the American theologian Theodore Parker, whose works she collected and edited for publication, and she wrote a number of widely acclaimed articles and books on theological and moral questions. A great lover of animals, she devoted much of her time and energy, especially in her later years, to the antivivisection crusade. Miss Cobbe's interest in social problems had been deepened by her early experience as Mary Carpenter's companion and helper in her work among the poor of Bristol. In London her friendships and her experiences as a journalist aroused her special interest in women's questions. She became a member of the Kensington Society, the London women's suffrage society, and the executive body of the Married Women's Property Committee, and she wrote many articles about women, some of which were later collected and published in two volumes under the titles *Duties of Women* and *Pursuits of Women*. She was especially concerned with the problem of battered wives, and her articles on 'Wife Torture' and her personal representations to members of the government helped to win passage of the Matrimonial Causes Act of 1878, with its provision that women whose husbands were convicted of aggravated assault upon them could obtain separation and maintenance orders from local magistrates.

Another among the prominent women supporters of the Married Women's Property Committee in London was Emilie Ashurst Venturi, who came from a well-known Radical family.[37] Her father was William Henry Ashurst, a solicitor famous for his championship of such causes as reform of the government of the City of London, postal reform, socialism, Chartism, and the abolition of slavery. At his home at Muswell Hill English reformers and political refugees from all countries found a hearty welcome. One of Ashurst's chief interests was the emancipation of the subject nationalities of Europe, and in particular the liberation and unification of Italy. His family were intimate friends of the exiled Mazzini, who brought them into contact with another of his great friends Jane Welsh Carlyle, and together with Peter Taylor the Ashursts played an active part in founding the Society of the Friends of Italy. Another of Ashurst's great interests was the emancipation of women. 'When asked why he had taken up the cause of women's rights, he would say that he had seen a girl tried for child murder, who had been betrayed by a man, was convicted by men, sentenced by a man, and hanged by a man.'

Bred in such an atmosphere, Ashurst's four daughters were considered 'bold and independent' and 'Mazzini noted that they all smoked, "a capital crime in English society."' The eldest daughter, Eliza, married a Frenchman named Bardonneau despite her family's disapproval. Matilda married Joseph Biggs, a well-known Radical of Leicester. Caroline Ashurst became the wife of James Stansfeld (later Sir James), a dedicated feminist who eventually sacrificed his promising career as a Liberal statesman to join with Josephine Butler in the campaign to win repeal of the Contagious Diseases Acts. Emilie Ashurst was married first to Sydney Hawkes, a lawyer friend of Stansfeld's and his partner in a brewing business which was dissolved because of disagreements and financial difficulties in 1853. Another brewery Hawkes set up went bankrupt the following year, and soon after this he and his wife parted company. In 1861 they were divorced. After their parting Emilie had devoted herself entirely to the Italian liberation movement and spent much of her time in Italy, and she had been the cause, at least indirectly, of a famous international incident of the time, the so-called Orsini Plot of 1858. The story goes that Stansfeld had complained to Mazzini about his friend Orsini's unwelcome attentions to Emilie Hawkes; Orsini then challenged Stansfeld to a duel, whereupon he was denounced by Mazzini and expelled from the Society of Italian Exiles in London; Orsini then left England determined to outshine Mazzini and proceeded to Paris, where he threw a bomb at the carriage of Emperor Napoleon III, who escaped unharmed although eight others were killed and 150 more were injured. The incident led to Orsini's execution and to angry charges by the French government that the British were harbouring alien terrorists. During her travels in Italy, Emilie Hawkes met and married Carlo Venturi, whom Thomas Carlyle described as 'a Tyrolese Venetian (ex-Austrian military cadet, and also Garibaldist to the bone, consequently in a bad Italian position), who had fallen in love at first sight, &c., &c.' The Venturis' marriage was tragically brief for shortly after their return to England to live, in 1866, Carlo died suddenly of a heart attack. Thereafter Emilie dedicated herself chiefly to the movement for repeal of the Contagious Diseases Acts, serving from 1871 to 1886 as editor of *The Shield*, the movement's official organ.

Two other women in the London circle of supporters of property-law reform may be briefly mentioned. One was Louisa Goldsmid, who had married her cousin Sir Francis Goldsmid, a distinguished financier and philanthropist like his father before him and a recognized leader and spokesman of the Jewish community, chiefly dedicated to removing their disabilities. Goldsmid was the first Jew to become a barrister and the first to become a queen's counsel, and in

1860, after passage of the bill opening parliament to Jews, he was elected member for Reading, which he represented till his death in 1878. Lady Goldsmid herself was a constant supporter of women's suffrage and women's education. She took a special interest in Girton College, founding a scholarship in her husband's memory and making other gifts to the college, and serving as a member of the governing body from 1872 until the year before her death in 1909. Frances Wedgwood, a daughter of Sir James Mackintosh, was the wife of Hensleigh Wedgwood, a grandson of Josiah Wedgwood of Etruria and cousin of Charles Darwin, and a scholar renowned as a philologist. Mrs Wedgwood, a great friend of Harriet Martineau, took a special interest in higher education for women. She served as a member of the council of Bedford College for Women and was also interested in Girton College, where in the early days one of her daughters, Julia, was a resident tutor in classics.[38]

Finally, mention should be made of two Irishwomen who worked for women's causes not only in their own country but also in England, both of them serving on the executive body of the Married Women's Property Committee. One was Isabella Tod of Belfast, who inherited from her liberal-minded mother 'the longing she felt from her youth up to improve the lot of women' and who 'studied diligently many things not usual with the girls of her day.' When the Social Science Association congress met in Belfast in 1867, Miss Tod was ready to be drawn into active work for women's education, women's suffrage, and repeal of the Contagious Diseases Acts as well as for property-law reform, and she began to pay annual visits to London during the parliamentary session to watch the legislative interests of Irishwomen. Josephine Butler hailed her as 'one of the ablest, and certainly the most eloquent, of our women workers,' and a fellow suffragist likewise paid tribute to the abilities and eloquence that made her 'foremost in the movement in Ireland' – 'the easy flow of well-chosen words, springing from the stores of a cultured and deeply religious mind, combined with some of the fighting temperament of her Scotch Presbyterian paternal ancestry.' The second of these women was Helena Pauline Downing, a niece of McCarthy Downing, who was MP for County Cork from 1868 till 1879. Especially active in the suffrage movement, 'this little bright-eyed Irishwoman never failed to win the sympathy of her hearers,' for her addresses were 'full of force and fire, mingled with pathos and humour.'[39]

Clearly the Married Women's Property Committee formed in the later 1860s was a much larger and more impressive group than Barbara Bodichon's little committee of the previous decade, those 'few literary ladies whose peculiar talents had placed them in a rather anomalous position,' as the *Saturday Review* described them. Given the circumstances of the time, it was a definite and perhaps a decisive advantage that this second Married Women's Property Committee, unlike its predecessor, included men as well as women in its membership. As Mill said, 'Women cannot be expected to devote themselves to the emancipation of women, unless men in considerable number are prepared to join them in the undertaking.'[40] And the men enlisted in the cause were important ones from all walks of public life – lawyers, members of parliament and of the bench, businessmen, scholars and educators, journalists, political economists, and political reformers generally. As for the women members of the committee, they benefited not only from this masculine support but also from the simple fact that they were a younger generation of workers in women's causes. The feminists of the fifties had provided them with models of intelligent and spirited women who first called public attention to the special needs of women and began work to remedy women's grievances. More directly, the younger women benefited from the friendly advice of those women who had been at work longer in the field and who had built up informal networks of relatives and personal friends as their supporters.

As a result of the interest and support of increasing numbers of women and men, the organized feminist movement, which had begun in the 1850s with the campaign to win reform of the married women's property law, had by now grown to encompass many other demands besides legal equality – demands for equality in education, in employment, in political life, and in sexual matters. There was always a good deal of specialization of labour among the workers in women's causes, so much so that some feminists came to be identified, at least in the public mind, as 'single-issue' people. For example, Josephine Butler was known in her own time and is remembered today chiefly for her campaigns against the Contagious Diseases Acts. But Mrs Butler also did important work for women's education and for property-law reform, so that her career, like many others, illustrates an interesting and important fact – that the proliferation of feminist demands had the effect of increasing rather than diminishing the support that could be mobilized for any one of these demands. Women and men who took up work for one of the women's causes almost invariably gave their time and talents to other women's causes as well, as occasion demanded and as opportunity afforded. Now, in 1868, all the forces that the Married Women's Property Committee could muster were called into action, and all the usual means of bringing pressure to bear upon public opinion and upon parliament were employed with good effect.

The Social Science Association continued to give its powerful support to the cause of property-law reform. At the association's annual congress held at Birmingham in the fall of 1868, three papers on the subject of the married women's property law were presented. The most important of these was the one by Arthur Hobhouse (later Sir Arthur), a most impressive recruit to the women's movement. In twenty years as a barrister he had built up a large Chancery practice and been named a queen's counsel. In 1866 he retired from active practice for reasons of health, and was appointed a member of the Charity Commission. Later he was to serve as a commissioner under the Endowed Schools Act of 1869, and then as a legal member of the council of the viceroy of India. In 1881 he became a member of the judicial committee of the Privy Council, a post he would hold for twenty years, and in 1885 he was elevated to the peerage as Baron Hobhouse of Hadspen. Hobhouse recalled afterward that the presentation of his paper to the Social Science Association in 1868 had elicited a great deal of discussion, during which all possible objections to reform were aired and found to be 'of a very flimsy character and admitting of obvious and specific answers.' Following this discussion a resolution was moved by Mary Johnson of Birmingham and seconded by Annie Robertson of Dublin, both of whom were active in the women's suffrage cause. Their resolution, condemning the 'injustice and inexpediency' of the common law and calling upon the council of the Social Science Association to continue its efforts to win parliamentary reform, was carried unanimously. In 1869 the Married Women's Property Committee held its second annual meeting in Bristol at the same time as the Social Science Association's congress and in conjunction with its first special Ladies' Conference. Among other business, a paper dealing with the Married Women's Property Bill then before parliament was presented by Alfred Hill, son of Matthew Davenport Hill. By the time the association held its congress in 1870, a Married Women's Property Bill had been passed by parliament.[41]

During this time there appeared a number of important books dealing with women's questions generally and including the question of married women's property rights. Overshadowing them all was Mill's *Subjection of Women*, a profound philosophical treatment of the whole question of the position of women, first published in 1869. In the same year there appeared a third edition of Barbara Bodichon's *Brief Summary ... of the Most Important Laws Concerning Women*, which had been revised to include material on the current agitation for reform of the married women's property law, although it emphasized chiefly the suffrage movement. Josephine Butler's *Woman's Work and Woman's Culture* was also published in 1869. Included were essays by Frances Power Cobbe on the moral responsibility of women; Elizabeth Wolstenholme on the education of girls; Jessie Boucherett on 'redundant women'; George Butler on education as a profession for women; Sophia Jex-Blake, pioneer of women doctors, on medicine as a profession for women; Julia Wedgwood on the suffrage movement; and John Boyd Kinnear, a member of the executive committee of the Married Women's Property Committee, on the social position of women. In particular, the volume included essays by Charles H. Pearson, 'On Some Historical Aspects of Family Life,' which dealt with the law of property, and by Herbert N. Mozley, another member of the executive of the Married Women's Property Committee, on 'The Property Disabilities of a Married Woman, and Other Legal Effects of Marriage.'

The power of the daily and periodical press was also called into play to stimulate interest in reform of the property law. Numerous leaders and important articles on the subject of reform appeared. Frances Power Cobbe's article entitled 'Criminals, Idiots, Women and Minors: Is the Classification Sound?' was published in *Fraser's Magazine* in 1868. In the same year the *Contemporary Review* published articles by two other members of the executive of the Married Women's Property Committee: 'The Marriage Laws of England and Scotland,' by John Boyd Kinnear, and 'The Injustice of the English Law as It Bears on the Relationship of Husband and Wife,' by Alfred Dewes, a clergyman of Manchester. These articles and some of the speeches that were delivered in parliament on the subject of reform were reprinted by the Married Women's Property Committee in the form of pamphlets, of which 8,000 copies were distributed in 1868 and 27,000 the following year.[42]

Press articles dwelt especially upon the practical hardships in everyday life that resulted from the state of the married women's property law, and one case in particular, which occurred in 1869, seemed providentially sent for propaganda purposes. This was the case of Susannah Palmer, a poor working woman who was convicted in the Recorder's Court in London of stabbing her husband, and was sentenced to imprisonment in Newgate. (Russell Gurney presided at her trial.) Her husband had treated her brutally for many years, beating her, turning her and their children out of the house into the streets at night and bringing in other women, and at last showing an incestuous interest in his own daughter. Susannah Palmer had finally left her husband in order to establish a new home and support herself and her children by her own efforts. But then her husband appeared and seized all her possessions, as he had every legal right to do, and at last she struck back. The facts of the case, detailed in court and publicized by Frances Power Cobbe in *The Echo* and by other writers, aroused such interest that a public subscription was raised to provide for Susannah Palmer and her children. Fortunately she had only wounded and not killed her husband, and when she was released from prison after a few months a post was found for her where she would be safe from him. But, a final irony, the money and articles of furniture collected for her could not be given to her legally, for then they would have been her husband's property, so that everything had to be put into the name of the sheriffs of London as the legal owners.[43]

On the whole, it seems, the leading newspapers and periodicals favoured reform. Among the exceptions were the *Saturday Review*, always a hopeless case from the feminist point of view, and *The Times*. However, the latter was inconsistent in its position, and its shifting stance was an interesting indication of changing political fortunes and public opinion – from adamant opposition to reform in 1868, to grudging admission of the need for some limited measure of reform the next year, to enthusiastic support of reform by 1870.

To impress parliament with the widespread feeling in the country in favour of reform, members of the Married Women's Property Committee undertook an extensive campaign of writing letters and circulating petitions. Sympathetic MPs received innumerable written pleas for reform, together with information and arguments to be used in the debates. Signatures were collected on petitions which were sent in to be presented in parliament. Millicent Garrett Fawcett later recalled her own experience of circulating a petition at a meeting of Liberal voters, held at her old family home in Suffolk and including chiefly farmers of the neighbourhood. One old man asked her, 'Am I to understand you, ma'am, that if the bill becomes law and my wife had a matter of a hundred pounds left her, I should have to *arst* her for it?' When she answered truthfully 'yes,' she got no more signatures. All together the Married Women's Property Committee presented 29 petitions with some 33,000 signatures to parliament in 1868. The following year the committee presented to the House of Commons 113 petitions with more than 42,000 signatures, including one petition signed by John Stuart Mill and nearly 1,400 others and one presented for Susannah Palmer by Russell Gurney, while 70 petitions with some 30,000 signatures were presented to the House of Lords.[44]

All of this work for and by women had the desired effect. Public interest in property-law reform was aroused, and the public conscience was pricked. Of greater immediate importance was the fact that parliament was now again prepared to deal with the question. Standing together with Mill and the other well-known friends of women's causes already mentioned were some of the ablest men in the House of Commons who, although they had not identified themselves with the work of the Married Women's Property Committee, now made reform of the property law their special concern.[45]

First among these was George John Shaw-Lefevre (afterward Baron Eversley), another of the young men of whom Mill expected great things. Son of a distinguished public servant and nephew of Sir Charles Eversley, an outstanding speaker of the House, Shaw-Lefevre was a lawyer who entered parliament in 1863 as Liberal member for Reading. He quickly made a great impression with his speeches expressing sympathy for the Union in the American Civil War and concern over British policy toward the United States, and in 1868 he carried an important resolution in favour of arbitration of the *Alabama* claims. The same year he became secretary to the Board of Trade, of which John Bright was president, and in 1873 he was named secretary to the admiralty. Shaw-Lefevre was also an early environmentalist and conservationist, the founder and almost lifelong chairman of the Commons Preservation Society, which included Mill and Fawcett among its distinguished members. Shaw-Lefevre never in fact attained the front rank in politics despite his early promise, serving only twice in the cabinet, as postmaster general after Fawcett's death in 1884 and as president of the Local Government Board under Rosebery. But at this time he was being talked of as a future prime minister, and it was he who introduced the Married Women's Property Bill in parliament in the spring of 1868.

Another of the women's important supporters was George Osborne Morgan (later Sir George), a brilliant lawyer and queen's counsel who entered parliament in 1868 as Liberal member for Denbighshire. He quickly became the acknowledged leader of the Welsh party in the Commons, and constantly pressed for home rule for Wales and disestablishment of the Welsh Church. Perhaps best known for his opposition to all religious disabilities, Morgan finally carried through parliament the Burials Bill, which removed a long-standing grievance of Dissenters by ending the requirement that the funeral services of Dissenters interred in Anglican cemeteries be conducted by Anglican clergymen. Morgan was to become judge advocate general in Gladstone's second ministry in 1880, and parliamentary undersecretary for the colonies in Gladstone's third ministry. He favoured improved education for women as well as reform of the married women's property law, but from the women's point of view he was by no means an entirely satisfactory champion, for he later opposed repeal of the Contagious Diseases Acts, perhaps because of his official interest in the army.

Rather surprisingly, property-law reform was also energetically and forcefully supported by the controversial Robert Lowe, Liberal member for Calne, who was by no means known for his democratic or Radical sympathies. As the minister in charge of education under Palmerston, Lowe had been forced to resign because of criticism of his policies, and he had led the dissident Liberals known as 'Adullamites' who opposed Lord John Russell's Reform Bill of 1866 and helped bring down Russell's government. But Lowe's talents were of a high order, and he could not be denied high office when the Liberals returned to power in 1868. He proved equally controversial as chancellor of the exchequer and then as home secretary, and the end of the Liberal government in 1874 also marked the effective end of his own political life. When the Liberals returned to office in 1880, Lowe was 'kicked upstairs' to the House of Lords as Viscount Sherbrooke.

Finally, a very important champion of the women's cause was Sir George Jessel. A highly successful lawyer, he entered parliament in 1868 as Liberal member for Dover, one of the first Jews to be elected to the House of Commons. Jessel's legal talents quickly attracted the attention of Gladstone, who named him solicitor general in 1871, and it was Jessel who was chiefly responsible for piloting through the Commons the great Judicature Bill of 1873. The same year he succeeded Lord Romilly as master of the rolls, and he proved to be one of the ablest men ever to hold that high judicial position, contributing significantly to the development of the doctrines of equity in the many leading cases which he decided.

Few important members of the House of Commons spoke in opposition to reform of the married women's property law. Next to the veteran antifeminist Beresford-Hope, the two most prominent and persistent opponents of reform were Henry Charles Lopes (later Sir Henry, and afterward Baron Ludlow) and Henry Cecil Raikes. A successful lawyer and queen's counsel who served as recorder of Exeter, Lopes was elected to parliament as a Conservative, at Launceston in 1868 and at Frome in 1874. Two years later he was appointed a justice of the new Supreme Court of Judicature, on which he served creditably but with no special distinction. Raikes had practised law for only a few years before his election to parliament in 1868 as Conservative member for Chester. He quickly won a place in Conservative counsels, and was chosen chairman of committees on the Conservatives' return to power in 1874. He was defeated at the election of 1880, but two years later re-entered parliament as member for Preston. He soon resigned this seat to become member for the University of Cambridge, and served ably as postmaster general from 1886 until his death five years later.

So in the early summer of 1868 the stage again was set for parliamentary action on the married women's property law and for the full-dress debate that the question of reform had not received a decade earlier. Before considering the course of parliamentary action, it will be well to look in some detail at the accompanying debate both within parliament and out-of-doors, for this was one of the first and most thorough public airings of the whole 'rights of women' question.

7

'The Burthen of Proof'
The Great Debate
on Reform

All of the arguments advanced by women and their friends in favour of property-law reform can be summed up in the words of the preamble of the Married Women's Property Bill which George Shaw-Lefevre introduced in the House of Commons in 1868 and Russell Gurney the following year – that the existing law was 'unjust in principle' and that it pressed 'with peculiar severity upon the poorer classes of the community.'[1]

In the debates Mill seized the high ground at once, basing his case for women upon the principle of liberty. 'The old theory was,' he said, 'that the least possible should be left to the choice of the individual,' but 'the modern conviction, the fruit of a thousand years of experience, is, that things in which the individual is the person directly interested, never go right but as they are left to his own discretion; and that any regulation of them by authority, except to protect the rights of others, is sure to be mischievous.' This being the modern conviction, Mill declared, then 'the burthen of proof is ... with those who are against liberty.' Robert Lowe likewise placed 'the burthen of proof' upon opponents of reform, challenging them to show how the existing law could be defended on 'any principles of equity or justice.'

Yet Mill had no illusions about the ease of arguing the case for women. 'So long as an opinion is strongly rooted in the feelings,' he said, 'it gains rather than loses in stability by having a preponderating weight of argument against it ... the worse it fares in argumentative contest, the more persuaded its adherents are that their feeling must have some deeper ground, which the arguments do not reach ...' A good example of this kind of reaction was the comment by one member of the Commons that 'there were more things with respect to this important relation [of man and woman] in heaven and earth "than were dreamt of in his [Mill's] philosophy,"' and that 'one of the greatest of philosophers had written the most fanciful and even the most irrational things with regard to women.' Nevertheless, Mill urged that the whole question of the position of women 'should not be considered as prejudged by existing fact and opinion, but open to discussion on its merits, as a question of justice and expediency,' adding that this should be 'a real discussion ... not resting satisfied with vague and general assertions.' But it was just the 'vague and general assertions' Mill denigrated that he and his supporters met with in the debates.

First, opponents of reform argued that the subjection of women was sanctioned by universal custom. Lord Penzance, the chief opponent of reform in the upper House of parliament, declared that 'the relations of husband and wife were founded upon a condition of things which had existed without exception in all times and in all parts of the earth – the husband being the protector and support of the wife and the latter subordinate to and reliant upon him ... and ... the law obviously ought to follow in the same track.'[2]

That women had lived in subjection to men since earliest times and in every place was no argument for their continuing in that state, Mill replied. The subjection of women 'never was the result of deliberation, or forethought, or any social ideas, or any notion whatever of what conduced to the benefit of humanity or the good order of society.' On the contrary, said Mill, women's subjection rested upon the fact that 'from the very earliest twilight of human society, every woman ... was found in a state of bondage to some man. Laws and systems of polity always begin by recognizing the relations they find already existing between individuals.'

According to Mill the root of women's legal inferiority to men lay in their physical inferiority to men, and their legal subjection was the last relic of the old 'law of the strongest' which placed 'right on the side of might.' A woman was indeed 'the actual bondservant of her husband,' said Mill, for she 'vows a lifelong obedience to him at the altar, and is held to it all through life by the law.' Jessel likewise pointed out that the legal position of a married woman was exactly that of a slave, a person who could not own property, enter into contracts, or sue for injuries, and who could be beaten and imprisoned by a master whose only obligation was that he must not let the other starve. Mill, together with Lowe and Gurney, also pointed out that one of the chief penalties imposed by marriage upon women, 'whom,' said Mill, 'we profess to desire to surround with marks of honour and dignity,' was the same as that imposed upon traitors and felons – that is, confiscation of their property. (This penalty for treason and felony was abolished in 1870.)

Opponents of reform could, however, turn these arguments about the physical inferiority of women the other way around. Denying that marriage and the marriage laws were the last vestiges of slavery, they maintained that, as *The Times* put it, the law 'followed nature, and ... laid a just foundation for marriage.'[3] The law, said Lopes, 'recognized the fact that the wife was the weaker vessel, that there ought to be only one head of the house, and that the husband was the proper head, being physically, at all events, better fitted to bear the brunt of the outer world than his wife.' Opponents of reform never quite said that women were the natural inferiors of men except in physical strength, although this opinion was implicit in much that they did say. What they argued was that women were meant by nature to be wives and mothers, and so they should be placed under the legal protection of their husbands.

To this argument that the subjection of women 'followed nature,' Mill replied first by asking 'was there ever any domination which did not appear natural to those who possessed it? ... So true it is,' he added, 'that unnatural generally means uncustomary, and that everything which is usual appears natural.' How long had absolute monarchy been considered the 'natural' form of government? How long had slavery itself seemed part of the 'natural' order of things? Now, these cases of the right of the 'stronger' to rule the 'weaker' had passed away, but not the subjection of women.

Developing the theme of the nature of women and of their 'natural' subjection further, Mill observed that the 'general opinion of men is supposed to be, that the natural vocation of a woman is that of wife and mother.' He added, 'I say, is supposed to be because, judging from acts ... one might infer that their opinion was the direct contrary ... and that the alleged vocation of women was of all things the most repugnant to their nature; insomuch that if they are free to do anything else ... there will not be enough of them willing to accept the condition said to be natural to them.' But women were not 'free to do anything else.' They were limited in their opportunities to obtain a sound education, and were constantly exhorted to cultivate the virtues of submission, dependence upon others, and self-sacrifice. They were hampered by social convention and in some cases prevented by law from entering occupations and professions outside the home. For them marriage was the only realistic option, the only socially acceptable career. This being true, Mill continued, it might seem that everything would have been done to make the condition of marriage as attractive to women as possible, 'that they might have no cause to regret being denied the option of any other.' Yet society 'has preferred to obtain its object by foul rather than fair means,' Mill said, citing in particular the laws relating to the custody of children and the property of married women.

On the whole question of the nature of women Mill denied that 'any one knows, or can know, the nature of the two sexes, as long as they have only been seen in their present relation to one another.' What was then called the 'nature of women,' he maintained, was 'an eminently artificial thing' for 'no other class of dependents have had their character so entirely distorted from its natural proportions by their relations with their masters.' Mill himself believed that the existing differences between men and women resulted from differences in their education and circumstances, and indicated 'no radical differences, far less radical inferiority, of nature.' Shaw-Lefevre summed up well on this point when he said, 'Let them have as far as possible fair play, remove unequal legislation, and women would then speedily find their true level, whatever that might be, for which by nature they were intended.'

But still opponents of reform argued that the subjection of wives to their husbands not only was natural and therefore universal, but also was sanctioned by religion. 'As in the eyes of the Church the two become one flesh [in marriage], so in the eyes of the law they become one person,' said *The Times*,[4] while in parliament Beresford-Hope, in his usual form, asserted, 'Old fashioned people like himself were not ashamed to declare that it was written in nature and in Scripture that the husband was and ought to be lord of his household, the regulator of its concerns, and the protector of its inmates ...'

To this argument Mill replied that 'every established fact which is too bad to admit of any other defence, is always presented to us as an injunction of religion.' The Church, he admitted, enjoined women's obedience to men in its formularies but, he maintained, 'it would be difficult to derive any such injunction from Christianity.' It was true that St Paul said, 'Wives, obey your husbands,' but he also said, 'Slaves, obey your masters,' and 'The powers that be are ordained by God.' St Paul's acceptance of the social institutions of the early Christian world, said Mill, was not 'to be construed as disapproval of attempts to improve them at the proper time.' No one any longer maintained, on the basis of Pauline pronouncements, that Christianity favoured the existence of slavery or that 'military despotism' was 'the Christian form of political government.' Why, then, maintain that the subjection of women was a basic tenet of Christianity? On the contrary, said Mill, 'the equality of human beings ... is the theory of Christianity,' but he added that Christianity would never teach this practically while it sanctioned 'institutions grounded on the arbitrary preference of one human being over another.'

Still, opponents of reform appealed to long experience of the existing state of things, and they were fond of extolling, besides the wisdom of the common law, its antiquity, its origins being traceable back to the Norman Conquest, and its slow, majestic growth. As *The Times* editorialized, 'Our present law is rough, as the inheritance of rough times ... But rude justice is often substantially just; and ... the sentiments of our forefathers on the present question afford an eminent instance of this rule.'[5]

In rebuttal Mill argued that the long experience of women's subjection under the law was no argument in favour of their subjection as opposed to their equality. 'Experience,' he said, 'cannot possibly have decided between two courses, so long as there has only been experience of one. If it be said that the doctrine of the equality of the sexes rests only on theory, it must be remembered that the contrary doctrine also has only theory to rest upon.' That is, until equality for women had been tried as well as subjection, no one could say which was the better state.

In addition Jacob Bright and Herbert Mozley pointed out that, however ancient and majestic, the common law relating to married women's property was inconsistent in principle. If it were based upon the supposed inferiority of women to men, then it should place unmarried women in the same position as married women by depriving them of the right to own property. If the law were based upon a husband's right to his wife's property, then it should allow him to take her real property as absolutely as he took her personal property.[6] In this connection George Hastings, together with John Westlake, a fellow lawyer and a colleague of his in the Social Science Association, suggested that the common law had originally embodied an ideal of partnership between husband and wife, since it protected the real property of married women at a time when this property was of paramount importance and personal property of little. But this ideal had been obscured with the passage of time, as personal property, which was not secured to married women by the law, increased so greatly in importance relative to real property.

Robert Lowe insisted that one must return to first principles, to the first question that needed to be asked about the law. That question, he said, was not whether the common law could be traced through 'a long succession of ages in the most barbarous times' but whether it was 'founded on justice and righteousness, equality and fairness, or ... on injustice, tyranny and oppression.'

But, opponents argued, public opinion supported the existing state of things. The law, Lopes declared, 'was in accordance with public feeling' generally, and Lord Penzance did not think that women themselves 'would desire a change in the order of Providence which was the source of the highest pleasures which either men or women could enjoy.'[7]

Mill agreed with his opponents on this point. It was his mission to change public opinion. Clearly the great majority of men favoured the existing laws. Those who 'have a real antipathy to the equal freedom of women,' Mill said, 'are afraid, not lest women should be unwilling to marry ... but lest they should insist that marriage should be on equal conditions; lest all women of spirit and capacity should prefer doing almost anything else, not in their own eyes degrading, rather than marry, when marrying is giving themselves a master, and a master too of all their earthly possessions.' Mill maintained that a great many women did not accept their present position gracefully and gratefully. Thousands of women, including some of the most eminent in the country, had petitioned parliament for the right to vote; women were claiming with increasing intensity their right to be educated as well as men were; women were demanding admission to professions and occupations that were closed to them. 'How many more women there are who silently cherish similar aspirations, no one can possibly know,' Mill said, 'but there are abundant tokens how many *would* cherish them, were they not so strenuously taught to repress them as contrary to the proprieties of their sex.'

Having demonstrated, to their own satisfaction at least, that the existing law was just – being in accord with universal custom, rooted in nature, sanctioned by religion, proved by long experience, and supported by public opinion – opponents proceeded to denounce the proposed reform of the property law as 'revolutionary.' *The Times* declared that reform would cause 'a social revolution' that would 'abolish families in the old sense' and 'break up society again into men and women.'[8] Reform, said Lopes, would create 'discomfort, ill-feeling, and distrust where hitherto harmony and concord prevailed.' It would, Raikes argued, 'disturb the peace of every family and destroy for ever that identity of interests between husband and wife, which had hitherto been regarded as the basis of the Christian family and the peculiar characteristic of English society.'

Opponents of reform seemed especially disturbed at the prospect that married women's increased independence of attitude and action, which would inevitably result from this 'revolutionary' reform, would lead to a great deal of 'immorality.' One member of the Commons asked nervously whether it would be 'conducive to the happiness of married life if a woman, perhaps a good woman, but still possessed of personal attractions was to go out into the world and be negotiating in shares or in other affairs of life with agents and people of various classes, who might not be notorious for their high notions as to what was right.' Another member suggested that financial independence 'would so free a woman from restraint in any quarrel she might have with her husband' that she could say, 'I have my own property, and if you don't like me I can go and live with somebody who does.'

To those fearful of increased 'immorality,' reformers were quick to respond. The danger of going 'out into the world' to negotiate in the 'affairs of life' would be no greater for married women that it was for unmarried women who managed their own property, and probably 'it would be less.' Jessel then asked whether opponents of reform were willing 'to act in the analogous case, and ... deprive the husband of his property because it sometimes was applied to support a mistress?' More generally, Mill remarked upon the fact that 'we are perpetually told that women are better than men, by those who are totally opposed to treating them as if they were as good,' adding that this was all 'tiresome cant, intended to put a complimentary face upon an injury.'

According to Robert Lowe, what opponents were really saying when they claimed that the reform was revolutionary and would destroy domestic tranquillity was that 'unless you put the whole property of a married couple into the hands of the husband and give him, like this House [of Commons], the power of stopping the supplies whenever he thinks proper, there is no chance of concord and harmony in the marriage state.' For his part, Gurney could not understand how 'any one who really knew what domestic harmony was' could make such claims. Mill realized that some people were 'sentimentally shocked' at the idea of separate property interests between husband and wife, as being inconsistent with 'the ideal fusion of two lives into one.' He added that he himself was 'one of the strongest supporters of community of goods, when resulting from an entire unity of feeling in the owners, which makes all things common between them.' But, he said, he had no relish for 'a community of goods resting on the doctrine that what is mine is yours but what is yours is not mine.'

It was not true, Mill continued, that 'in all voluntary association between two people, one of them must be the absolute master: still less that the law must determine which of them it shall be.' The law did not decree in other partnerships that one partner should have 'entire control of the concern' and that the others were 'bound to obey his orders.' The natural way, Mill argued, was 'a division of powers between the two ... [not] pre-established by the law, since it must depend on individual capacities and suitabilities.' In like vein Arthur Hobhouse maintained that a wife ought to have 'due weight in the family counsels,' that in many domestic matters 'women are better judges than men,' that many women 'are wiser and stronger than their husbands,' and that 'it is a monstrous thing to assume that the husband must always be right, and therefore to give him ... all ... the power.'[9]

In this connection one member of the Commons quipped that if the Married Women's Property Bill was passed, the marriage service would have to be changed; a woman could hardly promise to 'love, honour and obey' her husband, but would have to say that she would enter into a partnership with him on equal terms. To this Shaw-Lefevre retorted that the marriage service already needed changing for, as it stood, the husband said that he endowed his wife with all his worldly goods, but actually it was exactly the other way around.

The basic question here, as reformers clearly saw, was not one of property but of power – of 'sexual politics,' to use a twentieth-century phrase. As Priscilla Bright McLaren later observed, many husbands could not bear the thought of their wives' having property and therefore power.[10] The legal disabilities of women, said Mill, were 'only clung to in order to maintain their subordination in domestic life; because the generality of the male sex cannot yet tolerate the idea of living with an equal.'

Yet in the face of general male prejudice Mill went on to argue that equality for wives in marriage was not merely a matter of justice to them but was also the real source of domestic happiness. 'Even with true affection,' he said, 'authority on the one side and subordination on the other prevent perfect confidence,' and 'thorough knowledge of one another hardly ever exists, but between persons who, besides being intimates, are equals.' With special poignance, in view of his own married life, now ended, Mill said, 'What marriage may be in the case of two persons ... between whom there exists that best kind of equality ... I will not attempt to describe. To those who can conceive it, there is no need; to those who cannot, it would appear the dream of an enthusiast.' But, he concluded, 'I maintain, with the profoundest conviction, that this, and this only, is the ideal of marriage.'

Going beyond assertions that greater independence for women would tend to increase rather than to destroy domestic happiness, reformers argued that women's independence would improve the tone and condition of society generally. With their independence, said Jacob Bright, there would come 'an increase of respect for women, and of real respect, which is a hundred times more valuable than the conventional politeness which it is always so easy to pay.' Among the working classes in particular, a man 'would feel that the woman was not the mere drudge that she is now so often ... if she was a woman who had an independent existence and independent rights.'

Taking a much broader view than this, Mill held that the root of all 'the selfish propensities, the self-worship, the unjust self-preference' that existed, and the 'principal nourishment' of these, could be found in the existing relationship between men and women. 'Think what it is to a boy,' he said, 'to grow up to manhood in the belief that ... by the mere fact of being born a male he is by right the superior of ... an entire half of the human race ... Is it imagined,' he asked, 'that all this does not pervert the whole existence of the man, both as an individual and as a social being?' The family as it existed, he declared, was 'a school of despotism,' for it could not inculcate the 'true virtue of human beings,' which was 'fitness to live together as equals; claiming nothing for themselves but what they as freely concede to every one else ...' But the family 'justly constituted,' according to Mill, 'would be the real school of the virtues of freedom.' For parents it would be 'a school of sympathy in equality, of living together in love, without power on one side or obedience on the other,' and for children it would be 'a model' of 'feelings and conduct.' In short, said Mill, 'the moral regeneration of mankind will only really commence, when the most fundamental of the social relations is placed under the rule of equal justice, and when human beings learn to cultivate their strongest sympathy with an equal in rights.'

To sum up, Mill and his supporters could not truly deny their opponents' charge that the reform they favoured was 'revolutionary' – despite Mill's quip that the many distinguished statesmen and jurists on both sides of the House who supported the Married Women's Property Bill were, of course, 'eminent socialists and revolutionaries.' Gurney, for one, conceded that the bill was revolutionary, if this meant that it would effect a great change. Its passage would, in fact, represent a long step forward on the road to equality for women in marriage and in society generally, and the 'principle of perfect equality' of the sexes for which Mill and others spoke was indeed a revolutionary ideal.

Descending from the high plains of debate on matters of principle, opponents of reform next turned to practical matters, foreseeing a number of difficulties that would result from reform. For one thing, they argued that even if reform was enacted, a man would still be liable to support his wife, which was one sound reason why the existing law allowed him to have control of her property, and they suggested that a wife might refuse to pay anything out of her own property toward the expenses of maintaining the household and providing for the children.

Reformers had a good deal to say in reply to this objection. Lydia Becker, for one, argued that whether or not a wife brought her husband property upon marriage, she was entitled to be supported by him 'as an equivalent for services rendered' – that is, 'the performance by her of the duties of a wife.' In fact, Miss Becker maintained, a wife's position was not so good as that of a servant in her own household, for a cook or footman received wages as well as maintenance for services rendered, while a wife received only maintenance and no wages.[11] Other reformers agreed that if the law were to place upon men a real responsibility for support of their families, it would be only fair to place a similar responsibility upon women. But as things were, a man had only the legal obligation not to allow his wife and children to become charges on the parish. Questions of the strictly legal responsibility of a woman aside, *The Times*, now in its period of more lucid opinion, asked, 'Is there any reason to suppose that she [a married woman] will be less faithful to the marriage relation when she has the responsibility of property, and when society looks to her to advance the interests of her children, than when she is dependent for everything upon her husband ...?' There was no reason to fear, the writer continued, for 'a certain degree of pecuniary independence tends to the promotion of morality and the proper fulfillment of the duties of life.'[12]

Opponents next suggested that reform would 'revolutionize' the existing system of retail credit to the great peril of tradesmen, who would never know which of two marriage partners they were trusting for a debt or whether they would ever be paid. As Beresford-Hope put it, every household would be transformed into 'a limited company consisting of two partners, neither of whom could be fixed with liability for the debts of the establishment.'

Reformers easily countered this objection. Arthur Hobhouse stated that tradesmen at present encountered no difficulties when dealing with people who lived together but had separate property interests, as, for example, in the case of a daughter keeping house for her father, a sister for her brother, or even a servant for a master. If the law was changed, tradesmen would simply make it their business to know which of the partners in a marriage they were trusting for a debt.[13] In addition Gurney pointed out that as the law of agency stood, the law under which wives could contract debts in their husbands' names, it was always a matter for a jury to determine whether a wife had her own property – that is, separate property in equity – and if so, she was liable to pay for articles supplied to her by tradesmen.

Opponents argued too that reform, by giving married women the right to property, would also subject them to the liabilities of property. Specifically, women themselves and not their husbands would be liable to pay debts they incurred and damages for torts they committed, and would be liable to imprisonment for non-payment. Lopes and others conjured up gloomy pictures of husbands coming home to dinner at night only to find their wives dragged off to jail. (Imprisonment as a penalty for debtors was abolished in 1869.) Some opponents even argued that the proposed reform would have little effect, for the only 'right' which married women would gain would be the right to be sued. This clearly contradicted their simultaneous claim that the reform was 'revolutionary,' a contradiction which reformers were quick to point out.

In reply Mill spoke contemptuously of the law that made a man responsible for his wife's acts 'as a master is for the acts of his slaves or of his cattle.' George Hastings pointed out that even under the existing law married women could be imprisoned for debt, and that this occasionally happened. That is, a woman with separate property in equity who had been successfully sued and who refused to pay could be imprisoned; if a woman had no separate property, the courts would order her released. Hastings and Arthur Hobhouse submitted that imprisonment was not good for anybody, but it was good that people who did not meet their responsibilities should suffer the consequences – 'as they sow, so should they reap.' It was, in fact, a favourite theme of the reformers that equal rights for women did and must entail equal responsibilities as well. One writer went so far as to declare, 'It is not so much in the rights refused to them as in the obligations which are not imposed on them that consists the injury done to women by the law.'[14]

Opponents argued finally that the proposed reform would not effect the object sought – that is, the protection of married women and their property against their husbands. A brutal man, so Lopes and others suggested, would not be deterred by the new law from seizing his wife's property and earnings if he wished, while a more gentle type of husband could easily persuade his wife to give her property to him.

While law may not effectively deter acts which are considered immoral or undesirable, law can certainly punish such acts. As for a wife 'coaxed out of her money' by her husband, Jessel observed that 'at any rate she would get the benefit of the coaxing,' to which Osborne Morgan added that 'there was a vast difference between allowing persons to injure themselves and allowing the law to injure them. The one they could not prevent – the other they could and ought.'

To all the arguments about practical difficulties that would result from amendment of the married women's property law, reformers also replied that where this law had been amended, no difficulties had in fact arisen. One had only to look across the Atlantic, where both the United States and Canada had inherited the English common law and had seen fit to amend its provisions relating to married women's property. English reformers paid especially close attention to the results of reform in the important states of New York, which had amended its married women's property law in 1848 and again in 1860, and Massachusetts, which had done so in 1855. Inspired by the example of the United States and also, perhaps, by Sir Erskine Perry's Married Women's Property Bill of 1857, Canada had carried through reform in 1859. An interesting fact brought out in this connection was that in the southern United States, where many former slaves had hastened to marry after their emancipation, black women had soon begun to shun marriage, for they found they had simply exchanged one master for another. As slaves they could not legally marry, but they could hold property at their masters' pleasure; as freedwomen they could legally marry but they lost their property to their husbands, since many southern states had not amended the common law relating to married women's property.[15] The testimony from abroad was unanimous: wherever reform had been carried through it worked well, there was general satisfaction with the change, and no demands were heard for a return to the old system.

Predictably, opponents of reform in England were not impressed. 'It is notorious,' declared *The Times*, that in the United States 'the more normal relations of the sexes are for the time reversed. The men are more numerous than the women; and women, consequently, can assert a degree of independence which would be neither possible nor desirable for them in a settled country.'[16] Denying that he was about to raise 'an alarm cry against Americanizing our institutions,' Beresford-Hope proceeded to do precisely that. In particular, he claimed that in the United States 'free trade in divorce' prevailed, whereas in England 'indissoluble marriage' was the rule and married life was in a more 'pure and satisfactory condition,' and the reason must lie in the laws governing marriage. Lopes likewise appealed to his colleagues not to look for their models abroad but to consider 'the homes of England, nurtured and fostered under the existing law, and ... say where could be found so much domestic happiness, so much conjugal felicity.'

In vain did Gurney try to reassure his opponents that this was no 'leap in the dark' – the phrase Lord Derby had used to describe the Reform Bill of 1867 – but a reform of tried and proven value.

If opponents could not be persuaded by evidence of successful reform abroad, they were still faced by evidence of successful reform already carried out at home – that is, the existence of marriage settlements in equity, which provided for the wealthy classes relief from the provisions of the common law. The mere existence of such settlements, according to reformers, undermined their opponents' whole case, based as it was on the claim that the common law was just and that reform of the law would be revolutionary. Arthur Hobhouse declared, 'Those who contend that the principle of the common law is not bad are bound to give some satisfactory explanation of ... why all who can escape from it do so. No such explanation has ever been attempted.'[17] Every marriage settlement drawn up, said Lowe, was a tacit condemnation of the common law. No member of parliament would allow his own daughter to marry without a settlement, and now parliament should stand *in loco parentis* for all women, granting them the protection of their property which was available only to wealthy women. Jessel called it amazing that the common law on this subject had survived into the nineteenth century, and said that the only reason for this was that 'the laws of this country were made by the rich and for the rich, and wealthy women had no cause of complaint.' When Gurney conceded that the Married Women's Property Bill was 'revolutionary' in that it would effect a great change, he added that it simply followed the lead of bodies which were not noted for their revolutionary policies – that is, the courts of equity.

In turn Lopes and other opponents of reform denied that marriage settlements in equity implied condemnation of the common law and were analogous to the proposed amendment of the married women's property law. They were certainly on firm ground when they maintained that the purpose of marriage settlements was not to give married women absolute control over their property but to protect the property settled and make an inalienable provision for husbands and children as well as wives. Yet they could not deny that marriage settlements created separate property interests between husband and wife, protecting a married woman against her husband's common-law rights and giving her a great deal of control, if not absolute power, over her property. Nor did they meet Shaw-Lefevre's challenge to assert, as logically they should have done, that marriages among the upper classes, with their marriage settlements and separate property interests of husband and wife, were less happy than marriages among the lower classes, who could not escape the operation of the common law.

In addition to their argument that the existence of marriage settlements in equity bore witness to the injustice of the common law, reformers pointed out that the provisions of equity were subject to almost as much criticism as those of the common law. In the first place, marriage settlements were not really just to women and might not protect them fully. It was true, Mill said, that a marriage settlement prevented a husband from squandering his wife's capital, but this was done at the price of 'debarring the rightful owner from its use,' for in equity a wife's control over her separate property belonged, technically at least, to her trustee and not to her. It was also true, Mill said, that a marriage settlement precluded payment of the income from a wife's settled property to her husband, but 'if he takes it from her by personal violence as soon as she receives it, he can neither be punished, nor compelled to restitution.'

In the second place, reformers said, marriage settlements in equity allowed and even encouraged frauds. For example, Herbert Mozley reminded his readers that they had doubtless heard of cases of bankers who defrauded their customers by resorting to equity. Money deposited in a bank became legally the banker's property, customers then having the legal right to sue to recover their deposits as personal debts owed them. But the banker might, by equitable procedures, settle his customers' money upon his wife, and if she was not an accomplice to the fraud but acted in good faith, agreeing to the settlement as being made for a valuable consideration, that of marriage, then the settlement could not be set aside and the hapless customers of the bank would be, in effect but not in equity, robbed.[18] Also, John Westlake testified that married women with separate property in equity resorted to all sorts of 'shifts' to avoid having their financial obligations made good out of their separate property. This, he added, 'speaks very ill for the moral effect upon married women of the present condition of things, by which they are allowed ... the benefit, without the responsibility, of property.'

Finally, returning to their main theme, reformers emphasized that the remedies of equity, however imperfect, were financially beyond the reach of all but the wealthiest classes. 'Why,' asked one writer, 'should a yoke which the rich are enabled to throw off be fastened without remedy on the necks of the humbler classes? In short, why one law for the rich and another for the poor?' The Married Women's Property Bill, Jessel asserted, 'was emphatically a poor woman's Bill.' It was, declared *The Times*, now in its more enlightened period, 'a legitimate result of the doctrines of Equity applied to the poor. Those who oppose it ought to submit to Parliament a Bill disallowing the application of these doctrines in settling the property of the rich.'[19]

In this connection a writer in the *Spectator* suggested that those who opposed reform did so from motives that were hardly disinterested. The drawing up of a marriage settlement involved 'setting two firms of attorneys to squabble by letters at five shillings each, and long attendances at thirteen and fourpence,' so that 'a moderate bill for such services amounts to 150 1 ... Wherefore, then serveth the law? ... it is for the benefit of the lawyers.' This, the *Spectator* asserted, was 'a sufficient explanation of the "distaste" with which Mr. Lopes says the Bill is regarded by the majority of the legal profession.'[20]

The Times doubtless summed up the situation correctly when it said, in the year that Mill's *Subjection of Women* was first published, that 'theories now afloat respecting the equality of the sexes and the independence of women have not yet received the sanction, even if they have received the consideration, of the English people.'[21] This being so, it was fortunate for the cause of reform that it could be most forcefully presented not as amendment of a law that was merely 'unjust in principle,' but above all as a means of correcting a law which pressed 'with peculiar severity upon the poorer classes of the community.'

Abundant evidence was brought forward to support the reformers' claim that many poor women suffered grievously under the existing law. When Lopes and others argued, with careless disregard of facts, that few married women of the lower classes had any property to be protected – not one woman in 500, Lopes suggested – they were quickly reminded that the last census had revealed that in England and Wales one married woman in four, a total of over 800,000 married women, was employed outside the home. To be more precise, 838,856 wives were employed out of a total of 3,488,952 – that is, 24 per cent of all married women were employed – and these figures did not include wives of farmers, innkeepers, and such, who helped with their husbands' businesses.[22] Most of these married women worked outside the home because their husbands were unable or unwilling to support their families, and details were given of many 'very painful cases' that arose when husbands seized their wives' earnings and also their personal possessions, often squandering these on drink and leaving their families with no recourse but the workhouse.

The case of Susannah Palmer was notorious, but hers was only one among many. For example, a poor woman had to go out to work in order to support herself and her three children, for her husband, although he earned good wages, spent them mostly on drink. The woman had applied to a lady for a loan to buy some furniture, and this loan she had repaid by weekly instalments out of her own earnings. Again she applied to the lady for a loan to pay off a debt she had

incurred at a provision shop for food for her family, but the lady was advised to
refuse the request and tell the woman that her husband was legally liable for the
debt and the shopkeeper should sue him for it. The woman replied that her
husband had threatened to strip the house and sell every stick of her furniture,
and that he might carry out this threat if he were asked to pay the debt.[23]
Another woman who worked as a domestic servant had an idle and dissipated
husband. He lived apart from her, but did not desert her within the letter of the
law – that is, for a period of two years – and would swoop down upon her periodically to seize the money she had saved up during his absence. As a result, the
family of Arthur Hobhouse, who related this story, had to undertake to support
her.

Nor were cases of hardship confined to women of the lower classes. They were
also to be found among the middle and upper classes, as the following examples
show. A widow had been left by her husband at his death in possession of a
comfortable inn and the sum of £1,000 in the bank. She married again, but soon
afterward her husband ran off to Australia, taking the money, which he had
withdrawn from the bank. Still, she was able to earn a good living from the
business for herself and her daughter by her first marriage. Several years later
her husband returned, penniless and ill and professing penitence, and she agreed
to take him back and nursed him till he was well. One day the husband persuaded her and her daughter to take a carriage drive in the country by way of a
pleasant excursion. Upon their return they found the inn in the possession of a
stranger. He produced a bill of sale for the house and the business given him by
the husband, who had again disappeared. Mother and daughter were turned out
into the streets, homeless and penniless. Another woman possessed of a small
fortune married a solicitor, whom she trusted to draw up her marriage settlement, since she was an orphan and had no male relatives or friends to look after
her interests. Soon after the marriage a younger woman came to live in the
household as a sort of housekeeper or companion, and the story was given out
that the wife had been seriously ill and had become insane, but would be cared
for at home rather than being sent to an asylum. When the husband died a few
years later, his relatives took possession of the house and found the wife locked
in a garret, but quite sane. Her marriage settlement, whatever its provisions
might have been, had been destroyed, so that she was subjected to the common
law and thus to the terms of her husband's will, which left all her property to the
woman who had supplanted her and served as her jailer.[24]

Such cases were indeed deplorable, opponents of reform agreed, but they
maintained that these were exceptions to the general rule of marital happiness.
Lopes denounced the Married Women's Property Bill as being 'exceptional

legislation,' meaning that it would subvert the whole principle of the law applying to all women for the benefit of those exceptional cases of women who
suffered under the law. Raikes called the bill 'unjust and humiliating to Englishmen,' for it implied that they were all monsters who oppressed their wives and
despoiled them of their property.

Mill remarked upon the fact that defenders of the existing marriage law generally thought that 'any complaint is merely quarrelling with the evil which is
the price paid for every great good,' especially when 'they have not personally
experienced' the evil. Jessel answered Lopes by saying that the bill was, of
course, 'exceptional legislation.' Crime, said Jessel, was always exceptional or it
could not be legislated against, and it was always necessary to legislate against
the minority for the protection of the majority. To pass a law against theft did
not stigmatize all citizens as thieves, any more than passage of the Married
Women's Property Bill would brand all husbands as villains. To this, Mill added
that 'laws and institutions require to be adapted, not to good men, but to bad.'
Marriage was not for 'a select few,' and men who married were not required as a
preliminary 'to prove by testimonials that they are fit to be trusted with the
exercise of absolute power.'

In short, reform of the married women's property law was not merely a reform
based on abstract theories of justice and of the nature of marriage, and designed
to remove sentimental grievances. It was also, and above all, a measure to afford
relief for widespread suffering and hardship, especially among the poor. If the
Married Women's Property Bill was passed, said Jacob Bright, thousands of
homes would be less miserable, for many families would be supported by
mothers who otherwise would have been at the mercy of their husbands. Gurney
summed up eloquently, saying that parliament, in passing the bill, would
'receive the blessing of multitudes of toiling women who now, when they see the
hard [won] earnings of a fellow-workwoman swept away [by her husband],
gather together in the streets, saying, – "What is the use of a body striving?"'

Reading the debates in the House of Commons on the Married Women's Property Bill, one has the distinct impression that, as Osborne Morgan later said,
opponents of the bill objected to it 'not so much because of what, in reality,
would be its effect, as because of that to which they feared it would lead – the
development of the "women's rights" question, and looming behind that a parliament in petticoats.'[25] Opponents of reform were perhaps mindful of Mill's
comments that 'no enslaved class ever asked for complete liberty at once,' that it
was 'a political law of nature that those who are under any power of ancient
origin, never begin by complaining of the power itself, but only of its oppressive

exercise.' Raikes declared that supporters of the Married Women's Property Bill were really aiming at 'civil equality between men and women,' at 'what was called the emancipation of women,' and he warned darkly, 'The hand that introduced the measure was the hand of the right hon. Gentleman [the Conservative Gurney], but the voice that spoke in every clause was that of a very different sort of social reformer.'

Opponents of reform were certainly mindful of the concurrent agitation for women's suffrage. Raikes, for example, referred specifically to a public meeting held in London at which a lady had described the Married Women's Property Bill as merely a step in the direction of the enfranchisement of women. This was the first meeting to advocate women's suffrage held in London, in July 1869, with Clementia Taylor presiding. Both Mrs Taylor and Millicent Garrett Fawcett delivered speeches on the suffrage question, as did their husbands. Also present and speaking on this occasion were Mill, Sir Charles Dilke, Thomas Hare, Lord Houghton (Monckton Milnes), John Boyd Kinnear, and James Stansfeld.[26] If this lady's claim was true, Raikes said, then the bill 'aimed at destroying the mutual relations that had existed between men and women since time immemorial,' and would 'create a factitious, an artificial, and an unnatural equality' between the sexes. Another member warned more succinctly that if the bill became law, 'married women would be entitled to vote in respect of their property.'

In a sense, supporters of the Married Women's Property Bill capitalized upon their opponents' fears, engaging in a bit of gentle blackmail. Mill remarked that he and those who, like him, favoured extension of political rights to women should actually desire rejection of the bill, for this would give 'an extraordinary impulse' to the movement for women's suffrage, which had already advanced 'with so much vigour.' But, he added, 'I should like my own sex to have the credit of giving up unjust and impolitic privileges before they are brought under the influence of other motives than their own good feelings.' Gurney pointed out that he had to appeal on women's behalf to 'a Legislature elected exclusively by men,' and added, 'I trust that it will appear that the members of a Legislature, so elected, are as keen to discern the evil, and as earnest in applying a remedy, as if the appeal were made on behalf of those whose voices could be heard at elections, and whose votes could be recorded at the hustings.' And in a letter to *The Times* Lydia Becker said that if members of parliament passed the Married Women's Property Bill, they would, 'without affecting the justice of the claim of women to representation, destroy one of the strongest reasons for pressing it.'[27]

Mill correctly foresaw the actual course of events. 'This particular injustice and oppression to women,' he said, referring to the married women's property law, 'which is, to common apprehension, more obvious than all the rest, admits of remedy without interfering with any other mischief; and ... it will be one of the earliest remedied.' Reform of the married women's property law was carried, while the movement for women's suffrage was doomed to failure for many years to come.

8

'That Legislative Abortion' The Married Women's Property Act of 1870

During three successive sessions the question of reform of the married women's property law was before parliament. The hopes of feminists for passage of their bill were high in 1868 and rose higher still the next year and the next. Success seemed within their grasp in 1870. But then things went wrong, and their hopes were dashed. After more than two years' labour the parliamentary mountain brought forth a mouse.

In April 1868 Shaw-Lefevre, with Mill and Gurney as co-sponsors, introduced in the House of Commons the Married Women's Property Bill which had been drafted by Dr Richard Pankhurst for the Social Science Association. Seven weeks later the bill came on for its second reading. Of the debate on this occasion one writer commented, 'Our old friends, the "floodgates," and the "framework of society," were on active service ... All the old bugbears were rubbed up and paraded before a not inattentive House of Commons.' Another writer found 'the pompous platitudes about authority [of men] and subordination [of women], savouring strongly of the henpecked husband.' The Conservative attorney general, Sir John Karslake, said that he could not approve the bill because the change it proposed was so great and, like others, he suggested instead extension of the protection-order system instituted by the Divorce Act of 1857 to safeguard the property of women deserted by their husbands. The vote on the bill resulted in a tie, 123 to 123, whereupon the Speaker cast his deciding vote with the 'ayes,' in accordance with the custom that in such cases the House should have further opportunity to consider the measure.[1]

Late in June the bill was submitted to a select committee for study. The committee was chaired by Shaw-Lefevre and included among its fourteen members Gurney, Jacob Bright, Lowe, and, representing the Conservative government, Sir Robert Collier, the solicitor general. Collier was soon to succeed Karslake as attorney general and later, as Lord Monkswell, would serve as a member of the judicial committee of the Privy Council. Interestingly, Collier disagreed with his colleague Karslake about the Married Women's Property Bill. He had spoken in favour of property-law reform as early as the debate on Sir Erskine Perry's resolution in 1856, and now likewise favoured reform. Because of the lateness of the parliamentary session, the select committee met only five times and heard the testimony of only fourteen persons. Later Lopes commented sourly that there was not 'a single independent or unprejudiced opinion given by any of the witnesses.' Certainly the testimony was unanimously and enthusiastically in favour of reform.[2]

Ten of the witnesses who gave evidence before the select committee testified to the injustice and the generally unsatisfactory state of the married women's property law, drawing upon their own personal knowledge and experience. Appearing as expert legal witnesses and also as representatives of the Social Science Association were George Hastings, Arthur Hobhouse, and John Westlake. Speaking in favour of reform on behalf of both working men and working women was John Ormerod, president of the famed Rochdale Pioneer Co-operative Society, which was held to represent the best class of workers. Ormerod explained that married women were allowed to invest money in the society in their own names, and that this money was not paid out to husbands without their wives' consent, although this policy was of doubtful legality and the society had in fact been threatened with legal proceedings because of it. Anthony John Mundella, a large-scale hosiery manufacturer from Nottingham, likewise testified to the need and desire for reform among the working classes, saying that he never passed his factory gates without being asked by his women workers when parliament would pass the bill. Mundella was to enter parliament later in 1868 as Radical member for Sheffield and serve until his death in 1897, becoming vice-president of the Committee of the Privy Council on Education in Gladstone's second ministry and president of the Board of Trade in Gladstone's third and fourth ministries. Always concerned to improve the condition of the working classes, he played an important part in the passage of the Education Act of 1870, and he created the Labour Department of the Board of Trade.[3] The only woman among the witnesses was Isabella Tod, who had been drawn into the women's movement the previous year through her attendance at the Social Science Association congress in Belfast, and who would later serve on the executive committee of the Married Women's Property Committee. Now she explained that she and other ladies in Belfast and Dublin had taken up property-law reform in order to relieve the sufferings of the many poor married women who worked in the Irish linen mills. Two clergymen, on the basis of their long experience among the poor in their parishes in London's East End, testified to the sufferings of women under the existing law. One of these men, Septimus Hansard, rector of Bethnal Green, would later join the executive committee of the

Married Women's Property Committee. Finally, two other witnesses, one a police magistrate for the Marylebone district of London and the other a solicitor and clerk to a police magistrate in Liverpool, gave their opinion that the protection-order system established by the Divorce Act of 1857 had proved totally ineffective and that thorough reform of the property law should be enacted.

In addition to the testimony of these witnesses, the select committee also took evidence of the success of reform in Canada and the United States. Appearing before the committee were the Honourable John Rose, finance minister of Canada; Cyrus Field of New York, promoter of the Atlantic telegraph and brother of the distinguished jurist Dudley Field; and two lawyers from the United States who were visiting in England, one from Massachusetts and the other from Vermont. Their testimony was supported by letters sent to the committee by five eminent Americans – Dudley Field; Emory Washburn, professor of law at Harvard, former governor of Massachusetts, and former justice of the Massachusetts supreme court; G.S. Hillard, United States attorney for Massachusetts; John Wells, an associate justice of the Massachusetts supreme court; and Edward Atkinson, a cotton manufacturer and important civic leader from Lowell, Massachusetts.

The select committee presented its report in mid-July. First, the existing state of the law was summarized – the two distinct legal systems guided by different principles and administered by the separate courts of common law and of equity, the numerous cases of hardships arising under the common law, and, in turn, the shortcomings of equity. The committee was especially impressed by the evidence of reform successfully carried through abroad since, without such practical evidence, all arguments as to the results of reform were merely theoretical. In view of the experience abroad, and in view of the tendency of the provisions of equity to grant financial independence to wives, the committee concluded that reform of the married women's property law was as feasible as it was necessary. However, for lack of time the committee had not completed its consideration of the bill nor reached decisions on a number of questions that had been raised. For example, should the Poor-Law liability of fathers to support their children be extended to mothers as well? Therefore it was recommended that another select committee be appointed during the next session of parliament to finish work on the bill, which was now reported without amendment. A week later it was withdrawn because of the impending adjournment of parliament.

When the Married Women's Property Bill came before parliament in 1869, the political situation was completely changed. The general election of late 1868 had swept the Conservatives out of office and the Liberals in, and had dramatically altered the complexion of the House of Commons. More than one-third of the

members were new to parliament, including a sizable group of Radicals, followers of Mill and other friends of women's causes, among them Dilke, Jessel,
Morgan, and Mundella. Mill himself was defeated in his bid for re-election, but
his absence from the House proved no great loss to the Radicals, for his influence remained strong. Also, he was not personally disappointed, for he had
always considered himself a thinker standing apart from partisan politics rather
than as an effective practical politician. The new men in parliament were Radical, as the *Spectator* put it, in that they were 'disposed to try every institution by
its results, without reference to any consideration except those results.' The tone
and tactics of the new House were especially evident, remarked the *Spectator*, in
the debates on the Married Women's Property Bill.[4]

Mention must also be made of an event in 1869 which indirectly but pro-
foundly influenced the feminists' chances of success in winning reform of the
property law. This was the publication of the first report of the Judicature Commission, the royal commission appointed in 1867 to study the whole matter of
reform of the country's law and its superior courts. The commission's report
advocated the merger of the existing superior courts into one Supreme Court of
Judicature, which would fuse into a coherent whole the separate bodies of law
then administered in the separate courts and, in particular, would reconcile the
differences between the common law and equity. The report thus had important
implications for reform of the married women's property law, which illustrated
so well the scandalous differences existing between the common law and equity.
The Liberal government accepted the commission's report and thus was committed to translating its recommendations into statute. This was to be accomplished by passage of the Judicature Act of 1873.

In February 1869 the same bill Shaw-Lefevre had brought in the year before
was introduced in the Commons by Gurney, with Jacob Bright and Thomas
Emerson Headlam now its co-sponsors. Shaw-Lefevre had become secretary to
the Board of Trade in the new government, and felt unable now to assume
responsibility for piloting the bill through the Commons. Headlam, a successful
equity lawyer and queen's counsel, was Liberal member for Newcastle-upon-
Tyne from 1847 till 1874, and had served as judge advocate general for seven
years under Palmerston and Russell.[5]

The Married Women's Property Bill came on for its second reading in mid-
April. 'The debate was as hot as ever,' the *Spectator* commented, 'but the old
arguments were all laid aside.' Now no one, not even Beresford-Hope, argued for
'the Divine Right of a husband to confiscate his wife's property, or described the
family as an institution beyond discussion, or predicted that the new law would
weaken the authority of Scripture, and therefore of the Church, and therefore of
the Constitution.' Those who opposed the bill now did so as 'politicians discuss-

ing an injurious or imperfect measure, not as priests denouncing vengeance [sic] upon all who might approach the ark.'[6]

Speaking for the new Liberal government, Sir John Coleridge, the solicitor general, expressed hearty approval of the bill, and at his suggestion it was read a second time without a division and submitted to a select committee for consideration of its details. Coleridge was an impressive recruit to the women's cause. The son of a justice of the Court of Common Pleas and nephew of the poet Samuel Taylor Coleridge, he succeeded Collier as attorney general in 1871; two years afterward, as Lord Coleridge, he became chief justice of the Court of Common Pleas. Still later, he was the first lord chief justice of England, presiding over the new Supreme Court of Judicature. In 1869 he served as the women's counsel, with Richard Pankhurst as junior counsel, in the leading case of *Chorlton* v *Lings*, the case which determined that women householders could not vote under the provisions of the Reform Bill of 1867, and in parliament he was an important supporter of reform of the married women's property law. But eventually Coleridge's feminist sympathies disappeared. In 1889 he presided over the Court of Appeal when it rejected Lady Sandhurst's claim that her election to the London County Council should not be voided merely on the ground that she was a woman. Sylvia Pankhurst later remarked that 'it was whispered at the bar that Lord Coleridge's metamorphosis from being counsel for the women in one case to becoming head of the court that rejected their claims in another, was due to his second wife having been more of a Tartar than his first.'[7]

The select committee of 1869, chaired by Gurney and including among its members Jacob Bright, Headlam, Coleridge, and Robert Lowe, now chancellor of the exchequer, did not hear the evidence of witnesses but restricted itself to working over the details of the bill. After three weeks of deliberation the committee reported the bill with several amendments. As a sop thrown to conservative opponents of the bill, the preamble, which declared that the law was 'unjust in principle,' was replaced by the simple statement that it was 'desirable to amend the law.' No married woman was to be liable to imprisonment in execution of a judgment against her in a case involving a contract made or a civil act done by her during marriage. Husband and wife were not to be allowed to sue each other in tort except with respect to their property, and if either husband or wife brought such an action and the judge considered it 'frivolous or vexatious,' he could stay the proceedings. A married woman was made liable for the support of her husband, as he was liable for her support under the Poor Law Amendment Act of 1868, and she was likewise liable for the support of her children, although this was not to relieve the husband of liability for his children's support.[8]

Two months after presentation of the select committee's report, the amended
bill came on for its third reading in the Commons. Vainly Raikes proposed its
postponement for three months. In vain did Beresford-Hope urge that the bill
stand over till the next session, complaining that a measure 'vitally altering the
most important of all social relations' should be considered 'at past five o'clock
on a Wednesday late in July,' with the House exhausted and not really debating
and with the front bench on the opposition side empty and no cabinet minister
on the treasury bench. The bill passed by a vote of 131 to 33.[9]

Next day the bill was introduced in the upper House by Lord Penzance, and
a week later came on for its second reading. Penzance clearly disliked the bill
and recommended its approval by the Lords only as a gesture of courtesy to the
new government and because it was obviously too late for it to be passed during
that session. The bill was read a second time without a division, and there the
matter rested for another year.[10]

During the parliamentary session of 1870 the Commons had to consider not one
Married Women's Property Bill but two. In February Gurney introduced the
bill of the previous year as it had been amended by the select committee, while
Raikes, such a strong opponent of reform, introduced his own bill in an effort to
block passage of the other. Three months later, in mid-May, the two bills came
on together for a second reading in the Commons.[11]

Long and complicated, Raikes's bill differed basically from the simpler and
more comprehensive measure backed by the Social Science Association and the
Married Women's Property Committee and sponsored by Gurney. It embodied
suggestions made earlier in the Commons that married women could be best
protected not by giving them the same property rights as unmarried women but
by two other means: by applying to all married women the equitable principle of
a married woman's separate property held in trust, and by extending to more
women the protection-order system instituted by the Divorce Act of 1857.[12]
Specifically, Raikes's bill provided that where no marriage settlement existed, a
husband would be trustee for his wife's property, as he would be in equity if no
trustee was named when property was settled upon his wife. However, a husband's powers as trustee would be limited. For example, he could not dispose of
his wife's property without the approval of a county-court judge, and no payments could be made to him as his wife's trustee except by her signed order
allowing this. Moreover, a married woman could apply to a county court to have
her husband divested of his powers as her trustee and to have a new trustee
appointed. Raikes's bill also provided that a married woman could obtain from a
county-court judge a protection order against her husband if she could prove
that for six months she had been earning more than half of the family's

expenses. She would then have all the rights of an unmarried woman over the property she acquired after the order was issued.

The Married Women's Property Committee, fearful that Raikes's bill might be passed instead of their own, sprang into action. The committee members presented to the House of Commons 250 petitions with more than 46,000 signatures expressing support of Gurney's bill. They also reprinted in pamphlet form Arthur Hobhouse's article 'On the Forfeiture of Property by Married Women,' a version of his 1868 paper presented to the Social Science Association congress which had appeared in the February issue of the *Fortnightly Review*, and this was widely distributed.[13] Members of parliament had to be clearly informed as to which bill women really wanted, and had to be primed with arguments to use against the bill that women did not want. In the event, Raikes's bill was attacked in the Commons as being both unjust in principle and ineffective in its provisions.

First, the women's friends denounced Raikes's suggestion that the principle of equitable marriage settlements be extended to all married women. Hobhouse called this 'one of the first things to occur to lawyers more familiar with such arrangements than with the short and simple annals of the poor.' For the poor, much more than for the rich, it was essential that they have ready access to and use of any money they possessed, and it was not feasible to tie up this money in settlements. Such a scheme, Hobhouse continued, would mean the extension of paternal government into the most private affairs, 'a regular invasion by Mr. Raikes at the head of a posse of County Court judges, Vice-Chancellors and other trustees.' Then, too, as Jessel pointed out, Raikes's bill would transfer to a married woman's trustee all of her property except that which was transferable by mere delivery, but the property of poor women usually consisted of a few clothes, a little furniture, and perhaps a small sum of money, all of these transferable by mere delivery and therefore not protected from their husbands. Gurney added that Raikes's bill would afford relief to those few women of the wealthier classes who through ignorance or carelessness had not protected themselves by marriage settlements, but not relief to women of the poorer classes. It would 'protect the rich woman's Consols, but ... not protect the poor woman's mangle.'[14]

The women's friends in the Commons attacked with equal forcefulness Raikes's suggestion that the protection-order system of 1857 be extended. They began by pointing out that the existing protection-order system had not worked well in practice. Protection orders could be granted only to women whose husbands had deserted them for two years; orders did not prevent men from leaving their wives for lesser periods, returning to seize the property their wives had acquired in the meantime, and then deserting again. Also, protection orders secured to women only the property which they acquired after being deserted; they did not protect those wives whose husbands squandered their property before they left or who stole it when they deserted. Finally, protection orders could not be granted to women who left their husbands, even for good cause, as they could be granted to women whose husbands deserted them. For example, Susannah Palmer could not have obtained a protection order. In fact, very few protection orders were granted – only 100 in the first three years of the operation of the system.[15]

Next, it was argued that extension of the protection-order system would be inexpedient. To allow a wife who was living with her husband to apply for a protection order against him would create precisely that discord within families that opponents of reform were so anxious to avoid. Husbands would be encouraged to use force to prevent their wives from applying for an order, so that women would be too intimidated to seek relief. Also, as one writer observed, 'There is often ... actually a spirit of delicacy in hard working women, and the parade of domestic grievances in a public court is an ordeal from which all women, of however humble a station, naturally and instinctively shrink.'[16]

Finally, the women's friends argued that extension of the protection-order system would simply add injustice to existing injustice. Was it just, Arthur Hobhouse demanded, to provide that a husband's property was his as a matter of course while a wife could have her property only if she was courageous enough to embark upon court proceedings and lucky enough to succeed? 'Would you,' he challenged any advocate of this proposal, 'be content to mete it out to your own daughter? If she marries, will you consent to abstain from securing to her any property of her own [by a marriage settlement] ...?'[17]

Aware that he was fighting a losing battle, Raikes tried unsuccessfully to gain time. He pointed out that the government had promised to deal with the whole question of law reform, especially with a view to achieving a fusion of the common law and equity, and this would necessarily affect the law relating to married women's property. This, he urged, was sufficient reason for not pressing forward with Gurney's bill, a claim which Jessel quickly denied. Coleridge, the solicitor general, while remarking upon 'a great example of a Raikes' progress' – from opposition to reform, to introduction of his own measure of reform – urged acceptance of Gurney's bill instead. Raikes's measure was soundly defeated by a vote of 208 to 46, and Gurney's was approved.[18]

Now the scene of battle shifted to the upper House. In preparation for the upcoming debate on their bill, the members of the Married Women's Property Committee sent to every member of the House of Lords a 'carefully reasoned petition' about the measure before them. But their efforts proved unavailing, for the Married Women's Property Bill, when it came on for a second reading late in June, met with universal disapproval.[19]

Leading the opposition to the bill was Lord Penzance, who had introduced it so unenthusiastically the year before, and whose speech now, *The Times* reported, 'was greeted with approving laughter.' Penzance had now served for seven years as judge ordinary of the Divorce Court, and *The Times* suggested that since he was 'accustomed to see nothing but the ugly side of matrimonial nature,' he might be excused for 'taking a sort of Old Bailey view of the married state, and particularly for looking upon wives as a set of extravagant queans, with whom flirtation is only kept short of adultery by the fear of himself and the machinery he directs.'[20] Penzance questioned the wisdom of setting up in one household 'two holders of the purse, two powers, co-equal at first and likely to become adverse in the end.' If the bill passed and a married woman was able to deal with her property as she chose, a man might be startled to find that his wife had set up a rival shop to his and taken as a partner 'her cousin, who need not be a woman.' Penzance warned 'the advocates of what were popularly called the "rights of women," whose opinions, if not their hands, might be traced in these provisions,' that 'great evil' had resulted from 'marriages being less frequent than they used to be or possibly ought to be,' and that if the law held that 'a man in taking a wife took a partner with separate interests ... it was doubtful how far there would remain an inducement to the male portion of the community to enter into such a contract.' He was sure, he added, that 'if there was one race of people to whom it would be less agreeable than to another not to be masters in their own homes, it was the race represented by their Lordships.'

Seconding Penzance in opposition to the bill was Lord Westbury, who, *The Times* commented, was 'almost equally witty' and 'whose imagination was equally fertile.' Westbury was the same brilliant, arrogant, and irascible Sir Richard Bethell who had opposed Perry and 'strong-minded women' in 1857. He had risen to be lord chancellor in 1861, but resigned four years later when scandals involving corruption among some of his subordinate officials were revealed and were followed by a vote of censure in the House of Commons. A distinguished historian of the law has described Westbury as 'intellectually one of the greatest of our Chancellors, but by reason of his deficiency in manners, temper and moral sense one of the least admirable.'[21] Westbury declared that the Married Women's Property Bill 'seemed to have sprung from the sensationalism of the day, which delighted in extravagancies, and sought to carry them even into the amendment of the law,' and that its passage would mean 'an entire subversion of domestic rule which had prevailed in this country for more than 1,000 years.' He appealed to married men as to 'whether they would like this additional yoke' laid upon them, a yoke which for the unmarried would add 'a new terror' to the prospects of marriage. Westbury suggested that if a married woman could deal with her property freely, she might reject her husband's suggestion that she use it for the expenses of their household or for their children's education, and buy a diamond necklace and bracelets instead or, 'if there was some person for whom she had greater affection than for her legitimate lord, she might lavish the proceeds upon him.' In short, he said, passage of the bill as it stood was 'out of the question.'

Even that great humanitarian reformer Lord Shaftesbury joined in all this. The bill, he declared, 'struck at the root of domestic happiness, introducing insubordination, equality and something more.' He asked whether, if the bill passed, a woman might not quarrel with her husband, eject him from the house which was her property, and 'while keeping him out of it ... admit everyone else?' Again, he asked, if a married woman was to have her own property, 'what was to be the rule, if the husband thought it necessary to forbid her accepting presents from persons with whom he did not wish her to be on terms of intimacy?'

The tone of the debate in the upper House was such as to infuriate those who were sympathetic to the women's cause, and to disturb even those who were not especially sympathetic. For example, a writer in the *Spectator* replied to the comments of Westbury and Penzance by demanding, 'Suppose my Lord has a legacy of £20,000, does any law bind him to expend it "on the general comfort and maintenance of the household," or is he precluded from "dropping" it on a horse race, or expending it at Poole's, or giving it to a mistress?'[22] Both Lord Romilly, the master of the rolls, and Lord Cairns, the former lord chancellor, remonstrated with their colleagues who, said Cairns, 'had with great ingenuity conjured up spectres to frighten their Lordships.' Both pointed out that wealthy women with separate property in equity could already do the dastardly things suggested – spend their money on diamonds and lovers instead of on their families, keep their husbands out of their houses, and so on – but few women actually did.

The members of the upper House clearly believed that some measure of reform must be enacted in order to protect poor women. Lord Shaftesbury, when he had finished with his suggestions as to the improper uses that wealthy women might make of their own property, dwelt movingly on the sad plight of working women, who were too often victimized by their husbands. He compared such women, to their advantage, with women of the higher classes, because they had 'many more duties' to discharge than ladies, and had no nurses or other servants to help them. He compared them favourably, too, with men of their class, maintaining that they were much superior in tact, sound judgment, and economy. 'The wife of a working man,' said Shaftesbury, 'was the moving principle of the whole family.' For her, a measure of reform was of 'immense importance,' and 'even if it involved the violation of some sort of principle, this would be better than the continuance of the present evil.' Even Penzance and Westbury did not oppose amendment of the property law, but they objected to the doctrine of separate interests of husband and wife, and favoured instead adoption of the doctrine of community property of husband and wife such as existed in France.

At the same time it was equally clear that members of the upper House believed that the bill before them went much further than was necessary to correct existing evils. Lord Romilly suggested that it be submitted to a select committee and 'judiciously amended,' in the naively sanguine belief that the Commons 'would cheerfully accept it, as knowing that it had been carefully considered by noble and learned Lords who were well acquainted with the subject.' This suggestion was welcomed by Lord Hatherley, the genial and popular if not very forceful lord chancellor, who commented – here quoting Arthur Hobhouse – that it was doubtless 'monstrous' to say the husband was always right and therefore should have his wife's property, but that he himself held to 'the old-fashioned notion that the head of the family must be the husband.' Soon afterward the select committee was appointed, including among its members Penzance, Westbury, Cairns, Romilly, and Shaftesbury. The Married Women's Property Committee now asked to give evidence before the select committee, but were informed that no evidence would be taken and that the committee would merely modify the bill.[23]

The dominant figure on the committee and the chief author of its report, which was prepared in only a week's time, was Lord Cairns. A brilliant equity lawyer who had studied his profession under Sir Richard Malins, Cairns had entered parliament in the 1850s and had quickly become one of the leaders of the Conservative party and an acknowledged legal authority in the House of Commons. He served briefly as solicitor general and attorney general before accepting a post as lord justice of appeal in Chancery, with a peerage and a seat in the House of Lords, where he proved a distinguished defender of the Conservative government. In 1867, a testimonial to his enormous prestige, Cairns was named chairman of the important royal commission whose studies and reports led to passage of the Judicature Act of 1873. When Disraeli succeeded Derby as prime minister in 1868, he appointed Cairns lord chancellor. Cairns held the post only a few months before the government resigned, but he was to serve as lord chancellor again when the Conservatives returned to power. An enthusiastic Evangelical, Cairns actively supported the Church throughout his life, and the story goes that aspiring barristers assiduously attended prayer meetings at his home when he was lord chancellor, in hopes of obtaining from him appointments as county-court judges. But for his cold and ungenial manner, which made him personally unpopular, however respected he was professionally, Cairns might well have succeeded Disraeli as leader of the Conservative party.

Led by Lord Cairns, the select committee of the Lords tore the Commons' bill to shreds, striking out fourteen of its seventeen substantive clauses and replacing them with new provisions, and amending the other three.[24] In rewriting the bill the committee threw out the phrase 'her own property' applied to the property of a married woman, and substituted for it the words 'property held and settled to her separate use' or, more simply, her 'separate property.' Here the Lords were applying the principles and the exact language of equity to the property – or rather, some of the property – of married women who did not have marriage settlements. Doubtless they did this in a conscious effort to move with the current of legal reform around them – that is, in the direction of the fusion of law and equity and the superseding of the law by equity in case of conflict between the two. This, after all, was the basic recommendation of the royal commission over which Lord Cairns had presided and on which Penzance, Westbury, and Romilly had also served.

Specifically, the bill provided that married women without marriage settlements were to have as their 'separate property,' free from their husbands' control, property that fell into roughly three categories. The first and by far the most important of these categories comprised their earnings from 'any employment, occupation, or trade' in which they were engaged or which they carried on separately from their husbands; any money or property they acquired by the 'exercise of any literary, artistic, or scientific skill'; and 'all investments' of such earnings, money, and property. Second, married women were to have as their separate property money, and the proceeds from it, which were invested in several specified ways – in government annuities; in savings banks; in the public stocks and funds; in incorporated or joint-stock companies; in industrial, provident, friendly, building and loan societies; and in life insurance policies taken out by them on their own or their husbands' lives, or taken out by their husbands on their own lives for their wives' benefit. In no case could such investments be made by married women using their husbands' money without their consent, nor could they be made by husbands for their wives' benefit in order to defraud their creditors. Third, married women could have as their separate property, with qualifications, property coming to them from the estates of persons deceased.

In short, as Penzance happily observed, it was an entirely new bill which the select committee had constructed. This bill the Lords approved, despite efforts by Lord Houghton (Monckton Milnes) and a few others to insert substantial amendments. It was then sent down to the Commons.[25]

In view of these daunting developments, the Married Women's Property Committee called a special meeting in London at the offices of the Social Science Association, with Arthur Hobhouse presiding, to decide whether to accept or oppose the bill as amended by the Lords. Hobhouse later recalled that 'it wanted only the holding up of a little finger to prevent it going through the House of Commons.' Those who opposed the amended bill argued that its passage would make enactment of the thoroughgoing reform that women really wanted much more difficult. That is, the bill's most important provision would protect the earnings of poor women, and opponents of reform could then argue that there was no need to protect the property of other women. Earlier events had shown the likelihood of this happening. The first campaign for property-law reform in the fifties had failed at least partly because of passage of the Divorce Act of 1857, with its provision for the protection of property of deserted wives. However, as Hobhouse later said, the Married Women's Property Committee eventually 'determined to take the generous course ... and to get for our suffering country-women such a measure of benefit as the Lords' Bill might give them irrespective of consequences to others.' Another consideration influenced the committee's decision not to oppose the bill as amended by the Lords. The storm clouds had rolled up over Europe as France, on 19 July 1870, declared war on Prussia, and the committee feared the effects the worsening international situation would have upon the fortunes of reform at home. Also, it was now too late in the parliamentary session for the women's friends in the Commons to propose substantial amendments to the Lords' bill, and the opportunity for achieving even this limited measure of reform might not soon recur.[26]

So prompted by the Married Women's Property Committee, Gurney urged the House of Commons to approve the bill as amended by the Lords. But, he added prophetically, legislation must not end with this measure, for much would remain to be remedied.[27] The Commons did approve the bill, which received royal assent on 9 August and came into operation on that date – the Married Women's Property Act of 1870 (33 & 34 Vict., c 93). (For the text of the act, see appendix 5.)

The action of the House of Lords with respect to the Married Women's Property Bill was such as to enrage not only supporters of women's rights but also all those who were concerned about the balance of power in parliament in an age that was increasingly democratic in temper. The women's bill had been studied by two select committees of the Commons and had been passed in three successive sessions of the lower House, only to be emasculated by the Lords. Here was a clear case of obstruction of the popular will, as expressed in the House of Commons, by the hereditary and appointed upper House. A much more celebrated case was to occur the following year, when the Lords rejected a key provision of Cardwell's great scheme of army reform, the abolition of the purchase of officers' commissions, which had then to be carried through by royal warrant instead. Here one sees the beginnings, or rather the revival, of that conflict between Lords and Commons which was to increase in intensity over the years, as Liberal governments found themselves consistently thwarted by the Conservative Lords, and which culminated long afterward in passage of the Parliament Act of 1911.

As for the Married Women's Property Act itself, comment upon it, both in the House of Commons and outside of parliament, was scathing. 'That legislative abortion,' Arthur Arnold contemptuously called it. It 'proceeded on no principle whatever,' said one member of the Commons, while another member termed it merely 'a feeble compromise.' An eminent lawyer declared the act to be 'full of blots and itself a blot on our statute book, and the most absurd Act he had ever read.' Shaw-Lefevre echoed this opinion, saying that the act was 'so badly drawn, so faulty, and so absurd in many of its details' as to be 'unintelligible.' He added that judges who had recently inveighed from the bench against legislation hastily passed by parliament should remember that the Married Women's Property Act, with all its defects, was 'exclusively the handiwork of the Law Lords of the House of Lords.' Their lordships, said another member, apparently framed the act 'by contributing each a section, without any of them taking care that the different sections should be consistent one with another.'[28]

Reformers were quick to spell out in detail the many defects of the act, some of which were obvious in its wording while others became clear only as the act was interpreted by judicial decisions. In drafting the measure the Lords had been chiefly concerned to protect the earnings of poor working women. But as Elizabeth Wolstenholme pointed out, in a paper presented at the Social Science Association's congress later in 1870, the act's protection of married women's earnings was inadequate. This was so because the act specified as separate property 'the wages and earnings of any married woman' which were 'acquired or gained by her' after the passing of the act. That is, the money which a woman had saved from her earnings before she married, or had saved after marriage but before the act was passed, was not recognized as her separate property, unless she had invested it in the ways specified in the act – in savings banks, in friendly societies, and so on.[29]

Money so invested was the second category of property recognized as a married woman's separate property by the act, and therefore was protected. But Elizabeth Wolstenholme and Lydia Becker pointed out in a letter to *The Times* that this protection did not operate automatically. That is, under the act's provisions a married woman had to make special application to have her savings-bank deposits, friendly-society shares, and other investments registered as her separate property. Why, asked Coleridge in parliament, should not a married woman have as her separate property investments which were not specially registered as well as those that were? In any case, the act's provisions protecting a married woman's investments were of little practical value, so Lydia Becker told the Social Science Association. Bankers objected to taking the deposits of a married woman without her husband's signature, and hesitated or refused to honour her cheques if her husband forbade them to do so. Stockbrokers likewise, according to Miss Becker, objected to doing business with a married woman without her husband's consent.[30]

The third category of property secured to married women as their separate property by the act of 1870 was that which they inherited, but only with qualifications. A married woman could have as her separate property all property, both real and personal, of whatever amount which came to her as the next-of-kin of an intestate, but she could have a sum of money coming to her under any deed or will only if it did not exceed £200. The reason for this seemingly strange provision was that the Lords had followed to the letter the equitable rules relating to separate property which they had adopted as their model for reform. Equity generally allowed the whole of a legacy of less than £200 to be paid to a woman's husband, as being too small for her to claim her 'equity to a settlement,' while any legacy larger than £200 was subject to a wife's claim to a settlement and was usually divided equally between husband and wife. The Lords had written the law so as to allow married women to have as their separate property small legacies which otherwise would have gone to their husbands, while larger legacies would still be subject to equitable rules requiring that they be divided between husband and wife. Lord Houghton had tried unsuccessfully to amend the bill to allow married women to have as their separate property legacies of any amount, and he had been reproached for proposing to go beyond the protection which equity afforded to married women.[31]

But these provisions of the act were absurd, reformers declared. Coleridge, like Lord Houghton, wanted to know why a married woman should not have as her separate property the £500 she inherited by will as well as the £500 she earned. In this connection a writer in the *Spectator* commented that the Lords had 'sanctioned an innovation on the property law of the most dangerous kind,' by drawing a 'distinction between income derived from industry and income derived from inheritance,' adding that 'in the eyes of the most conservative and the richest group of men in the world the moral right to own extends only to the owner's earnings, the right to own inherited property being a mere creation of law.' The writer concluded, 'There are philosophers among us who will cordially welcome that admission, but whether the Peers will like the deductions from it which those philosophers will draw is a matter for their calmest consideration.'[32]

Earnings, specially registered investments, and certain inherited property – these were recognized by the act of 1870 as a married woman's separate property, free from her husband's control and obligations. But a court case in 1878 raised the question of whether this property was really protected against a woman's husband after all. This was the case of a certain Mrs McCarthy of Manchester, who tried to sue her husband in order to recover her separate property which he had taken; the stipendiary magistrate hearing her case dismissed it, saying he did not believe the Married Women's Property Act was intended 'to enable a woman to prosecute her husband.' This decision seemed to flout the clear provision in the act that, in order to protect her separate property, a married woman was to 'have in her own name, the same remedies, both civil and criminal' which an unmarried woman had, and 'against all persons whomsoever.' But presumably the magistrate was applying the old common-law rule that husband and wife were one person, and that therefore neither could steal from or sue the other.[33]

After defining the separate property of married women, however absurdly and anomalously, the act of 1870 had proceeded to spell out the responsibilities of married women with respect to this property. For one thing, the act imposed upon them the same liability for the support of their husbands and children that was imposed upon men for the support of their wives and offspring – the so-called Poor-Law liability. This provision had been included in the Married Women's Property Bill as passed by the Commons, and was almost the only one to survive the hatchet job performed upon the bill by the Lords. Reformers now objected to this provision on two grounds. First, Elizabeth Wolstenholme and Lydia Becker held that a wife should not be legally compelled to support her husband, arguing that a wife was entitled absolutely to be supported, since her maintenance was merely a money equivalent for the services she rendered her husband by managing his household. Second, Miss Wolstenholme argued that it was unfair to make a woman legally liable to support her children so long as the law recognized not her but her husband as the children's sole parent and guardian, with all the consequent privileges and prerogatives.[34]

Another responsibility which the act of 1870 laid upon married women with separate property was that of paying debts they had contracted before marriage, their husbands being relieved of liability for these. This provision, too, had been included in the bill passed by the Commons, and had escaped the Lords' hatchet wielding. The provision made sense in the context of the original bill, which gave married women all the rights and therefore all the responsibilities of unmarried women with respect to property, but it made no sense whatever in the act as passed, for a man might have acquired all his wife's property upon marriage but he was not liable to pay her antenuptial debts. Almost immediately cases arose in which, it was said, women who owed money would marry and then 'snap their fingers at their creditors.'[35]

Specifically, the problem was that the property women acquired by going into debt might not be of the kind recognized as separate property by the act of 1870, and therefore it would not be liable for settlement of their debts. The judicial decision in a case in 1871 made this problem clear. In this case a creditor sued a married woman to collect a debt she had incurred before marriage, and obtained a judgment against her, execution of which was being levied by seizure of her furniture. But her husband protested, claiming that the furniture was his property, and the presiding judge pointed out that the act designated as separate property a wife's earnings, specified investments, and inherited property, but said nothing about furniture. The creditor declined to incur the expense involved in an appeal of the case in order to clarify this point of law, and the judge ordered him to withdraw from possession.[36]

At the same time the act of 1870 did not impose upon married women with separate property responsibility for payment of the debts they incurred after marriage. This was made clear by the decision of the Court of Common Pleas in 1878 in the leading case of *Hancock* v *Lablache*. In this case Madame de Mérie Lablache, a noted actress and opera singer, who was separated from her husband, bought jewellery from a famous London firm, agreeing in writing to pay for it in instalments out of her separate property but soon defaulting. The court ruled that Madame Lablache could not be sued, for while the act of 1870 stated specifically that a married woman could sue with respect to her separate property, it did not say that she could be sued for debts incurred after marriage. The court believed this omission to be intentional, for the act did state specifically that a married woman could be sued for debts incurred before marriage, and also could be sued to enforce her responsibility for the support of her husband and children. On the other hand, the omission might well have been another of the blunders made by the Lords in drafting the measure. Press reports of the Lablache case inspired letters to the papers commenting upon its implications, including one from Elizabeth Wolstenholme, now Mrs Elmy, who pointed out that all such legal difficulties could have been avoided had the measure originally passed by the Commons been enacted.[37]

The fact that married women could not be sued for their debts – or could be sued only with doubtful prospects of success – was naturally a burden to hapless creditors and a boon to defaulting debtors. It was also a great hindrance to honest wives who wished to carry on a business or trade separate from their husbands. As Mrs Elmy pointed out before the Social Science Association, tradesmen were naturally loath to supply married women with goods for their businesses on credit, when they knew they might not be able legally to recover the money these women owed them.[38]

In view of these provisions and interpretations of the act of 1870, many people besides those who were identified as supporters of 'women's rights' could agree with Arthur Arnold's description of the act as a 'legislative abortion,' could second Coleridge when he asserted that the act was so bad that an amending bill must soon be passed. Yet with all its defects the act of 1870, like the Divorce Act of 1857 before it, was important in its recognition of the principle that married women should in certain circumstances own and control their property. As the *Annual Register* of 1870 noted rather wistfully, the act was 'a first recognition of a new principle, another small sign of the times ... that the old creeds were passing away, and, whether for good or evil, all things becoming new.'[39]

9

'What an Emancipation is This!'
The Married Women's Property Act of 1882

Feminists had lost an important battle in 1870, but they had not lost the war and they were determined to continue the fight. Speaking for the Married Women's Property Committee, Elizabeth Wolstenholme and Lydia Becker acknowledged that the act of 1870 was 'an important concession to the growing sentiment of justice,' but they refused to accept it as 'even a temporary settlement of the question.' Therefore, they said, their organization would remain 'intact and in working order' and would continue 'to press the subject upon public attention.'[1] Whether the members of the committee were optimistic about their chances of early success it is impossible to say. Whatever they expected, twelve long years of hard and frustrating labour lay before them.

One of the problems that faced the Married Women's Property Committee during these twelve years was that of keeping the organization 'intact and in working order,' for some of the most important supporters tended to drop away. Elizabeth Wolstenholme resigned as secretary and member of the executive committee in 1871. Three years later Lydia Becker gave up her post as treasurer and, together with Frances Power Cobbe, Isabella Tod, the Penningtons, and the Ashworth sisters, ceased to serve upon the executive committee. Also in 1874 Lady Amberley died. (For the changing membership of the executive committee, see appendix 3.) This loss of support was partly due to the changing political climate, which was increasingly unfavourable to reform, especially after the Conservative victory at the election of 1874. But the Married Women's Property Committee blamed chiefly the mistaken belief of the public and even of 'best friends' that the act of 1870 represented a victory for equal rights and responsibilities for women rather than being merely an 'ineffective compromise.' The committee reported receiving 'innumerable letters' showing that 'the greatest stumbling block in the way of real and vital reform is some half-measure, which whilst seeking to remedy the most flagrant abuses, really conceded as little as possible.' In short, what the members of the committee had feared would happen, when they reluctantly agreed to accept the emasculated bill of 1870, did happen. The momentum for reform was lost.[2]

Still, the Married Women's Property Committee did continue in existence, unlike Barbara Bodichon's little committee of the fifties, which disappeared after passage of the Divorce Act of 1857. Some of the committee's members served faithfully as long as it was in being, most notably Josephine Butler, Jacob and Ursula Bright, Richard Pankhurst, and Professor and Mrs Hodgson. Then, in the later 1870s, the committee regained its reforming vigour. Perhaps this was partly due to the obvious fact that the Conservative government could not remain in power much longer, and the belief that reform would fare better with the Liberals in office. But the committee gave credit for its revived energies chiefly to Ursula Bright, who had succeeded Lydia Becker as treasurer, and to Elizabeth Wolstenholme Elmy, who returned to her old post as secretary in 1880. Mrs Bright was able to increase both the number of subscribers and the amount of money subscribed. Before 1876 the largest number of subscribers did not exceed 64, but by 1876 the number had risen to 90, and among these were such important new supporters and members of the executive committee as Peter and Clementia Taylor, Arthur and Amelia Arnold, and Emilie Venturi. Also, the amount of money raised in 1876 was £180 more than the amount raised in any previous year. Still, the largest subscribers were Jacob Bright, his nieces the Ashworth sisters, and J.P. Mellor, Mrs Bright's father; and during the whole fifteen years of its existence, the committee collected and expended less than £3,200.[3]

The Married Women's Property Committee continued its campaign designed to 'press the subject upon public attention.' An important feature of this campaign was the presentation of papers on the subject of property-law reform. The congresses of the Social Science Association continued to be a favourite forum. Elizabeth Wolstenholme and Herbert N. Mozley presented papers at the congress of 1870, and the former, now Mrs Elmy, delivered another at the congress in 1875. At the association's meeting in 1877 in Aberdeen, a paper on the married women's property law in Scotland was presented by John McLaren, later lord advocate and later still, as Lord McLaren, a judge of the Court of Session; and another paper, on the law in England, was given by John Boyd Kinnear. Two years later Kinnear spoke again at the association's congress in Manchester. At the congress of 1880 in Edinburgh there were two extended discussions on the question of reform: one session, presided over by John McLaren, now lord advocate, included yet another paper by Kinnear, while the other session, presided over by the solicitor general for Scotland, J.B. Balfour, included presentations by Mrs Elmy and by Lydia Becker, and the former delivered still another talk on the subject at the association's congress in 1881. The audiences were always sympathetic, but the association itself, after twenty years' existence, was now clearly in decline and no longer a very effective organ for support of the women's cause.[4]

The publicity campaign of the Married Women's Property Committee also included the publication and distribution of pamphlets. One of these was a reprint of a lecture given at Birmingham in 1873 by Sir Henry Maine, the distinguished legal historian and professor of jurisprudence at Oxford, on 'The Early History of the Property of Married Women,' later included in one of his larger works. Another pamphlet was one by Arthur Arnold entitled *The Married Women's Property Committee, the Hon. Mrs. Norton and Married Women*, published in 1873, and yet another was a reprint of Arnold's article 'The Hon. Mrs. Norton and Married Women' which appeared in *Fraser's Magazine* in 1878 after Mrs Norton's death. Some of the speeches delivered at the annual meetings of the Married Women's Property Committee were also reprinted in pamphlet form, such as Sir Erskine Perry's speech of 1880. During the last seven years of its existence, the Married Women's Property Committee distributed half a million pamphlets, leaflets, and other papers.[5]

The committee was active, too, in circulating petitions for signatures and presenting these to parliament. During its last seven years the committee collected more than 1,600 petitions containing over 60,000 names. This work the committee believed to be 'of the highest educational value, so many of the signatures having only been given after long and deliberate consideration.'[6]

Meanwhile, in addition to its propaganda efforts, the committee naturally engaged in work that was more strictly political and legal. Its members studied the details and implications of legislation already enacted or under consideration by parliament that would affect the property of married women although it did not deal specifically with that property. Such legislation included, for example, bills relating to taxation and to the criminal law. The members were also active in giving and procuring legal advice about the provisions of the act of 1870 for persons who, as the committee's report said, wanted to prevent or redress a wrong or to guard against inflicting a wrong on others. The committee prompted questions in parliament on the subject of the married women's property law – as when Peter Taylor twice inquired about the Conservative government's attitude and intentions with respect to Mrs McCarthy's case in 1878, only to receive very unsatisfactory answers from the attorney general, Sir John Holker. Most important of all, the committee carefully calculated the chances of getting a reform bill introduced and passed in every session of parliament, while always on watch against undesirable bills.[7]

The question of further reform of the married women's property law did not come before parliament again until two years after passage of the act of 1870, and then the initiative was taken not by the women's friends but by their opponents. The bill of 1872 was introduced by Alexander Staveley Hill, a stauch Conservative who had entered parliament in 1868 and was to remain there for thirty-three years, representing first Coventry and then Staffordshire. A highly successful lawyer, Hill also served for many years as recorder of Banbury and as counsel to the admiralty and judge advocate of the fleet. Hill's proposed reform, which Henry Lopes and Henry Raikes co-sponsored, would have removed the anomaly created by the act of 1870 that a husband was relieved of liability for his wife's antenuptial debts although he might have received all of her property upon marriage. Hill did not propose to return to the situation obtaining before 1870 by making husbands solely responsible for their wives' debts contracted before marriage. Instead, his bill would impose a joint liability upon husband and wife, the husband being liable only to the extent of property he had acquired from his wife.[8]

The Married Women's Property Committee took counsel as to what course should be followed with respect to this bill. A special meeting of the committee was held in London at the rooms of the Social Science Association, with Frederick Pennington presiding. The general feeling was that Hill's measure was a bad one and should be opposed; it provided a remedy for the creditors of women who contracted debts and then married, thereby escaping liability, but it provided no remedy for the creditors of women who contracted debts after marriage, especially those who were carrying on businesses separate from their husbands. At the same time the committee hoped that the introduction of Hill's measure would be 'a favourable occasion for moving the legislature to remedy the evil complained of, together with all other hardships of the existing law, by passing a comprehensive measure annexing to all women the same rights and liabilities as to property and contract as appertain by law to men.'[9]

The women and their friends were able to defeat Hill's proposed reform. The second reading of his bill was postponed twice, first from 27 March to 27 May because of the Easter holidays, and then from 27 May, which was Derby Day, to 17 July. All this time Russell Gurney, who had introduced the women's comprehensive reform bill in 1869 and again the following year, was in the United States, occupied with his official duties as one of the arbitrators of American and British claims under the provisions of the Treaty of Washington. Immediately upon his return to England a deputation from the Married Women's Property Committee conferred with him about the situation. Gurney could not agree to lead the women's cause in parliament now because of his imminent return to the United States to resume his arbitration work, but he promised to find another member of parliament to help in his absence. This new helper of the women's cause was John Hinde Palmer, a successful barrister who had been named a queen's counsel and who, after four unsuccessful contests for a parliamentary seat, had been elected as Liberal member for Lincoln in 1868. He had actively supported the Education Act of 1870, and likewise favoured extension of house-hold suffrage to the counties, a reform carried through in 1884, and he wrote two books reflecting his interest in these important public issues. He sponsored and helped to carry through parliament several useful bills to amend the law of property, one of them popularly known as 'Hinde Palmer's Act.' He was to lose his seat in parliament in the election of 1874, then regain it in 1880 and serve until his death four years later. Now Palmer, on the women's behalf, announced his opposition to Hill's bill and proposed that the second reading be postponed for three months. He was taking advantage of a new rule of the House of Com-mons, the so-called 'half-past twelve rule,' under which no private member's bill could be taken up after that hour in the evening if opposition to it had been announced. Palmer's action in effect defeated Hill's measure, for at that late period of the parliamentary session every day was fully occupied with other business.[10] Unfortunately this 'half-past twelve rule' could be used against women as well as for them, as they were soon to learn.

With Hill's imperfect measure out of the way, the Married Women's Property Committee next tried to persuade the government to take up the cause of reform. When questioned, the women's old friend Coleridge, the attorney gen-eral, said that he himself could not undertake to bring in a reform bill. However, he did preside at the committee's fifth annual meeting in 1872, which was held in September at Plymouth in conjunction with the Social Science Association's congress. This meeting passed a resolution praying the government to deal with this 'question of social justice' during the next parliamentary session by intro-ducing a 'comprehensive measure' such as the women's original bill of 1870 to 'remedy all defects and hardships of the existing law.' Then, on the committee's behalf Coleridge forwarded to Gladstone a memorial containing the request for government support of reform, but the prime minister made no reply.[11]

Having failed to gain official support for reform, the members of the Married Women's Property Committee turned again to their new friend Hinde Palmer. During the previous parliamentary session Palmer had given notice of his inten-tion to bring in a reform bill in 1873, and he now honoured this pledge. Early in February Staveley Hill's measure of 1872, which had been reintroduced, received its second reading. Five days before this Palmer introduced the women's bill, with Jacob Bright, Osborne Morgan, and Sir Richard Amphlett as co-sponsors. Amphlett, an able equity lawyer, had sat in parliament since 1868 as member for East Worcestershire; in 1874 he was to be appointed a justice of the Exchequer Division of the High Court, and two years afterward promoted to the Court of Appeal. The women's bill of 1873 was a measure of thoroughgoing reform. It had been prepared on behalf of the Married Women's Property Committee by Dr Richard Pankhurst and was based on the women's original bill of 1870. It would have repealed eleven of the seventeen clauses of the act of 1870, replacing them with provisions securing to married women all property of whatever kind which they acquired both before and after marriage, with the same property rights and responsibilities as unmarried women.[12]

The women's bill came on for its second reading later in February. In the debates Palmer, Morgan, and Shaw-Lefevre dwelt upon the defects of the act of 1870 and the obvious need for its amendment, Palmer expressing the hope that the stock arguments against the bill would not be repeated now. But Lopes and a few others brought them all out again. Lopes agreed that the act of 1870 was bad – 'no worse Act of Parliament ... had ever become law' – but maintained that that was no reason for accepting Palmer's bill. Taking his examples and even some of the language he used from the remarks of Lord Penzance and Lord Shaftesbury during the debates of 1870, Lopes argued that if the bill was passed, a wife could turn her husband out of her house, set up a business in competition with her husband's and in partnership with 'a cousin' who 'need not be a woman, and might not be a cousin at all,' and so on. But Coleridge, on behalf of the government, expressed approval of the bill, which passed its second reading by a vote of 124 to 103, and then went into committee.[13]

Thereafter the bill was lost in the parliamentary mazes, and its troubled history can be briefly summarized. The committee to which it was referred sat on four occasions between the end of March and the end of June, amending the bill slightly and reporting progress three times. The bill was 'counted out' six times – that is, it failed for lack of a quorum. Referring to these occasions, the Married Women's Property Committee later remarked, 'This indifference to the fate of a measure affecting the property and personal rights of that half of the people which is unrepresented in Parliament illustrates the difficulty of obtaining the attention of members to the interests of a class which has no voice in their election.' The bill was postponed because of the 'half-past twelve rule' no less than fifteen times. Ironically the women's opponents, led by Lopes, took their cue from the women's friend Hinde Palmer, who had defeated Staveley Hill's bill the previous year by invoking this rule. Finally, the women's bill was postponed on six other occasions as well. All in all, it was a grueling ordeal, and at its annual meeting that year, held at the town hall in Manchester in October, the Married Women's Property Committee paid special tribute to Hinde Palmer: 'Early and late he has been at his post, and only one who knows the long and patient watching involved in the charge of such a Bill can appreciate the amount of personal sacrifice which has been cheerfully undergone by our zealous and indefatigable Parliamentary leader.'[14]

Still, the parliamentary session of 1873 was by no means a total loss to the women's cause. The most important business of the session was passage of the Judicature Bill. For nearly seven years, since appointment of the royal commission in 1867, the matter of thoroughgoing legal reform had been before parliament, and the Liberals were determined to carry through reform before they left office. The Judicature Bill, one of the greatest landmarks in English legal history, was passed, with its provisions for the merger of all superior courts in the new Supreme Court of Judicature, which would achieve a fusion of the different systems of law previously administered by the different courts and would, in particular, be guided by the principle that in any conflict between the common law and equity on the same matter, the rules of equity should prevail. These provisions meant that in time, inevitably, by judicial decisions, the old common-law rules which gave a married woman's property to her husband would be superseded by the equitable rules which recognized a married woman's separate property.

But the members of the Married Women's Property Committee were not content to await this inevitable but slow development. They were determined to press forward with legislation to amend the married women's property law immediately. Unfortunately for their hopes, the Liberals' tenure of power was ending. Once the Judicature Bill was safely through parliament, the government front bench, said Disraeli, resembled a row of extinct volcanoes, their reforming energies spent. In January 1874 Gladstone announced the dissolution of parliament, and the ensuing general election returned the Conservatives under Disraeli to office. Especially disheartening to women was the fact that more than eighty members who had supported reform between 1868 and 1873 were absent, among them such staunch friends as Jacob Bright, Henry Fawcett, and Hinde Palmer, while 'the opponents of such legislation were in strong force.'[15] (However, within two months' time Fawcett was returned to parliament as member for Hackney, the constituency which he represented until his death in 1884, while Bright was re-elected as member for Manchester in a by-election in 1876 and held this seat, except for one more brief interval, until 1895.) Women had already lost other powerful supporters. Sir George Jessel had left the Commons upon his appointment as master of the rolls in 1873, and in that year John Stuart Mill had died. Five years later Russell Gurney died.

Reform of the married women's property law fared ill under the Conservative government. To be sure, two acts dealing with married women's property were passed during the Conservatives' six-year tenure. But neither of these was a measure of thoroughgoing reform; each was, instead, a sort of tidying-up measure.

The first of these to be passed was a relatively minor amendment to the act of 1870. The measure as introduced was similar to the one brought in by Staveley Hill without success in the two preceding sessions of parliament. Its sponsors freely admitted that its purpose was not to protect married women but to protect the large numbers of businessmen who had petitioned parliament for reform. Wholesale dealers trading with shopkeepers all over the country had found it unsafe to do business with unmarried women, who could obtain goods on credit and then marry and transfer all their property to their husbands, thus escaping responsibility for payment. The members of the Married Women's Property Committee now decided not to oppose the measure, on the ground that they had no bill of their own before parliament. After the election of this year the committee had consulted 'long and anxiously' with friends in parliament, who felt it inexpedient to introduce a bill during the session of 1874. Also, probably the women were personally more favourably disposed to Samuel Morley, sponsor of the bill of 1874, than they had been to Staveley Hill. Morley, Liberal member for Bristol, was a large-scale hosiery manufacturer and one of the wealthiest men of the time. He was also one of the greatest philanthropists of his day. A devout Congregationalist and a model employer, he supported such causes as the building of chapels and the removal of religious disabilities, popular education, and the temperance movement, and was principal proprietor of the liberal *Daily News*. In fact Morley could be counted as one of the women's friends, for he had presided at the annual meeting of the Married Women's Property Committee in 1869. Morley's measure was approved on behalf of the new Conservative government by the attorney general, Sir Richard Baggallay, who was later to serve for more than a decade as a justice of the Court of Appeal. The bill passed its second reading without a division, was amended slightly by a select committee, and then passed through parliament in only two months' time.[16]

This Married Women's Property Act (1870) Amendment Act of 1874 (37 & 38 Vict., c 50) restored a husband's liability for his wife's antenuptial debts, but with the qualification that he was liable only to the extent of assets he had received from her upon marriage, these assets being specifically set forth in the act. Of the easy passage of the measure through parliament Arthur Arnold commented, 'That tradesmen – electors and fathers – should be cheated, was to Parliament intolerable.'[17] Women might well ponder the ease and speed with which a bill to remedy the grievances of the male business community was passed, compared to the unsuccessful attempts to remedy their own grievances.

The second reform to become law under the Conservatives was the act of 1877 amending the married women's property law in Scotland (40 & 41 Vict., c 29). (The Married Women's Property Act of 1870 applied to England, Wales, and Ireland but not to Scotland.) The Scots law relating to married women's property, which differed from the English law more in language than in substance, vested in the husband two legal rights upon marriage. The first of these was the *jus mariti*, which in practice transferred to the husband absolutely all of his wife's property except land, although he received the income from her land and also had a life interest in it under the curtesy. The second legal right vested in the husband, the 'right of administration,' made his consent necessary to any dealing by his wife with any of her property which did not become his upon marriage. In turn, a wife enjoyed the right of *terce*, which was analogous to the English dower right – a life interest in one-third of the income from her husband's land after his death. She also enjoyed the *jus relictae*, the right to at least one-third of her husband's personal property on his death or one-half if there were no children. At the same time, marriage settlements or marriage contracts drawn up to provide an escape from these provisions of the law were as common in Scotland as in England, so that in Scotland too there existed one law for the rich and another for the poor. The Scots law relating to married women's property had been amended only slightly up to this time. Under the Conjugal Rights Act of 1861 a wife deserted by her husband could obtain legal protection for the property she acquired after her desertion, just as deserted wives in England could obtain protection under the provisions of the Divorce Act of 1857. Under the same act of 1861 a wife living with her husband could claim provision for herself out of property coming to her during marriage, this being analogous to English wives' 'equity to a settlement.'[18]

At the request of the Married Women's Property Committee, a reform bill for Scotland was introduced in parliament in 1877 by George Anderson, Radical member for Glasgow, with Duncan McLaren as one of the co-sponsors. This bill was not the same as the English act of 1870 but represented an attempt to 'jump to one more perfect and complete.' Specifically, it would have created for married women in Scotland a 'separate estate' comprising their income from real property and their earnings and other personal property. Thus it would have gone considerably beyond the provisions of the English act of 1870.[19]

The Conservative government now refused to accept broader reform for Scotland than for England. This position was set forth implacably by the lord advocate, William Watson, an impressive opponent of the women's cause. Known as a staunch conservative and reputed to be the most learned lawyer in the country, he was to be raised to the peerage as Baron Watson in 1880 and appointed a lord of appeal in ordinary. Watson agreed to the second reading of Anderson's bill only on the condition that the government's amendments to it should be accepted. The bill was then submitted to a select committee which reduced it to two substantive clauses: one granted to married women in Scotland control over their earnings, a provision similar to one in the English act of 1870; the other, like the English act of 1874, made husbands liable for their wives' antenuptial debts only to the extent of property they had acquired from their wives. Thus the bill did not give wives in Scotland even so much protection as English wives, because it did not protect their investments and inherited property as well as their earnings. Still, the government promised to allow Anderson and his colleagues to bring the Scots law up to the level of the English law at a later date, and also indicated their own willingness to deal comprehensively with the question later on. In these circumstances the Married Women's Property Committee did not feel free to oppose the amended bill, which easily completed its passage through parliament.[20]

Reform of the Scots law came before parliament again in 1878, when George Anderson introduced a bill which would have assimilated the Scots law relating to married women's property to the existing English law. But the bill never obtained a second reading. As Anderson later told the story, Watson, the lord advocate, and Richard Assheton Cross (later Lord Cross), the home secretary, had agreed to his introduction of the bill, but then Watson put down notice of government opposition, and this blocked the bill from coming before the Commons.[21]

Still Anderson persisted in his efforts to push through a reform measure. When parliament met in December 1878, he introduced his bill again, and it came on for its second reading the following March. On this occasion Anderson commented that the sparse attendance in the House, despite the special request of women interested in the bill that members be present for the debate and vote, showed how little parliament cared for those who had no vote and no representation. He challenged the lord advocate and the home secretary, whom he accused of treachery in breaking their pledges to him, to allow his bill to pass or else to bring in a government bill. Watson and Cross were among the many members who were absent from the House, and the bill was read a second time without a division. But the government opposed the bill in its later stages. Then, to no avail, Anderson tried private negotiation with the lord advocate, who merely said that the government would legislate on the matter. Anderson introduced his bill yet again early in 1880. It was scheduled for a second reading in June, but before then parliament had been dissolved.[22]

Meanwhile the English reformers had fared no better than the Scots. In 1877, at the request of the Married Women's Property Committee, the bill which Hinde Palmer had introduced in the Commons four years before was brought before the upper House by Lord Coleridge, the former attorney general who was now chief justice of the Common Pleas Division of the Supreme Court. But Coleridge met with such a hostile reception in the House of Lords that he did not insist on a division on the second reading of the bill.[23]

The next year, 1878, the same bill was introduced again in the Commons, this time by John Tomlinson Hibbert (later Sir John), with Osborne Morgan and Sir Charles Dilke as co-sponsors. Lord Coleridge had recommended Hibbert to the

Married Women's Property Committee as the person to be asked to take charge of the measure. Hibbert was a lawyer who had entered parliament in 1862 and served as parliamentary secretary of the Local Government Board in Gladstone's first ministry. He had been defeated at the election of 1874 but had now regained his seat for Oldham at a by-election. He was to hold office in Gladstone's three later ministries as well – again as parliamentary secretary of the Local Government Board, as undersecretary of the Home Office, as financial secretary to the treasury, and as secretary to the admiralty. In 1884 Hibbert was to be forced by Gladstone to vote, against his convictions, against the women's suffrage amendment to the Reform Bill of that year, while his feminist colleagues in the government Dilke and Fawcett abstained from voting. Now, Hibbert could not get a day for the second reading of his bill until July, and by that time the government had pre-empted for its own business all the time remaining in the session.[24]

Still Hibbert, like his colleague George Anderson for Scotland, persisted in efforts to carry through a reform measure. When parliament met in December 1878, suddenly summoned for a short session, Hibbert, a widower who had just remarried, was absent from England on his wedding trip. He wrote to Osborne Morgan asking him to introduce the women's bill in his place, but delivery of his letter was delayed for two days, and by then all the time allotted for private members' bills had been taken up by others. Hibbert then consulted with the Married Women's Property Committee at its annual meeting in London in January 1879, and it was agreed that he should give notice in the Commons of a resolution declaring that 'the present statutes with respect to the property of married women being restricted and uncertain in their operation, are unsatisfactory and ought to be amended.' For discussion of his resolution Hibbert obtained time on a Friday night in mid-July. He went to the House with friends, prepared and hoping for a good debate, and found present a number of members far above the necessary quorum, including most of the cabinet members in their places. Now the government forced him to give way so that the Army Discipline Regulation Bill could be taken up. Hibbert relinquished his time with rather ill grace, pointing out that the government's measure affected only a comparatively small number of persons, while the reform he was promoting affected every man, woman, and child in the country. Hibbert introduced his bill again in February 1880, on the same day that Anderson reintroduced the women's bill for Scotland, but parliament was dissolved before the two could come on together for their second reading.[25]

Further reform of the married women's property law obviously stood no chance of success so long as the Conservatives were in power. George Anderson told the annual meeting of the Married Women's Property Committee in 1880 that, to judge by his own experience of the Conservative government's faithlessness, they could not get justice until a Liberal government was in office again.[26] Certainly the Conservatives did not oppose all domestic reforms, despite their claims while they themselves were out of power that the Liberals' reform measures were threatening the social fabric of the country. The Conservative government's earlier years produced legislation which proved Disraeli's strong interest in social problems – for example, legislation which protected the peaceful activities of trade unions, guarded the interests of tenant farmers, regulated the working conditions of merchant seamen, provided public housing for the working classes, and made elementary education compulsory and also free, at least for the poorest. Nor was the failure of property-law reform explained by the fact that the Conservatives found their time and energies more and more absorbed by Irish problems and foreign affairs – the increasingly militant agitation for home rule in depression-ridden Ireland and the emergence of an obstreperous Irish nationalist party in parliament under Parnell's leadership, and abroad such matters as the Zulu War, problems in Afghanistan, and especially the Balkan War and the ensuing Congress of Berlin, at which Disraeli played so large a role. The Liberals, too, had had to deal with Irish and foreign problems. Time for private members' bills – and all the Married Women's Property Bills were private members' measures – had been limited while the Liberals were in power as well as now when the Conservatives were in, yet reform bills had been carried under the Liberals in the sessions of 1869 and 1870, only to be dismembered at last by the Lords.

The real responsibility for the Conservatives' failure to permit passage of the Married Women's Property Bills seems to rest with Lord Cairns, now again lord chancellor, whom Disraeli so greatly respected and relied upon. Cairns was also the chief architect of the Married Women's Property Act of 1870. When Lord Coleridge introduced the Married Women's Property Bill in the upper House in 1877, Cairns responded irately that he trusted the Lords 'would not let it be thought out-of-doors that after all that had passed they were going to re-open this question again.' He concluded inexorably, 'It was settled seven years ago that married women were not to be unmarried so far as their property was concerned, and that they were yet to retain the marriage tie in other respects. The Act of 1870 had worked admirably, and, moreover, it remedied every grievance upon which any person could put his finger.'[27] In view of Cairns's attitude, reformers could only await the Liberals' return to power.

This came in 1880 after an election unprecedented in English history. In his famous Midlothian campaign Gladstone stumped the country personally, as no prime minister had ever done before, taking his case directly to the people. He also appealed especially to women, urging them to take an active part in his campaign, which, he said, 'so far from involving any departure from your character as women ... would serve to gild your future years with sweet remembrances and to warrant you in hoping that, each in your own place and sphere has raised her voice for justice, and has striven to mitigate the sorrows and misfortunes of mankind.' Women responded enthusiastically, serving as canvassers for the Liberals in most constituencies and speaking publicly in the Liberal cause in many places. In particular, during the campaign the Married Women's Property Committee communicated, directly or through friendly constituents, with a majority of the candidates to discover their views on property-law reform. With the growing economic discontent in the country resulting from the onset of the Great Depression, and the increasing seriousness of the Irish question, the Liberals swept back to power with a majority of 137, or a majority of more than 200 if one includes the Irish nationalists. Women were naturally heartened by these results, and especially by the fact that many of their old opponents were defeated, including Henry Raikes (although he was returned to parliament again at a by-election two years later), and many supporters of women's causes came in, among them Arthur Arnold, George Hastings, and, again, Hinde Palmer. In the new parliament the Married Women's Property Committee counted 300 known friends and not 100 known or presumed opponents of the cause.[28]

With the Liberals in office, reform of the married women's property law came on again in parliament, apparently with good chance of success. In May 1880 the English bill was introduced by Hinde Palmer, again the women's parliamentary leader now that Hibbert was a member of the new Liberal government. On the same day George Anderson introduced a bill embodying a more complete reform of the law in Scotland than had been contained in his measure of 1878, which would simply have assimilated the Scots law to the existing English law. The two bills came on together for their second reading early in June. Speaking for the new government, the attorney general, Sir Henry James (later Lord James of Hereford), gave approval to the principles of both bills but stated that some of their clauses should be amended in committee. Debate was brief, and both bills passed without a division. (Incidentally, James, a bachelor, was no friend to women's causes. He had attracted attention by his forceful speech against the women's suffrage bill introduced by Jacob Bright in 1871, and later he was to become an officer in an antisuffrage organization.) The women's bills progressed no further after their second reading, because of the pressure of other parliamentary business and, in particular, because notice of opposition to both bills was put down unexpectedly by a new opponent of reform so that under the half-past twelve rule they could not be considered. This new opponent was Sir

George Campbell, who had sat in parliament as Liberal member for Kirkcaldy since 1875. Campbell, a lawyer and a nephew of the great jurist Lord Campbell, had had a long and distinguished career as a public servant in India, where he was a judge of the high court of Bengal and then lieutenant governor of Bengal. But his career in politics after his return home was, in contrast, a failure, for he gained the reputation in the Commons of being both loquacious and cantankerous.[29]

From the women's point of view it clearly was not enough simply to have a Liberal government rather than a Conservative government in office, even one avowedly in favour of property-law reform. With the government's attention and concern absorbed elsewhere, there was little scope for private members' reform measures. Irish problems dominated home politics – the difficulties over an Irish Land Bill, first between the government and the Irish nationalists and then between the Commons and the Lords, and the government's resort to a policy of coercion in Ireland, which led at length to the arrest and imprisonment of Parnell. Abroad the dominant concern was the increasing British involvement in Egypt – the dispatch first of a British fleet to Alexandria and then of an army under Sir Garnet Wolseley to restore order in the country, which led in turn to British involvement in the Sudan as well, and finally to the disastrous failure to relieve Gordon at Khartoum.

What women needed from the government was not general sympathy for their cause, but active government support for passage of their reform bills. This fact was urged at the annual meeting of the Married Women's Property Committee in 1880 by Sir Erskine Perry, who spoke at the meeting at the special invitation of Amelia Arnold, because of his long connection with the reform movement, dating back to 1855. As Perry said, 'It is a matter essentially for the Government to take up ... for a private member to undertake it, especially in the enormous pressure of business that prevails in every Parliament that meets, would tax his powers to such a degree that it would be almost impossible to accomplish anything of importance ... it is only by the assistance of the Government that a large and comprehensive measure can be obtained.'[30]

But the women and their friends were understandably dubious about the likelihood of obtaining active government support, for Lord Selborne, the new lord chancellor, was believed to be as much opposed to reform as his Conservative predecessor Lord Cairns. Selborne, the former Sir Roundell Palmer, was one of the greatest equity lawyers of the century. He had served with distinction as solicitor general and then as attorney general under Palmerston and Russell, and after the Whig-Liberal government resigned in 1866, he emerged as one of the most important leaders of the opposition together with Gladstone. When Gladstone formed his first ministry in 1868, he offered Palmer, as he then was, the position of lord chancellor. But Palmer, the son of a clergyman and himself a devout Churchman, could not accept Gladstone's announced intention to disestablish the Church in Ireland; he did not become lord chancellor, as Lord Selborne, until Hatherley's resignation for reasons of health in 1872, after disestablishment had been carried through. Bertrand Russell, who together with his older brother Frank became a ward in Chancery after the early death of his parents the Amberleys, remembered Selborne as 'a deeply religious man.' Once, he recalled, when Frank had disobeyed his guardians, 'they sent him to the Lord Chancellor to be reasoned with; but he, finding reason unavailing, went on his knees and prayed that my brother might be granted a better spirit.' A conservative in all but name, and the despair of his more radical colleagues such as Dilke, Selborne had opposed reform of the married women's property law at the time when the act of 1870 was passed. In a widely noticed address as president of the Juridical Society, Selborne had expressed his belief that reform would tend to make wives independent of their husbands and 'unfeminine,' and therefore would not be conducive to domestic peace and harmony. He thought some legislation to give married women both protection for their earnings and a means of enforcing their husbands' responsibility for their support might be good, but beyond that he was 'not prepared to go.'[31]

Yet despite the reformers' misgivings, it was Lord Selborne's immense prestige and practical help in parliament that would carry their cause to victory. It was Selborne who at last adopted the women's bills as government measures and thereby assured their success. Early in January 1881, on behalf of the Married Women's Property Committee, a deputation led by Hinde Palmer and including Arthur Arnold, Jacob Bright, and Sir Arthur Hobhouse waited upon Selborne, and in a long conversation with him had the 'satisfaction of finding how substantial was his Lordship's agreement' with them, and of obtaining his commitment to confer with them about the prospects of reform in parliament. Two weeks later, at a meeting of the Law Amendment Society at which a paper on reform was presented by Charles McLaren, Hinde Palmer stated that he was not apprehensive about the chances of success because 'his Lordship took a favourable view of the principles upon which they proceeded.'[32]

That the conservative-minded lord chancellor had become a convert to the cause of women's rights is extremely doubtful. But Selborne was a jurist, an outstanding one, and doubtless he now viewed reform of the married women's property law as merely a logical consequence of the much broader legal reform which had already been enacted under his leadership. It was Selborne who in 1867 had urged appointment of the royal commission to study reorganization of the country's law and legal machinery, and he was the leading spirit on that distinguished body, whose recommendations were embodied in the great Judicature Bill of 1873. Again, it was Selborne as lord chancellor who was chiefly responsible for passage of that bill through parliament. Now, property-law reform must have seemed to him a practical instance of that fusion of the common law and equity which he himself had so actively and effectively promoted.

In 1881 Married Women's Property Bills for both England and Scotland came before parliament again. On the first day of the year George Anderson brought in the same bill for Scotland he had introduced the year before, and three days after leading the deputation to wait upon Selborne, Hinde Palmer introduced the English bill he had brought in the previous year. Both measures were scheduled to receive a second reading two days after introduction of the English bill, but Anderson and Palmer had to give way at the insistence of W.E. Forster, the chief secretary for Ireland. The debate on the address from the throne had not been concluded, and it was not customary for the House to consider controversial measures until this debate was over. Irish members were enraged by the government's proposal to resort to a policy of coercion in Ireland, and Parnell and his followers indulged in their notorious obstructionist tactics, repeatedly interrupting the proceedings amidst the Speaker's vain cries of 'Order!' The next day, however, the women's bills had their turn. The Scots bill came on late in the evening, and the attorney general, Sir Henry James, gave approval for its second reading on the understanding that it would be submitted to a select committee for amendment. Again Irish members threatened to disrupt proceedings, but were finally called off by Parnell and the bill was approved. Immediately afterward the English bill was read a second time, also without a division, and at Palmer's suggestion was submitted to a select committee for amendment.[33]

Within six months the Scots bill slipped through the parliamentary mazes and became law. The select committee that considered it was chaired by the new lord advocate, John McLaren, and included the solicitor general for Scotland, J.B. Balfour, and other eminent Scots jurists. They redrafted the bill and reported it to the Commons at the end of March. A month afterward, at a late evening hour, the redrafted bill was read a second time by a vote of 69 to 19, and the next evening, again after midnight, it received a third reading. In the upper House Lord Selborne himself took charge of the bill. To it were now added amendments advocated by the Married Women's Property Committee, and in this form it was read a second time without a division. The Lords in committee added a few more amendments, which the Commons accepted, and the measure received royal assent on 18 July (44 & 45 Vict., c 21). This act abolished the *jus mariti* of husbands in Scotland by providing that wives were to have as their separate property both their personal property and the income from their real property; however, a husband's 'right of administration' continued to the extent that his wife could not anticipate the income from her separate property or dispose of it without his consent. Thus the act did not accomplish everything that the reformers had wanted, but it did represent a 'considerable step in advance' and was welcomed as such.[34]

On the other hand, the English bill of 1881 came to an untimely end. The select committee which considered it was chaired by the attorney general, Sir Henry James, and included among its members the veteran feminists Jacob Bright, George Hastings, Osborne Morgan, Hinde Palmer, and George Shaw-Lefevre. They completed their business in less than a month's time, reporting the bill with amendments which the Married Women's Property Committee described as 'practically recasting the Bill as to form,' while still accepting the basic principle that a woman's right to property should not be affected by her marriage. Then, however, the bill ran into difficulties. Notice of opposition to it was put down by yet another new opponent of reform, Charles Nicholas Warton, a staunchly conservative lawyer who sat in parliament briefly as member for Bridport from 1880 until his retirement five years later. Because of his opposition and also because of the pressing problems of Ireland, the bill was repeatedly postponed and was finally withdrawn by Hinde Palmer in August. In that month a heavy blow fell upon the bill's supporters. While seated on the wool-sack, presiding in the House of Lords, Selborne, the lord chancellor, was suddenly taken seriously ill, apparently the victim of a stroke, and for the next several months he was absent from parliament, recuperating at his country home.[35]

Fortunately Selborne recovered his health rapidly, and by the beginning of 1882 was able to return to his official duties. At the request of the Married Women's Property Committee Hinde Palmer entered into communication with Selborne, and obtained his agreement to introduce the English reform bill in the House of Lords, just as, the year before, he had piloted the Scots bill through the upper House. In mid-February Selborne introduced in the Lords the bill as amended by the select committee of the Commons in the preceding parliamentary session, and by the end of May it had been passed. Even Lord Cairns, who had so staunchly defended the act of 1870, did not now oppose reform, whether personally persuaded by Selborne or merely won over by the same rather technical and legalistic considerations which had probably converted Selborne himself.[36]

But the women's bill had still to pass through the Commons, and here again difficulties arose. Early in June Osborne Morgan, now the judge advocate general, introduced the bill on behalf of the government, and six days later, at past one o'clock in the morning, it received a second reading without debate and without a division. It would speedily have passed its third reading as well, but for those two diehards Sir George Campbell and Charles Warton, who gave notice of their opposition in an attempt to defeat the bill. But by now, according to the Married Women's Property Committee, the Commons and the government were 'roused to the conviction that it was nothing less than a public scandal that the obstinacy of two men should be permitted any longer to stand in the way of a great social reform for which the action of both Houses of Parliament and the expressed voice of the country had shown that public opinion was fully ripe.' It was therefore arranged that the committee stage of the bill should be taken at a time to which the half-past twelve rule did not apply, for it was only this rule that enabled obstructionists to succeed.[37]

The Married Women's Property Bill came on for consideration by the House in committee of the whole in mid-August. Interrupted by cries of 'Oh, oh!' and 'No, no!' Campbell and Warton denounced the bill as certain to create a 'social revolution.' Campbell expressed regret that 'the "women righters" had been exceedingly energetic, whilst the friends of the poor married men were indolent.' Warton declared that the bill would 'make the woman, instead of a kind and loving wife, a domestic tyrant,' and unsuccessfully proposed amendment after amendment, including a facetious one to postpone for two years the date on which the enacted bill would come into operation 'in order to give people who were contemplating matrimony time to change their minds when they find the law altered.' Osborne Morgan responded angrily, declaring that Campbell and his constituents had no direct interest in the bill, since a Married Women's Property Act for Scotland had already been passed the year before, and that Warton 'blocked every Bill, good, bad, or indifferent.' Time was running out, for parliament was due to adjourn in a week's time. The House in committee added some amendments to the bill, which four days later was read a third time.[38] Three days after this, on the day that parliament recessed, the bill received the royal assent – the Married Women's Property Act of 1882 (45 & 46 Vict., c 75). (For the text of the act, see appendix 5.)

The act of 1882 sought to embody the principles for which women and their supporters had striven so long – that married women should have the same rights over property as unmarried women, and that husbands and wives should have separate interests in their property. Contrasted with the existing common-law rules relating to married women's property, these were revolutionary principles indeed. Yet these principles, as embodied in the act of 1882, were not set forth in revolutionary terms. Rather, they were couched in the familiar terms of the rules of equity relating to the property of married women. That is, the act of 1882, following the precedent set by the act of 1870, referred not to a married woman's 'own property' but to her 'separate property.' This was a change in the

reprinted from *Punch* 1882

measure which women and their friends favoured and which had been introduced in parliament again and again. The change had been made by the select
committee of the Commons in 1881, and here one surely sees the spirit, if not the
hand, of Lord Selborne. In effect, the act of 1882 bestowed an equitable marriage settlement upon every married woman who did not have one. (The act did
not interfere with existing settlements or with the power to make settlements in
future.) Every married woman without a settlement was to hold all her property
as 'her separate property, in the same manner as if she were a feme sole [unmar-
ried woman] without the intervention of any trustee.' Thus the Married Women's
Property Act of 1882 carried out the principles of the Judicature Act that the
common law and equity should be fused, and that in the event of a conflict
between them equity must prevail.

    The act spelled out precisely what, in the absence of a marriage settlement,
was to be treated as a married woman's separate property. Women who married

after the act came into effect on 1 January 1883 were to have all property, of whatever kind and from whatever source, which they possessed or were entitled to at the time of marriage and which they acquired or became entitled to after marriage. Women married before 1883 were to have all property which they acquired or became entitled to after the act came into effect, as well, of course, as the property they already held under the provisions of the act of 1870. (This act and that of 1874 were now repealed, although some of their provisions were incorporated into the act of 1882.) The act provided further that in case of a dispute between husband and wife over ownership of property, either of them could apply for a summary decision in the matter to the Supreme Court or to a county court, and this provision, the most useful of all those contained in the act, has been used frequently down to the present day.

The act of 1882 set forth the rights that married women were to have with respect to their separate property. They were made capable of 'acquiring, holding and disposing' of it 'by will or otherwise.' They were capable of entering into and making themselves liable on any contract, in respect of and to the extent of their separate property, and capable of suing and being sued alone, without their husbands' being joined with them as parties. In the case of any contract entered into by a married woman, this was to be deemed a contract entered into with respect to her separate property, unless the contrary could be shown. Married women were also specifically empowered to carry on trades and businesses separately from their husbands, using their separate property.

The act also spelled out the responsibilities of married women with separate property. They became primarily liable, to the extent of their separate property, for their antenuptial debts, contracts, and torts; their husbands were liable for these only to the extent of any property they had acquired from their wives. (This was a re-enactment, with additions, of the act of 1874.) The act expressly provided that no marriage settlement, including one subject to the restraint on anticipation, should prevent the property settled from being liable for satisfaction of a woman's antenuptial debts, and that no settlement made or entered into by a woman should be more valid against her creditors than a settlement made or entered into by a man would be valid against his creditors. The act also expressly made subject to the bankruptcy laws all married women who carried on trades and businesses separately from their husbands. In addition, married women were made as liable for the maintenance of their husbands as men were liable for the maintenance of their wives under the provisions of the Poor Law Amendment Act of 1868. Married women were likewise made as liable as men for the support of their children and grandchildren, although the act expressly stated that this was not to relieve husbands of their liability. (These provisions had been included in the act of 1870.)

Finally, the act made special provision for the protection of married women's separate property. It declared that a married woman should have 'in her own name against all persons whomsoever, including her husband, the same civil remedies, and also ... the same remedies and redress by way of criminal proceedings' as if she had been unmarried. With respect to husbands and wives, this provision was qualified in two ways. First, husband and wife could not sue each other in tort, although a wife could sue her husband to protect her separate property. For example, neither husband nor wife could sue the other for slander or for injuries suffered as a result of the other's negligence. Second, no criminal proceedings could be instituted by a wife against her husband while they were living together, or when they were living apart unless her husband had taken her property 'when leaving or deserting, or about to leave or desert.' Here the act specified that in proceedings taken by a wife against her husband, both were 'competent to give evidence against each other, any statute or rule of law to the contrary notwithstanding.' The act provided reciprocally that a husband could take criminal proceedings against his wife for acts done by her against his property. Interestingly, the first case to arise under the act was that of a husband who charged his wife with stealing some of his property and running off with another man.[39]

On 8 November 1882 the Married Women's Property Committee held its final meeting in London, with George Shaw-Lefevre presiding in the absence, because of illness, of Lord Coleridge. The meeting unanimously approved a resolution which declared the Married Women's Property Act of 1882 to be 'a great measure of justice advantageous to all classes of the community, and calculated to raise the dignity and stability of the marriage relationship in this country,' and tendered 'hearty thanks to the Lord Chancellor, and to the many earnest friends both in and out of Parliament whose labours have contributed to the passing of that Act.' Acknowledging this vote of thanks, Osborne Morgan declared that gratitude was really due to 'the devoted band of earnest-minded women, who, with very slender resources at their back and in the face of determined opposition, were resolved to secure for the poor women of this country that control over their own property which their richer sisters enjoyed.' Two of these 'earnest-minded women,' Ursula Bright and Elizabeth Wolstenholme Elmy, received a special address of appreciation and congratulations, presented to them on behalf of the National Society for Women's Suffrage. The final report of the Married Women's Property Committee also paid them tribute, citing Mrs Bright's 'energy and generosity ... capacity and unwearied devotion' and Mrs Elmy's 'intellectual power, legal knowledge, practical skill and unflagging energy.' To them, said the report, belonged 'the chief honour of this peaceful overthrow of a chartered Wrong in the name of a moral Right; of this first great victory of the principle of human equality over the unjust privilege of Sex; this bloodless and beneficent revolution.'[40]

On the first day of January 1883, an editorial in *The Times* declared, 'Today several Acts of great importance ... come into operation. Without denying their significance, we may truly say that all yield in practical consequence to the Married Women's Property Act of 1882, which ... in fact revolutionizes the law upon a vital subject [that] concerns every husband and wife ...' And years afterward another writer, commenting upon the changing legal position of women, said, 'January 1, 1883 is a great date in the annals of married women ... What an emancipation is this!'[41]

10

'The Equality of Two'
After the Acts

Now ... things have got somewhat put to rights ... and by and by
more will be done, till it is all worked through, and the theory of
marriage will be no longer based on the enslaving of one but on
the equality of two.
ELIZA LYNN LINTON[1]

Feminists had won a major victory with passage of
the Married Women's Property Act of 1882. For twenty-seven years they had
fought the good fight to win for wives the same property rights that were
enjoyed by men and unmarried women. They had struggled to end the 'virtual
slavery of marriage' imposed upon women, particularly those of the lower
classes, by the common law, and also to abolish the special, privileged status that
wealthy women enjoyed under the provisions of equity, 'the guardian of the
weak and unprotected.' When they denounced the existence of these two rival
and contradictory legal systems, which meant in practice 'one law for the rich
and another for the poor,' the feminists won a wide and sympathetic hearing.
This was so not only because of the obvious merits of the particular case they
argued but also because their voices were part of a much larger chorus demanding legal reform, and this became the order of the day. In short, feminists were
fortunately not swimming against the tide but were moving with the currents
charted by some of the finest minds of the time.

The English law and courts underwent fundamental revision in the Victorian
age, the reform of the married women's property law being but one part of this
great transformation. The superior courts inherited from earlier times were
swept away and replaced by one Supreme Court, which was to fuse the different
bodies of law previously administered in the separate courts and, in particular,
to see that in cases of conflict among these, the rules of equity should prevail.
When reform of the married women's property law came, therefore, it was

accomplished by applying to women of all classes the equitable provisions once limited to wealthy women. The reform, said A.V. Dicey, was 'simply one more application of the principle insisted upon by the historians of English law, that in England the law for the great men has a tendency to become the law for all men.'[2] The reform was not precisely what had been urged by feminists, who wanted not the extension of equity but the enactment of equal property rights for men and women. Nevertheless the Married Women's Property Act of 1882 was a great measure of reform, and feminists rightly claimed much of the credit for having won its passage.

Why, then, in this age of legal reform, did it take twenty-seven years to pass an effective Married Women's Property Act? One observer of the changing Victorian scene suggested that reform was enacted in 1882 and not earlier because, in effect, there was nothing so powerful as an idea whose hour had come. 'Twenty or thirty years ago, such an Act would have been considered revolutionary; a man who had dared to advocate the views [of independence for women embodied in it] would have been represented as a social firebrand, as an enemy to marriage, as throwing an apple of discord between husband and wife, as a disturber of the peace and harmony of family life.' But by the last decades of the nineteenth century a great revolution in public opinion had taken place. The ideas of Mill and other feminists were by then widely known and widely accepted, and the Married Women's Property Committee took pride in having been 'amongst the most active of the silent but potent forces which have effected this revolution.'[3]

This explanation of the long delay in reforming the married women's property law seems plausible at first, but in fact it will not stand critical scrutiny. Certainly during the first agitation for reform of the law in the 1850s, and again during the great debate on reform in the sixties, feminists were denounced as being social firebrands, enemies of marriage, and the like. But it is by no means certain that twenty or thirty years later feminist ideals of equality and independence for women were generally accepted, so that property-law reform inevitably resulted. In 1882 gloomy voices were still heard denouncing the reform enacted. To give but one example, a lawyer, in a letter to *The Times* signed simply 'Q.C.,' argued that the Married Women's Property Act would 'tend very much to lower the happiness of the marriage state, and reduce matrimony to a condition very little, if any, better than a state of concubinage, with the chill or stigma of that state removed.'[4] One remembers, too, that feminist claims for the parliamentary franchise went unrewarded in this period, that the final victory of the women's suffrage movement was achieved not by the late Victorians but by the next generation. More specifically, this 'intellectual climate' explanation of the delay in enacting property-law reform ignores the actual course of the reform movement in parliament. In 1857, despite a climate of opinion supposedly unfavourable to feminist claims, property-law reform was accepted by a majority in the House of Commons. The question remains, therefore, why a reform first approved in parliament in 1857 was not enacted until 1882.

Feminists, echoing Mill's comments in parliament in 1867 and judging by their own experience with parliament in succeeding years, maintained that the long-delayed reform of the married women's property law was proof that women needed the franchise to protect their interests and win passage of legislation for their benefit. If women had had votes and could have brought pressure directly to bear upon members of parliament and upon successive governments, reform of the married women's property law might have come much earlier than it actually did. As it was, however, feminists had to depend upon the sympathetic efforts of individual members of parliament, and upon the attitude of the government of the day and the state of parliamentary business. Between 1857 and 1882, twenty Married Women's Property Bills were introduced in parliament, all of them private members' bills. A majority in the Commons favoured reform, as shown by the fact that all the bills that came on for a second reading there passed easily, with the single exception of the bill of 1868. But only five bills were enacted into law, all with government support.[5] (For a summary of the legislation in parliament, see appendix 6.) So the further question arises as to why particular governments helped or hindered property-law reform. A more specific question is why it was that certain men in the successive governments of the day favoured or opposed reform, and there is room for interesting if idle speculation as to how different the course of reform might have been had these individuals been different.

The governments of the 1850s were committed to legal reform in general, and were committed in particular to ending some of the differences and conflicts between the common-law courts and the courts of equity and to abrogating the ecclesiastical courts' jurisdiction in matrimonial causes and testamentary matters. In the midst of public and parliamentary debate on these questions, especially the question of divorce, the first organized group of feminists in England, the little committee of Barbara Leigh Smith and her friends, had an excellent opportunity to present their case for property-law reform and to sow the 'germs of an effective movement' throughout the country. Palmerston was determined to carry through reform of the divorce law in 1857, and carried it was, despite the most strenuous opposition. If he had been as deeply committed to property-law reform, would this too have been carried? Palmerston was not so committed. He was always more interested in foreign affairs than internal problems, and there were many crises abroad to occupy his time and energies in these years.

Also, perhaps the strong opposition to passage of the Divorce Act deterred him from honouring the pledge given to feminists that his government would take up property-law reform as well. More probably Palmerston, like many others, felt that the Divorce Act afforded sufficient protection for women, since it safeguarded the property of those women who were judicially separated or divorced or were deserted by their husbands. Certainly passage of the Divorce Act 'took the wind out of the sails' of the feminists who were demanding property-law reform, and after their defeat in 1857 Barbara Leigh Smith's committee disbanded.

The years after 1865, when Palmerston died, were a time of renewed reform activity. The 'peculiar character' of this 'modern world' was the demand for individual freedom and equality; and two great public questions of the day were the widening of the parliamentary franchise and, again, the carrying through of legal reform, specifically the matter of complete amalgamation of the country's superior courts and of the different bodies of law which they administered. In these circumstances feminists once more had a fine chance to assert their claims that women should be treated as free and equal citizens under the law – that they be allowed to vote as well as to control their property – and they placed 'the burthen of proof' on their opponents to show why freedom and equality should not be granted women. A second Married Women's Property Committee, larger in membership and with more numerous and more powerful political connections than the first committee of the fifties, was formed to agitate for amendment of the property law. The Reform Bill of 1867 was passed, enlarging the electorate although not including women, and the first election held under its provisions was a great popular mandate for Gladstone's Liberals, who took office in 1868 committed to carrying through sweeping reform of the country's legal system and many other reforms as well. In 1870, with the blessing of the Liberal government, the first reform of the married women's property law was enacted. Gladstone himself, no friend of the feminists and the women's suffrage cause, perhaps took to heart the suggestion that if parliament enacted property-law reform, it would do away with one of the most important grievances which inspired women to demand the right to vote.

But the Married Women's Property Act of 1870 was a most unsatisfactory measure, a 'legislative abortion.' The bill favoured by the feminists, approved by Gladstone's government, and passed by the House of Commons had been amended beyond recognition by the law lords of the House of Lords, led by Lord Cairns. Their Lordships' action was motivated not by any desire to flout the wishes of the feminists and their friends in the Commons but by their wish to make the provisions of the bill more consistent with the equitable rules applying to married women's property. Their action, in turn, reflected the general trend of legal reform which culminated in passage of the Judicature Act of 1873 – the superseding of the common law by equity in case of conflict between them.

The principles of the act of 1870 were not carried through to their logical legal conclusion until twelve years later. When the Conservatives returned to office in 1874, Lord Cairns again became lord chancellor, and as the real author of the act of 1870 he was too professionally and personally involved in defending its wisdom and practical usefulness to countenance any suggestion that it be amended. In 1880, when the Liberals took office again, Lord Selborne succeeded Cairns as lord chancellor. Like Gladstone, Selborne was no feminist, but almost single-handedly, in the midst of the government's foreign and Irish problems, he carried through that sweeping reform of the married women's property law in 1882 which was hailed as such a great 'emancipation.' Doubtless he saw this reform not as a means to assert women's independence and equality but merely as a measure to tidy up the law of property in the wake of the Judicature Act, which he himself had so largely inspired. Indeed, in the context of the times it may have been as necessary as it was logical that meaningful reform of the married women's property law should follow and not precede the thorough-going reform of the judiciary in 1873. But if Selborne had died in 1881 or been permanently disabled by his illness, would property-law reform have been further and indefinitely delayed?

To trace the course of reform of the married women's property law is to suggest another question, tangential but intriguing. The campaign for property-law reform was closely connected, both logically and chronologically, with the women's suffrage movement. Why was it that reform of the property law succeeded and women's suffrage failed?

One of the most important of the suffragist arguments is especially interesting because of its direct connection with the question of women's property. This argument, which may be called the constitutional claim, was well presented by Helen Taylor in the earliest days of the suffrage movement – that in England possession of property had always been the qualification for voting.

It is hard to see how, if the law of England endows a woman with property, it can, consistently with this legal dictum, deprive her of the 'essential privilege' ... whereby her property is to be preserved ... If it be an advantage to be able to protect one's property by the power of voting for members of Parliament, the possession of this advantage must be good for all those who live and own property under Parliamentary Government. The good that would be done to women themselves is, in fact, not open to dispute, unless we dispute the advantage of Parliamentary Government and representation of property; and in that case we must dispute the advantage of the English system of government altogether.[6]

This constitutional claim was logically unanswerable, yet its practical implications and applications created differences of opinion among the supporters of women's suffrage. They agreed in principle that all women should be enfranchised, but they differed as to tactics – should they demand the vote for all women of property, with little chance of success, or should they claim the vote for unmarried women only, with some chance of success, and then press their claim for married women as well? The situation was complicated by the success of property-law reform. In 1866, when the women's suffrage movement began, few wives owned property that would have qualified them to vote; after passage of the Married Women's Property Acts of 1870 and 1882, many more wives owned property that was unrepresented in parliament.

This question of tactics was raised in the earliest days of the suffrage movement and led to a split among the first suffragists in London. According to Mill and Helen Taylor, the issue of married women's right to vote with respect to their property should not be interjected into the suffrage question. The first women's suffrage petition, which was drafted by Helen Taylor at Barbara Bodichon's request and presented by Mill in parliament in June 1866, simply asked the Commons to consider 'providing for the representation of all householders, without distinction of sex, who possess such property or rental qualification as your Honourable House may determine.' Similarly, Mill's suffragist amendment to the Reform Bill of 1867 provided only that women should be enfranchised on the same terms as men. Meanwhile a women's suffrage committee had been organized in London, its members including Barbara Bodichon, Jessie Boucherett, Frances Power Cobbe, Emily Davies, Elizabeth Garrett, Lady Goldsmid, Bessie Parkes, and Clementia Taylor. Headed by Miss Davies, this committee decided to claim the vote only for 'unmarried women and widows on the same conditions on which it is, or may be, granted to men.' As Miss Davies explained to Helen Taylor, 'We ask for what there is a remote chance of getting. If we ask for married women also, we get it neither for them nor for the smaller class [of unmarried women]. When the wedge is inserted, we can go on for more, including liberty for married women in other directions.' But Mill held that the committee's position of specifically excluding married women undermined the whole principle of equality of the sexes for which he stood, and he and Helen Taylor were glad to see the committee disband in June 1867, because of internal disagreements and personality clashes. Clementia Taylor soon formed a new committee, the nucleus of the London National Society for Women's Suffrage, with Mill as its nominal head and herself as secretary. She had complained earlier to Helen Taylor of being regarded by her suffragist colleagues as 'a dangerous go-ahead revolutionary person,' and none of the members of the first suffrage committee joined the successor group.[7]

In the years that followed, leadership of the suffrage movement passed from the suffragists of London to those of Manchester, and for a time the dispute over tactics was muted. In 1868 Mill was defeated in his bid for re-election to parliament, and Jacob Bright, new to parliament and as yet unknown to the public, became the parliamentary champion of the women's suffrage cause. Bright successfully carried an amendment to the Municipal Franchise Bill of 1869 providing that women could vote in municipal elections under the same conditions as men, and containing no specific mention of married women's right to vote. In 1870 Bright, seconded by Sir Charles Dilke, introduced a bill which, like Mill's proposal of 1867, would have given women the parliamentary vote on the same terms as men with no mention of married women's right. This bill, defeated in the Commons only by the Liberal government's tardy announcement of opposition to it, was reintroduced by Bright in the three succeeding sessions of parliament and defeated each time. Meanwhile, in 1870 the first Married Women's Property Act was passed, and as a result hundreds of married women who now owned property attempted to vote in the elections in Manchester, claiming that they had been enfranchised by the act of 1869. However, these women's claim was denied, and the Court of Queen's Bench, in the leading case of *R* v *Harrald* in 1872, ruled that marriage disqualified women of property from voting, that only single women who owned property could vote.

The year 1874 saw another division in the suffragist ranks, as the question of whether married women should be included, excluded, or simply not mentioned in suffrage bills surfaced again. At the general election that year the Conservatives were returned to control of parliament, and Jacob Bright lost his parliamentary seat. To succeed him as sponsor of the women's suffrage bills Lydia Becker secured the support of William Forsyth, a lawyer and queen's counsel who was Conservative member for Marylebone. But to Miss Becker's dismay and despite her remonstrations Forsyth insisted on including in the suffrage bill the so-called 'coverture clause' – a clause stating that women under coverture, that is, married women, were not to be enfranchised. Forsyth hoped by this means to disarm opposition to the bill, but it was defeated in the Commons in 1875 and again the following year. Meanwhile Jacob and Ursula Bright, Richard Pankhurst, and others dissociated themselves from Lydia Becker and her supporters, blaming them for sacrificing the women's original bill.[8] Doubtless these events explain Miss Becker's resignation from the executive committee of the Married Women's Property Committee in 1874, and her replacement as treasurer by Mrs Bright. In 1877 Jacob Bright briefly resumed charge of the women's suffrage bill, having regained his seat in parliament the year before, but he soon gave way as the parliamentary suffrage leader to Leonard Courtney.

Some years later a similar scenario was acted out. In the interim the Married Women's Property Act of 1882 had been passed, creating many more propertied wives without votes. Also, women had been given equally with men the right to vote in elections for the new county councils created by the Local Government Act of 1888, but in view of the decision in *R* v *Harrald* this meant that only single women of property could vote in these elections. As a result of these developments Lydia Becker and other leaders of the Central National Society for Women's Suffrage decided in 1889 to support a bill granting women the parliamentary franchise but including the 'coverture clause' barring married women. Three years later the society, headed by Millicent Fawcett since Miss Becker's death in 1890, adopted a suffrage bill which would have given the parliamentary vote to those women who were qualified to vote in local elections – that is, the unmarried. In protest against these bills, neither of which was passed by parliament, the supporters of married women's right to vote seceded from the society and formed the short-lived Women's Franchise League, its council including Jacob and Ursula Bright, Richard and Emmeline Pankhurst, Elizabeth and Ben Elmy, Josephine Butler, and Clementia Taylor.[9]

The divisive issue of votes for all women of property or for single women only was finally resolved in 1894. The Local Government Act of that year creating district and parish councils gave women equally with men the right to vote for these councils. The act also included a clause, proposed by Walter McLaren at the insistent urging of Ursula Bright and other supporters of married women's rights, providing that marriage should not disqualify women from voting in any local elections. The act thus reversed the decision in *R* v *Harrald* and ensured that all women of property, the married as well as the unmarried, could participate freely in local elections. Only the parliamentary franchise still eluded women, for another quarter-century.[10]

Meanwhile, the continually revived proposal to restrict the parliamentary franchise to single women of property had not only distracted and divided the suffragist ranks, but had also provided antisuffragists with ammunition for their attacks. Some argued that unmarried women were, of all women, the least qualified to vote intelligently. The Countess of Galloway, for one, remarked snidely that a spinster had 'hardly any experience of life beyond managing each her own maid-servant and her own cat – if indeed the cat and the maid-servant do not manage her.' Gladstone observed that wives were no less intelligent and able than their unmarried sisters and were, moreover, better fitted to vote by their 'life-long habit of responsible action.' Millicent Fawcett defended her position as best she could, pointing out that women were not divided irrevocably into two classes, the married and the unmarried. Single women were every day getting married, while married women were every day becoming widows. There would always be the closest identity of feeling and interests between these two constantly changing categories, and thus there was little danger that the single women who were enfranchised would neglect the interests of married women.[11]

More serious than their speculations about the ability of single women to vote intelligently was the antisuffragists' valid argument that the claim of the vote for single women of property only was both illogical and unconstitutional. And in this connection many antisuffragists claimed that the whole suffrage question had been made more difficult by passage of the Married Women's Property Acts, especially the act of 1882. As one writer vehemently expressed this view:

However excellent and necessary that act is on its merit it causes serious complication relating to woman suffrage. There is no escape from this dilemma: either you refuse a vote to a wife possessing large property ... Then you violate the whole principle ... that *property* should be represented ... Or ... you render the voting wife politically, as well as pecuniarily, independent of her husband. The vote becomes a curse; the husband becomes a mere appendage without authority, a cipher, a nonentity in his own house.[12]

To such tirades Millicent Fawcett replied calmly and sensibly, 'There is nothing unwomanly in recording a vote ... and between man and wife it would make no more difference than does the fact that a woman may now hold separately property of her own.'[13] But in this matter the majority of suffragists had sacrificed principle to expediency, and still they had won no practical advantage.

All this time, suffragists were putting forward another argument for their cause which, like their constitutional claim for the representation of women of property, was closely connected with the question of married women's property rights. This was the utilitarian argument, used first by Mill in parliament in 1867 and heard frequently thereafter both within parliament and out-of-doors – that women needed the vote to protect their interests, and that this need was amply demonstrated by the lack of legal protection for the property of married women and by the long delay in reforming the property law. As one suffragist declared dramatically:

It took a male Parliament just twenty-seven years to see any wrong in the Common Law which proclaimed a married woman a nonentity and a slave ... Would this have been the case if women had been in possession of the vote? Why, of course not ... Every measure of so-called justice to woman has only been wrung after years of toil, in mutilated form, from the British Parliament ... where man sits jealously guarding the domains, privileges and rights which he has usurped. And in thus acting, man has grossly wronged women, and his only honest course is to frankly come forward, and having acknowledged it, give us the human right of having a voice in the making of our own laws. We need the vote for self-protection.[14]

Yet this utilitarian argument, like the suffragists' constitutional claim, could be easily countered by antisuffragists. Even when women could not vote and so bring pressure to bear upon parliament, reforms that women desired were carried through by parliament. Reform of the married women's property law was enacted, and many other reforms as well, such as laws to allow mothers custody of their children and to protect women whose husbands treated them cruelly or failed to support them. As Gladstone wrote to another member of parliament in 1892 in a letter that was printed as a pamphlet and widely circulated by the antisuffragists, 'I admit that we have often, as legislators, been most unfaithful guardians of her [woman's] rights to moral and social equality. And I do not say that full justice has in all things yet been done; but such great progress has been made in most things, that in regard to what may still remain, the necessity for violent remedies [i.e., women's suffrage] has not yet been shown.'[15]

Ironically, then, it can be argued that the success of the campaign to win reform of the married women's property law caused the defeat of the women's suffrage movement. Property-law reform muddied the waters of debate by raising the question of whether, since property was the constitutional qualification for voting, all women of property or only the unmarried should be included in the suffragist claims. This question in turn divided the suffragist ranks and dissipated their energies for nearly thirty years, and justified the antisuffragist argument that the majority of suffragists were supporting an illogical and unconstitutional proposal. Also, property-law reform removed one of the most important grievances which led women to demand the vote, and to that extent deprived them of a telling argument in favour of votes for women. But to argue so is to give too much weight to the importance of suffragist and antisuffragist arguments, and too little weight to the actual business of getting a women's suffrage bill passed by parliament. Reforms, after all, are not carried through by debates but by the machinery controlled by political parties and their leaders. One can understand the failure of the suffrage movement, just as one can understand the success of property-law reform, only by considering the situation in parliament.

To win the vote, as to win reform of the property law, women had to depend upon the sympathy and efforts of individual members of parliament and upon the attitude of the successive governments of the day. Women always hoped for help from the Liberals, who, especially the Radicals among them, usually

"NOT AT HOME."

Miss Sarah Suffrage (*indignantly*). "OH! '*OUT*' IS HE!"   Eight-Hours Bill (*angrily*). "YES!—AND HE WON'T GET '*IN*,' IF *I* CAN HELP IT!!!"

[Mr. Gladstone has lately published an unsympathetic Pamphlet on "Female Suffrage," and has declined to receive a Deputation on the "Eight Hours Day" question.]

reprinted from *Punch* 1892

seemed more sympathetic to women's causes than the Conservatives. Many rank-and-file Liberals favoured women's suffrage, but they could not persuade their party leaders. Gladstone set his face resolutely against votes for women, to the discomfiture of his feminist colleagues such as Dilke and Fawcett and Hibbert. Aside from purely personal prejudice, the antisuffragist attitude of Gladstone and other Liberal leaders may well have been due to their fear that if women were enfranchised on the same terms as men – that is, on the basis of property qualifications – these women of property would be likely to vote Conservative rather than Liberal. On the other hand, a number of Conservative leaders, including Disraeli and Salisbury, personally favoured women's suffrage, but the majority of Conservative backbenchers did not, perhaps fearful that the women who would vote when enfranchised would be precisely the more emancipated who would support the Liberals rather than the Conservatives. For Liberals and Conservatives alike, practical politicians as they were, the prospect of enfranchising a large and untried body of voters was frightening, even though in debate many of them tried to laugh it off as ridiculous or to scorn it as subversive.[16] In contrast, reform of the married women's property law would not be politically unsettling, and it might even disarm the suffragists. Much more important, property-law reform as finally enacted was a logical result of the wider reform of the legal system which had been carried through with the support of both political parties.

Accounts of the Victorian women's movement have traditionally given so much attention to the suffrage campaign that that movement and that campaign have often appeared to be identical. But one should not lose sight of the fact that the suffrage campaign was only one part of a much wider movement which won other important reforms long before women gained the parliamentary vote in 1918. The 'first point in the women's charter' was not the right to vote but the right of married women to own and control property. It was of much greater immediate importance to women that their property be secured to them throughout their married lives than that they be able to cast a ballot at certain intervals in their lives. Reform of the married women's property law, said one Victorian, was 'not so attractive and showy' a matter as voting, public speech making and the like, but, he added, 'Until married women's property is protected by the same laws that protect the property of the rest of Her Majesty's subjects, it is idle to talk of the emancipation of women.'[17] Clearly reform of the married women's property law was one of the greatest achievements, if not the greatest, of the Victorian women's movement.

In fighting to win this reform, feminists had argued chiefly that it would do great practical good, that it would relieve widespread hardship and suffering among women, especially those of the lower classes. What, then, were the practical effects of the Married Women's Property Acts? They were sweeping measures, for they affected every married person in the country and, it might be added, touched them in a very sensitive spot, namely their pocketbooks. An interesting speculation in this connection is suggested by a comment made by Lord Shaftesbury during the debates of 1870. He estimated that if roughly 800,000 wives were employed at wages of, say, £20 a year, then it was a matter of £16 million annually that needed to be protected from these women's husbands.[18] If one could know and add to this £16 million the value of property other than their earnings which belonged to women and would also have passed to their husbands but for the Married Women's Property Acts, one would come up with a very large sum indeed. It is therefore not too much to suggest that these acts quietly and undramatically carried through one of the greatest expropriations and reallocations of property in English history. At the same time, one cannot know the number of women in England who, but for passage of the acts, would have been abused and despoiled of their property by their husbands. Perhaps it is enough to know that cases such as that of Susannah Palmer could no longer occur.

The practical effects of the Married Women's Property Acts were enormous but, interestingly, contemporaries, both those who favoured and those who opposed reform, stressed chiefly their psychological effects. One writer, speaking of the 'novel sense of independence' that married women would now feel, declared, 'The difference caused by mental change is much greater than the difference caused by material change, and the mental change will be very great ... This increase of individuality is about to accrue, moreover, when women are seeking individuality with a sort of passion, when they are crying for "rights" which are all rights to be separate and unmerged in their husbands.' In similar vein another writer said that the act of 1882 would cause women eventually to lose that 'spaniel-like submission' to their husbands which could be traced to the fact that 'the law of the land affords them little or no protection for their money,' and would 'modify the marriage relationship, giving wives a more pronounced individuality of character and position.' Yet another writer, a lawyer who was by no means enthusiastic about the act of 1882, believed that as a result of its passage women would 'dwell more upon their rights, and resent their husbands' interference' and would not be content to 'follow the conventional ways of married life.' Now, he continued, there was 'no further legal difficulty in the way of their carrying out the most advanced views which have been promulgated of late years.' If the husband 'is no longer the head of the wife (and, as far as property goes he is so no longer), there seems no reason why wives should not have independent views, an independent profession, independent society, and independent interests.' Moreover, since property was the qualification for voting, 'it may occur to her that she ought to have a separate vote also.'[19] In short, as feminists always claimed, emancipation was not only a matter of fact but also, and perhaps above all, a state of mind. That was the feminists' second great argument in favour of reform of the married women's property law.

In a more immediate and specific way the Married Women's Property Acts, and the campaign which led to their passage, had a liberating effect upon women. To work for property-law reform, feminism as an organized movement appeared in England in the 1850s. For the first time women, and men as well, were working together in the cause of women. The personal friendships that were formed, the political alliances that were made, the practical experience that was gained in publicizing the women's cause and in pushing for parliamentary action – all of these were of tremendous importance in launching and sustaining an effective women's movement. The interest aroused, the energies called into action, the abilities displayed by women were soon focused upon many other important matters in addition to property-law reform – women's education, the employment of women, and the suffrage question, to name but a few. In their work for reform women felt a unity of interests and purpose that was totally new in their experience, and their success in winning property-law reform brought a thrilling sense of practical achievement that encouraged them to continue the good fight for other feminist causes. As the final report of the Married Women's Property Committee summed up, 'there are rights more sacred than even the right of property, wrongs more flagrant than even the forfeiture of a wife's property by marriage, which yet remain unredressed, but of the redress of which they rejoice to believe that they see in the passing of the [Married Women's Property] Act [of 1882] the sure pledge and herald.'[20]

The act of 1882 was a landmark in English legal history and an important milestone on the road to women's emancipation, and it stood as the basic law on the subject for more than fifty years. Yet this act, like all works of human hands, was far from perfect. Indeed it soon occasioned comments as fiercely derogatory as any that the act of 1870 had inspired. A few years after its passage one lawyer denounced it as 'an ill-conceived and ill-drawn Act, sanctioned by the ignorance and stupidity of Parliament, and rendered more complicated by the subtlety of judicial interpretation.' Some years after this, a county-court judge by the name of Snagge declared that the act 'had opened the door to the most monstrous frauds,' adding that if parliament did not soon correct the situation 'he could do no more than cry in the wilderness of his Courts.' (Snagge was commenting upon a case involving a bankrupt who sold his business to his wife in order to defeat his creditors; the act allowed creditors to impeach only gifts and not sales made by a husband to his wife in order to defeat them.) Nearly half a century after the act's passage a justice of the Supreme Court who, incidentally, was a bachelor, said, 'I find nothing but confusion, obscurity and inconsistency. I find privileges given to the wife which are denied to a husband, and I find that upon the husband has fallen one injustice after another.'[21]

Stated in more temperate terms and seen from the historical point of view, the problem was that 'when the legislature adopted the equitable rules [relating to married women's separate property], and applied them with some modifications to all married women [by the Act of 1882], many curious legal rules, many doubtful problems, and some injustice resulted from the imperfect fusion of these two antagonistic sets of legal principles' – that is, the common law and equity.[22] From 1882 until the present day, therefore, it has been the concern of parliament and of the courts, in the midst of changing circumstances, to work out the practical applications of the principles of separate property rights for married women and of marriage as a partnership of equals, principles which the act of 1882 only imperfectly embodied.

The first problem arising under the act to which parliament turned its attention was that of legal proceedings between husband and wife. Confusion arose here because of two unclear if not exactly contradictory sections of the act of 1882. Section 12, which empowered a married woman to take both civil and criminal proceedings 'against all persons whomsoever, including her husband' in order to protect her separate property, specifically stated that in any such proceedings husband and wife were competent to give evidence against each other, 'any statute or rule of law to the contrary notwithstanding.' (Legislation as early as 1853 had settled that in civil proceedings one spouse was both a competent and a compellable witness against the other.) However, section 16 of the act, which gave a husband the reciprocal right of taking criminal proceedings against his wife in order to protect his property, made no mention of the competence of spouses to give evidence against each other.

To clear up this matter, Hinde Palmer, the women's champion, and Richard Cross, the former Conservative home secretary and opponent of reform, introduced in parliament in 1884 a brief Married Women's Property Act (1882) Amendment Bill. As introduced, the bill provided that in any criminal proceedings brought by a husband against his wife under the act of 1882, he was competent to give evidence against her, 'any statute or rule of law to the contrary notwithstanding.' As amended by the Lords and finally passed (47 & 48 Vict., c 14), the act provided that in criminal proceedings arising under the act of 1882 both husband and wife were competent witnesses and, except when the defendant, were compellable to give evidence.[23] Making assurance doubly sure, the Criminal Evidence Act of 1898 made wives competent witnesses against their husbands in certain specified cases, including cases arising under the act of 1882. These two acts were further blows to the old common-law rule of the identity of husband and wife.

Yet another blow to the old rule was dealt by the Theft Act of 1968. This act made it possible for husband or wife to bring criminal charges against the other for stealing his or her property. (The act of 1882 did not allow criminal proceedings for theft between spouses while they were living together, or when they were living apart unless a husband had taken his wife's property 'when leaving or deserting, or about to leave or desert.') However, under the 1968 act such criminal proceedings can be instigated only with the consent of the Director of Public Prosecutions, unless husband and wife were judicially separated at the time the offence was committed.

Passage of the act of 1882 gave rise to a new legal question, that of the validity of contracts between husbands and wives. In a leading case in 1885 the Court of

Appeal ruled that the Married Women's Property Act had not affected the practice in equity before the act's passage – that is, that a woman could contract with her husband with respect to her separate property and could sue or be sued by him – and this ruling was upheld by another decision of the court in 1908. But the practical question remained, and still does, as to what exactly is a contract between married persons. The decision of the House of Lords in a leading case in 1919 held that mutual promises made between husband and wife are not legally binding contracts. That is, 'the Courts prefer to regard such domestic promises as falling outside the realm of contract on the ground that neither spouse at the time intended to create a contractual legal relationship' and that the parties are bound in honour but not in law 'unless the context very clearly indicates an intention to contract.'[24]

Passage of the act of 1882 also gave rise to the new legal question of the validity of gifts made between married persons. Before 1882 it was legally impossible for married persons to make gifts to each other, for in law they were one person. However, such gifts might be upheld in equity. For example, a wife who allowed her husband to receive and use her separate property was deemed in equity to have surrendered the property to him absolutely by her action, while a husband could make a gift to his wife of property which would be deemed her separate property in equity, the husband thereby constituting himself his wife's trustee. Clearly the act of 1882, by creating separate property interests between husbands and wives, made gifts between them a legal possibility and thereby gave rise to a new type of litigation.

Cases involving the validity of such gifts were likely to arise in two different sets of circumstances. One was the event of a creditor's making a claim against husband or wife, when the property of each had to be determined before the creditor could obtain anything in satisfaction of his claim. The other was the event of termination of a marriage, by judicial separation or divorce or by the death of one of the spouses, when the assets of the parties to the marriage had to be separated and distributed. However, such cases no longer arise in the event of separation or divorce since passage of the Matrimonial Proceedings and Property Act of 1970, under which the assets of both spouses are pooled and then divided between them fairly by the court.

Decisions in cases involving gifts between husband and wife were especially difficult for a variety of reasons. For one thing, when married persons live together amicably in the same household it is difficult to determine when a gift has been legally made – that is, when a legal change of ownership has taken place. This is so because at law a merely verbal agreement to bestow a gift is not sufficient; actual delivery of the gift is required to effect a legal change of ownership, except in the case of bulky goods, when delivery by symbol may suffice.

Therefore cases involving the validity of gifts between husbands and wives involve questions of evidence of delivery.

Another difficulty which might arise in such cases was related to the question of 'undue influence,' for any gift is voided by such influence. In equity the presumption was that in certain family and other confidential relationships the influence of the receiver of a gift over the giver procured the transfer, and the person seeking to uphold the transfer had to prove that there was no undue influence. (If there was no special relationship between giver and receiver, the presumption was reversed – that is, the person who alleged undue influence had to prove it.) During the nineteenth century contradictory judicial decisions were handed down in cases involving the question of a husband's exercising undue influence over his wife in order to obtain gifts from her. The Court of Appeal finally settled the question in 1909 by ruling that there was no presumption of a husband's undue influence over his wife. As one of the justices stated, business simply could not go on if in every business transaction involving a wife's gift to her husband, he must prove that he had exerted no undue influence over her.

Passage of the act of 1882 raised questions not only regarding gifts between husbands and wives but also questions relating to gifts made to a married couple by a third party. The old common-law rule was that for the purposes of acquisition of property, husband and wife were one person. For example, if someone gave property in equal shares to three persons, two of whom were husband and wife, the property was divided not into three shares but into two, husband and wife taking one share and the third person taking the other. A series of court decisions after 1882 upheld the validity of the old rule, but amended its application in practice. Under these decisions the one share going to husband and wife was divided into two parts, one of which was the wife's separate property. The Law of Property Act of 1925 finally corrected this situation by treating husband and wife as individual and separate persons in the acquisition of property. Thereafter, in a similar case, property going to a husband and wife and a third person would be divided into three shares, husband, wife, and the third person each taking one share.

By far the most important kind of problems arising under the Married Women's Property Act of 1882 involved questions of the extent of a married woman's responsibilities with respect to her property. The reform of 1882, by failing to bestow upon wives the same property rights as upon unmarried women and by following instead the precedent established in 1870 of bestowing upon them a special status as owners of separate property governed by equitable principles, raised many practical difficulties. In short, a wife had all the rights but not all the liabilities of independence.

For one thing, the act of 1882 had made the separate property of married women liable for the satisfaction of their antenuptial torts; husbands were freed from liability for these except to the extent of any property they had received from their wives. However, the question was certain to arise as to whether husbands were also freed from liability for their wives' torts committed after marriage. In 1925 the House of Lords, upholding the decisions in a series of earlier cases, ruled that the act of 1882 did not in fact relieve husbands from liability for their wives' torts and that they were still liable to be sued jointly with their wives. Commenting on the decision, one of the law lords said that the act of 1882 was 'a Married Woman's Property Act, not a Married Man's Relief Act' and that a husband could escape his 'inexorable doom only by parting with his spouse, his money or his life.' The decision was based upon the fact that the act of 1882 merely gave a plaintiff the choice of suing a married woman alone, when she had separate property out of which her damages could be paid, or of suing her jointly with her husband. Usually a plaintiff would sue husband and wife jointly, for the damages a wife was liable to pay were limited to the extent of her separate property, and any difference between the amount of her separate property and the amount of damages awarded the plaintiff would then have to be paid by her husband. (The plaintiff could not first sue the wife alone and, failing to have his claim satisfied by her separate property, sue her husband in turn.)[25]

As serious as questions concerning a married woman's responsibility for her torts were questions relating to her power of entering into contracts. Judicial decisions in a number of cases that soon arose under the act of 1882 revealed anomalies resulting from the fact that a married woman's contractual capacity was not personal but proprietary. A court decision in 1886 held that a married woman could not be committed to prison under the Debtors Act of 1869 for failure to pay money for which a judgment had been recovered against her, for her contracts did not bind her personally but bound only her separate property. The decisions in two other leading cases in the 1880s held that a married woman's contracts were not valid if she possessed no separate property at the time of contracting, that her contracts bound only the separate property which she had at the time of contracting and not that which she afterward acquired, and that her contracts bound only her separate property that was not subject to the restraint on anticipation. Later decisions held that a married woman's contracts did not bind property freed from the restraint on anticipation by her husband's death, or property that came to her after the termination of her marriage either by her husband's death or by divorce; in both these cases such property was not technically her separate property, and only her separate property could be bound by her contracts. Finally, a married woman could not be made a bankrupt except, as the act of 1882 provided, in the case that she was carrying on a trade or business separately from her husband using her separate property.

The first attempt to put some of these matters straight came with passage of the brief Married Women's Property Act of 1893 (56 & 57 Vict., c 63). This act provided that every contract entered into by a married woman other than as agent for her husband bound her separate property whether or not she had such property at the time of contracting, and also that it bound all separate property which she acquired afterward and not merely the separate property which she had at the time of contracting. However, her contract did not bind her separate property that was subject to restraint on anticipation.

More thoroughgoing reform designed to clarify questions of a married woman's proprietary responsibilities did not come until the passage in 1935 of the Law Reform (Married Women and Tortfeasors) Act (25 & 26 Geo. V, c 30). This measure, the first major amendment of the act of 1882, returned to the principle for which Victorian feminists had fought so long and unsuccessfully – that a married woman should have the same rights and responsibilities with respect to her property as an unmarried woman. To accomplish this, the act of 1935 repealed those sections of the 1882 act which referred to a married woman's 'separate property' or 'separate estate' and replaced them with provisions which referred instead to a 'married woman's property.' As one lawyer commented at the time, 'It is supposed that this was a concession to feminist feeling that a man and his wife being separate persons (and not one as considered by the old Common Law) it was as anomalous to speak of a wife's separate estate as it would be to speak of a husband's ... In short, the old Norman-French phrase "feme covert" seems to have been abolished.'[26]

The act of 1935 rendered a married woman responsible for all her torts and contracts. It did so by releasing her husband from all responsibility for these, the only qualification being that he was responsible for his wife's postnuptial contracts to the extent that she was acting as his agent in entering into these. The act also specifically rendered a married woman subject to the bankruptcy laws in all cases, not merely in the case that she was carrying on a trade or business separate from her husband, and she was likewise specifically made liable to imprisonment if she failed to comply with judgments and orders made against her as a result of suits brought against her.

One anomaly with respect to a married woman's contracts and torts which survived passage of the act of 1935 was the old restraint on anticipation. The act did prohibit the imposition of restraints after its passage, but did not interfere with the restraints then existing or with those coming into effect before 1946 in wills which were executed before 1936. The Married Women (Restraint on Anticipation) Act of 1949 (12, 13 & 14 Geo. VI, c 78) at last abolished restraints completely and immediately. The occasion of its passage was Lady Mountbatten's promotion of a private bill to remove the restraint imposed upon her large fortune, in view of the expenses connected with her public position. The more general measure was enacted to enable married women to use their property to meet the burdens of increased post-war taxation and to reduce the liability of their property for death duties by disposing of the property during their lifetimes.

Another anomaly to survive the act of 1935 was the general inability of husband and wife to sue each other in tort. The legislation of 1935 reaffirmed the rule contained in the Married Women's Property Act of 1882 that a wife could sue her husband in tort to protect her property, although he did not have a reciprocal right to sue her. The Law Reform (Husband and Wife) Act of 1962 (10 & 11 Eliz. II, c 48) abolished this rule by declaring that each spouse has a right to sue the other in tort as if they were not married. The chief reason for passage of this act was to enable a husband or wife to collect damages for injuries suffered through the fault of the other, such as injuries resulting from an automobile accident, since damages would usually be paid not by the other spouse personally but by his or her insurance company. Apparently, however, little advantage has been taken of this particular reform.

After passage of the Married Women's Property Act of 1882, the law continued to presume that despite the separate property interests of his wife, a husband was primarily responsible for her maintenance and that of their children. This legal presumption, which 'like so much of English family law ... originates in the economic and social conditions of Victorian England,' continues today in a vastly different society.[27] After 1882, as before, a wife had the right, acting as her husband's agent, to pledge his credit for the supply of necessaries. (The act of 1882 specifically provided that a married woman's separate property was liable for satisfaction of her contracts, except those which she entered into as her husband's agent.) It was necessary to keep alive the idea of the wife's agency in order to protect creditors. Originally the law of agency held that a wife had the right to act as her husband's agent only so long as she did not leave him without cause and refuse to return, and so long as she did not commit adultery, although if her husband received her back after her adultery her right to pledge his credit revived. However, in a leading case in 1955 the Court of Appeal ruled that a wife's right to maintenance is indestructible so long as the marriage lasts.

In the nineteenth century the law also presumed, and today it still does, that a married couple's standard of living is fixed by the husband, whose income is chiefly responsible for maintenance of the household. A court ruling in a leading case in 1960 denied a wife's claim to receive a certain allowance from her husband, declaring that she had only the right 'to be supported by being given bed and board,' which is enforced by her right to act as her husband's agent. That is, if a man is a millionaire who chooses a miserly rather than a magnificent lifestyle, his wife has no legal grounds for complaint. A wife apparently has not even the right to know what her husband's financial situation is. All of this has prompted a present-day critic of the law to declare:

Marriage is a partnership; no commercial partnership would exist if the partners did not have the *right* to see the books, even if it is a right which they choose not to exercise. It is over 100 years since John Stuart Mill wrote that 'no one would enter into partnership on terms which would subject him to the responsibilities of a principal, with only the powers and privileges of a clerk or agent.' Yet women are still required to enter marriage on terms which would be regarded as backward – in these days of participation – by any self-respecting clerk (or executive, as he would no doubt now be called).[28]

Twentieth-century legislation has amended the law relating to a wife's right to maintenance during marriage in only two instances. The first of these amendments was the short Married Women's Property Act of 1964 (c 19), designed to remedy a particular grievance. In leading cases in 1943 and 1949 the Court of Appeal had ruled that the money a wife had saved out of the housekeeping allowance given her by her husband was not her property but his. The court thus upheld a decision handed down as early as 1856, when a woman unsuccessfully claimed that the savings from her housekeeping allowance should be deemed her separate property in equity. The reason for these decisions, arising from the law of agency, was that an agent is not permitted to make a profit unknown to the principal. To rule otherwise, the courts would have had to abandon the idea of the wife's agency. To set this matter straight the act of 1964 provided that when any money is saved by a wife from the housekeeping allowance given her by her husband, each is entitled to half the money unless there is an agreement to the contrary. Interestingly, the act bestowed a right only upon women; a man does not have the right to ownership of half the savings from an allowance given him by his wife.

The second twentieth-century amendment of the law relating to a wife's right to maintenance was the Matrimonial Homes Act of 1967 (c 75), which like the act of 1964 was designed to remedy a particular grievance. The House of Lords had ruled in a leading case in 1965 that a husband was obligated to provide his wife with housing and she could obtain an injunction to prevent his selling their house, but if a sale took place without her knowledge she had no recourse. The act of 1967 sought to prevent recurrences of such situations, and also to prevent a husband from mortgaging the family home, then getting into financial difficulties and being forced to sell, leaving his wife homeless. The act provided that both husband and wife have the right of occupation of the matrimonial home, that either can apply to a court for an order declaring, enforcing, or restricting the other's right, and that neither can be evicted during the marriage except by a court order. The act also provided that when there is a mortgage in the name of either of the spouses on a house which they occupy, the other spouse may make any payment due on the mortgage; this provision thus allows a wife whose husband has defaulted on his mortgage payments to make the payments herself and so retain her right of occupation. Finally, the rights of husband and wife under the act are personal; that is, they cannot be assigned to others, and they terminate with the death of a spouse or the ending of the marriage.

Since a man was legally responsible for the support of his wife and children, the question arose as to how this responsibility was to be enforced by means other than his wife's right as his agent to pledge his credit for the supply of necessaries. One such means was action by the public assistance authorities. The nineteenth-century Poor Law had provided that a wife whose husband did not support her could obtain poor relief, and the Poor Law guardians could then collect as a debt owed them by the husband the amount of any relief provided. The National Assistance Act of 1948 (11 & 12 Geo. VI, c 29), which replaced the old Poor-Law system, continued the provision for the relief of wives, the National Assistance Board being empowered to recover sums paid to an assisted person from anyone liable for his or her support.

In addition, as has been seen, a series of laws which were enacted, the first in 1878, to provide cheap and speedy relief short of divorce for wives cruelly treated or deserted by their husbands contained important provisions relating to these women's right to maintenance by their husbands. Under these laws married women could apply to local magistrates' courts for separation orders having the legal effect of judicial separations, and also for maintenance orders compelling their husbands to contribute to their own and their children's support. After 1949 such orders could also be obtained in the High Court. Later legislation made husbands liable to imprisonment and to attachment of their wages if they failed to make payments under maintenance orders. As a result of these and other reforms, the Matrimonial Proceedings and Property Act of 1970 (c 45) abolished as anachronistic the old common-law rule that a wife deserted by her husband became his 'agent of necessity' with the continuing right to pledge his credit for her support.

If marriage is a partnership of equals, it would seem that a husband should have the reciprocal right to be supported by his wife, but the law hardly recognizes this. The Married Women's Property Act of 1882 did impose on wives the same obligation then applied to husbands – namely, the so-called Poor-Law liability not to allow spouses, children, or grandchildren to become charges on the parish. This was supplemented in 1908 by a brief Married Women's Property Act (8 Edw. VII, c 27) which reversed a court decision of two years before by making a married woman with separate property responsible for the support of her parents as well. The National Assistance Act of 1948 replacing the old Poor Law also imposed on women as well as men the liability to support their spouses and children. But long before this, the law of maintenance with respect to husbands and wives had diverged as, beginning in 1878, women in specified cases were given the right to obtain maintenance orders as well as separation orders against their husbands, and the same right was not given to men. For example, if a wife deserted her husband, he could not obtain an order compelling her to contribute to his support, as she could do if he deserted her. Not until passage of the Matrimonial Proceedings (Magistrates' Courts) Act of 1960 (8 & 9 Eliz. II, c 48) was this situation rectified to a degree by allowing a husband to obtain an order for his wife to maintain him, but only if he could prove that his earning capacity had been impaired through age, illness, or disability of mind or body so that it was reasonable to expect his wife to support him. It should be added that a husband still has no legal right to pledge his wife's credit for his support under the law of agency, as she has the right to pledge his credit. The legal presumption continues to be that 'the husband's duty to maintain his wife is a normal incidence of marriage, whilst her obligation to maintain him results from abnormal and pathological situations.'[29]

There remain to be considered questions which arose after 1882 with respect to the disposition of a married woman's property after her death. The act of 1882 gave to married women the same right to dispose of their separate property by will as they had to dispose of this property during their lifetime. But here too, as in the case of a married woman's contractual capacity, difficulties arose because of the technicalities relating to separate property in equity. After 1882, as before, a married woman's will was not valid if she had no separate property at the time the will was made, and her will disposed only of the separate property she had at the time of making her will and not the separate property she acquired afterward. The same Married Women's Property Act of 1893 which attempted to set straight matters relating to a wife's contracts also contained provisions relating to her will. Under this act a married woman's will was valid even if she had no separate property when the will was made, and it bound all the separate property which was hers at the time of her death and not merely that which she had at the time her will was made. Further, a married woman's will no longer required re-execution after her husband's death. The possibility of confusion in this area of law, as in the area of contract, was ended only by passage of the Law Reform (Married Women and Tortfeasors) Act of 1935.

Absolute freedom of testation had long been the rule of English law for men and unmarried women, and after 1882 it was the rule for married women as well. This freedom to dispose of one's property by will was first abrogated by the Inheritance (Family Provision) Act of 1938 (1 & 2 Geo. VI, c 45). This act did not require a testator to make certain reasonable provisions out of his or her estate for the surviving members of the family. It merely empowered the court, in cases where no reasonable provision was made, to order an allowance paid out of the net estate of the deceased for the benefit of the surviving spouse, minor sons, unmarried daughters, or children who were physically or mentally incapacitated. Such allowances would end with the remarriage of the spouse, the sons' coming of age, the daughters' marriage, or the end of the children's disability respectively. This act has been amended several times, most recently by the Inheritance (Provision for Family and Dependents) Act of 1975 (c 63). This legislation still does not require that particular shares of the estate of the deceased be given to surviving family members. Under its provisions application to the court for relief can be made by certain dependents of the deceased – the surviving spouse, a former spouse who has not remarried, a child, any person who was treated as a child of the family, and any person who was wholly or partly maintained by the deceased – and the court is empowered to make orders with respect to the disposition of the property of the deceased, rather than merely ordering periodical payments or the payment of lump sums as before the act.

As for the disposition of the property of husbands and wives who died intestate, the old common-law rules obtaining before 1882 continued to apply after 1882. (The Married Women's Property Act of 1882 contained no specific provisions relating to the disposition of married women's separate property in cases of their intestacy. Technically a wife's separate property ceased to exist when her marriage was ended, whether by her own or her husband's death or otherwise.) Under the old rules a woman's legal heirs succeeded to her real property subject to her husband's right by the curtesy to a life interest in this property, while the rest of her property – personal property, chattels real, and choses in action – went to her husband absolutely. In continuing contrast to these rules relating to wives' property were the rules applying in the cases of husbands who died intestate. In such a case the widow had a life interest in one-third of her husband's real property by virtue of her right of dower; as for his other property, she received one-third and her child or children two-thirds, or she received half if there was no child, the remainder going to the husband's near relatives or to the crown. The Intestates' Estates Act of 1890 (53 & 54 Vict., c 29) amended these rules in the interest of wives by allowing a widow the first £500 of her husband's estate, the division of the remainder being governed by the earlier rules, or granting her the whole estate if it was less than £500 in value.

Not until passage of the Administration of Estates Act of 1925 (15 & 16 Geo. V, c 23) were the rules of succession in cases of intestacy radically remodelled and husbands and wives placed on an equal footing. This act abolished the distinction so long made between real and personal property, and in so doing abolished the old common-law rights of dower and curtesy. Thereafter a surviving spouse was to receive all the personal chattels of the deceased, a 'statutory legacy' originally set at £1,000 (later legislation greatly increased this amount; it is now £15,000), and a life interest in half the residue of the estate, the remainder being held in 'statutory trust' for the child or children. If there were no children of the marriage, the surviving spouse received the personal chattels, a much larger statutory legacy (now £40,000), and half the remainder, the other half going to the close relatives of the deceased – parents, or brothers and sisters or their children. If there were neither children of the marriage nor close relatives of the deceased, the surviving spouse received the whole estate.

As the result of successive amendments of the law of property, the old common-law rule of the identity of husband and wife lingers on now in only one area – namely, the tax law. Under the Income and Corporation Taxes Act of 1970 (c 10) the incomes of husband and wife are aggregated for the purpose of calculating their liability for taxes. However, the Finance Act of 1971 (c 68) provided that husband and wife could jointly, not singly, choose to have their incomes taxed separately and therefore at a lower rate. Interestingly, as one commentator has remarked, 'This is the first time since 1882 that the English legislature has given a man power to consent or refuse assent to his wife's legal actions.'[30]

Today, a century after passage of the Married Women's Property Act of 1882, it may seem that 'it is all worked through,' or nearly so, and that both the theory and the practice of the marriage laws are based no longer on 'the enslaving of one' but on 'the equality of two.' Yet this is not the case, for today, just as a hundred years ago, feminists are denouncing existing property laws and demanding changes to ensure equality for women. One critic calls the laws 'confused and inconsistent,' and another describes them as 'patchwork, a series of responses to the needs of the moment,' pointing out that 'the problem of matrimonial property has never been tackled systematically.'[31] (For a summary of legislation relating to married women's property, see appendix 7.) Thus, with respect to the property law one seems to have come full circle.

The reason for present-day demands for reform is clear when one remembers the historical development of the property law. The first thoroughgoing reform of the common law affecting married women's property came in the later nineteenth century as a response to the changed position of women in a modern industrialized society. The great need at that time was to protect against the common-law rights of husbands the earnings of wives who worked outside their homes. The only model for such protection of wives that existed in England was the model afforded by equity, with its doctrine of 'separate property' for married women. The idea of establishing instead 'a *régime matrimonial* such as had been part of the living law across the Channel for centuries and was codified in the Code Napoleon' was favoured by a few, but such a regime of 'community property' was too exotically foreign to the traditions of English law to be seriously considered. It was natural, then, that the Married Women's Property Act of 1870, designed to protect working women in particular, should apply the equitable doctrine of separate property interests of husbands and wives, and that this doctrine should be extended to all wives by the Married Women's Property Act of 1882 and by later legislation and judicial decisions. One student of the law sums it up thus: 'Since 1870 the basic principle of English law is that marriage has no effect on the spouse's property rights,' but 'in the same way as the Common Law failed to provide adequate rights when capital began to be invested in wealth other than land, and just as the rules of Equity failed to provide for wage earners, so the system of separation has failed to deal adequately with the economic realities of married life in the twentieth century.'[32]

What, then, are 'the economic realities of married life' to which the present law of separate property interests of husband and wife fails to respond? For one thing, there has been another economic and social revolution, analogous to the revolution in family life which was caused by industrialization in the nineteenth century and which prompted the first reform of the married women's property law. In the nineteenth century the great majority of people lived on their earnings and had no or only small savings – hence the great need to protect the earnings of married women. But the twentieth century has witnessed 'a revolutionary transformation in consumption.' People in the affluent countries of the industrialized Western world live in a consumer-oriented society in which the 'acquisition for family use of durable assets, immovable and movable, is one of the dominant features of economic life.' Moreover, married women are now playing a much larger role in economic life. When agitation for reform of the married women's property law began in the nineteenth century, only about one-fourth of all wives worked outside the home; today nearly three-fifths of all married women are so employed.[33]

Present-day critics maintain that the existing property law is basically flawed because it 'ignores social groups, above all the family as a social group – it deals with society as if it was an agglomeration of atoms rather than a structure of molecules.' (One is reminded of the words of *The Times*, which objected to the reform proposed in the nineteenth century because it would 'abolish families in the old sense' and 'break up society again into men and women.')[34] Now, husbands and wives have assets as members of a family rather than as individuals – a house and its furnishings, and various forms of liquid capital which are used for the benefit of the family as a whole – although these assets are financed by the earnings of individual members of the family. But the law assigns ownership of property to the individual whose assets purchased it, not to husband and wife jointly or to the whole family. The question of ownership and division of the family assets may seldom arise in ongoing marriages, but it becomes acute when a marriage is terminated, especially by divorce or judicial separation. And today, when the number of divorces petitioned for annually is a hundred times greater than the number at the turn of the century – more than 50,000 today compared with 500 in 1900 – the question of ownership and division of family assets is especially acute.

The present law, according to its critics, discriminates against women in two ways when it comes to deciding ownership of property and dividing family assets between husband and wife. First, it ignores the fact that wives usually earn less than their husbands, and therefore cannot contribute as much financially to the family and cannot gain legal title to as much property as their husbands. This is so because women generally receive much lower pay than men – women, comprising one-third of the labour force, earn about 55 per cent of men's earnings – and because their working lives are interrupted by domestic cares and duties, especially child bearing and child rearing.[35] Second, the law ignores the value of the important but unpaid labour which wives, much more than husbands, contribute to the functioning of the household, because the value of this labour is not quantifiable in money terms.

Given the present state of the property law, with its theoretical equality but real inequality for married women, the trend of judicial decisions for more than two decades and of a few parliamentary enactments has been in the direction of recognition of a new legal principle relating to the property of husband and wife. This is the principle of 'matrimonial property' or 'family assets' as a special kind of property. Such property and assets may be defined as 'those things which are acquired by one or the other or both of the parties, with the intention that there should be continuing provision for them and their children during their joint lives, and used for the benefit of the family as a whole.' In practice, application of this principle means that both husband and wife, but more usually the wife, acquire 'rights in matrimonial property legal ownership of which has remained vested in only one of them during the marriage ... rights which would not have been acquired under general property law.' This principle derives in turn from the broader principle that 'equality is equity.'[36]

Two recent statutes are good examples of this new principle put into practice. One is the Matrimonial Homes Act of 1967, which gives both husband and wife during marriage a legal right of occupation which arises from the fact of marriage and not from general property law. The other is the Matrimonial Proceedings and Property Act of 1970, which gives the court, in cases of marital breakdown, wide discretion to distribute the joint assets of husband and wife between them on a fair and equal basis, having regard to several specific factors, including the contribution made by each to the welfare of the home and children. Until passage of this act the court had almost no powers to readjust the family assets, and disputes about these assets between husband and wife were solved by reference to the ordinary law of property – that is, by determining which of the two had legal title to the property. In dividing family assets judges have generally awarded the wife one-third rather than half, and the Court of Appeal, in a leading case in 1973, accepted this 'traditional one-third' as a simple guide to be followed. The reason for this decision was that, in the opinion of the court, the husband would normally have greater expenses than the wife. He would have to maintain his former wife's household as well as his own, and would need to hire a housekeeper, or he might remarry and have another wife and other children to provide for. His wife might go out to work but usually would do the housework herself rather than employing a housekeeper, and she might remarry and be provided for by her new husband.[37]

The new principle of 'matrimonial property' or 'family assets' may eventually replace completely the old rule of equity that equality is ensured by recognition of the separate property interests of husband and wife, the rule embodied in the Married Women's Property Acts of 1870 and 1882. But this new principle is far from being completely accepted and implemented now. That further reform is needed seems especially clear in view of the decision of the House of Lords in a leading case in 1970. Section 17 of the Married Women's Property Act of 1882 gave both husband and wife the right to apply to the High Court or to a county court for a summary decision in any question arising between them as to the title or possession of property, and this section had been frequently used to resolve such questions. But in 1970 the law lords denounced as 'heretical' the idea that this section of the act meant that the court had a 'free hand to do what is just' in all circumstances, ignoring the strict legal rules relating to the title to property. So feminist demands for further reform of the law continue. 'In effect what women are saying, and saying with considerable male support, is: "We are no longer content with a system whereby a wife's rights in family assets depend on the whim of her husband or on the discretion of a judge. We demand definite property rights, not possible discretionary benefits."'[38]

   Victorian feminists who struggled to win passage of the Married Women's
Property Act of 1882 would surely appreciate the efforts of latter-day feminists
to win further reform of the property law. After all, they too always insisted that
the law must be amended to meet the changing needs of a new day. In winning
passage of the act of 1882 Victorian reformers believed that they had achieved
equality for married women. Time has shown that they had not. The act represented not the end of the journey but merely a way station on women's long road
to liberation.

APPENDIXES
NOTES
BIBLIOGRAPHY
INDEXES

Appendix 1

Petition for Reform of the
Married Women's
Property Law
Presented to Parliament
14 March 1856

To the Honourable the House of Peers [and House of Commons] in Parliament assembled. The Petition of the undersigned Women of Great Britain, Married and Single, Humbly Sheweth – That the manifold evils occasioned by the present law, by which the property and earnings of the wife are thrown into the absolute power of the husband, become daily more apparent. That the sufferings thereupon ensuing, extend over all classes of society. That it might once have been deemed for the middle and upper ranks, a comparatively theoretical question, but is so no longer, since married women of education are entering on every side the fields of literature and art, in order to increase the family income by such exertions.

That it is usual when a daughter marries in these ranks, to make, if possible, some distinct pecuniary provision for her and her children, and to secure the money thus set aside by a cumbrous machinery of trusteeship, proving that few parents are willing entirely to entrust the welfare of their offspring to the irresponsible power of the husband, to the chances of his character, his wisdom, and his success in a profession.

That another device for the protection of women who can afford to appeal, exists in the action of the Courts of Equity, which attempt, within certain limits, to redress the deficiencies of the law; but that trustees may prove dishonest or unwise in the management of the funds entrusted to their care, and Courts of Equity may fail in adjusting differences which concern the most intimate and delicate relation of life; – that legal devices, patched upon a law which is radically unjust, can only work clumsily, and that here, as in many other departments of justice, a clearance of the ground is the chief thing necessary. That since this is a truth, which has gradually come to be recognised in regard to protective restrictions upon trade, to titles of property in land, and to the legal machinery for conveying such property from one owner to another, &c., we would hope that, before long, it will also come to be recognised in matrimonial legislation.

That it is proved by well known cases of hardship suffered by women of station, and also by professional women earning large incomes by pursuit of the arts, how real is the injury inflicted.

That if these laws often bear heavily upon women protected by the forethought of their relatives, the social training of their husbands, and the refined customs of the rank to which they belong, how much more unequivocal is the injury sustained by women in the lower classes, for whom no such provision can be made by their parents, who possess no means of appeal to expensive legal protection, and in regard to whom the education of the husband and the habits of his associates offer no moral guarantee for tender consideration of a wife.

That whereas it is customary, in manufacturing districts, to employ women largely in the processes of trade, and as women are also engaged as sempstresses, laundresses, charwomen, and in other multifarious occupations which cannot here be enumerated, the question must be recognised by all as of practical importance.

That newspapers constantly detail instances of marital oppression, 'wife-beating' being a new compound noun lately introduced into the English language, and a crime against which English gentlemen have lately enacted stringent regulations.

But that for the robbery by a man of his wife's hard [won] earnings there is no redress, – against the selfishness of a drunken father, who wrings from a mother her children's daily bread, there is no appeal. She may work from morning till night, to see the produce of her labour wrested from her, and wasted in a gin-palace; and such cases are within the knowledge of every one.

That the law, in depriving the mother of all pecuniary resources, deprives her of the power of giving schooling to her children, and in other ways providing for their moral and physical welfare; it obliges her in short, to leave them to the temptations of the street, so fruitful in juvenile crime.

That there are certain portions of the law of husband and wife which bear unjustly on the husband, as for instance, that of making him responsible for his wife's debts contracted before marriage, even although he may have no fortune with her. Her power also, after marriage, of contracting debts in the name of her husband, for which he is responsible, is too unlimited, and often produces much injustice.

That in rendering the husband responsible for the entire maintenance of his family, the law expresses the necessity of an age, when the man was the only money-getting agent; but that since the custom of the country has greatly changed in this respect the position of the female sex, the law of maintenance no longer meets the whole case. That since modern civilisation, in indefinitely extending the sphere of occupation for women, has in some measure broken down their pecuniary dependence upon men, it is time that legal protection be thrown over the produce of their labour, and that in entering the state of marriage, they no longer pass from freedom into the condition of a slave, all whose earnings belong to his master and not to himself.

That the laws of various foreign countries are in this respect much more just than our own, and afford precedent for a more liberal legislation than prevails in England; – and your Petitioners therefore humbly pray that your Honourable House will take the foregoing allegations into consideration, and apply such remedy as to its wisdom shall seem fit –

And your Petitioners will ever pray.

Anna Blackwell	Anna Mary Howitt
Isa Blagden	Anna Jameson
Elizabeth Barrett Browning	Geraldine Jewsbury
Sarianna Browning	Mrs Loudon
Mrs Carlyle	Mrs Lovell
Mary Cowden Clarke	Harriet Martineau
Charlotte Cushman	Hon. Julia Maynard
Amelia B. Edwards	Mary Mohl
Eliza F. Fox	Bessie Rayner Parkes
Mrs Gaskell	Mrs Reid
Matilda M. Hays	Barbara Leigh Smith
Mary Howitt	Miss Sturch

Appendix 2

Provisions Relating to Women's Property in the Divorce Act of 1857

(20 & 21 Vict., c 85)

XVII ... the [Divorce] Court or Judge to which such Petition [for restitution of conjugal rights or judicial separation] is addressed ... may decree such Restitution of Conjugal Rights or Judicial Separation accordingly, and where the Application is by the Wife may make any Order for Alimony which shall be deemed just ...

XXI A Wife deserted by her Husband may at any Time after such Desertion, if resident within the Metropolitan District, apply to a Police Magistrate, or if resident in the Country to Justices in Petty Sessions, or in either Case to the [Divorce] Court, for an Order to protect any Money or Property she may acquire by her own lawful Industry, and Property which she may become possessed of, after such Desertion, against her Husband or his Creditors, or any Person claiming under him; and such Magistrate or Justices or Court, if satisfied of the Fact of such Desertion, and that the same was without reasonable Cause, and that the Wife is maintaining herself by her own Industry or Property, may make and give to the Wife an Order protecting her Earnings and Property acquired since the Commencement of such Desertion, from her Husband and all Creditors and Persons claiming under him, and such Earnings and Property shall belong to the Wife as if she were a Feme Sole: Provided always, that every such Order, if made by a Police Magistrate or Justices at Petty Sessions, shall, within Ten Days after the making thereof, be entered with the Registrar of the County Court within whose Jurisdiction the Wife is resident; and that it shall be lawful for the Husband, and any Creditor or other Person claiming under him, to apply to the Court, or to the Magistrate or Justices by whom such Order was made, for the Discharge thereof: Provided also, that if the Husband or any Creditor of or Person claiming under the Husband shall seize or continue to hold any Property of the Wife after Notice of any such Order, he shall be liable at the Suit of the Wife (which she is hereby empowered to bring), to restore the specific Property, and also for a Sum equal to double the Value of the Property so seized or held after such Notice as aforesaid: If any such Order of Protection be made, the Wife shall during the Continuance thereof be and be deemed to have been during such Desertion of her, in the like Position in all respects, with regard to Property and Contracts, and suing and being sued, as she would be under this Act if she obtained a Decree of Judicial Separation.

XXIII Any Husband or Wife, upon the Application of whose Wife or Husband, as the Case may be, a Decree of Judicial Separation has been pronounced, may, at any Time thereafter, present a Petition to the Court praying for a Reversal of such Decree on the Ground that it was obtained in his or her Absence, and that there was reasonable Ground for the alleged Desertion, where Desertion was the Ground of such Decree; and the Court may, on being satisfied of the Truth of the Allegations of such Petition, reverse the Decree accordingly, but the Reversal thereof shall not prejudice or affect the

Rights or Remedies which any other Person would have had in case such Reversal had not been decreed, in respect of any Debts, Contracts, or Acts of the Wife incurred, entered into, or done between the Times of the Sentence of Separation and of the Reversal thereof.

XXIV In all Cases in which the Court shall make any Decree or Order for Alimony, it may direct the same to be paid either to the Wife herself or to any Trustee on her Behalf, to be approved by the Court, and may impose any Terms or Restrictions which to the Court may seem expedient, and may from Time to Time appoint a new Trustee, if for any Reason it shall appear to the Court expedient so to do.

XXV In every Case of a Judicial Separation the Wife shall, from the Date of the Sentence and whilst the Separation shall continue, be considered as a Feme Sole with respect to Property of every Description which she may acquire or which may come to or devolve upon her; and such Property may be disposed of by her in all respects as a Feme Sole, and on her Decease the same shall, in case she shall die intestate, go as the same would have gone if her Husband had been then dead; provided, that if any such Wife should again cohabit with her Husband, all such Property as she may be entitled to when such Cohabitation shall take place shall be held to her separate Use, subject, however, to any Agreement in Writing made between herself and her Husband whilst separate.

XXVI In every Case of a Judicial Separation the Wife shall, whilst so separated, be considered as a Feme Sole for the Purposes of Contract, and Wrongs and Injuries, and suing and being sued in any Civil Proceeding; and her Husband shall not be liable in respect of any Engagement or Contract she may have entered into, or for any wrongful Act or Omission by her, or for any Costs she may incur as Plaintiff or Defendant; provided, that where upon any such Judicial Separation Alimony has been decreed or ordered to be paid to the Wife, and the same shall not be duly paid by the Husband, he shall be liable for Necessaries supplied for her Use; provided also, that nothing shall prevent the Wife from joining, at any Time during such Separation, in the Exercise of any joint Power given to herself and her Husband.

XXXII The [Divorce] Court may, if it shall think fit, on any such Decree [for dissolution of marriage], order that the Husband shall to the Satisfaction of the Court secure to the Wife such gross Sum of Money, or such annual Sum of Money for any Term not exceeding her own Life, as, having regard to her Fortune (if any), to the Ability of the Husband, and to the Conduct of the Parties, it shall deem reasonable, and for that Purpose may refer it to any one of the Conveyancing Counsel of the Court of Chancery to settle and approve of a proper Deed or Instrument to be executed by all necessary Parties; and the said Court may in such Case, if it shall see fit, suspend the pronouncing of its Decree until such Deed shall have been duly executed; and upon any Petition for Dissolution of Marriage the Court shall have the same Power to make interim Orders for Payment of Money, by way of Alimony or otherwise, to the Wife, as it would have in a Suit instituted for Judicial Separation.

XXXIII Any Husband may either in a Petition for Dissolution of Marriage or for Judicial Separation, or in a Petition limited to such Object only, claim Damages from any Person on the Ground of his having committed Adultery with the Wife of such Petitioner ... and after the Verdict has been given the Court shall have power to direct in what Manner such Damages shall be paid or applied, and to direct that the whole or any Part thereof shall be settled for the Benefit of the Children (if any) of the Marriage, or as a Provision for the Maintenance of the Wife.

XLV In any Case in which the Court shall pronounce a Sentence of Divorce or Judicial Separation for Adultery of the Wife, if it shall be made appear to the Court that the Wife is entitled to any Property either in possession or reversion, it shall be lawful for the Court, if it shall think proper, to order such Settlement as it shall think reasonable to be made of such Property or any Part thereof, for the Benefit of the innocent Party, and of the Children of the Marriage, or either or any of them.

Appendix 3

Members of the Executive Committee of the Married Women's Property Committee, 1868-1882

Compiled from the *Annual Reports* of the MWPC. All members are mentioned in the text except those whose names are marked *, about whom I have been unable to discover information.

* Mrs Addey, 1876-82
Lady Amberley, 1871-4
Arthur Arnold, 1879-82
Mrs Arthur Arnold, 1879-82
Miss Anne Ashworth, 1873-4
Miss Lilias Ashworth, 1873-4
Lydia Becker, 1868-74
Jacob Bright, 1868-82
Mrs Jacob Bright, 1868-82
Josephine Butler, 1868-82
* Thomas Chorlton, 1868-82
Frances Power Cobbe, 1871-4
L.H. Courtney, 1879-82
Rev. Alfred Dewes, 1868-82
Sir Charles W. Dilke, 1871-82
Miss Downing, 1880-1
Elizabeth Wolstenholme Elmy, 1868-71, 1880-2
* Mrs Gell, 1876-82
Lady Goldsmid, 1881-2
* Miss Hacking, 1871-2
Rev. Septimus Hansard, 1871-82

Thomas Hare, 1871-82
* Ida Hardcastle, 1879-82
W.B. Hodgson, 1869-81
Mrs W.B. Hodgson, 1869-82
J. Boyd Kinnear, 1871-7
* William Malleson, 1876-82
* Mrs Moore, 1869-82
Herbert N. Mozley, 1871-82
Dr Richard Pankhurst, 1868-82
Mrs Richard Pankhurst, 1881-2
Frederick Pennington, 1871-2
Mrs Pennington, 1869-72
* Mrs Shearer, 1881-2
* Mrs Sutcliffe, 1871-82
Peter A. Taylor, 1876-82
Mrs Peter A. Taylor, 1876-82
* Thomas Taylor, 1871-81
Miss Tod, 1873-4
Mrs Venturi, 1876-82
Mrs Hensleigh Wedgwood, 1871-7
* Alice Wilson, 1869-82
* Lucy Wilson, 1876-82

Appendix 4

Married Women's Property Act, 1870

(33 & 34 Vict., c 93)

AN ACT TO AMEND THE LAW RELATING TO THE PROPERTY
OF MARRIED WOMEN (9 AUGUST 1870)

1 The wages and earnings of any married woman acquired or gained by her after the passing of this
Act in any employment, occupation, or trade in which she is engaged or which she carries on
separately from her husband, and also any money, or property so acquird by her through the
exercise of any literary, artistic, or scientific skill, and all investments of such wages, earnings,
money or property, shall be deemed and be taken to be property held and settled to her separate
use, independent of any husband to whom she may be married, and her receipts alone shall be a
good discharge for such wages, earnings, money, and property.

2 Notwithstanding any provision to the contrary in the Act of the tenth year of George the Fourth,
chapter twenty-four, enabling the Commissioners for the Reduction of the National Debt to
grant life annuities and annuities for terms of years, or in the Acts relating to savings banks and
post office savings banks, any deposit hereafter made and any annuity granted by the said Commissioners under any of the said Acts in the name of a married woman, or in the name of a
woman who may marry after such deposit or grant, shall be deemed to be the separate property
of such woman, and the same shall be accounted for and paid to her as if she were an unmarried
woman; provided that if any such deposit is made by, or such annuity granted to, a married
woman by means of moneys of her husband without his consent, the Court may, upon an application under section nine of this Act, order such deposit or annuity or any part thereof to be paid to
the husband.

3 Any married woman, or any woman about to be married, may apply to the Governor and
Company of the Bank of England, or to the Governor and Company of the Bank of Ireland, by a
form to be provided by the governor of each of the said banks and company for that purpose,
that any sum forming part of the public stocks and funds, and not being less than twenty pounds,
to which the woman so applying is entitled, or which she is about to acquire, may be transferred
to or made to stand in the books of the governor and company to whom such application is made
in the name or intended name of the woman as a married woman entitled to her separate use, and
on such sum being entered in the books of the said governor and company accordingly the same
shall be deemed to be the separate property of such woman, and shall be transferred and the
dividends paid as if she were an unmarried woman; provided that if any such investment in the
funds is made by a married woman by means of moneys of her husband without his consent, the
Court may, upon an application under section nine of this Act, order such investment and the
dividends thereof, or any part thereof, to be transferred and paid to the husband.

4   Any married woman, or any woman about to be married, may apply in writing to the directors
    or managers of any incorporated or joint stock company that any fully paid-up shares, or any
    debentures or debenture stock, or any stock of such company, to the holding of which no
    liability is attached, and to which the woman so applying is entitled, may be registered in the
    books of the said company in the name or intended name of the woman as a married woman
    entitled to her separate use, and it shall be the duty of such directors or managers to register
    such shares or stock accordingly, and the same upon being so registered shall be deemed to
    be the separate property of such woman, and shall be transferred and the dividends and
    profits paid as if she were an unmarried woman; provided that if any such investment as last
    mentioned is made by a married woman by means of moneys of her husband without his
    consent, the Court may, upon application under section nine of this Act, order such investment
    and the dividends and profits thereon, or any part thereof, to be transferred and paid to the
    husband.

5   Any married woman, or any woman about to be married, may apply in writing to the committee
    of management of any industrial and provident society, or to the trustees of any friendly society,
    benefit building society, or loan society, duly registered, certified, or enrolled under the Acts
    relating to such societies respectively, that any share, benefit, debenture, right, or claim whatso-
    ever in, to, or upon the funds of such society, to the holding of which share, benefit, or debenture
    no liability is attached, and to which the woman so applying is entitled, may be entered in the
    books of the society in the name or intended name of the woman as a married woman entitled to
    her separate use, and it shall be the duty of such committee or trustees to cause the same to be so
    entered, and thereupon such share, benefit, debenture, right, or claim shall be deemed to be the
    separate property of such woman, and shall be transferable and payable with all dividends and
    profits thereon as if she were an unmarried woman; provided that if any such share, benefit,
    debenture, right or claim has been obtained by a married woman by means of moneys of her
    husband without his consent, the Court may, upon an application under section nine of this Act,
    order the same and the dividends and profits thereon, or any part thereof, to be transferred and
    paid to the husband.

6   Nothing hereinbefore contained in reference to moneys deposited in or annuities granted by
    savings banks or moneys invested in the funds or in shares or stock of any company shall as
    against creditors of the husband give validity to any deposit or investment of moneys of the
    husband made in fraud of such creditors, and any moneys so deposited or invested may be
    followed as if this Act had not passed.

7   Where any woman married after the passing of this Act shall during her marriage become
    entitled to any personal property as next of kin or one of the next of kin of an intestate, or to any
    sum of money not exceeding two hundred pounds under any deed or will, such property shall,
    subject and without prejudice to the trusts of any settlement affecting the same, belong to the
    woman for her separate use, and her receipts alone shall be a good discharge for the same.

8   Where any freehold, copyhold, or customaryhold property shall descend upon any woman mar-
    ried after the passing of this Act as heiress or co-heiress of an intestate, the rents and profits of
    such property shall, subject and without prejudice to the trusts of any settlement affecting the
    same, belong to such woman for her separate use, and her receipts alone shall be a good discharge
    for the same.

9   In any question between husband and wife as to property declared by this Act to be the separate
    property of the wife, either party may apply by summons or motion in a summary way either to
    the Court of Chancery in England or Ireland according as such property is in England or
    Ireland, or in England (irrespective of the value of the property) the judge of the County Court

of the district in which either party resides, and thereupon the judge may make such order, direct such inquiry, and award such costs, as he shall think fit; provided that any order made by such judge shall be subject to appeal in the same manner as the order of the same judge made in a pending suit or on an equitable plaint would have been, and the judge may, if either party so require, hear the application in his private room.

10 A married woman may effect a policy of insurance upon her own life or the life of her husband for her separate use, and the same and all benefit thereof, if expressed on the face of it to be so effected, shall enure accordingly, and the contract in such policy shall be as valid as if made with an unmarried woman.

A policy of insurance effected by any married man on his own life, and expressed upon the face of it to be for the benefit of his wife or of his wife and children, or any of them, shall enure and be deemed a trust for the benefit of his wife for her separate use, and of his children, or any of them, according to the interest so expressed, and shall not, so long as any object of the trust remains, be subject to the control of the husband or to his creditors, or form part of his estate. When the sum secured by the policy becomes payable, or at any time previously, a trustee thereof may be appointed by the Court of Chancery in England or in Ireland according as the policy of insurance was effected in England or in Ireland, or in England by the judge of the County Court of the district, or in Ireland by the Chairman of the Civil Bill Court of the division of the country, in which the insurance office is situated, and the receipt of such trustee shall be a good discharge to the office. If it shall be proved that the policy was effected and premiums paid by the husband with intent to defraud his creditors, they shall be entitled to receive out of the sum secured an amount equal to the premiums so paid.

11 A married woman may maintain an action in her own name for the recovery of any wages, earnings, money, and property by this Act declared to be her separate property, or of any property belonging to her before marriage, and which her husband shall, by writing under his hand, have agreed with her shall belong to her after marriage as her separate property, and she shall have in her own name the same remedies, both civil and criminal, against all persons whomsoever for the protection and security of such wages, earnings, money, and property, and of any chattels, or other property purchased or obtained by means thereof for her own use, as if such wages, earnings, moneys, chattels, and property belonged to her as an unmarried woman; and in any indictment or other proceeding it shall be sufficient to allege such wages, earnings, money, chattels, and property to be her property.

12 A husband shall not, by reason of any marriage which shall take place after this Act has come into operation, be liable for the debts of his wife contracted before marriage, but the wife shall be liable to be sued for, and any property belonging to her for her separate use shall be liable to satisfy, such debts as if she had continued unmarried.

13 Where in England the husband of any woman having separate property becomes chargeable to any union or parish, the justices having jurisdiction in such union or parish may, in petty sessions assembled, upon application of the guardians of the poor, issue a summons against the wife, and make and enforce such order against her for the maintenance of her husband as by the thirty-third section of The Poor Law Amendment Act, 1868, they may now make and enforce against a husband for the maintenance of his wife who becomes chargeable to any union or parish. Where in Ireland relief is given under the provisions of the Acts relating to the relief of the destitute poor to the husband of any woman having separate property, the cost price of such relief is hereby declared to be a loan from the guardians of the union in which the same shall be given and shall be recoverable from such woman as if she were a feme sole by such and the same actions and proceedings as money lent.

14 A married woman having separate property shall be subject to all such liability for the maintenance of her children as a widow is now by law subject to for the maintenance of her children; provided always, that nothing in this Act shall relieve her husband from any liability at present imposed upon him by law to maintain her children.

15 This Act shall come into operation at the time of the passing of this Act.

16 This Act shall not extend to Scotland.

17 This Act may be cited as the 'Married Woman's Property Act, 1870.'

Appendix 5

Married Women's Property Act, 1882

(45 & 46 Vict., c 75)

(18 August 1882)

1 (1) A married woman shall, in accordance with the provisions of this Act, be capable of acquiring, holding, and disposing by will or otherwise, of any real or personal property as her separate property, in the same manner as if she were a feme sole, without the intervention of any trustee.

(2) A married woman shall be capable of entering into and rendering herself liable in respect of and to the extent of her separate property on any contract, and of suing and being sued, either in contract or in tort, or otherwise, in all respects as if she were a feme sole, and her husband need not be joined with her as plaintiff or defendant, or be made party to any action or other legal proceeding brought by or taken against her; and any damages or costs recovered by her in any such action or proceeding shall be her separate property; and any damages or costs recovered against her in any such action or proceeding shall be payable out of her separate property, and not otherwise.

(3) Every contract entered into by a married woman shall be deemed to be a contract entered into by her with respect to and to bind her separate property, unless the contrary be shown.

(4) Every contract entered into by a married woman with respect to and to bind her separate property shall bind not only the separate property which she is possessed of or entitled to at the date of the contract, but also all separate property which she may thereafter acquire.

(5) Every married woman carrying on a trade separately from her husband shall, in respect of her separate property, be subject to the bankruptcy laws in the same way as if she were a feme sole.

2 Every woman who marries after the commencement of this Act shall be entitled to have and to hold as her separate property, and to dispose of in manner aforesaid, all real and personal property which shall belong to her at the time of marriage, or shall be acquired by or devolve upon her after marriage, including any wages, earnings, money, and property gained or acquired by her in any employment, trade, or occupation, in which she is engaged, or which she carries on separately from her husband, or by the exercise of any literary, artistic, or scientific skill.

3 Any money or other estate of the wife lent or entrusted by her to her husband for the purpose of any trade or business carried on by him, or otherwise, shall be treated as assets of her husband's estate in case of his bankruptcy, under reservation of the wife's claim to a dividend as a creditor for the amount or value of such money or other estate after, but not before, all claims of the other creditors of the husband for valuable consideration in money or money's worth have been satisfied.

4 The execution of a general power by will by a married woman shall have the effect of making the property appointed liable for her debts and other liabilities in the same manner as her separate estate is made liable under this Act.

5 Every woman married before the commencement of this Act shall be entitled to have and to hold and to dispose of in manner aforesaid as her separate property all real and personal property, her title to which, whether vested or contingent, and whether in possession, reversion, or remainder, shall accrue after the commencement of this Act, including any wages, earnings, money, and property so gained or acquired by her as aforesaid.

6 All deposits in any post office or other savings bank, or in any other bank, all annuities granted by the Commissioners for the Reduction of the National Debt or by any other person, and all sums forming part of the public stocks or funds, or of any other stocks or funds transferable in the books of the Governor and Company of the Bank of England, or of any other bank, which at the commencement of this Act are standing in the sole name of a married woman, and all shares, stock, debentures, debenture stock, or other interests of or in any corporation, company, or public body, municipal, commercial, or otherwise, or of or in any industrial, provident, friendly, benefit, building, or loan society, which at the commencement of this Act are standing in her name, shall be deemed, unless and until the contrary be shown, to be the separate property of such married woman; and the fact that any such deposit, annuity, sum forming part of the public stocks or funds, or of any other stocks or funds transferable in the books of the Governor and Company of the Bank of England or of any other bank, share, stock, debenture, debenture stock or other interest as aforesaid, is standing in the sole name of a married woman shall be sufficient prima facie evidence that she is beneficially entitled thereto for her separate use, so as to authorize and empower her to receive or transfer the same, and to receive the dividends, interest, and profits thereof, without the concurrence of her husband, and to indemnify the Postmaster General, the Commissioners for the Reduction of the National Debt, the Governor and Company of the Bank of England, the Governor and Company of the Bank of Ireland, and all directors, managers, and trustees of every such bank, corporation, company, public body, or society as aforesaid, in respect thereof.

7 All sums forming part of the public stocks or funds, or of any other stocks or funds transferable in the books of the Bank of England or of any other bank, and all such deposits and annuities respectively as are mentioned in the last preceding section, and all shares, stock, debentures, debenture stock, and other interests of or in any such corporation, company, public body, or society as aforesaid, which after the commencement of this Act shall be allotted to or placed, registered, or transferred in or into or made to stand in the sole name of any married woman shall be deemed, unless and until the contrary be shown, to be her separate property, in respect of which so far as any liability may be incident thereto her separate estate shall alone be liable, whether the same shall be so expressed in the document whereby her title to the same is created or certified, or in the books or register wherein her title is entered or recorded or not.

Provided always that nothing in this Act shall require or authorize any corporation or joint stock company to admit any married woman to be a holder of any shares or stock therein to which any liability may be incident, contrary to the provisions of any Act of Parliament, charter, bye-law, articles of association, or deed of settlement regulating such corporation or company.

8 All the provisions hereinbefore contained as to deposits in any post office or other savings bank, or in any other bank, annuities granted by the Commissioners for the Reduction of the National Debt or by any other person, sums forming part of the public stocks or funds, or of any other stocks or funds transferable in the books of the Bank of England or of any other bank, shares, stock, debentures, debenture stock or other interests of or in any such corporation, company, public body, or society as aforesaid respectively, which at the commencement of this Act shall be standing in the sole name of a married woman, or which, after that time, shall be allotted to, or placed, registered, or transferred to or into, or made to stand in, the sole name of a married

woman, shall respectively extend and apply, so far as relates to the estate, right, title, or interest of the married woman, to any of the particulars aforesaid which, at the commencement of this Act, or at any time afterwards, shall be standing in, or shall be allotted to, placed, registered, or transferred to or into, or made to stand in, the name of any married woman jointly with any persons or person other than her husband.

9 It shall not be necessary for the husband of any married woman, in respect of her interest, to join in the transfer of any such annuity or deposit as aforesaid, or any sum forming part of the public stocks or funds, or of any other stocks or funds transferable as aforesaid, or any share, stock, debenture, debenture stock, or other benefit, right, claim, or other interest of or in any such corporation, company, public body, or society as aforesaid, which is now or shall at any time hereafter be standing in the sole name of any married woman, or in the joint names of such married woman and any other person or persons not being her husband.

10 If any investment in any such deposit or annuity as aforesaid, or in any of the public stocks or funds, or in any other stocks or funds transferable as aforesaid, or in any share, stock, debenture, or debenture stock of any corporation, company, or public body, municipal, commercial, or otherwise, or in any share, debenture, benefit, right, or claim whatsoever in, to, or upon the funds of any industrial, provident, friendly, benefit, building, or loan society, shall have been made by a married woman by means of moneys of her husband, without his consent, the Court may, upon an application under section seventeen of this Act, order such investment and the dividends thereof, or any part thereof, to be transferred and paid respectively to the husband; and nothing in this Act contained shall give validity as against creditors of the husband to any gift, by a husband to his wife, of any property, which, after such gift, shall continue to be in the order and disposition or reputed ownership of the husband, or to any deposit or other investment of moneys of the husband made by or in the name of his wife in fraud of his creditors; but any moneys so deposited or invested may be followed as if this Act had not passed.

11 A married woman may by virtue of the power of making contracts hereinbefore contained effect a policy upon her own life or the life of her husband for her separate use; and the same and all benefit thereof shall enure accordingly.

A policy of assurance effected by any man on his own life, and expressed to be for the benefit of his wife, or of his children, or of his wife and children, or any of them, or by any woman on her own life, and expressed to be for the benefit of her husband, or of her children, or of her husband and children, or any of them, shall create a trust in favour of the objects therein named, and the moneys payable under any such policy shall not, so long as any object of the trust remains unperformed, form part of the estate of the insured, or be subject to his or her debts; provided, that if it shall be proved that the policy was effected and the premiums paid with intent to defraud the creditors of the insured, they shall be entitled to receive, out of the moneys payable under the policy, a sum equal to the premiums so paid. The insured may by the policy, or by any memorandum under his or her hand, appoint a trustee or trustees of the moneys payable under the policy, and from time to time appoint a new trustee or new trustees thereof, and may make provision for the appointment of a new trustee or new trustees thereof, and for the investment of the moneys payable under any such policy. In default of any such appointment of a trustee, such policy, immediately on its being effected, shall vest in the insured and his or her legal personal representatives, in trust for the purposes aforesaid. If, at the time of the death of the insured, or at any time afterwards, there shall be no trustee, or it shall be expedient to appoint a new trustee or new trustees, a trustee or trustees or a new trustee or new trustees may be appointed by any Court having jurisdiction under the provisions of the Trustee Act, 1850, or the Acts amending and extending the same. The receipt of a trustee or trustees duly appointed, or, in default of any such appointment, or in default of notice to the insurance office, the receipt of the legal personal representative of the insured shall be a discharge to the office for the sum secured by the policy, or for the value thereof, in whole or in part.

12 Every woman, whether married before or after this Act, shall have in her own name against all persons whomsoever, including her husband, the same civil remedies, and also (subject, as regards her husband, to the proviso hereinafter contained) the same remedies and redress by way of criminal proceedings, for the protection and security of her own separate property, as if such property belonged to her as a feme sole, but, except as aforesaid, no husband or wife shall be entitled to sue the other for a tort. In any indictment or other proceeding under this section it shall be sufficient to allege such property to be her property; and in any proceeding under this section a husband or wife shall be competent to give evidence against each other, any statute or rule of law to the contrary notwithstanding; provided always, that no criminal proceeding shall be taken by any wife against her husband by virtue of this Act while they are living together, as to or concerning any property claimed by her, nor while they are living apart, as to or concerning any act done by the husband while they were living together, concerning property claimed by the wife, unless such property shall have been wrongfully taken by the husband when leaving or deserting, or about to leave or desert, his wife.

13 A woman after her marriage shall continue to be liable in respect and to the extent of her separate property for all debts contracted, and all contracts entered into or wrongs committed by her before her marriage, including any sum for which she may be liable as a contributory, either before or after she has been placed on the list of contributories, under and by virtue of the Acts relating to joint stock companies; and she may be sued for any such debt and for any liability in damages or otherwise under any such contract, or in respect of any such wrongs; and all sums recovered against her in respect thereof, or for any costs relating thereto, shall be payable out of her separate property; and, as between her and her husband, unless there be any contract between them to the contrary, her separate property shall be deemed to be primarily liable for all such debts, contracts, or wrongs, and for all damages or costs recovered in respect thereof; provided always, that nothing in this Act shall operate to increase or diminish the liability of any woman married before the commencement of this Act for any such debt, contract, or wrong, as aforesaid, except as to any separate property to which she may become entitled by virtue of this Act, and to which she would not have been entitled for her separate use under the Acts hereby repealed or otherwise, if this Act had not passed.

14 A husband shall be liable for the debts of his wife contracted, and for all contracts entered into and wrongs committed by her, before marriage, including any liabilities to which she may be so subject under the Acts relating to joint stock companies as aforesaid, to the extent of all property whatsoever belonging to his wife which he shall have acquired or become entitled to from or through his wife, after deducting therefrom any payments made by him, and any sums for which judgment may have been bona fide recovered against him in any proceeding at law, in respect of any such debts, contracts, or wrongs for or in respect of which his wife was liable before her marriage as aforesaid; but he shall not be liable for the same any further or otherwise; and any Court in which a husband shall be sued for any such debt shall have power to direct any inquiry or proceedings which it may think proper for the purpose of ascertaining the nature, amount, or value of such property; provided always, that nothing in this Act contained shall operate to increase or diminish the liability of any husband married before the commencement of this Act for or in respect of any such debt or other liability of his wife as aforesaid.

15 A husband and wife may be jointly sued in respect of any such debt or other liability (whether by contract or for any wrong) contracted or incurred by the wife before marriage as aforesaid, if the

plaintiff in the action shall seek to establish his claim, either wholly or in part, against both of them; and if in any such action, or in any action brought in respect of any such debt or liability against the husband alone, it is not found that the husband is liable in respect of any property of the wife so acquired by him, or to which he shall have become so entitled as aforesaid, he shall have judgment for his costs of defence, whatever may be the result of the action against the wife if jointly sued with him; and in any such action against husband and wife jointly, if it appears that the husband is liable for the debt or damages recovered, or any part thereof, the judgment to the extent of the amount for which the husband is liable shall be a joint judgment against the husband personally and against the wife as to her separate property; and as to the residue, if any, of such debt and damages, the judgment shall be a separate judgment against the wife as to her separate property only.

16 A wife doing any act with respect to any property of her husband, which, if done by the husband with respect to property of the wife, would make the husband liable to criminal proceedings by the wife under this Act, shall in like manner be liable to criminal proceedings by her husband.

17 In any question between husband and wife as to the title to or possession of property, either party, or any such bank, corporation, company, public body, or society as aforesaid in whose books any stocks, funds, or shares of either party are standing, may apply by summons or otherwise in a summary way to any judge of the High Court of Justice in England or in Ireland, according as such property is in England or Ireland, or (at the option of the applicant irrespectively of the value of the property in dispute) in England to the judge of the county court of the district, or in Ireland to the chairman of the civil bill court of the division in which either party resides, and the judge of the High Court of Justice or of the county court, or the chairman of the civil bill court (as the case may be) may make such order with respect to the property in dispute, and as to the costs of and consequent on the application as he thinks fit, or may direct such application to stand over from time to time, and any inquiry touching the matters in question to be made in such manner as he shall think fit; provided always, that any order of a judge of the High Court of Justice to be made under the provisions of this section shall be subject to appeal in the same way as an order made by the same judge in a suit pending or on an equitable plaint in the said court would be; and any order of a county or civil bill court under the provisions of this section shall be subject to appeal in the same way as any other order made by the same court would be, and all proceedings in a county court or civil bill court under this section in which, by reason of the value of the property in dispute, such court would not have had jurisdiction if this Act or the Married Woman's Property Act, 1870, had not passed, may, at the option of the defendant or respondent to such proceedings, be removed as of right into the High Court of Justice in England or Ireland (as the case may be), by writ of certiorari or otherwise as may be prescribed by any rule of such High Court; but any order made or act done in the course of such proceedings prior to such removal shall be valid, unless order shall be made to the contrary by such High Court; provided also, that the judge of the High Court of Justice or of the county court, or the chairman of the civil bill court, if either party so require, may hear any such application in his private room; provided also, that any such bank, corporation, company, public body, or society as aforesaid, shall, in the matter of any such application for the purposes of costs or otherwise, be treated as a stakeholder only.

18 A married woman who is an executrix or administratrix alone or jointly with any other person or persons of the estate of any deceased person, or a trustee alone or jointly as aforesaid of property subject to any trust, may sue or be sued, and may transfer or join in transferring any such annuity or deposit as aforesaid, or any sum forming part of the public stocks or funds, or of any other stocks or funds transferable as aforesaid, or any share, stock, debenture, debenture stock, or other

benefit, right, claim, or other interest of or in any such corporation, company, public body, or society in that character, without her husband, as if she were a feme sole.

19 Nothing in this Act contained shall interfere with or affect any settlement or agreement for a settlement made or to be made, whether before or after marriage, respecting the property of any married woman, or shall interfere with or render inoperative any restriction against anticipation at present attached or to be hereafter attached to the enjoyment of any property or income by a woman under any settlement, agreement for a settlement, will, or other instrument; but no restriction against anticipation contained in any settlement or agreement for a settlement of a woman's own property to be made or entered into by herself shall have any validity against debts contracted by her before marriage, and no settlement or agreement for a settlement shall have any greater force or validity against creditors of such woman than a like settlement or agreement for a settlement made or entered into by a man would have against his creditors.

20 Where in England the husband of any woman having separate property becomes chargeable to any union or parish, the justices having jurisdiction in such union or parish may, in petty sessions assembled, upon application of the guardians of the poor, issue a summons against the wife, and make and enforce such order against her for the maintenance of her husband out of such separate property as by the thirty-third section of the Poor Law Amendment Act, 1868, they may now make and enforce against a husband for the maintenance of his wife if she becomes chargeable to any union or parish. Where in Ireland relief is given under the provisions of the Acts relating to the relief of the destitute poor to the husband of any woman having separate property, the cost price of such relief is hereby declared to be a loan from the guardians of the union in which the same shall be given, and shall be recoverable from such woman as if she were a feme sole by the same actions and proceedings as money lent.

21 A married woman having separate property shall be subject to all such liability for the maintenance of her children and grandchildren as the husband is now by law subject to for the maintenance of her children and grandchildren; provided always, that nothing in this Act shall relieve her husband from any liability imposed upon him by law to maintain her children or grandchildren.

22 The Married Women's Property Act, 1870, and the Married Women's Property Act, 1870, Amendment Act, 1874, are hereby repealed; provided that such repeal shall not affect any act done or right acquired while either of such Acts was in force, or any right or liability of any husband or wife, married before the commencement of this Act, to sue or be sued, under the provisions of the said repealed Acts or either of them, for or in respect of any debt, contract, wrong, or other matter or thing whatsoever, for or in respect of which any such right or liability shall have accrued to or against such husband or wife before the commencement of this Act.

23 For the purposes of this Act the legal personal representative of any married woman shall in respect of her separate estate have the same rights and liabilities and be subject to the same jurisdiction as she would be if she were living.

24 The word 'contract' in this Act shall include the acceptance of any trust, or of the office of executrix or administratrix, and the provisions of this Act as to liabilities of married women shall extend to all liabilities by reason of any breach of trust or devastavit committed by any married woman being a trustee or executrix or administratrix either before or after her marriage, and her husband shall not be subject to such liabilities unless he has acted or intermeddled in the trust or administration. The word 'property' in this Act includes a thing in action.

25 The date of the commencement of this Act shall be the first of January one thousand eight hundred and eighty-three.

26 This Act shall not extend to Scotland.

27 This Act may be cited as the Married Women's Property Act, 1882.

Appendix 6

Married Women's Property Bills in Parliament, 1857-1882

YEAR	TITLE	SPONSORS	ACTION IN PARLIAMENT
1857	Married Women's Property Bill	Lord Brougham	*Lords* First reading 13 Feb.
1857	Married Women's Property Bill	Sir T.E. Perry M. Milnes	*Commons* First reading 14 May Second reading 15 July Dropped
1868	Married Women's Property Bill	G.J. Shaw-Lefevre R. Gurney J.S. Mill	*Commons* First reading 21 Apr. Second reading 10 June Select Committee 23 June–17 July Withdrawn 24 July
1869	Married Women's Property Bill (same as 1868 bill)	R. Gurney T.E. Headlam Jacob Bright	*Commons* First reading 25 Feb. Second reading 14 Apr. Select Committee 22 Apr.–13 May Third reading 21 July *Lords* First reading 22 July Second reading 30 July Dropped
1870	Bill to Protect Property of Married Women	H.C. Raikes S. Hill	*Commons* First reading 14 Feb. Second reading 18 May defeated
1870	Married Women's Property Bill (same as 1869 bill as amended by Select Committee)	R. Gurney T.E. Headlam Jacob Bright	*Commons* First reading 11 Feb. Second reading 18 May Third reading 30 May

YEAR	TITLE	SPONSORS	ACTION IN PARLIAMENT
			Lords
			First reading 31 May
			Second reading 21 June
			Select Committee 4-11 July
			Third reading 22 July
			Commons
			Acceptance of Lords' amendments 3 Aug.
			Royal assent Aug. 9, 33 & 34 Vict., c 93
1872	Bill to Amend Married Women's Property Act	S. Hill H.C. Raikes H.C. Lopes G. Goldney	*Commons* First reading 16 Feb. Dropped
1873	Bill (no. 1) to Amend Married Women's Property Act of 1870	J. Hinde Palmer Sir R.P. Amphlett O. Morgan Jacob Bright	*Commons* First reading 1 Feb. Second reading 19 Feb. House in committee 28 Mar.–27 June Dropped
1873	Bill (no. 2) to Amend Married Women's Property Act of 1870 (same as 1872 bill)	S. Hill H.C. Raikes G. Goldney	*Commons* First reading 7 Feb. Second reading 12 Feb. House in committee 9 July Dropped
1874	Bill to Amend Married Women's Property Act of 1870	S. Morley Sir J. Lubbock Sir C. Mills	*Commons* First reading 20 Mar. Second reading 15 Apr. Select Committee 24 Apr.–18 May Third reading 2 June *Lords* First reading 4 June Second reading 16 June Third reading 26 June Royal assent 30 July, 37 & 38 Vict., c 50
1877	Married Women's Property (Scotland) Bill	G. Anderson Sir R. Anstruther D. McLaren O. Ewing	*Commons* First reading 9 Feb. Second reading 18 Apr. Select Committee report 15 May Third reading 19 July

YEAR	TITLE	SPONSORS	ACTION IN PARLIAMENT
			Lords
			First reading 20 July
			Second reading 24 July
			Third reading 27 July
			Royal assent 2 Aug., 40 & 41 Vict., c 29
1877	Married Women's Property Bill	Lord Coleridge	*Lords* First reading 15 May Second reading 21 June, no division
1878	Married Women's Property (Scotland) Bill	G. Anderson Sir R. Anstruther O. Ewing D. McLaren	*Commons* First reading 18 Jan. Dropped
1878	Married Women's Property Act (1870) Amendment Bill (similar to 1873 bill no. 1)	J.T. Hibbert O. Morgan G. Goldney Sir C. Dilke	*Commons* First reading 18 Jan. Withdrawn 24 July
1879	Married Women's Property (Scotland) Bill (same as 1878 bill)	G. Anderson Sir R. Anstruther O. Ewing D. McLaren	*Commons* First reading 6 Dec. 1878 Second reading 5 Mar. Dropped
1880	Married Women's Property Acts Consolidation Bill (same as 1878 bill no. 1)	J. Hinde Palmer Sir G. Goldney Jacob Bright W. Williams	*Commons* First reading 21 May Second reading 9 June Withdrawn 28 July
1880	Married Women's Property (Scotland) Bill	G. Anderson D. McLaren Sir D. Wedderburn J. Stewart	*Commons* First reading 21 May Second reading 9 June Dropped
1881	Married Women's Property Acts Consolidation Bill (same as 1880 bill)	J. Hinde Palmer Sir G. Goldney Jacob Bright H. Davey	*Commons* First reading 10 Jan. Second reading 13 Jan. Select Committee 9 Feb.–10 Mar. Withdrawn 15 Aug.
1881	Married Women's Property (Scotland) Bill (same as 1880 bill)	G. Anderson D. McLaren Sir D. Wedderburn	*Commons* First reading 1 Jan. Debate on second reading 13 Jan. Select Committee appointed 11 Feb. Second reading 25 Apr. Third reading 29 Apr.

YEAR	TITLE	SPONSORS	ACTION IN PARLIAMENT
			Lords
			First reading 5 May
			Second reading 27 May
			House in committee 16 June
			Third reading 24 June
			Commons
			Agreement to Lords' amendments 30 June
			Royal assent 18 July, 44 & 45 Vict., c 21
1882	Married Women's Property Acts Consolidation Bill (same as 1881 bill as amended by Select Committee)	Lord Selbourne	*Lords*
			First reading 14 Feb.
			Second reading 7 Mar.
			Third reading 19 May
		O. Morgan	*Commons*
			First reading 2 June
			Second reading 8 June
			House in committee 11 Aug.
			Third reading 15 Aug.
			Royal assent 18 Aug., 45 & 46 Vict., c 75

Appendix 7

Legislation Relating to Married Women's Property

This listing is not exhaustive; it includes only acts referred to in the text.

1833	Dower Act (3 & 4 Wm. IV, c 105)
1857	Matrimonial Causes Act (20 & 21 Vict., c 85)
1859	Matrimonial Causes Act (22 & 23 Vict., c 61)
1870	Married Women's Property Act (33 & 34 Vict., c 93)
1873	Judicature Act (36 & 37 Vict., c 66)
1874	Married Women's Property Act (1870) Amendment Act (37 & 38 Vict., c 50)
1877	Married Women's Property (Scotland) Act (40 & 41 Vict., c 29)
1878	Matrimonial Causes Act (41 & 42 Vict., c 19)
1881	Married Women's Property (Scotland) Act (44 & 45 Vict., c 21)
1882	Married Women's Property Act (45 & 46 Vict., c 75)
1884	Married Women's Property (1882) Amendment Act (47 & 48 Vict., c 14)
1884	Matrimonial Causes Act (47 & 48 Vict., c 68)
1886	Married Women (Maintenance in Case of Desertion) Act (49 & 50 Vict., c 52)
1890	Intestates' Estates Act (53 & 54 Vict., c 29)
1893	Married Women's Property Act (56 & 57 Vict., c 63)
1895	Summary Jurisdiction (Married Women) Act (58 & 59 Vict., c 39)
1907	Matrimonial Causes Act (7 Edw. VII, c 12)
1908	Married Women's Property Act (8 Edw. VII, c 27)
1923	Matrimonial Causes Act (13 & 14 Geo. V, c 19)
1925	Law of Property Act (15 & 16 Geo. V, c 20)
1925	Administration of Estates Act (15 & 16 Geo. V, c 23)
1925	Summary Jurisdiction (Separation and Maintenance) Act (15 & 16 Geo. V, c 51)
1935	Law Reform (Married Women and Tortfeasors) Act (25 & 26 Geo. V, c 30)
1937	Matrimonial Causes Act (1 Edw. VIII & 1 Geo. VI, c 57)
1938	Inheritance (Family Provision) Act (1 & 2 Geo. VI, c 45)
1948	National Assistance Act (11 & 12 Geo. VI, c 29)
1949	Married Women (Restraint on Anticipation) Act (12, 13 & 14 Geo. VI, c 78)
1949	Married Women (Maintenance) Act (12, 13 & 14 Geo. VI, c 99)
1952	Magistrates' Courts Act (15 & 16 Geo. VI & 1 Eliz. II, c 55)
1960	Matrimonial Proceedings (Magistrates' Courts) Act (8 & 9 Eliz. II, c 48)
1962	Law Reform (Husband and Wife) Act (10 & 11 Eliz. II, c 48)
1963	Matrimonial Causes Act (c 45)

1964	Married Women's Property Act (c 19)
1967	Matrimonial Homes Act (c 75)
1969	Divorce Reform Act (c 55)
1970	Income and Corporation Taxes Act (c 10)
1970	Matrimonial Proceedings and Property Act (c 45)
1971	Finance Act (c 68)
1973	Matrimonial Causes Act (c 18)
1975	Inheritance (Provision for Family and Dependents) Act (c 63)

Notes

1 'THE FIRST POINT IN THE WOMEN'S CHARTER'

1 Cobbe *Life of Frances Power Cobbe* 2: 70-1; Great Britain, Hansard, *Parliamentary Debates* 3d series, 195 (1869) 765 (hereafter cited as Hansard, with appropriate volume and column numbers and dates); Fawcett *What I Remember* 62

2 Apparently there are only three works that deal with married women's property rights in historical and non-technical terms. One is the excellent study by Dicey in his *Lectures on the Relation between Law and Public Opinion in England during the Nineteenth Century*. Another is the present writer's 'Victorian Wives and Property: Reform of the Married Women's Property Law, 1857-1882,' in Vicinus *A Widening Sphere: Changing Roles of Victorian Women*. The third is Beard's somewhat mistitled *Woman as Force in History: A Study in Traditions and Realities*, which deals at length, *inter alia*, with the laws affecting married women's property, especially on the American scene, and accuses feminists of misunderstanding or at least misstating the law. Beard fails to do justice to this subject for two reasons. First, she does not give due weight to the fact that the language and the underlying assumptions of the common law were a powerful psychological depressant to women. Second, she does not study in detail the extent to which equity had in practice superseded the common law, and therefore fails to prove her contention that the common law did not in fact inflict great material injury upon married women. The present study contends that it was both the psychological burden of the law and the practical hardships arising under it that stirred up feminists to fight for reform in the United States as in England.

For specialized legal treatises on the property rights of married women, and for works dealing with the legal status of women generally, see bibliography.

3 'Married Women's Property' 93. For general histories of women and the women's movement, see bibliography.

4 Census of 1831, British Parliamentary Papers (1833) 36: 1-12 (hereafter cited as Parl. Papers, with appropriate dates and volume and page numbers)

5 Ibid. 13
6 Census of 1851, Parl. Papers (1852-3) 88 (Part 1): lxxxviii-lxxxix
7 On this large and important subject, see the magisterial work of Sir William
   Holdsworth, *History of English Law*. The account which follows is based upon this
   work, especially vol. 1, and upon the work of Jenks, *A Short History of English
   Law from the Earliest Times to the End of the Year 1938*.

2 'THE VIRTUAL SLAVERY OF MARRIAGE'

1 'The Modern Revolt' 147
2 The account of the common law in this chapter is based upon the works of Dicey,
   Holdsworth, and Jenks mentioned above, and upon those of Cleveland, Denning,
   Graveson and Crane, Redman, Underhill, and Wharton cited in the bibliography.
3 Quoted in Strachey '*The Cause*' 15
4 Quoted in Graveson and Crane *A Century of Family Law* 178
5 Ibid. 116, 178-80

3 'THE GUARDIAN OF THE WEAK
AND UNPROTECTED'

1 Graveson and Crane *A Century of Family Law* 140. The account of equity in this
   chapter is based upon the same works used for the account of the common law in
   the preceding chapter.
2 Special Report from the Select Committee on the Married Women's Property Bill,
   Parl. Papers (1867-8) 7: 360, 363
3 'Married Women and Their Property' 488; Hansard 142 (1856) 410
4 Dicey *Lectures on the Relation between Law and Public Opinion* 383

4 'THE GERMS OF AN EFFECTIVE MOVEMENT'

1 Dicey *Lectures on the Relation between Law and Public Opinion* 384-6; Census of
   1851, Parl. Papers (1852-3) 88 (Part 1): lxxxviii-lxxxix
2 Perkins *The Life of Mrs. Norton* 149.
3 Cecil *Melbourne* 224
4 For Lyndhurst, see Holdsworth *History of English Law* 16: 5-27.
5 Perkins *Life of Mrs Norton* 248
6 Burton *Barbara Bodichon* 92. Burton's is the only biography of this important
   woman. Additional material on her life can be found in the following works:
   Betham-Edwards *Mid-Victorian Memories* and *Reminiscences*; Haight *George Eliot: A
   Biography* and *George Eliot and John Chapman*; Sharp *Hertha Ayrton, 1854-1923*;
   and Barbara Stephen *Emily Davies and Girton College*.

7 There is no biography of Miss Parkes (Madame Belloc), but a good deal of biographical material is contained in the charming books by her daughter, Mrs Belloc Lowndes, '*I, Too, Have Lived in Arcadia*' and *Where Love and Friendship Dwelt*; and also in *The George Eliot Letters*. For her father, see Finlayson 'Joseph Parkes of Birmingham, 1796-1865.'

The story of the 'ladies of Langham Place,' as they have been called because of the location of the offices of the *Journal* and the SPEW, is briefly told by Gallagher 'A Coterie of Victorian Pre-Suffragists' and by Maison 'Insignificant Objects of Desire.' The history of the group can be traced in the pages of the *Journal*, in the *Annual Reports* of the SPEW, and in the *Transactions* of the National Association for the Promotion of Social Science, with which the SPEW was affiliated. For the Emigration Society, see Hammerton *Emigrant Gentlewomen*.

Of the five other women mentioned here, two – Mary Howitt and Anna Jameson – have been the subjects of biographies which are cited in the bibliography. Details of the life of Anna Mary Howitt may be gleaned from the works about her mother, and from Beaky's 'Letters of Anna Mary Howitt.' Details about Eliza Fox can be found in the biography of her father by R. and E. Garnett, *The Life of W.J. Fox*. The work of Elizabeth Reid is described in Tuke's *History of Bedford College for Women*.

8 See Hawes *Henry Brougham*.

9 R. and F. Davenport-Hill *The Recorder of Birmingham* 250

10 Ibid. 266

11 *Dictionary of National Biography*

12 Quoted in Cornwallis 'The Property of Married Women' 347

13 Quoted in Stephen *Emily Davies and Girton College* 43

14 The examples given here are found in Cornwallis 'The Property of Married Women' 342-4; Cornwallis 'Capabilities and Disabilities of Women'; Hansard 144 (1857) 608-9; and Hansard 146 (1857) 1516-17.

15 *Dictionary of National Biography*. The quotations which follow are taken from these articles. For another woman's response to Miss Cornwallis, see the two articles by Oliphant, 'The Laws Concerning Women' and 'The Condition of Women.'

16 Howitt *An Autobiography* 2: 116

17 Ibid. 115. Of the distinguished women described here, several have written their autobiographies, have been the subjects of biographies, and have had their letters edited and published – Elizabeth Barrett Browning, Elizabeth Gaskell, Harriet Martineau, Mary Cowden Clarke, Geraldine Jewsbury, Jane Carlyle, Mary Mohl, George Eliot, and Charlotte Cushman (see bibliography). Material on Sarianna Browning and Isabella Blagden can be gleaned from the works about Mrs Browning, material on Anna Blackwell from the works about her family and her famous sister Elizabeth, and material about Matilda Hays from the studies of her intimate

friend Charlotte Cushman. The *Dictionary of National Biography* contains sketches
of the husbands of Jane Loudon and Mary Ann Lovell. The material here about
Amelia Edwards is taken from Kunitz and Haycraft *British Authors of the Nine-
teenth Century* and from Betham-Edwards *Mid-Victorian Memories* and *Reminiscences.*
Finally, the material on Julia Maynard is taken from the mention of her family in
Debrett's *Peerage.*

18 Browning *The Letters of Elizabeth Barrett Browning* 1: 312, 330; 2: 388
19 Ibid. 2: 255
20 Gaskell *The Letters of Mrs. Gaskell* 419, 808
21 Ibid. 113, 142
22 Ibid. 379
23 Quoted in Webb *Harriet Martineau* 180
24 Garnett *Life of W.J. Fox* 310
25 Altick *The Cowden Clarkes* 88-9
26 Carlyle *New Letters and Memorials of Jane Welsh Carlyle* 2: 126; Howe *Geraldine
    Jewsbury: Her Life and Errors* 19, 105; Jewsbury *Selections from the Letters of Geral-
    dine Endsor Jewsbury to Jane Welsh Carlyle* 321, 341-2, 347
27 Carlyle *Letters and Memorials of Jane Welsh Carlyle* 1: 95; 2: 253
28 Quoted in L. and E. Hanson *Necessary Evil* 106
29 Ibid. 169, 197, 269-70
30 Ibid. 435
31 Quoted in O'Meara *Madame Mohl, Her Salon and Her Friends* 145-6
32 Ibid. 127-32
33 *George Eliot Letters* 2: 227
34 Ibid. 2: 438-9
35 Howitt *An Autobiography* 2: 116-17; Hansard 141 (1856) 120-1; Married Women's
    Property Committee *Final Report* (1882) 7. The petition is reprinted in Burton
    Barbara Bodichon 70-1, and in Cornwallis 'The Property of Married Women,'
    336-8.
36 Stephen *Emily Davies and Girton College* 41; *The Times* (London) 2 June 1856, 5

5 'THE WIND OUT OF OUR SAILS'

1 Hansard 142 (1856) 1273-6
2 Married Women's Property Committee *Annual Report* (1880) 11. For Malins,
   Chambers, and Phillimore, see *Dictionary of National Biography*; for Phillimore, see
   Holdsworth *History of English Law* 15: 359-60. The quotations here are from Hansard 142 (1856) 1278-9, 1282-3.
3 Hansard 142 (1856) 1277-81. For Cockburn, see Holdsworth *History of English
   Law* 15: 429-43.

4 Hansard 142 (1856) 1284

5 Hansard 144 (1857) 605-19. Brougham's bill was not the same as that introduced
   by Perry in the Commons three months later. It is not printed in the Parliamentary Papers, but according to the summary of its provisions in *The Times* (London) 18 February 1857, 7, it would have treated a married woman's property as
   her 'separate estate' and thus foreshadowed the course which reform of the law
   actually took in 1870 and 1882. For Lord Campbell, see Holdsworth *History of
   English Law* 15: 405-29.

6 Parl. Papers (1857) session 2, 3: 245-8; National Association for the Promotion of
   Social Science *Sessional Proceedings* (1867-8) 196; Special Report from Select Com-
   mittee on Married Women's Property Bill, Parl. Papers (1867-8) 7: 375; Perry
   'Rights and Liabilities of Husband and Wife'

7 Hansard 145 (1857) 266-73; 146 (1857) 1520-3

8 Milnes is the subject of biographies by Pope-Hennessy and Reid (see bibliography). For Drummond, see *Dictionary of National Biography*.

9 *Dictionary of National Biography*

10 Hansard 145 (1857) 278-80. The *Saturday Review* is quoted in Burton *Barbara Bodichon* 68-9, and in Stephen *Emily Davies and Girton College* 43.

11 Hansard 145 (1857) 280

12 Ibid. 277

13 Married Women's Property Committee *Annual Report* (1880) 12

14 The account of the divorce law which follows is based upon the works of Cleveland, Graveson and Crane, Holdsworth, Kitchin, McGregor, Miller, and Wharton
   cited in the bibliography.

15 Hansard 134 (1854) 1 ff, 1436 ff; 142 (1856) 401 ff, 1968 ff; 143 (1856) 230 ff,
   308-9, 319, 710; 145 (1857) 483 ff, 780 ff; 146 (1857) 227-8. For Cranworth, see
   Holdsworth *History of English Law* 16: 57-64.

16 Hansard 147 (1857) 413, 1602, 1720 and passim

17 Hansard 142 (1856) 410

18 Hansard 145 (1857) 799-800; 147 (1857) 1227-36. For St Leonards, see Holdsworth *History of English Law* 16: 39-57.

19 Hansard 147 (1857) 1889

20 Hansard 142 (1856) 412-13; 145 (1857) 496, 501-5; Graveson and Crane *A Century
   of Family Law* 319

21 Garnett *Life of W.J. Fox* 325; Hansard 142 (1856) 421

22 Graveson and Crane *A Century of Family Law* 318, 322-8; O.R. McGregor *Divorce
   in England* 29-31

23 Hansard 142 (1856) 412; Dicey *Lectures on the Relation between Law and Public
   Opinion* 347; Saleeby *Woman and Womanhood* 294-5; Graveson and Crane *A
   Century of Family Law* 12-13, 307

24 The account of these laws here is based upon the works of Graveson and Crane and of McGregor, already cited. For the problem of battered wives in the nineteenth century, see the study by Gibson and the article by Tomes cited in the bibliography.

25 For these developments, see Graveson and Crane *A Century of Family Law* and the works by Cretney, Lesser, Sachs and Wilson, and Stone cited in the bibliography.

26 'Property of Married Women' *English Woman's Journal* 59

27 Quoted in Arnstein *Britain Yesterday and Today* 81

6 'THE PECULIAR CHARACTER
OF THE MODERN WORLD'

1 There are various editions of Mill's *Subjection of Women*. The edition used for this study is the easily accessible one published in John Stuart Mill and Harriet Taylor Mill *Essays on Sex Equality*. The quotation here is from pp. 142-3 of this edition.

2 Mill *Autobiography* 198. There have been numerous studies of Mill, for which see the bibliography.

3 Mill *Letters* 1: 58-9

4 Mill *Autobiography* 130-1, 172 and *Subjection of Women* 235

5 Mill *Autobiography* 185-6

6 Mill *Letters* 2: 336-7. The lengthy report of the Schools Inquiry Commission is published in Parl. Papers (1867-8) 28.

7 Stephen *Emily Davies and Girton College* 106-8. For works on the suffrage movement, see bibliography.

8 Hansard 187 (1867) 817 ff; Mill *Autobiography* 213 and *Letters* 2: 157

9 Hansard 187 (1867) 817, 828-9

10 Mrs Elmy tried with little success to ensure that she would be recognized and remembered as an important feminist leader. Under her pseudonym Ellis Ethelmer she wrote an autobiographical sketch entitled 'A Woman Emancipator,' which was published in the *Westminster Review*. The material and quotations here are taken from this article.

11 In addition to her own *Personal Reminiscences of a Great Crusade*, there are numerous studies of Mrs Butler and her work, for which see bibliography. The quotations that follow are found in G.W. and L.A. Johnson *Josephine E. Butler* 20, 34, 58-9, 85-6, 135, 252; and in Petrie *A Singular Iniquity* 28-9.

12 There is no biography of this important woman. The material here is taken from the *Dictionary of National Biography*; Blackburn *Women's Suffrage* 50; and Stanton *The Woman Question in Europe* 90-1. Miss Boucherett's activities can also be traced in the pages of the *English Woman's Journal* and the *Englishwoman's Review*, in

the *Annual Reports* of the Society for Promoting the Employment of Women, and in the *Transactions* of the National Association for the Promotion of Social Science. See also Holcombe *Victorian Ladies at Work* 5-16.

13 See Ritt 'The Victorian Conscience in Action.'

14 Quoted in Hawes *Henry Brougham* 293. See Frances Power Cobbe 'Social Science Congresses, and Women's Part in Them.'

15 Ritt 'The Victorian Conscience in Action' passim

16 National Association for the Promotion of Social Science *Transactions* 11 (1867) 292

17 Married Women's Property Committee *Annual Report* (1869) 3-4 and *Final Report* (1882) 12; Hansard 191 (1868) 1016; Special Report from Select Committee on Married Women's Property Bill, Parl. Papers (1867-8) 7: 375; Davenport-Hill *The Recorder of Birmingham* 112, 331. Besides Miss Wolstenholme, Mrs Butler, and Miss Boucherett, a fourth woman, a Mrs Gloyn, also took part in organizing the memorial to the Social Science Association, but I have been unable to discover any information about her.

18 Married Women's Property Committee *Annual Report* (1869) 3-4 and *Final Report* (1882) 12; National Association for the Promotion of Social Science *Sessional Proceedings* (1867-8) 189-98; A Bill to Amend the Law with Respect to the Property of Married Women, Parl. Papers (1867-8) 3: 375-8; Hansard 191 (1868) 1015-25

19 Married Women's Property Committee *Annual Report* (1869) 3-4, and *Final Report* (1882) 13

20 There is no full-scale biography of Miss Becker, but a good deal of material about her is contained in Blackburn's *Women's Suffrage*.

21 Apparently there is no biography of Pankhurst, but material about him can be found in books by and about his family, which are cited in the bibliography. The quotations here are from Emmeline Pankhurst's *My Own Story* 9, and from David Mitchell's *The Fighting Pankhursts* 19.

22 Both Jacob and Ursula Bright were referred to frequently by their contemporaries, but there is no biography of either and they remain rather shadowy figures. The *Dictionary of National Biography* contains a brief sketch of Jacob Bright, as do the *Spectator* 81 (1898) 642-3, and *Vanity Fair* 17 (1877) 279. A good deal of information about the Bright family can be found in the biographies of John Bright cited in the bibliography.

23 Trevelyan *The Life of John Bright* 23

24 *Dictionary of National Biography*; Blackburn *Women's Suffrage* 64-5

25 Fawcett *What I Remember* 119

26 See *The Amberley Papers*.

27 See *Dictionary of National Biography*; also *George Eliot Letters* passim and Haight *George Eliot* passim.

28 See Fawcett *What I Remember* and Strachey *Millicent Garrett Fawcett*.

29 See the biographies by Gwynn and Tuckwell and by Jenkins cited in the biblio-
    graphy.
30 *Dictionary of National Biography*
31 Ibid.
32 Stenton *Who's Who of British Members of Parliament* 1 (1832-85) 307
33 *Dictionary of National Biography* and Stephen *Emily Davies and Girton College*
    passim. For the Gurneys' work for medical women, see the works on Elizabeth
    Blackwell and Elizabeth Garrett Anderson, and the studies by Bell, Jex-Blake,
    Newman, and Todd cited in the bibliography.
34 *Dictionary of National Biography* .
35 Ibid.
36 See her autobiography *Life of Frances Power Cobbe by Herself.*
37 There is no biography of Emilie Venturi. The material and quotations here come
    from the sketch of her father in the *Dictionary of National Biography*; from the
    biography of her brother-in-law by Hammond and Hammond *James Stansfeld: A
    Victorian Champion of Sex Equality*; and from *Letters and Memorials of Jane Welsh
    Carlyle* 2: 340.
38 *Dictionary of National Biography* and Stephen *Emily Davies and Girton College* 365,
    372
39 Butler *Personal Reminiscences of a Great Crusade* 189-90; Blackburn *Women's Suffrage*
    130, 166, 209
40 Mill *Subjection of Women* 215
41 *Dictionary of National Biography*; National Association for the Promotion of Social
    Science *Transactions* 12 (1868) 238-49, 281, and 13 (1869) 199-202
42 Married Women's Property Committee *Annual Report* (1869) 5, and *Final Report*
    (1882) 14
43 Cobbe *Life of Frances Power Cobbe by Herself* 2: 70-1; Hansard 195 (1869) 765
44 Fawcett *What I Remember* 61-2; Married Women's Property Committee *Annual
    Report* (1869) 5 and *Final Report* (1882) 14
45 Of the six men described here, the four supporters of reform and the two leading
    opponents, all are the subjects of sketches in the *Dictionary of National Biography*.
    In addition, a biography of Shaw-Lefevre by Wood and biographies of Lowe by
    Sylvester and Winter are cited in the bibliography; and a good brief account of
    Jessel can be found in Holdsworth *History of English Law* 16 121-6.

7 'THE BURTHEN OF PROOF'

1 A Bill to Amend the Law with Respect to the Property of Married Women, Parl.
   Papers (1867-8) 3: 375, and (1868-9) 3: 427. It would be cumbersome and tedious
   to cite individually every point of opinion and quotation contained in this chapter.

Unless otherwise noted, all material here is derived from three sources: the House of Commons debates of 1868-70, as cited in the bibliography; the Special Report from the Select Committee on the Married Women's Property Bill, Parl. Papers (1867-8) 7: 339-465; and Mill's *Subjection of Women*.

2 Hansard 198 (1869) 982
3 *The Times* (London) 15 April 1869, 8
4 Ibid. 12 June 1868, 9
5 Ibid. 31 July 1869, 9
6 Mozley 'The Property Disabilities of a Married Woman, and Other Legal Effects of Marriage' in Butler *Woman's Work and Woman's Culture* 205
7 Hansard 198 (1869) 982
8 *The Times* (London) 15 April 1868, 8
9 Hobhouse 'On the Forfeiture of Property by Married Women' 182
10 National Association for the Promotion of Social Science *Transactions* 24 (1880) 199
11 Becker 'The Political Disabilities of Women' 58
12 *The Times* (London) 22 June 1870, 9
13 Hobhouse *On the Laws Relating to the Property of Married Women* 12-13
14 Ibid. 12; 'The Legal Position of Women and Its Moral Effects' 93
15 *The Times* (London) 15 June 1868, 6
16 Ibid. 15 April 1869, 8, and 31 July 1869, 9
17 Hobhouse 'On the Forfeiture of Property by Married Women' 184
18 Mozley 'The Property Disabilities of a Married Woman' 209
19 'The Property of Married Women' 54; *The Times* (London) 19 May 1870, 9
20 'Married Women and Their Property' 488; 'The House of Commons on Wives' Property' 471
21 *The Times* (London) 31 July 1869, 9
22 Census of 1861, Parl. Papers (1863) 53 (Part 1) 33
23 Becker 'The Political Disabilities of Women' 62
24 Ibid. 57-8; Mozley 'The Property Disabilities of a Married Woman' 246
25 Hansard 214 (1873) 677
26 Stanton *The Woman Question in Europe* 10-11
27 *The Times* (London) 4 August 1870, 12

8 'THAT LEGISLATIVE ABORTION'

1 A Bill to Amend the Law with Respect to the Property of Married Women, Parl. Papers (1867-8) 3: 375-8; Hansard 191 (1868) 1015-25, 192 (1868) 1352-78; 'Married Women's Property' 90; 'Married Women and Their Property' 489. For Karslake, see Holdsworth *History of English Law* 15: 509.

2 Select Committee on Married Women's Property Bill, Parl. Papers (1867-8) 7: 40;
   Special Report from Select Committee on Married Women's Property Bill, Parl.
   Papers (1867-8) 7: 339-465; Hansard 142 (1856) 1282, and 195 (1869) 778. For
   Collier, see Holdsworth *History of English Law* 16: 167.

3 See the biography of Mundella by Armytage, cited in the bibliography.

4 'The House of Commons on Wives' Property' 471

5 A Bill to Amend the Law with Respect to the Property of Married Women, Parl.
   Papers (1868-9) 3: 427-34; Hansard 194 (1869) 331; *Dictionary of National Biography*

6 Hansard 195 (1869) 760-98; 'The House of Commons on Wives' Property' 471

7 Blackburn *Women's Suffrage* 83-5; Sachs and Wilson *Sexism and the Law* 26, 41.
   For Coleridge, see Holdsworth *History of English Law* 15: 460-6.

8 Hansard 195 (1869) 798; A Bill to Amend the Law with Respect to the Property
   of Married Women, Parl. Papers (1868-9) 3: 427-34; Report from Select Committee on Married Women's Property Bill, Parl. Papers (1868-9) 8: 771

9 Hansard 198 (1869) 401-5

10 Ibid. 979-87

11 Bill to Amend the Law Relating to the Property of Married Women, Parl. Papers
    (1870) 2: 657-60; Bill to Protect the Property of Married Women, Parl. Papers
    (1870) 2: 671-8; Hansard 201 (1870) 878-92

12 Hansard 192 (1868) 1357, 1369, 1373, 195 (1869): 774, 779

13 Married Women's Property Committee *Final Report* (1882) 16-17

14 Hobhouse 'On the Forfeiture of Property by Married Women' 185, and *On the
    Forfeiture of Property by Married Women* 15-16; Hansard 201 (1870) 886, 890-1

15 Hansard 192 (1868) 1371; Special Report from Select Committee on Married
    Women's Property Bill, Parl. Papers (1867-8) 7: 419, 426; 'Married Women's
    Property' 90; Returns Ordered by the Commons with respect to the number of
    causes filed for divorce, judicial separation, restitution of conjugal rights, annul-
    ments and protection orders, Parl. Papers (1862) 44: 515-16

16 Special Report from Select Committee on Married Women's Property Bill, Parl.
    Papers (1867-8) 7: 365, 429; 'Married Women's Property' 90

17 Hobhouse 'On the Forfeiture of Property by Married Women' 183-4

18 Hansard 201 (1870) 888-92

19 Married Women's Property Committee *Final Report* (1882) 18. The Lords' debate,
    from which the quotations that follow are taken, can be found in Hansard 202
    (1870) 600-22.

20 *The Times* (London) 23 June 1870, 9. For Penzance, see Holdsworth *History of
    English Law* 16: 155-6.

21 *The Times* (London) 23 June 1870, 9; Holdsworth *History of English Law* 16:
    70-90

22 'The Peers and the Married Women' 772

23 Married Women's Property Committee *Final Report* (1882) 18. For the law lords Cairns, Romilly, and Hatherley, see Holdsworth *History of English Law* 15: 240 ff, 16: 90-7, 105-12, 119-20, 155-6. For Shaftesbury, see the biographies by Battiscombe and Best cited in the bibliography.

24 Bill to Amend the Law Relating to the Property of Married Women as Amended by the Lords, Parl. Papers (1870) 2: 663-70

25 Hansard 203 (1870) 395-401, 622-3

26 Married Women's Property Committee *Annual Report* (1876) 10; *Annual Report* (1879) 33-4; *Final Report* (1882) 22

27 Hansard 203 (1870) 1488

28 Arnold *Social Politics* 345, 358-9; Hansard 214 (1873) 669, 676-9, 682; and 218 (1874) 611

29 National Association for the Promotion of Social Science *Transactions* 14 (1870) 549-52

30 *The Times* (London) 25 August 1870, 11; Hansard 214 (1873) 688; National Association for the Promotion of Social Science *Transactions* 24 (1880) 194-5

31 Hansard 203 (1870) 400

32 Hansard 214 (1873) 687; 'The Peers and the Married Women' 772

33 Hansard 243 (1878) 306, 853; *The Times* (London) 24 January 1879, 8

34 Becker 'The Political Disabilities of Women' 58; National Association for the Promotion of Social Science *Transactions* 19 (1875) 268-9, and 24 (1880) 191

35 Hansard 218 (1874) 607-8

36 *The Times* (London) 18 September 1871, 10, and 21 September 1871, 5

37 *The Times* (London) 11 March 1878, 9; 12 March 1878, 5; 13 March 1878, 11; and 14 March 1878, 11

38 National Association for the Promotion of Social Science *Transactions* 19 (1875) 267

39 Hansard 214 (1873) 669; *Annual Register* (1870) 80

9 'WHAT AN EMANCIPATION IS THIS!'

1 *The Times* (London) 25 August 1870, 11

2 Married Women's Property Committee *Annual Report* (1871) 6, and *Final Report* (1882) 28-9

3 Married Women's Property Committee *Annual Report* (1876) 11-14, and *Final Report* (1882) 29, 52

4 National Association for the Promotion of Social Science *Transactions* 14 (1870) 242-4, 549-52, 19 (1875) 265-9, 24 (1880) 270, 25 (1881) 248-9; Married Women's Property Committee *Final Report* (1882) 30, 43, 45. For the end of the Social

Science Association, see Ritt 'The Victorian Conscience in Action' 'Coroner's Inquest.'

5 Married Women's Property Committee *Final Report* (1882) 27, 51-2

6 Ibid. 51-2

7 Married Women's Property Committee *Annual Report* (1880) 6-12, and *Final Report* (1882) 52; *The Times* (London) 24 January 1879, 8, and 5 February 1880, 9; Hansard 243 (1878) 306, 853

8 Bill to Amend the Married Women's Property Act (1870) so far as It Relates to Debts Contracted by Women Who Afterwards Marry, Parl. Papers (1872) 3: 9-11. For Hill, see *Dictionary of National Biography*.

9 Married Women's Property Committee *Annual Report* (1872) 4-5, and *Final Report* (1882) 25

10 Married Women's Property Committee *Annual Report* (1872) 5-6, and *Final Report* (1882) 25. For Hinde Palmer, see Stenton *Who's Who of British Members of Parliament* vol. 1, 300.

11 Married Women's Property Committee *Annual Report* (1872) 6-7; *Annual Report* (1873) 3; *Final Report* (1882) 25-6

12 Married Women's Property Committee *Annual Report* (1873) 3, and *Final Report* (1882) 26; Bill to Amend the Married Women's Property Act (1870), Parl. Papers (1873) 3: 59-61. For Amphlett, see *Dictionary of National Biography*.

13 Hansard 214 (1873) 667-89

14 Bill [as amended in committee] to Amend the Married Women's Property Act (1870), Parl. Papers (1873) 3: 63-6; Married Women's Property Committee *Annual Report* (1873) 4-5, 10, and *Final Report* (1882) 26

15 Married Women's Property Committee *Annual Report* (1876) 4, and *Final Report* (1882) 27

16 Bill to Amend the Married Women's Property Act (1870), Parl. Papers (1874) 3: 265-70; Married Women's Property Committee *Annual Report* (1869) 6, *Annual Report* (1876) 4, and *Final Report* (1882) 27. For Morley and Baggallay, see *Dictionary of National Biography*.

17 Arnold *Social Politics* 360

18 Married Women's Property Committee *Final Report* (1882) 39-42

19 Bill to Amend the Married Women's Property Law in Scotland, Parl. Papers (1877) 4: 25-7; Married Women's Property Committee *Annual Report* (1880) 20

20 Hansard 233 (1877) 1414-16; Married Women's Property Committee *Annual Report* (1880) 20, and *Final Report* (1882) 42-3; Bill [as amended by the select committee] to Amend the Married Women's Property Law in Scotland, Parl. Papers (1877) 4: 29-30. For Watson, see *Dictionary of National Biography*.

21 Bill to Amend the Married Women's Property Law in Scotland, Parl. Papers (1878) 5: 57-8; Hansard 244 (1879) 260

22 Hansard 244 (1879) 257-64; Married Women's Property Committee *Annual Report* (1879) 5-6, *Annual Report* (1880) 20-1, and *Final Report* (1882) 44; Bill to Amend the Married Women's Property Law in Scotland, Parl. Papers (1880) 5: 89-91

23 Hansard 235 (1877) 71-81

24 Bill to Amend the Married Women's Property Act, 1870, Parl. Papers (1878) 5: 53-6; Married Women's Property Committee *Final Report* (1882) 29. For Hibbert, see *Dictionary of National Biography*.

25 Married Women's Property Committee *Annual Report* (1879) 3-5, 38, *Annual Report* (1880) 3-4, and *Final Report* (1882) 30, 44; the Married Women's Property Acts 1870 and 1874, Amendment Bill, Parl. Papers (1880) 5: 69-74

26 Married Women's Property Committee *Annual Report* (1880) 20-2

27 Hansard 235 (1877) 80

28 Fawcett *What I Remember* 112; Stanton *The Woman Question in Europe* 25; Married Women's Property Committee *Final Report* (1882) 30

29 The Married Women's Property Acts Consolidation Bill, Parl. Papers (1880) 5: 77-83; Bill to Amend the Married Women's Property Law in Scotland, Parl. Papers (1880) 5: 89-91; Hansard 252 (1880) 1533-53; Married Women's Property Committee *Final Report* (1882) 31, 44. For James and Campbell, see *Dictionary of National Biography*.

30 Married Women's Property Committee *Annual Report* (1880) 10, 14

31 Selborne *Memorials*; Holdsworth *History of English Law* 16: 97-104; *The Amberley Papers* 1: 542; *The Times* (London) 27 January 1870, 10

32 Married Women's Property Committee *Final Report* (1882) 31; *The Times* (London) 8 January 1881, 10, and 24 January 1881, 6

33 Bill to Consolidate and Amend the Acts Relating to the Property of Married Women, Parl. Papers (1881) 4: 37-43; Bill to Amend the Married Women's Property Law in Scotland, Parl. Papers (1881) 4: 53-5; Hansard 251 (1881) 551-89, 706-14

34 Bill [as amended by the select committee] to Amend the Married Women's Property Law in Scotland, Parl. Papers (1881) 4: 57-9; Report from the Select Committee on the Married Women's Property Bill for Scotland, Parl. Papers (1881) 9: 653-726; Hansard 260 (1881) 1179-81, 1521-7; 261 (1881) 1438-40; 262 (1881) 627-8, 1751; Married Women's Property Committee *Final Report* (1882) 47-9

35 Bill [as amended by the select committee] to Consolidate and Amend the Acts Relating to the Property of Married Women, Parl. Papers (1881) 4: 45-51; Married Women's Property Committee *Final Report* (1882) 32; Selborne *Memorials* part 2, 2: 27-33. Selborne does not mention the Married Women's Property Bills in his lengthy autobiography, but his editor does, in a footnote – part 2, 2: 90. For Warton, see Stenton *Who's Who of British Members of Parliament* vol. 1 399.

36 Married Women's Property Committee *Final Report* (1882) 33; Bill ... to ... Amend the Acts Relating to the Property of Married Women, Parl. Papers (1882) 4: 11-22; Hansard 267 (1882) 316-17

37 Hansard 270 (1882) 616-18; Married Women's Property Committee *Final Report* (1882) 34

38 Hansard 273 (1882) 1603-12, 1844-7

39 *The Times* (London) 16 February 1883, 4

40 Married Women's Property Committee *Final Report* (1882) 53, 63; *The Times* (London) 21 November 1882, 3

41 *The Times* (London) 1 January 1883, 7; Birrell 'Woman under the English Law' 334-5

10 'THE EQUALITY OF TWO'

1 'The Modern Revolt' 148

2 Dicey *Lectures on the Relation between Law and Public Opinion* 395

3 'The Married Women's Property Act (1882),' 819; Married Women's Property Committee *Final Report* (1882) 51

4 *The Times* (London) 5 January 1883, 8

5 The twenty bills introduced included eleven measures of broad reform applying to England and five applying to Scotland; the three bills which led to passage of the limited act of 1874 for England; and Raikes's bill of 1870. The five bills which became law were the acts of 1870, 1874, and 1882 for England, and the acts of 1877 and 1881 for Scotland. Of the fifteen bills not passed, five were introduced but did not obtain a second reading; six received a second reading and then were dropped; two were read a second time and were considered by select committees, but were not proceeded with further during the session in which they were introduced; one – the bill of 1869 – was passed by the Commons but not by the Lords; and one – Raikes's bill of 1870 – was defeated.

6 'The Ladies' Petition' 69-70

7 Rosen 'Emily Davies and the Women's Movement' 110-12, 116-20

8 Blackburn *Women's Suffrage* 135-7

9 Ibid. 195; *The Life of Emmeline Pankhurst* 27-9

10 Blackburn *Women's Suffrage* 205; Graveson and Crane *A Century of Family Law* 273-4; Pankhurst *Life of Emmeline Pankhurst* 31

11 Galloway, 'Women and Politics' 568; *Female Suffrage: A Letter from the Rt. Hon. W.E. Gladstone* 3; Fawcett 'Women's Suffrage: A Reply' 747-8

12 Allan *Woman Suffrage Wrong in Principle, and Practice* 253-4

13 'Women's Suffrage: A Reply' 747

14 *Woman's Position, and the Objects of the Women's Franchise League* 5-7

15 *Female Suffrage* 7-8
16 See the excellent study by Rover *Women's Suffrage and Party Politics in Britain, 1866-1914.*
17 'Married Women's Property' 89, 93
18 Hansard 203 (1870) 397
19 'Moneyed Wives' 10; 'The Married Women's Property Act (1882)' 820; Thicknesse 'The New Legal Position of Married Women' 216-20
20 Married Women's Property Committee *Final Report* (1882) 52
21 Graveson and Crane *A Century of Family Law* 88-9, 124; *The Times* (London) 18 January 1898, 12; Redman, *A Concise View of the Law of Husband and Wife* 70
22 Holdsworth *History of English Law* 3: 533. For the reforms in the married women's property law since 1882 discussed in this section, see the works by the following: Cretney, Denning, Dicey, Graveson and Crane, Holdsworth, Jenks, Kahn-Freund, Marshall, Redman, Stone, and Underhill, cited in the bibliography.
23 Parl. Papers (1884) 5: 153, 157
24 Graveson and Crane *A Century of Family Law* 126, 202; Underhill *The Law Reform (Married Women and Tortfeasors) Act* 70
25 Graveson and Crane *A Century of Family Law* 95; Underhill *The Law Reform (Married Women and Tortfeasors) Act* 49-50
26 Underhill *The Law Reform (Married Women and Tortfeasors) Act* 24
27 Cretney 'The Maintenance Quagmire' 666
28 Ibid. 674
29 Kahn-Freund 'Matrimonial Property and Equality before the Law' 494-5
30 Marshall 'Some Economic Aspects of Family Property Rights Reform' 30-7
31 Cretney 'The Maintenance Quagmire' 662; Kahn-Freund 'Recent Legislation on Matrimonial Property' 605
32 Kahn-Freund 'Recent Legislation on Matrimonial Property' 601; Cretney *Principles of Family Law* 255, 258
33 Kahn-Freund 'Recent Legislation on Matrimonial Property' 605-6; Holcombe *Victorian Ladies at Work* 217
34 Kahn-Freund 'Matrimonial Property and Equality before the Law' 502-3; *The Times* (London) 15 April 1868, 8
35 Stone 'The Status of Women in Great Britain' 598
36 Cretney *Principles of Family Law* 187; Lesser 'Acquisition of *inter vivos* Matrimonial Property Rights in English Law' 150-1, 172, and passim
37 Cretney *Principles of Family Law* 195-8, 253
38 Ibid. 268, 303

Bibliography

OFFICIAL PUBLICATIONS

PARLIAMENTARY PAPERS

1857   Bill to Amend the Law with Respect to the Property of Married Women, session 2, 3: 245-8

1862   Returns Ordered by the Commons with Respect to the Number of Causes Filed for Divorce, Judicial Separation, Restitution of Conjugal Rights, Annulments and Protection Orders, 44: 515-16

1867-68 Bill to Amend the Law with Respect to the Property of Married Women, 3: 375-8

Special Report from the Select Committee on the Married Women's Property Bill, 7: 339-465

Schools Inquiry Commission, 28 (8 volumes in one)

1868-69 Bill to Amend the Law with Respect to the Property of Married Women, 3: 427-34

Report from the Select Committee on the Married Women's Property Bill, 8: 769-74

1870   Bill to Amend the Law Relating to the Property of Married Women, 2: 657-60. Bill as Amended by the Lords, 2: 663-70

Bill to Protect the Property of Married Women, 2: 671-8

1872   Bill to Amend the Married Women's Property Act (1870) so far as It Relates to Debts Contracted by Women Who Afterwards Marry, 3: 9-11

1873   Bill to Amend the Married Women's Property Act (1870), 3: 59-61. Bill as Amended in Committee, 3: 63-6

Bill to Amend the Married Women's Property Act (1870), 3: 67-9

1874   Bill to Amend the Married Women's Property Act (1870), 3: 265-6. Bill as Amended by the Select Committee, 3: 269-70

1877   Bill to Amend the Married Women's Property Law in Scotland, 4: 25-7. Bill as Amended by the Select Committee, 4: 29-30

1878   Bill to Amend the Married Women's Property Act, 1870, 5: 53-6
            Bill to Amend the Married Women's Property Law in Scotland, 5: 57-8
1878-79   Bill to Amend the Married Women's Property Law in Scotland, 4: 381-2
1880   The Married Women's Property Acts, 1870 and 1874, Amendment Bill, 5:
            69-74
            The Married Women's Property Acts Consolidation Bill, 5: 77-83
            Bill to Amend the Married Women's Property Law in Scotland, 5: 89-91
1881   Bill to Consolidate and Amend the Acts Relating to the Property of Married
            Women, 4: 37-43. Bill as Amended by the Select Committee, 4: 45-51
            Bill to Amend the Married Women's Property Law in Scotland, 4: 53-5.
            Bill as Amended by the Select Committee, 4: 57-9. Lords' Amendments to
            the Bill, 4: 61
            Report from the Select Committee on the Married Women's Property Bill
            for Scotland, 9: 653-726
1882   Bill ... to ... Amend the Acts Relating to the Property of Married Women, 4:
            11-22

HANSARD, PARLIAMENTARY DEBATES (ALL VOLUMES SERIES 3)
1856   Divorce Bill
            First reading in Lords, 141: 870. Second reading in Lords, 142: 401-27.
            Report of Select Committee to Lords, 142: 1968-87. Amendments moved
            by Bishop of Oxford, 143: 230-52. Third reading in Lords, 143: 308-9.
            First reading in Commons, 143: 319. Second reading in Commons, 143:
            710
1856   Sir Erskine Perry's Resolution on Married Women's Property
            Debate in Commons, 142: 1273-84
1857   Lord Brougham's Married Women's Property Bill
            Introduction in Lords, 144: 605-19
1857   Sir Erskine Perry's Married Women's Property Bill
            First reading in Commons, 145: 266-81. Second reading in Commons,
            146: 1515-23
1857   Divorce Bill
            Second reading in Lords, 145: 483-537. Lords in Committee of the Whole,
            145: 780-807. Third reading in Lords, 146: 227-8. Second reading in Com-
            mons, 147: 373-415, 718, 775. Commons in Committee of the Whole, 147:
            1055 ff, 1153 ff, 1226 ff, 1534 ff, 1625 ff, 1717 ff, 1785 ff, 1866 ff, 1887 ff.
            Lords' Consideration of Commons' Amendments, 147: 1962 ff, 2005 ff.
            Lords' Amendments Accepted by Commons, 147: 2063 ff
1867   John Stuart Mill's Proposed Women's Suffrage Amendment to Reform Bill
            Debate in Commons, 187: 817-43

1868   Married Women's Property Bill
        Introduction in Commons, 191: 1015-25. Second reading in Commons,
        192: 1352-78
1869   Married Women's Property Bill
        Introduction in Commons, 194: 331. Second reading in Commons, 195:
        760-98. Third reading in Commons, 198: 401-5. Second reading in Lords,
        198: 979-87
1870   Married Women's Property Bill
        First reading in Commons, 199: 284-5. Second reading in Commons, 201:
        878-92. Second reading in Lords, 202: 600-22. Lords in Committee of the
        Whole, 203: 395-401. Report of Amendments in Lords, 203: 622-3. Com-
        mons' Agreement to Lords' Amendments, 203: 1488-9
1873   Married Women's Property Bill, No. 1 (Palmer)
        Second reading in Commons, 214: 667-89
1873   Married Women's Property Bill, No. 2 (Raikes)
        Second reading in Commons, 214: 328-30. Commons in Committee of the
        Whole, 214: 1364-5
1874   Married Women's Property Bill
        Second reading in Commons, 218: 607-14
1877   Married Women's Property Bill for Scotland
        Second reading in Commons, 233: 1404-19. Second reading in Lords,
        235: 1736-7
1877   Married Women's Property Bill (England)
        Debate on second reading in Lords, 235: 71-81
1878   Questions by Peter A. Taylor to Attorney General Sir John Holker
        243: 306, 853
1879   Married Women's Property Bill for Scotland
        Second reading in Commons, 244: 257-64
1880   Married Women's Property Bill
        Second reading in Commons, 252: 1533-45
1880   Married Women's Property Bill for Scotland
        Second reading in Commons, 252: 1548-53
1881   Married Women's Property Bill (England)
        Second reading in Commons, 257: 714
1881   Married Women's Property Bill for Scotland
        Second reading in Commons, 257: 551-89, 706-14. Consideration in Com-
        mittee of Commons, 260: 687-8, 1179-81. Third reading in Commons,
        260: 1521-7. Second reading in Lords, 261: 1438-40. Lords in Committee
        of the Whole, 262: 627-8. Commons' consideration of Lords' Amend-
        ments, 262: 1751

1882   Married Women's Property Bill (England)
        Second reading in Lords, 267: 316-17. Second reading in Commons, 270:
        616-18. Commons in Committee of the Whole, 273: 1603-12. Commons'
        consideration of bill as amended in Committee of the Whole, 273: 1844-7

GENERAL WORKS ON WOMEN

Acland, Alice *Caroline Norton* (London, Constable 1948)

Allan, James McGrigor *Woman Suffrage Wrong in Principle, and Practice: An Essay*
    (London, Remington 1890)

Altick, Richard D. *The Cowden Clarkes* (London, Oxford University Press 1948)

Amberley, K. 'The Claims of Women' *Fortnightly Review* 15 (1871) 95-110
    The Amberley Papers: The Letters and Diaries of Lord and Lady Amberley Bertrand and
    Patricia Russell eds 2 vols (London, Hogarth Press 1937)

Amos, Sheldon 'The Subjection of Women' *Westminster Review* 93 (1870) 63-89

Anderson, Louisa Garrett *Elizabeth Garrett Anderson, 1837-1917* (London, Faber and
    Faber 1939)

Anderson, Michael *Family Structure in Nineteenth-Century Lancashire* (New York,
    Cambridge University Press 1971)

'An Appeal against Female Suffrage' *Nineteenth Century* 25 (1889) 781-8

Armytage, Walter H.C. *A.J. Mundella, 1825-1897: The Liberal Background to the
    Labour Movement* (Toronto, McClelland and Stewart 1951)

Arnold, Arthur 'The Hon. Mrs. Norton and Married Women' *Fraser's Magazine* new
    series 17 (1878) 493-500. Reprinted in his *Social Politics* as 'The Legal Position of
    Married Women'

–   *The Married Women's Property Committee, the Hon. Mrs. Norton and Married Women*
    (London 1873)

–   'The Political Enfranchisement of Women' *Fortnightly Review* 17 (1872) 204-14.
    Reprinted in his *Social Politics*

–   *Social Politics* (London, C. Kegan Paul 1878)

Arnstein, Walter L. *Britain Yesterday and Today, 1830 to the Present* vol 4 of *A History
    of England* Lacey Baldwin Smith ed (Lexington, Mass. 1971)

August, Eugene R. *John Stuart Mill: A Mind at Large* (New York, Charles Scribner's
    Sons 1975)

Ausubel, Herman *John Bright, Victorian Reformer* (New York, John Wiley and Sons
    1966)

Banks, J.A., and Olive Banks *Feminism and Family Planning in Victorian England*
    (New York, Schocken 1964)

Barker, Dudley *Prominent Edwardians* (New York, Atheneum 1969)

Battiscombe, Georgina *Shaftesbury: The Great Reformer, 1801-1885* (Boston, Houghton Mifflin 1975)

Bauer, Carol, and Lawrence Ritt eds *Free and Ennobled: Source Readings in the Development of Victorian Feminism* (New York, Pergamon Press 1979)

Beaky, Lenore A. 'The Letters of Anna Mary Howitt to Barbara Leigh Smith Bodichon' (PhD dissertation, Columbia University 1977)

Beard, Mary *Woman as Force in History: A Study in Traditions and Realities* (New York, Macmillan 1946)

Becker, Lydia 'Female Suffrage' *Contemporary Review* 4 (1867) 307-16

Bell, E. Moberly *Josephine Butler, Flame of Fire* (London, Constable 1962)

– *Storming the Citadel: The Rise of the Woman Doctor* (London, Faber and Faber 1939)

Bellis, H. *Elizabeth Garrett Anderson* (London, Newnes 1953)

Best, Geoffrey F.A. *Shaftesbury* (New York, Arco 1964)

Betham-Edwards, Matilda *Mid-Victorian Memories* (London, John Murray 1919)

– *Reminiscences* (London, George Redway 1898)

Birrell, Augustine 'Woman under the English Law' *Edinburgh Review* 184 (1898) 322-40

Blackburn, Helen *Women's Suffrage: A Record of the Women's Suffrage Movement in the British Isles with Biographical Sketches of Miss Becker* (London, Williams and Norgate 1902)

Blackwell, Elizabeth *Pioneer Work in Opening the Medical Profession to Women: Autobiographical Sketches* (London and New York, Longmans, Green 1895)

Blake, Matilda M. 'The Lady and the Law' *Westminster Review* 137 (1892) 364-70

Blake, Robert *Disraeli* (New York, St Martin's 1967)

Bodichon, Barbara Leigh Smith *An American Diary, 1857-58* Joseph W. Reed, Jr ed (London, Routledge and Kegan Paul 1973)

Branca, Patricia *Silent Sisterhood: Middle Class Women in the Victorian Home* (Pittsburgh, Carnegie-Mellon University Press 1975)

– *Women in Europe since 1750* (New York, St Martin's 1978)

Bridenthal, Renate and Claudia Koonz eds *Becoming Visible: Women in European History* (Boston, Houghton Mifflin 1977)

Bristow, Edward J. *Vice and Vigilance: Purity Movements in Britain since 1700* (Totowa, NJ, Rowman and Littlefield 1977)

Brittain, Vera *Lady into Woman: A History of Women from Victoria to Elizabeth II* (London, Andrew Dakers 1953)

Browne, Matthew [pseud] 'The Subjection of Women' *Contemporary Review* 14 (1870) 273-86

Browning, Elizabeth Barrett *The Letters of Elizabeth Barrett Browning* Frederic G. Kenyon ed 2 vols in one (New York and London, Macmillan 1899)

Burton, Hester *Barbara Bodichon, 1827-1891* (London, John Murray 1949)

Butler, A.S.G. *Portrait of Josephine Butler* (London, Faber and Faber 1954)

Butler, Josephine E. *Personal Reminiscences of a Great Crusade* (London, Horace Marshall and Son 1896)

– ed *Woman's Work and Woman's Culture: A Series of Essays* (London, Macmillan 1869)

Butler, Melissa 'Early Liberal Roots of Feminism: John Locke and the Attack on Patriarchy' *American Political Science Review* 72 (1978) 135-50

Bryce, James *Studies in History and Jurisprudence* 2 vols (New York, Oxford University Press 1901)

Caine, Barbara 'John Stuart Mill and the English Women's Movement' *Historical Studies* 18 (1978) 52-67

Carlyle, Jane Welsh *I Too Am Here: Selections from the Letters of Jane Welsh Carlyle* Alan and Mary McQueen Simpson eds (New York, Cambridge University Press 1977)

– *Jane Welsh Carlyle: Letters to Her Family, 1839-1863* Leonard Huxley ed (Garden City, NY, Doubleday 1924)

– *Letters and Memorials of Jane Welsh Carlyle* James Anthony Froude ed 2 vols in one (New York, Charles Scribner's Sons 1883)

– *New Letters and Memorials of Jane Welsh Carlyle* Alexander Carlyle ed 2 vols (London and New York, John Lane, Bodley Head 1903)

Carroll, Berenice ed *Liberating Women's History: Theoretical and Critical Essays* (Urbana, University of Illinois Press 1976)

Cecil, David *Melbourne* (Indianapolis, Bobbs-Merrill 1954)

Chambers, Peggy *A Doctor Alone, A Biography of Elizabeth Blackwell: The First Woman Doctor, 1821-1910* (London, Bodley Head 1956)

Chapman, Theo 'Women's Suffrage' *Nineteenth Century* 19 (1886) 561-9

Checkland, S.G. *The Gladstones: A Family Biography, 1764-1851* (New York, Cambridge University Press 1971)

Cleveland, Arthur Rackham *Women under the English Law from the Landing of the Saxons to the Present Time* (London, Hurst and Blackett 1896)

Cobbe, Frances Power 'Criminals, Idiots, Women and Minors: Is the Classification Sound?' *Fraser's Magazine* 78 (1868) 777-94

– *Life of Frances Power Cobbe by Herself* 2 vols (London, Richard Bentley and Son 1894)

– 'Social Science Congresses, and Women's Part in Them' *Macmillan's Magazine* 5 (1861) 82-93

Collis, John Stewart *The Carlyles: A Biography of Thomas and Jane Carlyle* (London, Sidgwick and Jackson 1971 and New York, Dodd, Mead 1972)

Cook, Sir Edward *Florence Nightingale* 2 vols (London, Macmillan 1913)

Cornwallis, Caroline Frances 'Capabilities and Disabilities of Women' *Westminster Review* 67 (1857) 42-72

- 'The Property of Married Women: Report of the Personal Laws Committee (of the Law Amendment Society) on the Laws Relating to the Property of Married Women' *Westminster Review* 66 (1856) 331-60

Cowden Clarke, Mary *My Long Life* (New York, Dodd, Mead 1896)

Cretney, Stephen M. 'The Maintenance Quagmire' *Modern Law Review* 33 (1970) 662-83

- *Principles of Family Law* 2d ed (London, Sweet and Maxwell 1976)

Crow, Duncan *The Victorian Woman* (New York, Stein and Day 1972)

Cunnington, C. Willet *Feminine Attitudes in the Nineteenth Century* (New York, Macmillan 1936)

Cushman, Charlotte *Charlotte Cushman: Her Letters and Memories of Her Life* Emma Stebbins ed (1879; reprinted New York, Benjamin Blom 1972)

Davenport-Hill, Rosamond and Florence *The Recorder of Birmingham: A Memoir of Matthew Davenport Hill* (London, Macmillan 1878)

Davidoff, Leonore *The Best Circles: Women and Society in Victorian England* (London, Croom Helm 1973)

Davis, Richard W. *Disraeli* (Boston, Little, Brown 1977)

Delamont, Sara, and Lorna Duffin eds *The Nineteenth-Century Woman* (London, Croom Helm 1978)

Denning, Sir Alfred *The Changing Law* (London, Stevens and Sons 1953)

- *The Equality of Women* (Liverpool, Liverpool University Press 1960)

Dicey, A.V. *Lectures on the Relation Between Law and Public Opinion in England During the Nineteenth Century* (London, Macmillan 1920)

Dictionary of National Biography

Easson, Angus *Elizabeth Gaskell* (London and Boston, Routledge and Kegan Paul 1979)

The Economic Foundations of the Women's Movement ... by M.A. (London, Fabian Society 1914)

Eliot, George *The George Eliot Letters* Gordon S. Haight ed 7 vols (New Haven, Yale University Press 1954-5)

Elmy, Elizabeth C. Wolstenholme 'The Present Legal Position of Women in the United Kingdom' *Westminster Review* 163 (1905) 513-39

- 'A Woman Emancipator: A Biographical Sketch' *Westminster Review* 145 (1896) 424-8. Autobiographical sketch published under the pseudonym Ellis Ethelmer.

Engels, Friedrich *The Origin of the Family, Private Property, and the State* (New York, International Publishers 1942. First published in 1884)

Erskine, Mrs Steuart ed *Anna Jameson: Letters and Friendships (1812-1860)* (New York, E.P. Dutton n.d.)

Evans, Richard J. *The Feminists: Women's Emancipation Movements in Europe, America and Australasia, 1840-1920* (New York, Barnes and Noble 1977)

Fahnestock, Jeanne Rosenmayer 'Geraldine Jewsbury: The Power of the Publisher's Reader' *Nineteenth-Century Fiction* 28 (1973) 253-72

Fawcett, Millicent Garrett 'The Electoral Disabilities of Women' *Fortnightly Review* 13 (1870) 622-32

– *A Reply to the Letter of Mr. Samuel Smith, M.P., on Women's Suffrage* (London, Central Committee of the National Society for Women's Suffrage 1892)

– *What I Remember* (New York, G.P. Putnam's Sons 1925)

– 'Women and Representative Government' *Nineteenth Century* 14 (1883) 285-91

– 'Women's Suffrage: A Reply' *Nineteenth Century* 19 (1886) 740-8

– *Women's Suffrage: A Short History of a Great Movement* (London and Edinburgh, T.C. and E.C. Jack 1911)

– 'The Women's Suffrage Movement' in *The Woman Question in Europe: A Series of Original Essays* Theodore Stanton ed (New York and London, G.P. Putnam's Sons 1884)

– *The Women's Victory and After: Personal Reminiscences, 1911-18* (London, Sidgwick and Jackson 1920)

– and M.M. Dilke 'Reply to Appeal against Female Suffrage' *Nineteenth Century* 26 (1889) 86-103

Feaver, George *From Status to Contract: A Biography of Sir Henry Maine, 1822-1888* (New York, Humanities Press 1969)

Feuchtwanger, E.R. *Gladstone* (New York, St Martin's 1975)

Figes, Eva *Patriarchal Attitudes* (New York, Stein and Day 1970)

Finlayson, G.B.A.M. 'Joseph Parkes of Birmingham, 1796-1865: A Study in Philosophic Radicalism' *Bulletin of the Institute of Historical Research* 46 (1973) 186-201

Finnegan, Frances *Poverty and Prostitution: A Study of Victorian Prostitutes in York* (New York, Cambridge University Press 1979)

Flexner, Eleanor *Mary Wollstonecraft: A Biography* (New York, Coward, McCann and Geoghegan 1972)

Fulford, Roger *Votes for Women* (London, Faber and Faber 1957)

Gallagher, Alicia E. 'A Coterie of Victorian Pre-Suffragists, 1850-1875' (MA essay, Columbia University 1943)

Ganz, Margaret *Elizabeth Gaskell: The Artist in Conflict* (New York, Twayne 1969)

Garnett, Richard and Edward *The Life of W.J. Fox: Public Teacher and Social Reformer, 1786-1864* (London and New York, John Lane 1910)

Gaskell, Elizabeth Stevenson *The Letters of Mrs. Gaskell* J.A.V. Chapple and Arthur Pollard eds (Cambridge: Harvard University Press 1967)

George, Margaret *One Woman's 'Situation': A Study of Mary Wollstonecraft* (Urbana, University of Illinois Press 1970)

Gerin, Winifred *Elizabeth Gaskell: A Biography* (Oxford, Clarendon Press 1976)

Gibson, Ian *The English Vice: Beating, Sex and Shame in Victorian England and After* (London, Duckworth 1978)

Gladstone, William Ewart *Female Suffrage: A Letter from the Rt. Hon. W.E. Gladstone, M.P., to Samuel Smith, M.P., 11 April 1892* (London, John Murray 1892)

Goode, William J. *World Revolution and Family Patterns* (New York, Free Press 1963)

Graveson, R.H., and F.E. Crane eds *A Century of Family Law, 1857-1957* (London, Sweet and Maxwell 1957)

Gross, George C. 'Mary Cowden Clarke, "The Girlhood of Shakespeare's Heroines," and the Sex Education of Victorian Women' *Victorian Studies* 16 (1972) 37-58

Guettel, Charnie *Marxism and Feminism* (Toronto, Canadian Women's Educational Press 1976)

Gwynn, Stephen, and Gertrude M. Tuckwell *The Life of the Rt. Hon. Sir Charles W. Dilke, Bart., MP* 2 vols (New York, Macmillan 1917)

Haight, Gordon S. *George Eliot: A Biography* (New York, Oxford University Press 1968)

– *George Eliot and John Chapman* (New Haven, Yale University Press 1940)

Haldane, Elizabeth *Mrs. Gaskell and Her Friends* (New York, D. Appleton 1931)

Halevy, Elie *The Growth of Philosophic Radicalism* (Boston, Beacon Press 1955)

Halliday, R.J. *John Stuart Mill* (London, George Allen and Unwin and New York, Barnes and Noble 1976)

Hamburger, Joseph *Intellectuals in Politics: John Stuart Mill and the Philosophic Radicals* (New Haven, Yale University Press 1965)

Hamilton, Margaret 'Opposition to the Contagious Diseases Acts, 1864-1886' *Albion* 10 (1978) 14-27

– 'Opposition to Woman Suffrage in England, 1865-1884' *Victorian Institute Journal* 4 (1975) 59-73

Hamilton, Roberta *The Liberation of Women: A Study in Patriarchy and Capitalism* (Boston and London, Allen 1978)

Hammerton, A. James *Emigrant Gentlewomen: Genteel Poverty and Female Emigration, 1830-1914* (London, Croom Helm and Totowa, NJ, Rowman and Littlefield 1979)

Hammond, J.L., and Barbara Hammond *James Stansfeld: A Victorian Champion of Sex Equality* (London and New York, Longmans, Green 1932)

Hanson, Lawrence and Elisabeth *Necessary Evil: The Life of Jane Welsh Carlyle* (London, Constable 1952)

Hareven, Tamara K. 'The Family as Process: The Historical Study of the Family Cycle' *Journal of Social History* 7 (1974) 322-9

Harrison, Brian *Separate Spheres: The Opposition to Women's Suffrage in Britain* (London, Croom Helm and New York, Holmes and Meier 1978)

Hartman, Mary S. and Lois W. Banner eds *Clio's Consciousness Raised: New Perspectives on the History of Women* (New York, Harper 1974)

Haw, Reginald *The State of Matrimony: An Investigation of the Relationship between Ecclesiastical and Civil Marriage in England* (London, Macmillan 1953)

Hawes, Frances *Henry Brougham* (London, Jonathan Cape 1957)

Hayek, F.A. ed *John Stuart Mill and Harriet Taylor: Their Correspondence and Subsequent Marriage* (Chicago, University of Chicago Press 1951)

Hayes, Elinor Rice *Those Extraordinary Blackwells: The Story of a Journey to a Better World* (New York, Harcourt, Brace and World 1967)

Hewitt, Margaret *Wives and Mothers in Victorian Industry* (1958; reprinted Westport, Conn., Greenwood 1975)

Hewlett, Dorothy *Elizabeth Barrett Browning* (London, Cassell 1953)

Hill, Georgiana *Women in English Life: From Medieval to Modern Times* 2 vols (London, Richard Bentley 1896)

Himmelfarb, Gertrude *Victorian Minds* (London, Weidenfeld and Nicholson and New York, Knopf 1968)

'History of the Married Women's Property Bill' *Englishwoman's Review* (1873) 177-84

Hobhouse, Arthur 'On the Forfeiture of Property by Married Women' *Fortnightly Review* 13 (1870) 180-6. Reprinted as a pamphlet by the Married Women's Property Committee, Manchester 1870

— *On the Laws Relating to the Property of Married Women (A Paper Read at the Social Science Congress, Birmingham, October 1868)* (Manchester 1870)

Holcombe, Lee *Victorian Ladies at Work: Middle-Class Working Women in England and Wales, 1850-1914* (Hamden, Conn., Archon and Newton Abbot, Devon, David and Charles 1973)

Holdsworth, Sir William *History of English Law* 16 vols (London, Methuen and Boston, Little, Brown 1923-1966)

Hollis, Patricia ed *Pressure from Without in Early Victorian England* (New York, St Martin's 1974)

— *Women in Public: Documents of the Victorian Women's Movement, 1850-1900* (London, Allen 1979)

Houghton, Walter E. *The Victorian Frame of Mind* (New Haven, Yale University Press 1957)

'The House of Commons on Wives' Property' *Spectator* 42 (1869) 470-1

Howe, Susanne *Geraldine Jewsbury: Her Life and Errors* (London, George Allen and Unwin 1935)

Howitt, Mary *Mary Howitt: An Autobiography* Margaret Howitt ed 2 vols (Boston and New York, Houghton Mifflin 1889)

Hutchins, B.L. *Conflicting Ideals: Two Sides to the Woman's Question* (London, Thomas Murby 1913)

Hynes, Samuel *The Edwardian Turn of Mind* (Princeton, Princeton University Press 1968)

'The Issues of Two Debates: Suffrage and Married Women's Property' *Englishwoman's Review* (1879) 97-103

Jameson, Anna *The Communion of Labour: A Second Lecture on the Social Employments of Women* (London, Longman, Brown, Green, Longmans and Roberts 1856)

– Sisters of Charity Catholic and Protestant, Abroad and at Home (London, Longman, Brown, Green and Longmans 1855)

Jenkins, Roy *Sir Charles Dilke: A Victorian Tragedy* rev ed (London, Collins 1965)

Jenks, Edward *A Short History of English Law from the Earliest Times to the End of the Year 1938* 6th ed (London, Methuen 1949)

Jewsbury, Geraldine Endsor *Selections from the Letters of Geraldine Endsor Jewsbury to Jane Welsh Carlyle* Mrs. Alexander Ireland ed (London and New York, Longmans, Green 1892)

Jex-Blake, Sophia *Medical Women: A Thesis and a History* 2d ed (Edinburgh, Oliphant, Anderson and Ferrier and London, Hamilton, Adams 1886)

Johnson, George W. and Lucy A. eds *Josephine E. Butler: An Autobiographical Memoir* (Bristol, J.W. Arrowsmith and London, Simpkin, Marshall, Hamilton, Kent 1909)

'Judicial Sex-Bias' *Westminster Review* 149 (1898) 147-60, 279-88

Kahn-Freund, Otto 'Matrimonial Property and Equality before the Law: Some Sceptical Reflections' *Revue des droits de l'homme* 4 (1971) 493-510

– 'Recent Legislation on Matrimonial Property' *Modern Law Review* 33 (1970) 601-31

Kamm, Josephine *John Stuart Mill in Love* (New York, Atheneum 1977)

– Rapiers and Battleaxes: The Women's Movement and Its Aftermath (London, George Allen and Unwin 1966)

Kanner, Barbara ed *The Women of England from Anglo-Saxon Times to the Present: Interpretive Bibliographical Essays* (Hamden, Conn., Archon 1979)

Kingsley, Charles 'Women and Politics' *Macmillan's Magazine* 20 (1869) 552-61

Kitchin, S.B. *A History of Divorce* (London, Chapman and Hall 1912)

Klein, Viola *The Feminine Character: History of an Ideology* (London, Routledge and Kegan Paul 1946)

Kunitz, Stanley J. and Howard Haycraft eds *British Authors of the Nineteenth Century* (New York, H.W. Wilson 1936)

'The Law in Relation to Women' *Westminster Review* 128 (1887) 698-710

'The Laws of Marriage and Divorce' *Westminster Review* 82 (1864) 442-54

Leach, Joseph *Bright Particular Star: The Life and Times of Charlotte Cushman* (New Haven, Yale University Press 1970)

Lee, Amice *Laurels and Rosemary: The Life of William and Mary Howitt* (London, Oxford University Press 1955)

'The Legal Position of Women' *Westminster Review* 105 (1876) 315-39

'The Legal Position of Women and Its Moral Effects' *Meliora* 8 (1865) 93-102

Leigh Smith, Barbara *A Brief Summary, in Plain Language, of the Most Important Laws Concerning Women, Together with a Few Observations Thereon* (London, Chapman and Hall 1854)

Lesser, Henry 'Acquisition of *inter vivos* Matrimonial Property Rights in English Law: A Doctrinal Melting Pot' *University of Toronto Law Journal* 23 (1973) 148-214

Levine, David *Family Formation in an Age of Nascent Capitalism* (New York, Academic Press 1977)

Levine, Richard A. *Benjamin Disraeli* (New York, Twayne 1968)

Liddington, Jill, and Jill Norris *One Hand Tied Behind Us: The Rise of the Woman's Suffrage Movement* (London, Virago 1978)

Linton, Eliza Lynn 'The Modern Revolt' *Macmillan's Magazine* 23 (1870) 142-9

– 'The Wild Women as Politicians' *Nineteenth Century* 30 (1891) 79-88

The Lords and the Married Women's Property Bill (Manchester 1870)

Lowndes, Mrs. Belloc *'I, Too, Have Lived in Arcadia': A Record of Love and of Childhood* (New York, Dodd, Mead 1942)

– *Where Love and Friendship Dwelt* (New York, Dodd, Mead 1943)

McGregor, O.R. *Divorce in England: A Centenary Study* (London, William Heinemann 1957)

– 'The Social Position of Women in England, 1850-1914: A Bibliography' *British Journal of Sociology* 6 (1955) 48-60

McHugh, Paul *Prostitution and Victorian Social Reform* (New York, St Martin's 1980)

McKendrick, Neil 'Home Demand and Economic Growth: A New View of the Role of Women and Children in the Industrial Revolution' in *Historical Perspectives: Studies in English Thought and Society in Honour of J.H. Plumb* (London, Europa 1975)

McLaren, W.S.B. 'The Political Emancipation of Women' *Westminster Review* 128 (1887) 165-73

McLennon, John *The Patriarchal Theory* (London, Macmillan 1885)

Macpherson, Gerardine *Memoirs of the Life of Anna Jameson* (London, Longmans, Green 1878)

Maison, Margaret M. 'Insignificant Objects of Desire' *The Listener* 86 (1971) 105-7

Manton, Jo *Elizabeth Garrett Anderson* (New York, E.P. Dutton 1965)

– *Mary Carpenter and the Children of the Streets* (London, Heinemann 1976)

'Married Women and Their Property' *Spectator* 41 (1868) 488-9

'Married Women's Property' *All the Year Round* 24 (1870) 89-93

'The Married Women's Property Act (1882)' *Chambers's Journal* 4th series 19 (1882) 819-21

Married Women's Property Committee *Annual Reports* (1868-82). Sometimes published under the title *Proceedings at the Annual Meetings*

Marshall, G.P. 'Some Economic Aspects of Family Property Rights Reform' *British Tax Review* (Jan.-Feb. 1974) 30-37

Martin, Anna *The Married Working Woman* (London, National Union of Women's Suffrage Societies 1911)

Martineau, Harriet *Autobiography* Maria Weston Chapman ed 2 vols (Boston, James R. Osgood 1877)

– 'Female Industry' *Edinburgh Review* 109 (1859) 293-336

Martyn, Elizabeth 'Women in Public Life' *Westminster Review* 132 (1889) 282-5

Marx, Karl, and Friedrich Engels *The Communist Manifesto* (first published in 1848, various later editions)

Mill, John Stuart *Autobiography* (New York, Columbia University Press 1924)

– *Letters* Hugh S.R. Elliot ed 2 vols (London, Longmans, Green 1910)

– and Harriet Taylor Mill *Essays on Sex Equality* Alice S. Rossi ed (Chicago: University of Chicago Press 1970)

Miller, Gareth 'Maintenance and Property' *Law Quarterly Review* 87 (1971) 66-85

Millett, Kate *Sexual Politics* (Garden City, NY, Doubleday 1970)

Milne, John Duguid *Industrial and Social Position of Women, in the Middle and Lower Ranks* (London, Chapman and Hall 1857)

Minge-Kalman, Wanda 'The Industrial Revolution and the European Family: The Industrialization of "Childhood" as a Market for Family Labor' *Comparative Studies in Society and History* 20 (1978) 454-68

Minton-Senhouse, R.M. 'Married Women: An Historical Sketch' *Westminster Review* 131 (1889) 355-66

'Mr. Jacob Bright' *Spectator* 81 (1898) 642-3

Mitchell, David *The Fighting Pankhursts: A Study in Tenacity* (New York, Macmillan 1967)

Mitchison, Naomi 'Elizabeth Garrett Anderson' in *Revaluations: Studies in Biography* (London, Humphrey Milford 1931)

'Moneyed Wives' *Spectator* 56 (1883) 9-10

Morgan, David *Suffragists and Liberals: The Politics of Woman Suffrage in England* (Totowa, NJ, Rowman and Littlefield 1975)

Morrison, N. Brysson *True Minds: The Marriage of Thomas and Jane Carlyle* (London, Dent 1974)

Myrdal, Alva, and Viola Klein *Women's Two Roles: Home and Work* (London, Routledge and Kegan Paul 1956)

National Association for the Promotion of Social Science *Sessional Proceedings* (1857-86)

– *Transactions* (1857-86)

Neff, Wanda Fraiken *Victorian Working Women: An Historical and Literary Study of Women in British Industries and Professions, 1832-1850* (New York, Columbia University Press 1929)

'The New Law of Divorce' *English Woman's Journal* 1 (1858) 186-9

'New Objections to Women's Suffrage' *Englishwoman's Review* (1870) 55-78

Newman, Charles *The Evolution of Medical Education in the Nineteenth Century* (London, Oxford University Press 1957)

Norton, Caroline *English Laws for Women in the Nineteenth Century* (London 1854)

- *A Letter to the Queen on Lord Chancellor Cranworth's Marriage and Divorce Bill* (London 1855)
- *The Letters of Caroline Norton to Lord Melbourne* James O. Hoge and Clark Olney eds (Columbus, Ohio University Press 1974)
- *A Plain Letter to the Lord Chancellor on the Infant Custody Bill* (London 1839)

Odgers, W. Blake, and Walter Blake Odgers *The Common Law of England, Being the 10th Edition of Broom's Commentaries on the Common Law* 2 vols (London, Sweet and Maxwell 1911)

Oliphant, Margaret 'The Condition of Women' *Blackwood's Edinburgh Magazine* 83 (1858) 138-54
- 'Grievances of Women' *Fraser's Magazine* new series 21 (1880) 698-710
- 'The Laws Concerning Women' *Blackwood's Edinburgh Magazine* 79 (1856) 379-87
- 'Mill on the Subjection of Women' *Edinburgh Review* 130 (1869) 291-306

O'Meara, Kathleen *Madame Mohl, Her Salon and Her Friends: A Study of Social Life in Paris* (London, Richard Bentley and Son 1885)

O'Neill, William L. *The Woman Movement: Feminism in the United States and England* (New York, Barnes and Noble 1969)

Pankhurst, Emmeline *My Own Story* (1914; reprinted New York, Kraus 1971)

Pankhurst, Estelle Sylvia *The Life of Emmeline Pankhurst: The Suffragette Struggle for Women's Citizenship* (1935; reprinted New York, Kraus 1969)
- *The Suffragette Movement: An Intimate Account of Persons and Ideals* (London, Longmans 1931)

Pankhurst, Richard K.P. *Sylvia Pankhurst, Artist and Crusader: An Intimate Portrait* (New York, Paddington Press 1959)

Pankhurst, Richard Marsden 'The Right of Women to Vote under the Reform Act, 1867' *Fortnightly Review* 10 (1868) 250-4

'The Peers and the Married Women' *Spectator* 43 (1870) 772-3

Perkins, Jane Gray *The Life of Mrs Norton* (London, John Murray 1910)

Perry, Sir Thomas Erskine 'Rights and Liabilities of Husband and Wife' *Edinburgh Review* 105 (1857) 181-205

Pethick Lawrence, F.W. *Women's Fight for the Vote* 2d ed (London, The Women's Press 1911)

'Petitions for Extension of the Elective Franchise to Women' *Englishwoman's Review* (1870) 198-210

Petrie, Glen *A Singular Iniquity: The Campaigns of Josephine Butler* (New York, Viking 1970 and London, Macmillan 1971)

Pfeiffer, Emily 'Suffrage for Women in England' *Contemporary Review* 47 (1885) 418-35
- 'Woman's Claim' *Contemporary Review* 39 (1881) 265-77

Pinchbeck, Ivy *Women Workers and the Industrial Revolution, 1750-1850* (1930; reprinted New York, Augustus M. Kelley 1969)

Pope-Hennessy, James *Monckton Milnes* 2 vols (London, Constable 1949, 1951)

'Property of Married Women' *English Woman's Journal* 1 (1858) 58-9

'The Property of Married Women' *Meliora* 12 (1869) 51-60

'Public Opinion in the Press on Women's Suffrage' *Englishwoman's Review* (1873) 29-32

Pugh, Evelyn L. 'John Stuart Mill and the Women's Question in Parliament, 1865-1868' *Historian* 42 (1980) 399-418

Rabb, Theodore K., and Robert I. Rotberg eds *The Family in History: Interdisciplinary Essays* (New York, Harper and Row 1971)

Raeburn, Antonia *The Militant Suffragettes* (London, Michael Joseph 1973)

– *The Suffragette View* (New York, St Martin's 1976)

Ramelson, Marian *The Petticoat Rebellion: A Century of Struggle for Women's Rights* (London, Lawrence and Wishart 1967)

Redinger, Ruby *George Eliot: The Emergent Self* (New York, Knopf 1975)

Redman, Joseph Haworth *A Concise View of the Law of Husband and Wife as Modified by the Married Women's Property Acts ...* (London, Reeves and Turner 1883)

Rees, Barbara *The Victorian Lady* (London, Gordon and Cremonesi and New York, Atheneum 1977)

Reid, T. Wemyss *The Life, Letters and Friendships of Richard Monckton Milnes, First Lord Houghton* 2 vols (New York, Cassell 1891)

Reiss, Erna *The Rights and Duties of Englishwomen: A Study in Law and Public Opinion* (London, Sherratt 1934)

Richards, Eric 'Women in the British Economy since about 1700: An Interpretation' *History* 59 (1974) 337-57

Ridley, Jasper *Lord Palmerston* (New York, E.P. Dutton 1970)

Ritt, Lawrence 'The Victorian Conscience in Action: The National Association for the Promotion of Social Science' (Ph D dissertation, Columbia University 1959)

Robbins, Keith *John Bright* (Boston, Routledge and Kegan Paul 1979)

Robson, John M., and Michael Laine eds *James and John Stuart Mill: Papers of the Centenary Conference* (Toronto, University of Toronto Press 1976)

Rosen, Andrew 'Emily Davies and the Women's Movement, 1862-1867' *Journal of British Studies* 19 (1979) 101-21

– *Rise Up, Women! The Militant Campaign of the Women's Social and Political Union, 1903-1914* (Boston, Routledge and Kegan Paul 1974)

Rosenberg, Charles E. ed *The Family in History* (Philadelphia, University of Pennsylvania Press 1975)

Ross, Ishbel *Child of Destiny: The Life Story of the First Woman Doctor* [Elizabeth Blackwell] (New York, Harper and Brothers 1949)

Rover, Constance *Women's Suffrage and Party Politics in Britain, 1866-1914* (Toronto, University of Toronto Press and London, Routledge and Kegan Paul 1969)

Rowbotham, Sheila *Hidden from History: Rediscovering Women in History from the Seventeenth Century to the Present* (New York, Pantheon 1975)

Ryan, Alan *J.S. Mill* (Boston, Routledge and Kegan Paul 1975)
– *John Stuart Mill* (New York, Pantheon 1970)
Sachs, Albie, and Joan Hoff Wilson *Sexism and the Law: A Study of Male Beliefs and Judicial Bias in Britain and the United States* (New York, Free Press 1978)
Saleeby, C.W. *Woman and Womanhood: A Search for Principles* (New York and London, Mitchell Kennerley 1911)
Sampson, Ronald V. *The Psychology of Power* (New York, Pantheon 1965)
Selborne, Earl of [Roundell Palmer] *Memorials* 4 vols (London, Macmillan 1898)
Sharp, Evelyn *Hertha Ayrton, 1854-1923: A Memoir* (London, Edward Arnold 1926)
Shaw, Bernard *The Intelligent Woman's Guide to Socialism, Capitalism, Sovietism, and Fascism* (London, Constable and New York, Brentano's 1928)
Shklonik, Esther Simon 'Petticoat Power: The Political Influence of Mrs. Gladstone' *Historian* 42 (1980) 631-47
Shore, Louisa 'The Emancipation of Women' *Westminster Review* 102 (1874) 137-74
Simcox, Edith 'On the Influence of John Stuart Mill's Writings' *Contemporary Review* 22 (1873) 297-317
Smelser, Neil J. *Social Change in the Industrial Revolution: An Application of Theory to the Lancashire Cotton Industry, 1770-1840* (Chicago, University of Chicago Press 1959)
Smith, Goldwin 'Female Suffrage' *Macmillan's Magazine* 30 (1874) 139-50
Snowden, Ethel *The Feminist Movement* (London, Collins 1913)
Society for Promoting the Employment of Women *Annual Reports* 1859-
Southgate, Donald *'The Most English Minister': The Policies and Politics of Palmerston* (New York, St Martin's 1966)
Speech of Sir Thomas Erskine Perry at the Annual Meeting of the Married Women's Property Committee, 4th February 1880 (Manchester, Alexander Ireland 1880)
Squibb, G.D. *Doctors' Commons: A History of the College of Advocates and Doctors of Law* (New York, Oxford University Press 1977)
Stanton, Theodore ed *The Woman Question in Europe: A Series of Original Essays* (New York and London, G.P. Putnam's Sons 1884)
'Statesmen. No. CCII. Mr. Jacob Bright, M.P.' *Vanity Fair* 17 (1877) 279
Stenton, Doris Mary *The English Woman in History* (London, George Allen and Unwin 1957)
Stenton, Michael ed *Who's Who of British Members of Parliament* vol 1 1832-1885 (Atlantic Highlands, NJ, Humanities Press 1977)
Stephen, Barbara *Emily Davies and Girton College* (London, Constable 1927)
– *Girton College, 1869-1932* (Cambridge, at the University Press 1933)
Stone, Olive W. 'The Status of Women in Great Britain' *American Journal of Comparative Law* 20 (1972) 592-621
Strachey, Ray *'The Cause': A Short History of the Women's Movement in Great Britain* (London, G. Bell and Sons 1928. Published in the United States as *Struggle: The*

Stirring Story of Women's Advance in England New York, Duffield 1930. Reprinted Port Washington, NY, Kennikat Press 1969)

– *Millicent Garrett Fawcett* (London, John Murray 1931)

Sylvester, D.W. *Robert Lowe and Education* (New York, Cambridge University Press 1974)

Tabor, M.C. 'On the Condition of Women as Affected by the Law' *English Woman's Journal* 10 (1862) 124-7

Taplin, Gardner *The Life of Elizabeth Barrett Browning* (New Haven, Yale University Press 1958)

Taylor, Barbara 'Lords of Creation: The Attitudes of Utopian and Marxist Socialists toward Feminism' *New Statesman* 99 (1980) 361-2

Taylor, Harriet 'The Enfranchisement of Women' *Westminster Review* 55 (1851) 289-301. Reprinted in *Essays on Sex Equality*.

Taylor, Helen 'The Ladies' Petition: Petition Presented to the House of Commons by Mr. J. Stuart Mill, June 7th, 1866' *Westminster Review* 87 (1867) 63-79

Taylor, Sir Henry 'Mr. Mill on the Subjection of Women' *Fraser's Magazine* new series 1 (1870) 143-65

Thicknesse, Ralph 'The New Legal Position of Married Women' *Blackwood's Edinburgh Magazine* 133 (1883) 207-20

Thomas, Clara *Love and Work Enough: The Life of Anna Jameson* (Toronto, University of Toronto Press 1967)

Thompson, Dennis F. *John Stuart Mill and Representative Government* (Princeton, Princeton University Press 1976)

Thomson, Patricia *The Victorian Heroine: A Changing Ideal, 1837-1873* (New York, Oxford University Press 1956)

Tilly, Louise A. and Joan W. Scott *Women, Work and Family* (New York, Holt 1978)

Todd, Margaret *Life of Sophia Jex-Blake* (London, Macmillan 1918)

Tomes, Nancy 'A "Torrent of Abuse": Crimes of Violence between Working-Class Men and Women in London, 1840-1875' *Journal of Social History* 11 (1978) 328-45

Travers, Richard Lawrence *Husband and Wife in English Law* (London, Duckworth 1956)

Trevelyan, George Macaulay *The Life of John Bright* (1913; reprinted Westport, Conn., Greenwood 1971)

Tufte, Virginia and Barbara Myerhoff eds *Changing Images of the Family* (New Haven, Yale University Press 1979)

Tuke, Margaret J. *A History of Bedford College for Women, 1849-1937* (London, Oxford University Press 1939)

Turner-Samuels, Moss *The Law of Married Women* (London, Thames Bank 1957)

Underhill, Sir Arthur *The Law Reform (Married Women and Tortfeasors) Act 1935 and the Unrepealed Sections of the Married Women's Property Acts 1882 to 1908 as Amended* (London, Butterworth 1936)

Vicinus, Martha ed *Suffer and Be Still: Women in the Victorian Age* (Bloomington, Indiana University Press 1972)
- *A Widening Sphere: Changing Roles of Victorian Women* (Bloomington, Indiana University Press 1977)
Walkowitz, Judith R. *Prostitution and Victorian Society: Women, Class, and the State* (New York, Cambridge University Press 1980)
Wardle, Ralph *Mary Wollstonecraft: A Critical Biography* (Lawrence, University of Kansas Press 1951)
Webb, R.K. *Harriet Martineau: A Radical Victorian* (New York, Columbia University Press 1960)
Wedgwood, Barbara, and Hensleigh Wedgwood *The Wedgwood Circle, 1730-1897: Four Generations of a Family and Their Friends* (London, Studio Vista and Westfield, NJ, Eastview 1980)
Wharton, J.J.S. *An Exposition of the Laws Relating to the Women of England: Showing Their Rights, Remedies and Responsibilities, in Every Position of Life* (London, Longman, Brown, Green and Longmans 1853)
Williford, Miriam 'Bentham on the Rights of Women' *Journal of the History of Ideas* 36 (1975) 167-76
Wilson, Dorothy Clarke *Lone Woman: The Story of Elizabeth Blackwell, the First Woman Doctor* (Boston, Little, Brown 1970)
Winter, James *Robert Lowe* (Toronto, University of Toronto Press 1976)
Wohl, Anthony S. ed *The Victorian Family: Structure and Stresses* (London, Croom Helm 1977 and New York, St Martin's 1978)
Woman's Position, and the Objects of the Women's Franchise League. Lecture by Lady Florence Dixie Delivered in the Christian Institute, Glasgow, on Tuesday, 21st April 1891 (Dundee n.d.)
'Women's Rights' *Saturday Review* 29 (1870) 662-4
'Women's Rights as Preached by Women' *Westminster Review* 116 (1881) 469-78
'Women's Suffrage: A Reply' *Fortnightly Review* 52 (1889) 123-39
Wood, Joy L.O. 'George John Shaw Lefevre, Lord Eversley: A Liberal Reformer and Founder of the Conservation Movement in England' (PhD dissertation, Texas Christian University 1978)
Woodham-Smith, Cecil *Florence Nightingale, 1820-1910* (New York, McGraw-Hill 1951)
Woodring, Carl Ray *Victorian Samplers: William and Mary Howitt* (Lawrence, University of Kansas Press 1952)
Wyndham, Horace *Feminine Frailty* (London, Ernest Benn 1929)
Ziegler, Philip *Melbourne: A Biography of William Lamb, Second Viscount Melbourne* (New York, Knopf 1976)

General Index

Index of
Law and Legislation